Britain's War Against
the Slave Trade

Britain's War Against the Slave Trade

The Operations of the Royal Navy's West Africa Squadron 1807–1867

Anthony Sullivan

FRONTLINE BOOKS

First published in Great Britain in 2020 by
Frontline Books
An imprint of
Pen & Sword Books Ltd
Yorkshire – Philadelphia

ISBN 978 1 52671 793 1

Printed and bound in the UK by TJ International Ltd,
Padstow, Cornwall.

Pen & Sword Books Limited incorporates the imprints of Atlas,
Archaeology, Aviation, Discovery, Family History, Fiction, History,
Maritime, Military, Military Classics, Politics, Select, Transport,
True Crime, Air World, Frontline Publishing, Leo Cooper, Remember
When, Seaforth Publishing, The Praetorian Press, Wharncliffe
Local History, Wharncliffe Transport, Wharncliffe True Crime
and White Owl.

For a complete list of Pen & Sword titles please contact

PEN & SWORD BOOKS LIMITED
47 Church Street, Barnsley, South Yorkshire, S70 2AS, England
E-mail: enquiries@pen-and-sword.co.uk
Website: www.pen-and-sword.co.uk

Or

PEN AND SWORD BOOKS
1950 Lawrence Rd, Havertown, PA 19083, USA
E-mail: Uspen-and-sword@casematepublishers.com
Website: www.penandswordbooks.com

Contents

Maps

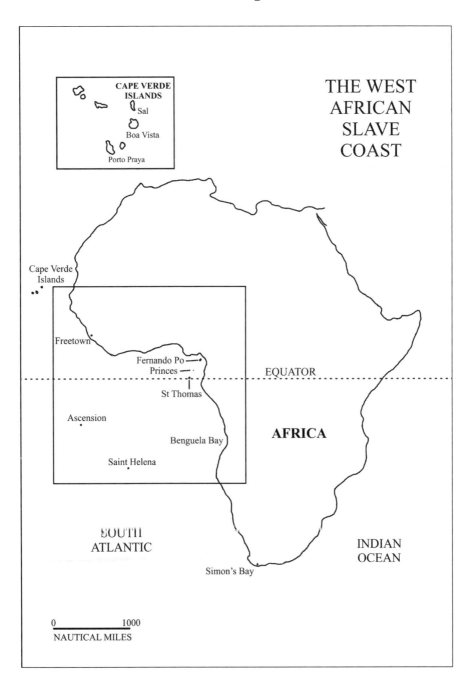

CAPE VERDE ISLANDS

Sal

Boa Vista

Porto Praya

THE WEST AFRICAN SLAVE COAST

Cape Verde Islands

Freetown

Fernando Po

Princes

St Thomas

EQUATOR

Ascension

AFRICA

Benguela Bay

Saint Helena

SOUTH ATLANTIC

INDIAN OCEAN

Simon's Bay

0   1000

NAUTICAL MILES

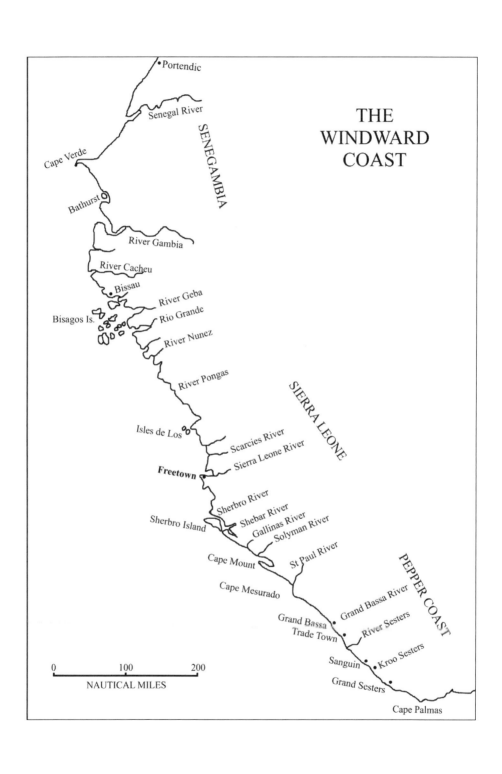

THE
WINDWARD
COAST

Portendic

Senegal River

SENEGAMBIA

Cape Verde

Bathurst

River Gambia

River Cacheu

Bissau

River Geba

Bisagos Is.

Rio Grande

River Nunez

River Pongas

SIERRA LEONE

Isles de Los

Scarcies River

Sierra Leone River

Freetown

Sherbro River

Shebar River

Sherbro Island

Gallinas River

Solyman River

Cape Mount

St Paul River

Cape Mesurado

PEPPER COAST

Grand Bassa River

Grand Bassa
Trade Town

River Sesters

Sanguin

Kroo Sesters

Grand Sesters

Cape Palmas

0   100   200
NAUTICAL MILES

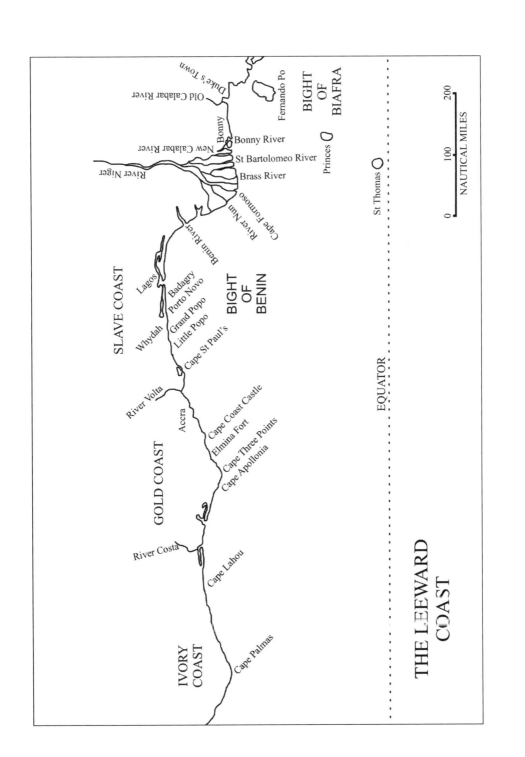

THE LEEWARD COAST

IVORY COAST

Cape Palmas
Cape Lahou
River Costa

GOLD COAST

Accra
River Volta
Cape Coast Castle
Elmina Fort
Cape Three Points
Cape Apollonia

SLAVE COAST

Lagos
Whydah
Badagry
Porto Novo
Grand Popo
Little Popo
Cape St Paul's

BIGHT OF BENIN

Benin River
River Niger
River Nun
Cape Formoso

New Calabar River
Bonny
St Bartolomeo River
Brass River
Bonny River
Old Calabar River
Duke's Town

BIGHT OF BIAFRA

Fernando Po
Princes
St Thomas

EQUATOR

0   100   200
NAUTICAL MILES

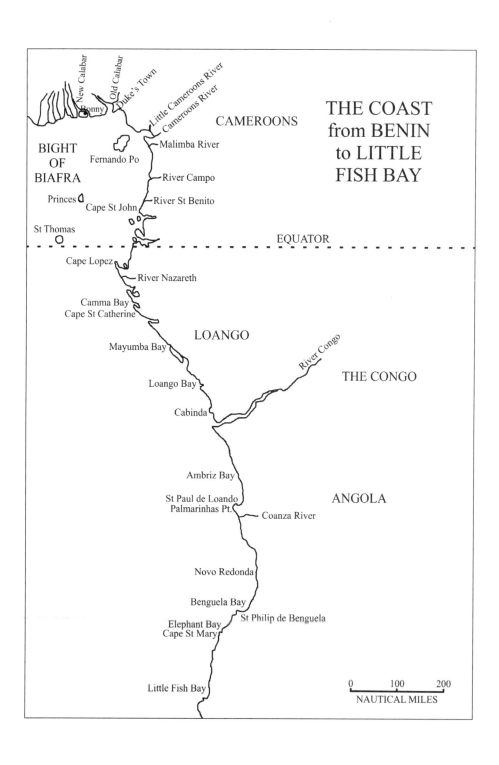

New Calabar
Old Calabar
Duke's Town
Little Cameroons River
Cameroons River

CAMEROONS

THE COAST
from BENIN
to LITTLE
FISH BAY

Bonny

Malimba River

BIGHT
OF
BIAFRA

Fernando Po

River Campo

Princes

River St Benito

Cape St John

St Thomas

EQUATOR

Cape Lopez

River Nazareth

Camma Bay
Cape St Catherine

LOANGO

Mayumba Bay

River Congo

THE CONGO

Loango Bay

Cabinda

Ambriz Bay

ANGOLA

St Paul de Loando
Palmarinhas Pt.

Coanza River

Novo Redonda

Benguela Bay

St Philip de Benguela

Elephant Bay
Cape St Mary

Little Fish Bay

0	100	200

NAUTICAL MILES

Drawings

A SHIP'S BOATS

Based on sketches from *Naval Costume*s (1840) by Sir William Symonds, R. N.

barge, 32 feet, lateen-rigged

launch, 30 feet

gig, 30 feet

first and second cutter, 25 feet

TYPES OF SAILING VESSEL

Unless otherwise stated, based on sketches from *Naval Costumes* (1840)

16-gun brig

16-gun brigantine
(from the lithograph *Hove to, on the larboard tack*)

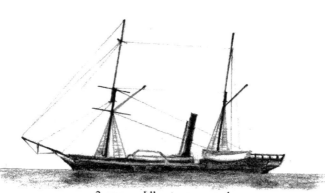

3-gun paddle steam-vessel
(based on an original photograph of HMS *Albert*)

sixth rate frigate (20-32 guns)
(various sources)

American topsail schooner

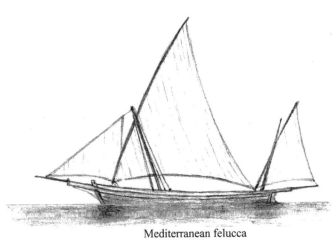

Mediterranean felucca

Acknowledgements

I would like to thank the staff of the National Archives, Kew, for their assistance whilst researching this book. The online British Newspaper Archive was also a valuable source of information as were the digitised *Papers Presented To Parliament* detailing the operations of various Mixed-Commission and Vice-Admiralty courts (including those at St Helena not eaten by termites!).

Since the release of Christopher Lloyd's *The Navy and the Slave Trade* in 1949 there has been surprisingly little written about the Royal Navy's six-decade-long suppression campaign and I am indebted to Peter Grindal for his recent, meticulously researched work, *Opposing the Slavers*. Other authors whose work I found most useful include Leslie Bethell, Bernard Edwards, Jenny S. Martinez, Andrew Pearson and Siân Rees. Finally, I would like to thank all at Pen and Sword Books, especially John Grehan for initially suggesting the project and Lisa Hoosan and Stephen Chumbley for their help in the preparation of this book.

Excerpts from *Opposing the Slavers* are © Grindal, P. 2016, *Opposing the Slavers: The Royal Navy's Campaign against the Atlantic Slave Trade*, I.B. Tauris, used by permission of Bloomsbury Publishing Ltd. Excerpts from *Royal Navy Versus the Slave Traders* are © Edwards, B. *Royal Navy Versus the Slave Traders: Enforcing Abolition at Sea 1808–1898* (Pen and Sword Books, 2007). Excerpts from *Sweet Water and Bitter* are © Siân Rees 2009, *Sweet Water and Bitter: The Ships that Stopped the Slave Trade*, first published in Great Britain by Chatto & Windus in 2009.

Glossary

aft:	To the rear of a vessel.
amidships:	The central part of the ship.
athwart:	At right angles to the ship's centreline.
barque:	A vessel with three or more masts. The aft mast fore-and-aft rigged, the others square rigged.
beak:	Projection at head of a ship beneath the bowsprit, to which is attached the ship's figurehead.
beam:	The width of the ship.
bear:	To turn relative to the direction of the wind; i.e. bear to or bear away from the wind.
beat:	To sail into the wind by repeatedly tacking.
bowsprit:	A spar projecting forward from the bows upon which yards can be set.
brig:	A vessel with two square-rigged masts.
brig-sloop:	A two-masted sailing vessel, square rigged on both masts.
brigantine:	A two-masted vessel, the aft mast fore-and-aft rigged.
broad pennant:	A long, swallow-tailed flag flown by a commodore.
bulkhead:	Internal partition in a vessel.
burthen:	Internal volume of a ship.
cable:	(i) Strong, heavy rope.
	(ii) Measure of distance, 200 yards.
careen:	To heave a ship down onto her side by her masts for cleaning.
chains:	Narrow platforms that provided a fixing point for the rigging outside the hull of the ship.
commodore:	Senior captain placed in command of a squadron or division.
cordage:	Rope or rigging.

cutter:	A single-masted vessel with more than one forward set fore-and-aft rigged sail.
draught:	Depth of water in which a ship floats.
fathom:	6ft.
felucca:	A small, two-masted Mediterranean vessel used for coastal trading, sometimes also equipped with oars.
fish:	A long piece of timber lashed to a mast or yard to strengthen it.
flagship:	Ship of the officer in command of a squadron or fleet, and flying his flag.
fleet:	Several squadrons of ships combined under the command of a single officer.
forecastle:	Originally castellated, the structure at the front of the ship around the foremast.
foremast:	Furthest-forward mast on a ship with two or more masts.
frigate:	Single-decked, square-rigged warship. Fast sailing and lightly armed.
gaff:	Uppermost spar supporting a fore-and-aft rigged sail.
gig:	Ship's boat. A captain or commanding officer's personal transport, usually crewed by four oarsmen.
guardship:	Ship with reduced crew and guns placed to guard an anchorage.
gun-brig:	*see* brig-sloop.
hawser:	Rope fitted between a cable and a tow-line.
heave to:	Set the sails so that a ship makes no headway.
jolly boat:	The smallest type of ship's boat. Used for transporting people and goods to and from the shore.
kedge anchor:	A small anchor that is used to manoeuvre a vessel.
knot:	One nautical mile an hour.
langrage:	A type of shot composed of pieces of irregular-shaped iron, designed to do maximum damage to sails, rigging and men on deck.
larboard:	Old term for port (left hand side of vessel facing forwards).
leeward:	In the direction towards which the wind is blowing.
long gun:	Main armament on a ship.

luff: Order given to helmsman to bring the ship's head more to windward.

mainmast: Tallest mast in a vessel with two or more masts.

master: (i) warrant officer responsible for the sailing and navigation of a Royal Navy vessel.

                 (ii) Commanding officer of a merchant vessel.

mate: (i)   warrant rank held by Royal Navy midshipmen passed for lieutenant and awaiting promotion.

                 (ii) responsible for assisting the master or other warrant officer (boatswain, gunner etc).

                 (iii) Officer in the merchant navy lower in rank to the master.

mizzenmast: Usually the rearmost mast on a vessel with two or more masts.

offing: Distant horizon at sea.

ordinary: A ship laid up with guns and stores removed and masts partially dismantled.

pinnace: A ship's boat, usually with eight oars, often used as a tender.

polacca: A brig or ship-rigged Mediterranean vessel.

poop deck: A short deck above the quarterdeck at the stern of the ship.

port: Left-hand side of a ship (facing forward).

post captain: Captain of a Sixth-Rate ship or above.

privateer: Merchant vessel with a military commission to capture enemy shipping.

prize: Captured enemy vessel.

quarter: Towards the stern of a vessel.

quarterdeck: Part of the deck astern of the mainmast. The command centre of the vessel.

rake: To fire at the bow or stern of a ship that is at right angles to one's own ship.

rate: Designation, used by most navies, based on size and number of guns a ship carried. A First Rate had 100+ guns, a Second Rate 90–98, a Third Rate 64–80, a Fourth Rate 50–60, a Fifth Rate 32–48 and a Sixth Rate 20–32 guns.

rigging:	Fixed ropes used to support masts and adjustable ropes used to control yards and sails.
road, roadstead:	Place of open anchorage some way from the main harbour or shore.
run:	To sail in roughly the same direction as the wind.
schooner:	A vessel with two or more masts all fore-and-aft rigged.
ship:	Large, three-masted vessel, square rigged on all three masts.
shoal:	Shallow water in which a ship can run aground.
shot:	Metal projectiles fired by guns.
shrouds:	Rigging ropes used as support either side of the masts.
sloop:	small vessel with main guns on the upper deck. Divided into two categories, three masted ship-sloops and two-masted brig-sloops.
spring tides:	Tides occurring in the second and fourth quarters of the moon, producing higher high water and lower low water than average.
squadron:	Group of ships smaller in size than a fleet and under the control of a senior officer.
square rigged:	Sails set at a right angle to the centreline of the vessel.
starboard:	Right-hand side of a ship (facing forward). Side of a vessel to which a steering board used to be fixed.
strike:	To haul down a ship's flag to indicate its surrender.
sumaca:	Small coastal trading schooner.
sweeps:	Large, heavy oars, employed on a ship's boats.
tack:	To change direction by pointing the ship through the wind so that the wind comes over the opposite side of the vessel.
tender:	A vessel that services an armed vessel of a navy, supplying provisions and munitions and carrying mail and dispatches.
topsail schooner:	A schooner with one or two square-rigged topsails on her foremast
warp:	To move a vessel by hauling on ropes attaching to anchors, buoys or other vessels.
yard:	Horizontal spar on a mast to which the sails are attached.

Prologue

On the morning of 27 February 1845 the 18-gun brig-sloop *Wasp*, Commander Sydney Ussher, was cruising 50 miles to the south of Lagos. Patrolling the Bight of Benin under light and variable winds in a vessel that was a poor sailer in anything but a strong breeze, Ussher held out little hope of catching any of the slave-carrying vessels he had been tasked with arresting as an officer in the Royal Navy's West Africa Squadron. However, around mid-morning a strange sail was sighted off *Wasp*'s bow and Ussher immediately gave chase, the vessel eventually revealing herself to be a topsail schooner, a type notorious for its use by the human traffickers on the coast. By midday *Wasp* was close enough to the Brazilian-flagged vessel for Ussher to send his boats, commanded by Lieutenant Robert Stupart and Midshipman Thomas Palmer, away. After a long hard pull it was around 8.00pm before *Wasp*'s cutter and gig finally drew alongside the schooner and Stupart led his men up her side. Armed with just two pistols and five cutlasses between them, the fifteen British sailors and marines received little resistance from the schooner's crew of twenty-eight men. Their captain, Joaquim Cerquira, protested against the boarding, but allowed for his vessel, *Felicidade*, to be searched. It was quickly established that there were no slaves aboard the schooner but a search of her hold revealed typical slave provisions, farina and casks of water, hidden beneath a deck made of loose boards. When questioned, Cerquira admitted he had been waiting off the coast for a cargo of slaves to transport to Brazil and had previously been chased by several Royal Navy cruisers, *Wasp* included, but had always evaded capture due to the superior sailing qualities of his vessel. However, on this occasion he had a boat ashore which he had been loath to abandon.

The following morning *Felicidade*'s crew, save for Cerquira and the cook, Janus Mayaval, were transferred to *Wasp* and the schooner, now under the command of Stupart with a prize crew of sixteen men, departed for Sierra Leone, where she was to be adjudicated by the court at Freetown.

Heading north, on the morning of 1 March Stupart spotted a strange sail to windward and gave chase. The pursuit continued throughout the day and into the night and by the following morning Stupart was close enough to the vessel, now identified as a Brazilian brigantine, to order her to heave to, threatening to open fire on her with *Felicidade*'s guns if she did not comply. The brigantine, *Echo*, shortened sail but when she was boarded her master, Francisco Serva, complained that he was on a legitimate trading voyage. However, a search of the vessel soon revealed 430 slaves crammed below her decks. Dividing his sixteen men between two vessels, Stupart gave command of *Felicidade* to the 15-year-old Palmer, with just one pistol and one cutlass between the young midshipman and the nine members of his prize crew, the other men arming themselves with iron bars. Fourteen of *Echo*'s crew of twenty-eight men were sent across to *Felicidade* and seven of these men were placed in a boat that was towed astern of the schooner. The remaining seven prisoners were placed under guard in the forepeak with the exception of Serva who was allowed to remain on deck with Cerquira. Palmer now allocated his men their duties. One man was placed at the helm, two men were stationed forward, another amidships and one as sentry along the hatchway. Having raided *Felicidade*'s spirit room, three of Palmer's men were soon asleep, one very drunk. The prize crew also included two Kroomen, skilled African sailors employed by the Navy to serve on board its cruisers. As both vessels sailed in company for Freetown on the evening of 2 March, Palmer was on deck speaking to his ageing quartermaster when Serva went over to the hatchway where the drunken sentry was now asleep and called for his men to come up. Seeing one of the prisoners appearing at the hatchway brandishing a knife, the quartermaster went across and struck him on the head with his iron bar. Grabbing a handspike he now defended himself against five other knife-wielding prisoners who had appeared on deck. Palmer, panicking at the appearance of the prisoners, was run through with a long knife and thrown overboard by the cook, Mayaval, who had come on deck from the cabin where he had been making bread. The drunken British sailor was stabbed through the chest; another was partly thrown overboard, clinging desperately to the fore sail until his fingers were hacked away. The quartermaster was eventually overpowered, his throat was slit and he was thrown overboard as Serva encouraged his crew to more violence. The two Kroomen escaped by jumping over the side of the ship and were never seen again. When the last British sailor had been killed Serva ordered the Brazilian ensign to be raised on board *Felicidade* and for the schooner to give chase to *Echo*.

Stupart's men were busy handing out food and water to the emaciated slaves on board *Echo* when the lookouts spotted *Felicidade* bearing down on them. Thinking that Palmer wished to hail him, Stupart shortened sail in order to speak to the midshipman. However, as *Felicidade* came up Stupart was alarmed to see she was once again flying the Brazilian flag. Furthermore, there was no sign of Palmer or any of his men on deck. Stupart was now hailed by Serva who demanded that he heave to. Ignoring this command Stupart sailed on but moments later *Felicidade* opened fire on *Echo* with several rounds of grapeshot. Stupart was preparing for another broadside when the schooner unexpectedly veered away and sailed off under a full spread of canvas. Stupart attempted to give chase but *Felicidade* was a far superior sailer to his brigantine and soon disappeared from sight, leaving *Echo* to resume her course for Freetown where Stupart would report the retaking of the schooner to his commander-in-chief, Commodore William Jones.

There was still English blood on *Felicidade*'s decks when four days later she fell in with the Royal Navy brig *Star*, Commander Robert Dunlop. After a short chase a warning shot was fired across *Felicidade*'s bows and she came to. Her crew had fled below and the boarding party, led by Lieutenant Etheridge, discovered her weather deck deserted apart from the man at the helm and a drunken Serva who insisted he was a passenger on board the schooner which, he informed Etheridge, was called *Virginie*. Etheridge and his men went below and soon discovered the nervous-looking crew in their various hiding places. Four sailors had head wounds and rather unconvincingly explained that a spar had fallen on them, although it seemed more likely to Etheridge that the wounds, which were nearly all alike, had all been made by a cutlass or similar edged weapon. There were also fresh bloodstains and bloody footprints on the deck along with a boat anchor marked with a broad arrow, denoting it was British government property. Searching the after cabin for the ship's papers, Etheridge discovered various items of Royal Navy clothing and an English book on astronomy with the name 'R.D. Stupart' written inside. Suspecting foul play, Dunlop ordered Serva and his men to be placed in irons and taken on board *Star*. Meanwhile Lieutenant John Wilson was placed in command of *Felicidade* with a prize crew of nine men and she was dispatched to Freetown

Heading out to sea to pick up the south-east trade winds, Wilson soon discovered that *Felicidade* was damaged below the waterline. On the night of 16 March the schooner was hit by a violent squall which descended out of nowhere, throwing the vessel, which had all her sails set, on her beam ends. *Felicidade* soon began to sink, leaving Wilson and his prize crew clinging to the forecastle rails which had settled just above the water. Wilson counted heads then set his men about the task of quickly building a life raft. With just three knives between them they cut cordage from the rigging which was used to lash planks and spars together. The main boom was retrieved by the three Kroomen who cut at the gear underwater and a piece of shredded canvas was turned into a makeshift sail. Several attempts were made to bring up food and water from the schooner but these proved unsuccessful. Just as the men finished building the raft *Felicidade* sank from view beneath them.

The hastily-assembled raft had no rudder or oars and Wilson no compass to steer by, but he had a rough idea of their position and he knew that if he kept the wind astern they should end up somewhere off the coast in the Bight of Benin. *Felicidade*'s shipwrecked crew spent the next twenty days afloat on their tiny raft, their half-naked bodies being burned black beneath the blisteringly hot sun during the day and frozen at night. Occasionally it rained and the men collected just enough water in a shoe to quench their thirsts. During the night flying fish landed on the raft and four sharks that followed the raft were caught with bowline knots and eaten raw. After several weeks afloat the three Kroomen and a British sailor went mad from the effects of drinking salt water and threw themselves overboard, just days prior to the raft being spotted by the brig *Cygnet* off Lagos on 5 April. Wilson and the remaining members of his prize crew were discovered barely alive, their emaciated bodies blackened by the sun and covered in salt water sores. Another sailor, a Brazilian, died just hours after coming aboard Commander Henry Layton's brig.

On 5 March *Echo* had fallen in with *Wasp* and Ussher put a fresh prize crew on board the brigantine along with a supply of water for the slaves prior to her departure for Sierra Leone, still under the command of Stupart. *Echo* arrived at Freetown on 11 April and her surviving 417 slaves were landed, forty-five of their number requiring hospital treatment. The court having heard the evidence, including a statement from Stupart regarding the attack on *Echo* by *Felicidade*, on 21 April the brigantine was condemned, 412 slaves surviving to be emancipated and handed over to the Liberated African Department.

On 3 July the brig *Rapid*, Commander Edmund Wilson, arrived at Portsmouth with the 'Spanish Pirates' as they were now known by the press – Francisco Serva, Janus Mayaval, Maria Alvares, Florenco Ribeira, Juan Francisco, Jose Martines, Antonio Joaquim, Manuel Antonio, Jose Antonio and Sebastian De Santos. On 24 July the ten prisoners appeared at the packed Crown Court in Exeter charged 'that with force and arms upon the high seas, in and upon one Thomas Palmer, in the peace of God and our Lady the Queen, then being in a certain vessel known as the *Felicidade*, did feloniously and wilfully make an assault'.[1] With Mr Justice Baron Platt presiding, Stupart, Wilson and Cerquira gave evidence against the accused, Cerquira's testimony being corroborated by Serva's two black servants, Emanuel Rossigre and Sobrina da Costa. After a lengthy trial Manuel Antonio, Jose Antonio and Sebastian De Santos were acquitted and released but the remaining prisoners were found guilty of the murder of Palmer and seven of *Wasp*'s crew. However, this was not the end of the matter. An appeal was launched on the premise that the boarding of *Felicidade*, an empty slaver, had been carried out against the terms of the treaty with Brazil and was therefore illegal. Furthermore it was argued that the retaking of the vessel, using whatever means necessary, was legally justified. On 20 November, just four days before the prisoners were due to be executed, there was a retrial. Of the thirteen judges on the bench, just two, Lord Chief Justice Denman and Baron Platt, upheld the original conviction for murder and the men were ordered to be freed and sent back to Brazil at the expense of the government. The decision caused uproar in Britain, newspapers decried the verdict and questions were raised in the House but the ruling of the appeal court could not be overturned. On the Coast boardings of suspected Brazilian slavers now began with cries of 'Remember the *Felicidade*!', encouraging the sailors of the West Africa Squadron to fight with greater resolve than ever before.

Chapter 1

Slavers and Abolitionists

uropeans did not introduce slavery to Africa; it had existed there long before the arrival of the first Portuguese ships in the fifteenth century. In African society slaves were the only form of private, revenue-producing property recognised by law, holding the equivalent status to land in European legal systems. The enslaving of prisoners taken in battle had, for thousands of year, been a way by which African chiefs could improve their own power and prestige and this was the sole purpose of many raiding parties into neighbouring territories. Slavery was firmly entrenched in tribal culture and was used both as a form of punishment for crimes against the community and as a form of payment for any debts.

Athletic, black-skinned Africans had been a common sight in the slave markets of Greece and ancient Rome and when Arab traders arrived in the continent in the seventh century they began exporting a large number of slaves to work their plantations in Mesopotamia, modern-day Iraq, adding this human cargo to the huge caravans of ivory, gold and spices making the long journey out of Africa to the Arab peninsula. Muslims saw manual labour as beneath them and Islam also forbid the enslavement of fellow Muslims. However, sharia law sanctioned slavery, imposing a religious duty on masters to convert their slaves. Africans were more than happy to sell their slaves to the Muslim traders, the geographer Al Yaqubi noting 'the kings of the blacks sell their own people without justification or in consequence of war'.[1] Beguiling tribal chiefs with what were, in reality, largely worthless trinkets, the Arabs purchased male slaves, castrated to stop them reproducing, to be employed as servants, soldiers or labourers in the Muslim states in North Africa and the Middle East, whilst female slaves were sold as concubines or servants.

In 1415, Prince Henry of Portugal, better known to history as Henry the Navigator, captured the Moroccan city of Ceuta, home to the Barbary pirates who for centuries had caused depredations along the Portuguese coast, kidnapping locals to be sold as slaves in Africa. In the 1420s Henry, who had already set up a school of navigation at Cape Sagres, began funding voyages of exploration down Africa's west coast, hoping to find the fabled kingdom of Prester John and to establish Portuguese colonies (one was eventually founded on Madeira). However, at that time the only vessels at his disposal were small two-masted vessels known as *barcas* which were intended for inshore fishing and as such were totally unsuited to the rigours of the Atlantic Ocean. Under Henry's direction a new, much lighter ship, the *caravela* or *caravel*, was designed. Three-masted, square rigged on the fore and main mast and lateen rigged on the mizzen, these ships, which unlike the *barcas*, were capable of tacking into the wind, soon became the envy of other European nations, indeed they were the forerunners of the Spanish, British and French ships that eventually fought against one another during the lengthy wars of the eighteenth and nineteenth centuries. It was by sailing further out to sea in these new *caravelas* and finding more favourable winds that the previously impassable Cape Bojador in Morocco was finally rounded by Gil Eannes in 1433. Eight years later Antão Gonçalves dropped anchor 150 miles further south off the West African coast near the Rio de Oro. When Gonçalves's ship eventually sailed for home it had gained a cargo of skins, salt, gold dust and ten Africans, presented to Gonçalves, so Henry's chamberlain claimed, by an Arab on a camel. Thus it was that Antão Gonçalves became the first European to purchase slaves from Africa.

At that time Portugal, like much of Europe, was suffering from a chronic shortage of manpower caused by the Black Death (the first outbreak in 1348 had killed a third of the population) and it was not long before Portuguese ships returned to the African coast in search of more slaves. In 1444 six ships under the command of Lançarote de Freitas, the revenue officer for Lagos, sailed from Sagres, dropping anchor off Senegal. Local villages were attacked and the Portuguese returned to Lagos with 235 slaves who were taken to the outskirts of the city and auctioned. Threatened by the advance of Islam, in January 1455 Pope Nicolas V issued a papal bull that confirmed Portuguese dominion over the recently discovered lands south of Cape Bojador and encouraged the taking of slaves in order to convert them to Christianity. By this time the number of Africans being offered a 'better' Christian life had reached around 1,000 a year. In 1461 the Portuguese built their first trading post on an island in the Bay of Arguin.

In the 1440s the Portuguese began growing sugar on Madeira. Popular throughout Europe, this super-sweet and highly addictive crop quickly became the island's major source of wealth. As demand increased production was taken over by slave labour and by the sixteenth century the number of Africans on Madeira was equal to 10 per cent of the island's population. Seeing the potential of this crop, it was brought to Jamaica by the Spanish where conditions were ideal for its production. The harvesting of sugar was, however, notoriously back-breaking work and most of the indigenous population soon died from exhaustion or fled from the plantations. A local missionary, Las Casas, suggested that African slaves, saved from their heathen lives by conversion to Christianity, be brought in to work the plantations (Las Casas would eventually argue against the practice due to the mistreatment of the slaves). Rather than bring the Africans across themselves, the Spanish government contracted the work out, initially to the Portuguese. This drastically increased the number of slaves carried by Portuguese ships. Inevitably, as demand grew the various West African kingdoms, who in 1494 had all signed trade agreements with John II, began warring with one another in order to make more slaves. Between 1450 and 1500 an estimated 81,000 slaves were exported from Africa and during the next hundred years this number rose to 328,000, climbing even further to 1,348,000 during the seventeenth century.

In March 1500, a year after Vasco de Gama's voyage to India via the Cape of Good Hope, a fleet of thirteen ships and 1,200 men under the command of Pedro Alvares Cabral set off from Lisbon for India. However, wind conditions forced Cabral's fleet further west than intended, resulting in the accidental discovery of Brazil, which was immediately claimed by Cabral for the Portuguese Crown. Within fifty years the first Portuguese settlers had begun to exploit the natural resources of this country, which, with its rich fertile soil, was capable of producing vast crops of coffee, sugar or tobacco. All that was lacking was a labour force to work the land. The Portuguese of course had an immediate solution to this problem and by the early seventeenth century were importing African slaves from Angola at a rate of 10,000 a year, their possession on the south-west coast of Africa eventually earning itself the nickname the 'black mother of Brazil'.

In 1555 the British trader John Lok brought back five slaves from Ghana to England for display following a voyage to Africa. Two years later William Towerson sailed to Guinea from Plymouth, returning with gold and more slaves. In 1562 Plymouth merchant John Hawkins set up a syndicate, purchased three ships and set sail for the Guinea Coast where he captured around 300 slaves from several Portuguese vessels. Departing Africa for the Caribbean, Hawkins successfully traded his slaves in Santo Domingo before returning home in September 1563. Having made a profit of around 60 per cent for his investors, Hawkins returned to sea in October 1564, this time having gained the backing of the Earls of Leicester and Pembroke and Queen Elizabeth who leased him one of her ships, the 300-ton *Jesus of Lubeck*. During this voyage Hawkins raided several coastal villages and he departed Africa for Venezuela in late January 1565 having captured around 400 slaves. Following his arrival at Venezuela Hawkins discovered that the Spanish, who had a monopoly on trade in the region, had forbidden the colonists from trading with foreigners. In response Hawkins went ashore, 'captured' various towns, sold his slaves, then sailed for home, returning to England in September 1565. On Hawkins's final expedition in October 1567 he was accompanied by his cousin, Francis Drake. Sailing from Africa, their ships once again laden with slaves, a severe storm suddenly blew up, forcing Hawkins to change direction and head for San Juan de Ulloa in Mexico. Here the British were attacked by the Spanish forts and ships in the harbour who were awaiting the imminent arrival of a Spanish treasure fleet. Hawkins lost four of his six ships including *Jesus of Lubeck*. This final voyage had been a disaster but Hawkins's reputation remained intact and on his return to England he was appointed Treasurer of the Navy. In 1618 Elizabeth's successor, James I, formed the Company of Adventurers to Guinea and Benin and ten years later the first African slaves began to arrive in Virginia, North America.

By 1600 half the sugar being transported from Brazil to Europe was being shipped aboard Dutch vessels. In 1612 the Dutch Guinea Company built Fort Nassau, just 15 miles from the Portuguese fortress at Elmina. Five years later the Dutch purchased the island of Goree at Cape Verde from the Portuguese. In the 1623 the Dutch West Indies Company captured the Brazilian port of Bahia and began developing plantations in north-east Brazil, shipping slaves across from the west coast of Africa to work the fields. In 1637 a Dutch expedition captured Elmina and in 1641 a subsequent expedition captured St Paul de Loando and Benguela, temporarily seizing control of the slave supply in Angola from the Portuguese.

As a result of a dynastic crisis following the death in battle of King Sebastian, in 1580 Portugal became united with Spain and for the next sixty years was prohibited from engaging in the slave trade as a carrier. When Portugal finally regained her independence she turned to Mozambique for a fresh source of slaves in order to compete with the Dutch who now led the Atlantic slave trade. Following the Restoration of Charles II in 1660 a new British company was formed, the Royal Adventurers into Africa, with the Duke of York as its president. The company, which seized the Cape Verde Islands from the Dutch, undertook to supply slaves to Barbados, claimed for the English crown in 1625. Disputes between Britain and the Netherlands over trading rights on the Guinea Coast were one of the reasons for the Second Dutch War of 1665–7. Sugar, brought over to Barbados by Dutch setters expelled from Brazil, had begun to take over from tobacco as the main crop from the 1650s. Initially indentured servants or slaves from Britain were brought over to work the crops, but as in the case of Madeira, many died from exhaustion or disease. As the cost of labour from England increased the plantation owners looked for other cheaper sources of manpower. In 1644 there were around 800 Africans on the island, around 3 per cent of the population. Just sixteen years later around 27,000 people, over half the island's population, were of African descent. African chiefs had to be increasingly inventive in order to cope with the increase in demand for slaves to work these plantations. Wars between kingdoms continued apace and the number of crimes punishable by sale into bondage suddenly increased. One of these crimes was adultery and many African kings made sure that they always had at least half a dozen young wives whom they intentionally left unsatisfied.

France, with its colonies in North and South America, had been involved in small-scale slave trading since the 1540s, with an estimated 200 ships sailing from France to Sierra Leone between 1540 and 1578. However, the first French ship confirmed to have carried slaves was *L'Esperance* of La Rochelle, which, in 1594, transported slaves from Gabon to Brazil. In 1672 the Compagnie du Senegal was formed to control trade between the colonial ports of St Louis and Goree in Africa and North America, maintaining a monopoly on the slave trade for most of the eighteenth century. With the introduction of sugar plantations to its colonies in the West Indies in the mid to late seventeenth century, French involvement in the trade increased dramatically. Between 1675 and 1700 around 55,000 slaves were shipped to its Caribbean possessions and slaves were also purchased from the British and Dutch Caribbean islands. By the 1680s there were around 2,000 African slaves on San Domingo which was now the French empire's largest sugar producer. A century later the slave population stood at 460,000 and the island was producing two-thirds of all French exports in the West Indies.

In 1649 the Swedish company Svenska Afrikanska Kompaniet was formed. Operating along the lines of the Dutch West Indies Company it built several trading posts in Africa including Fort Carolusbug on the Gold Coast. In 1657 Denmark formed the Danish Africa Company, capturing the Swedish forts and building several of its own. Whilst Sweden eventually pulled out of Africa Denmark continued to prosper, supplying 4,000 slaves to the sugar island of St Thomas during the period of 1675–1700. Prussia was also briefly involved in the Trade, building several forts on the Guinea Coast and selling slaves to the Portuguese, Dutch and Danes. However, facing stiff competition from the other slaving nations Prussia abandoned the enterprise in 1720.

In 1698 the struggling Royal African Company, formed after the collapse of the Adventurers Company, lost its monopoly. Other merchants began to enter the Trade and by the 1730s Bristol had overtaken London as the main English slaving port. Following the Treaty of Utrecht in 1713 Spain awarded its 'Asiento' to the British South Sea Company which undertook to supply the Spanish colonies in America with 4,800 slaves annually for the next thirty years. Of the 170,000 slaves carried aboard British ships between 1730 and 1740, 60,000 of them were destined for the Spanish empire and 40,000 for the British colonies in North America. By the end of the following decade Liverpool had become the main slaving port and a further 60,000 slaves had been exported to Virginia and the Carolinas. The 'Asiento' was renewed in 1748 but, following the War of Jenkins' Ear and the subsequent Treaty of Madrid, was finally ended by mutual agreement two years later.

By the late eighteenth century around 80,000 Africans were being transported across the Atlantic per year by all the major slaving nations using the now well-established triangular trade system. Portugal, Spain, Britain, America, France, Denmark and Holland were all involved in this trade but more than half the slaves were now being carried aboard British vessels. Ships left their home ports laden with a variety of goods such as cotton, iron, muskets, gunpowder, brandy, rum, cowrie shells, bracelets and beads which were bartered for slaves in Africa. These slave ships now began the long journey to the colonies in North America or the West Indies where their human cargoes were exchanged for sugar, tobacco and rum for the return journey home. Taken in their entirety these voyages could last up to a year and cover 12,000 miles. The ships employed were typically small vessels of around 200 tons known as guinea-men, rigged either as schooners or brigs. Upon their arrival off the coast of Africa the guinea-men were converted for the three-month journey across the Atlantic with a temporary deck, reducing the headroom to around 30in, installed between decks to allow more slaves to be carried aboard. Branded and stripped naked to avoid overheating, the slaves, up to 500 on some voyages, were laid side by side as tightly as possible, manacled two by two, men in one section, women in another. Often a slave ship would have to wait off the coast of Africa for several months before she had enough slaves aboard to proceed with the next part of her journey. In his *An Account of the Slave Trade on the Coast of Africa*, published in 1788, the slave doctor Alexander Falconbridge described the conditions for the slaves during the Middle Passage:

> … they are frequently stowed so close as to admit no other posture than lying on their side. Neither will the height between decks, unless directly under the grating, permit them the indulgence of any erect posture … The hardships and inconveniences suffered by the Negroes during their passage are scarcely to be enumerated or conceived. They are far more violently affected by the seasickness than the Europeans. It frequently terminates in death, especially amongst the women. But the exclusion of fresh air is among the most intolerable … The confined air, rendered noxious by the effluvia exhaled from their bodies, and by being repeatedly breathed, soon produces fevers and fluxes, which generally carries off great numbers of them.[2]

Once out of sight of land the usual practice was to allow the slaves on to the top deck to eat and exercise, weather permitting. Male slaves remained manacled but female slaves had their chains removed and were also allowed to remain on the top deck during daylight hours. However, ships often encountered foul weather, whereupon ports were closed, hatches were battened down and the slaves spent days, sometimes weeks, manacled below decks in stifling heat with seasickness now added to the list of complaints.

It was estimated that around 15 per cent of a slaver's cargo would die during the Middle Passage, falling victim to such diseases as smallpox, yellow fever, cholera and dysentery. Others went blind through opthalmia. Whilst conditions for slaves were appalling, they were at least considered a valuable cargo: the same, however, could not be said for the ship's crew. Often these men came from the crimping houses where they had been plied with alcohol and induced to enlist aboard the slave ships. They were worked hard for poor pay (generally the weak West Indies currency) and wretched food and they slept wherever there was space aboard ship, more often than not on the open top deck. Olaudah Equiano, a slave who eventually gained his own freedom, witnessed one crew member aboard his ship being flogged to death and his body unceremoniously dumped over the side. It was estimated that around 20 per cent of a slaver's crew would die from disease, flogging or murder by mutinous slaves. An equal number would return from a cruise permanently crippled. Of the 5,000 British sailors employed in the slave trade during 1786, 1,130 men died and a further 1,550 were discharged or deserted ship in the West Indies or Africa.

An incident in 1819 gives some idea of the hardships endured by slaves and crew alike during the Middle Passage. In April of that year the French slave ship *Rodeur* sailed from Africa for Guadeloupe with a crew of twenty-two and a cargo of 160 slaves. Just a few days out of Africa the most common of all slave diseases, opthalmia, suddenly swept through the vessel, blinding slaves and crew alike, the ship's captain included. With only one member of the crew able to see, the ship drifted helplessly for ten days until she came upon another slaver, the Spanish ship *San Leone*. Calling across for assistance *Rodeur*'s crew were shocked to discover that the Spaniard had suffered exactly the same fate and almost all of her crew were also blind. Leaving *San Leone*, which was never heard of again, *Rodeur* sailed on and by the time she reached Guadeloupe half her crew had regained their vision. The captain, who could now see out of one eye, ordered all the slaves on deck. Having ascertained that his cargo was insured, he ordered the mate to pick out the slaves who were still completely blind, thirty-nine in all. Weights were tied to their legs and they were summarily thrown over the side of the ship.

The captain of *Rodeur* was unfortunately not the only slaver who resorted to disposing of his cargo in this manner. On 6 September 1781 the

British slave ship *Zong*, Captain Luke Collingwood, departed the island of St Thomas in the Bight of Biafra, bound for Jamaica with a cargo of 442 African slaves. Two weeks out of port *Zong* hit the Doldrums, a region of light, variable winds around the equator, and her progress slowed to barely a dozen or so miles west every day. It took *Zong* six weeks to break free of the Doldrums and pick up the north-east trade winds. By the time the coast of Brazil finally came into sight the crew were surviving on rancid salt beef and the slaves were being fed a mash of ground cassava root. What water there was left aboard ship was green and barely drinkable. Whilst Collingwood waited for a fresh wind to take him into the Caribbean sixty dead slaves were thrown overboard and they were soon joined by seven of *Zong*'s crew. On 18 November *Zong* reached the Caribbean and land was sighted. However, there was now a disagreement between Collingwood and his First Mate, James Kelsal, as to whether the land was the eastern end of Jamaica, or as Collingwood insisted, the southern tip of Hispaniola, some 270 miles further east. With a storm in the offing Collingwood decided to head to leeward, away from land. Forced to cut the water ration once more, the slaves now began to die at an alarming rate. With any chance of a profit from the voyage rapidly disappearing, Collingwood decided on a radical course of action. Maritime law stated that a cargo could be disposed of over the side of a ship in case of an emergency, the loss of which could be then charged to the insurer. Collingwood consulted with his officers and despite the protestations of Kelsal it was agreed that, as the slaves were in essence a form of cargo, any who were ill should be thrown over the side of the ship. Fifty-two slaves were tossed overboard on 29 November and another forty-two followed them the next day. It now began to rain and there was no longer a shortage of water aboard ship but on 1 December a further twenty-six slaves were thrown overboard, with ten more following several days later. Three weeks later, with enough water on board for crew and slaves to be on half rations, *Zong* finally arrived at Jamaica. When the vessel eventually returned to Liverpool and details of Collingwood's treatment of his slaves came out the case went to court. At the trial it was concluded that Collingwood had acted lawfully, the Lord Chief Justice, Lord Mansfield, commenting that, 'the case of the slaves was the same as if horses had been thrown overboard'.[3] The owners of *Zong*, William Gregson and George Case, eventually received payments from the underwriters of £30 for each of the 130 slaves that had been thrown over the side of their ship.

Thankfully not all slave masters were men like Collingwood or the captain of *Rodeur* who placed profits over the lives of their slaves. Others made their profits by ensuring that the majority of their cargoes made it across the Atlantic alive. Born in 1765, the British slaver Hugh Crow had first gone to sea aged seventeen. Known as 'Mind Your Eye Crow' through the loss of an eye in a childhood accident, Crow had first been persuaded to join a slave ship in 1790 and on his first voyage to the Gold Coast witnessed the funeral of the King of Anomabo and the ritualised slaughter of his twenty-three wives. Crow rose to become master of his own slave ship and for the next eighteen years commanded vessels for Aspinall's of Liverpool. In his memoirs, published posthumously in 1830 Crow declared: 'In the African trade, as in all others, there were individuals bad as well as good, and it is but injustice to discriminate, and not condemn the whole for the delinquencies of the few.'[4] Crow considered the transportation of slaves to the colonies as a necessary evil and, like many of his generation, seems to have been sincere when he expressed the opinion that slaves in the bountiful West Indies were better off than free men in Africa who were 'subject to the caprices of their native princes'.[5] Crow ensured his slaves were well fed and exercised and that their quarters were regularly cleaned out. He also looked after the health of his crews and slaves by issuing both with lime juice to ward off scurvy and very rarely lost a man through sickness. When he brought a slave ship into port the word soon went round: 'Crow has come again and as usual his whites and blacks are as plump as cotton bags.'[6]

Fellow British slaver John Newton went further than Crow and eventually argued against the trade he had once been part of. Born in London on 24 July 1725, Newton first went to sea aged 11. The son of a sea captain, he remained aboard merchant ships until 1744, when during a brief spell ashore he was unfortunate enough to be pressed into the Navy, rising to the rank of midshipman. Newton took the first opportunity to desert, but he was soon recaptured, demoted and publicly flogged. Soon after this Newton left the Navy and eventually made his way to Sierra Leone, becoming the servant of a slave trader. Treated cruelly, in 1748 he found passage home in a merchant ship whose captain had known his father. Newton eventually became the master of his own slave ship, then, whilst returning to England in May 1748, his ship encountered a terrible storm. His vessel close to foundering, Newton recalled sinking to his knees and pleading to God for salvation. The storm suddenly blew itself out, leaving Newton to reflect on what could only be described as divine intervention. Newton carried on slaving until 1755 but was forced to retire due to poor health. He spent the next five years as Inspector of the Tides at Liverpool where he met the evangelical preacher George Whitefield. Newton had taught himself Latin during the endless hours at sea and he now began religious studies. In 1760 Newton was ordained as a clergyman and appointed curate of the parish of Olney in Buckinghamshire. In 1767 he met the poet William Cowper and the pair began writing hymns for Newton's increasingly popular prayer meetings. Their most famous composition was 'Amazing Grace'. In 1780 Newton left Olney to become rector of St Mary Woolnoth in London. His meetings, many of which concerned the abolition of the slave trade, drew huge congregations. Amongst those drawn to his sermons was a young MP who had recently undergone his own religious conversion, William Wilberforce.

Born in Hull on 24 August 1759, Wilberforce was the son of a wealthy merchant and grandson of a former mayor of Hull. With a sizeable inheritance following the death of his grandfather to fall back on, Wilberforce had little interest in studying, preferring to spend most of his time at university drinking and gambling. After Cambridge Wilberforce followed his friend William Pitt into politics and in 1780 became Member of Parliament for Hull, aged 21. A skilled public speaker, he soon became known as 'the nightingale of the House of Commons'.[7] Wilberforce's life changed dramatically in October 1784, when, during a tour of France and Switzerland, he began discussing religion with his travelling companion, Isaac Milner, who urged him to read *The Rise and Progress of Religion in the Soul*, by the Nonconformist Philip Doddridge. On his return home Wilberforce sought guidance on his new-found faith from John Newton who recalled his previous life as a slaver and his own conversion. In mid-May 1787 Wilberforce and Pitt, who was now Prime Minister, first discussed the issue of slavery at Pitt's home in Holwood, Croydon. Pitt, a keen abolitionist, encouraged Wilberforce to meet fellow Cambridge graduate Thomas Clarkson, founding member of The Committee for Effecting the Abolition of the Slave Trade, set up earlier that year with the assistance of the Quakers who had been the driving force behind the British abolitionist movement for nearly sixty years.

On the urging of fellow MP Sir Charles Middleton, Wilberforce agreed to lead the abolitionist cause in Parliament, leaving Clarkson free to begin a lengthy fact-finding mission, visiting all the major slaving ports and interviewing slavers and slave merchants. Through Wilberforce's friendship with the Prime Minister, Clarkson was also able to gain access to state papers. Having studied the muster rolls of 20,000 seamen it was clear that high mortality amongst the slaving crews was draining the Royal Navy of essential manpower. This information was enough for a committee of the Privy Council to be set up to look in to the matter. In early May 1788 Pitt introduced a Private Member's Bill to investigate the Trade. His bill failed but a subsequent bill introduced by Sir William Dolben, basing the number of slaves carried at sea on a ship's tonnage, fared better and after a fairly tortuous passage scraped through the Lords with the backing of Pitt later that year.

In May 1789 the Commons debated the Privy Council report on the slave trade. Introducing the debate, Wilberforce, displaying his usual eloquence, declared slavery to be a 'national iniquity'[8] and went on to describe the destructive effects of the Trade on its victims, Africa and the colonies. Unsurprisingly, he received a great deal of opposition from the Members of Parliament from London, Bristol and Liverpool. As a delaying tactic they proposed that the House hear its own evidence and Wilberforce reluctantly agreed. That autumn Clarkson travelled to Paris, hoping to convince the revolutionary French government to abolish the Trade. Meanwhile Wilberforce had speeded up the hearings by gaining approval for a smaller select committee to investigate the matter and in April 1791 he introduced the first parliamentary bill to abolish the slave trade with a four-hour speech backed up by speeches from Pitt and the prominent MPs Edmund Burke and Charles Fox. However, following two days of debates the motion was defeated by 88 votes to 163.

Following this setback the abolition movement received a major fillip when, in early 1792, the Danish government announced it was to ban the import of slaves from Africa to its possessions in the Caribbean following a ten-year moratorium. Encouraged by this news, Wilberforce introduced his second abolition bill in April 1792. In what was widely regarded as one of the greatest legislative debates that the House had ever seen, the Treasurer of the Navy and close personal friend of Pitt, Henry Dundas, suggested a gradual abolition over a number of years and the Commons eventually voted 230 to 85 in favour of his amended motion. In February 1793 another vote was defeated by just eight votes, but later that month

Britain went to war against France and the whole question of abolition was put on the Parliamentary back-burner. In February 1794 the National Convention of the new French Republic abolished slavery in all French territories and in 1796, the date originally agreed on in Dundas's bill for the abolition of the slave trade, Wilberforce introduced another bill calling for an end to the Trade the following year. By this time, Clarkson, for so many years the driving force behind the Abolition movement, had collapsed from exhaustion and Wilberforce was losing support due to his opposition to the war. The bill was defeated by four votes and further defeats followed in 1797, 1798 and 1799.

The Peace of Amiens in 1802 saw the reintroduction of slavery into the French colonies by Napoleon. The abolitionists now lost their association with the revolutionaries in France and, with Wilberforce also forgiven his opposition to the war, they were no longer looked on with suspicion by Parliament. At the same time Denmark confirmed that it was to abolish slavery by the end of the year. Clarkson had also recovered and had returned to work, adding fresh impetus to the campaign. In 1804 Wilberforce introduced a new bill. It was passed by the Commons but was defeated in the Lords by the anti-abolitionists who were led by Dundas, now Lord Melville, and the ageing Lord Chancellor, Edward Thurlow. The following year Melville was impeached for mismanagement of funds whilst Treasurer of the Navy and the abolition bill did not make it past the Commons, largely due to the absence of Pitt who was now preoccupied by the problems of his friend Melville. In January 1806 Pitt died from exhaustion and was replaced as prime minister by Lord Grenville. Grenville had spoken out against the Trade in all the Parliamentary debates and he gave fellow abolitionists prominent positions in his Cabinet. In March 1806 the new Attorney-General, Sir Arthur Pigott, quietly introduced a bill prohibiting the importation of slaves to British foreign territories by British ships and the use of any British ships, capital or credit in the foreign slave trade. This time Wilberforce did not speak during the debate and so did not raise the suspicions of the anti-abolitionists. In fact hardly any turned up to vote and the bill was passed in the Commons by thirty-five votes to thirteen. The Lords better understood the full implications of the bill but it still received a majority, becoming law on 23 May 1806. Prior to 1806 British ships had been carrying around 50,000 slaves to the Americas each year but Pigott's bill effectively brought three-quarters of British slavery to an end.

In January 1807 Grenville decided that the time was right to introduce a bill in the Lords for the abolition of slavery, declaring that the Trade was not only detestable but also criminal. The Prime Minister faced stiff opposition from the Duke of Clarence and Lords Westmorland, St Vincent (commander-in-chief of the Channel Fleet) and Hawkesbury but he gained the support of the Duke of Gloucester and his bill was passed by 100 votes to 34. In the Commons debates that followed, fears were expressed by some MPs that the bill would be damaging to Britain's overseas colonies and might even lead to slave revolts. However, on the morning of 24 February the abolitionists won a crushing victory with a majority of 283 votes to sixteen, the whole House rising to applaud Wilberforce. On 25 March the bill received royal assent and on 1 May 1807 the African slave trade became illegal throughout the British Empire, with a £100 fine for every slave found and confiscation of any vessel found to be involved in the Trade.

Early on in the abolition debates a proposal had been put forward by Granville Sharp to set up a colony for freed slaves at Sierra Leone on the West Coast of Africa. With financial support from both the Quakers and government, four vessels carrying 290 black men, forty-one black women and seventy white women (reportedly London prostitutes forced to marry the black settlers) sailed from Portsmouth in April 1787 escorted by the sloop *Nautilus*, Commander Thomas Bouldon Thompson. Upon their arrival in Sierra Leone the settlers constructed houses on a strip of land purchased from the local chief, King Tom, that had previously been used as a slave market. Unfortunately, delays prior to sailing had resulted in the settlers arriving in Sierra Leone in the middle of the rainy season, the worst for many years. Within a year half had succumbed to diseases such as malaria and dysentery. With little to do except watch their crops die, some succumbed to alcoholism while others simply gave up and deserted to join the local slave traders. The remaining colonists fled when their newly-established town was burned down by King Tom's successor in 1789. Unperturbed by these failures, in 1791 the Sierra Leone Company was formed, with a board of directors that included Clarkson and Wilberforce. The colonists returned to Sierra Leone to rebuild Granville Town and in January 1792 they were joined by 1,190 freed blacks from Nova Scotia and New Brunswick. The convoy that carried them across the Atlantic was led by Lieutenant John Clarkson, Thomas Clarkson's brother, who briefly acted as the colony's first Governor. The settlers from North America built a new capital, Free Town (later renamed Freetown) and the new colony flourished under Clarkson's successor, Governor Zachary Macauley. In 1808 Sierra Leone became a full dependency of the Crown.

In America, as in Britain, the Quakers had been the driving force behind calls for the abolition of the slave trade and had been agitating for change since the 1750s. There were also concerns that an increase in slave numbers would eventually lead to large-scale revolts of the kind witnessed in Jamaica in 1760. The Constitution of the United States, signed in September 1787, established a requirement for a debate on slavery in 1807, a compromise date arrived at to avoid the secession of the southern states. Pennsylvania had begun to introduce measures to ban slavery in 1780 and by the end of the decade Rhode Island, Massachusetts, Connecticut and New York had all prohibited the Trade, although it continued largely unchecked at Rhode Island. In 1790 Congress prohibited foreigners from fitting out slave ships and banned the Trade to foreign ports. Other measures introduced during the remainder of the decade forbade US citizens from carrying slaves to other nations and made it illegal for them to have shares in a slave vessel trading in foreign ports. However, slavery remained alive and well in North and South Carolina and Georgia and the establishment of Mississippi as a state in 1798 together with the sale of French Louisiana to the United States in 1803 further increased the number of slaving states.

In his annual address to the nation in December 1806 President Thomas Jefferson condemned those 'violations of human rights which have been so long continued on the unoffending inhabitants of Africa'.[9] These were strong words from a president who had both employed and even sold slaves himself and who had, up to this point, never made his position on slavery clear. The day after Jefferson's statement, 17 December, Senator Stephen Bradley of Vermont introduced an abolition bill. The ensuing debate concentrated on how the bill would be implemented (there were questions on what to do with any illegally-imported slaves and how to punish the slavers) rather than the principles behind it. It was passed by the Senate on 27 January, by the House of Representatives on 11 February and signed by the President on 2 March. The bill, which would come in to effect on 1 January 1808, prohibited the introduction into the United States of any 'negro, mulatto, or person of colour, as a slave'[10] and made it illegal for any US citizen to equip or finance any slave vessel operating out of the United

States. However, there was as yet no mechanism in place to enforce these new regulations. With successive governments showing little inclination to back up the anti-slavery legislation with action, the Trade in the southern states and Cuba would persist, albeit on a small scale, for decades to come.

British anti-slavery enforcement was more effective than that of the United States, several slave ships being seized by the Royal Navy squadron in the West Indies soon after the abolition bill was passed, but British slavery was a centuries-old affair and would not simply die overnight. Several large firms in Liverpool and London chose to invest in Portuguese vessels whilst others continued to sell equipment to foreign traders. Between December 1807 and July 1809 an estimated thirty-five suspected slave ships sailed from Liverpool under Portuguese colours. The most popular flag of convenience was initially the Stars and Stripes but this subterfuge ended with the arrest of several American vessels by the Royal Navy in 1808. However, rather than risk hefty fines or the loss of their vessels, the majority of British merchants quickly abandoned slavery and turned to more legitimate forms of commerce. Ivory, gold and spices once again began to be traded in large quantities and these were joined by new items such as beeswax, acacia gum and palm oil, which was used for making soap, candles and most importantly of all lubricants, demand for which was steadily increasing as the Industrial Revolution gained pace.

Britain and the United States of America had now, officially at least, turned their backs on slavery but the same could not be said for the other slaving nations. In April 1807 the British minister in Lisbon, Lord Strongford, sought to persuade the Portuguese to abolish the Trade but was informed by their Foreign Minister, the Count of Barca, that such a decision would be impractical. Furthermore, worries over their supply lines being cut by the Royal Navy had caused a sudden surge in the Portuguese Trade, which received a further boost in November 1807 when the Portuguese royal family relocated from Lisbon to Rio de Janeiro prior to Napoleon's invasion of the Iberian peninsula. Rio now became the seat of the Portuguese government and, having received the full backing of the Prince Regent, Dom Joao, the Trade quickly doubled in size from 10,000 to 20,000 slaves per year. Whilst France and Spain remained at war with Britain the Royal Navy could keep a check on these countries' trade through the blockade of their ports but in June 1808 the suppression campaign received a further setback when Britain and Spain signed a peace agreement and Spanish slavers were free to trade again.

The responsibility for enforcing Britain's new anti-slavery legislation was to be shared by the Lords Commissioners of the Admiralty and the Secretary of State for War and the Colonies. However, in 1807 these officials and their departments were understandably more concerned with the ongoing war with France, The Navy had very few ships to spare for anti-slavery operations and the First Lord, Charles Grey, who had replaced the abolitionist Lord Barham in 1806, treated the issue largely as an unfortunate distraction from more important matters. However, the Secretary of State for War and the Colonies, Lord Castlereagh, had been a close ally of Pitt and was therefore more responsive to the demands of his friend Wilberforce, who, in October 1807, wrote to the Colonial Office suggesting that a Vice-Admiralty court be set up in Sierra Leone to try cases concerning slave ships and their cargoes captured off the West Coast of Africa. He also suggested to Castlereagh that it might be possible to raise new black regiments in Africa by recruiting released slaves to the British Army. A Vice-Admiralty court was eventually set up at Freetown in March 1808. Vessels condemned by the court there were to be confiscated and sold whilst their human cargoes would be liberated in Sierra Leone, maintained at government expense for a year. They would also be given the choice of volunteering in the British West Indies as apprenticed labourers, working on the plantations for low wages, or as recruits to the British Army. The Order of Council that had set up the Vice-Admiralty court also laid out the regulations concerning 'Head Money', the money that would be paid out to the officers and men of the Royal Navy following the condemning of a slave ship. The regulations distinguished between two types of capture. The first was a slave cargo taken as a prize of war. Under these circumstances head money would be £40 for a male slave, £30 for a female and £10 for a child under 14. If a ship was seized under the Abolition Act the head money would be half that made for a prize of war. The distribution of the head money would be in accordance with the payment of prize money; a sliding scale where captains and officers received the lion's share of the money.

   On 27 July 1807 the last legal British slaver, *Kitty Amelia*, sailed from Liverpool for the coast of Africa, her clearance certificate having been signed just days before the abolition bill was passed. When *Kitty Amelia*'s captain, Thomas Forrest, died en route, her supercargo, Hugh Crow, who was in charge of purchasing and looking after the slaves, took over command of the vessel. Arriving at the Bonny after a voyage of seven weeks, the local chieftain, King Holiday, boarded the vessel and immediately demanded to know if the rumours that Britain had abolished the slave trade were true. His suspicions being confirmed by Crow, Holiday declared: 'We tink trade no stop, for all we Ju-Ju men say you country can niber pass God A'mighty.'[11] For Holiday and the other African chiefs it seemed inconceivable that Britain would attempt to end a trade that had lasted for nigh on 350 years and which was now responsible for three-quarters of the region's exports.

By the early nineteenth century slaves were being exported from every creek and estuary along 3,300 miles of West African coast from Cape Verde at latitude 14° North to Cape Frio at 18° South. Goree at Cape Verde had, for many centuries, been fought over between the major powers but had recently been recovered from France by Britain. Further south lay the mouth of the river Gambia with French and British factories situated 130 miles upstream. South of the Gambia was a region that had been dominated by the Portuguese since the fifteenth century, with slaving taking place along the Casamance, Cacheu, Geba and Rio Grande rivers. Most trade was carried out along the Cacheu, a river that was navigable for 100 miles once a ship had made her way past the entrance with its shallow banks and irregular shoals, features common to most of the rivers in West Africa. Fresh meat, fruit and rice was available at Bissau, situated at the mouth of the Geba, and ships could also stop here to water. South-east of the Rio Grande lay the infamous slaving rivers the Pongas and the Nunez, which, between them, had been responsible for a tenth of the total number of slaves exported from Africa during the eighteenth century. The Pongas was a particularly difficult river to navigate as its features seemed to change with every rainy season. On the bulge of Africa lay the mountains of Sierra Leone, the river of the same name providing one of the best harbours along this stretch of coast. To the south of this British-held territory lay another hot spot of Portuguese slave trading, the Gallinas River. Between the Gallinas and its neighbouring river, the Solyman, there was an extensive system of lagoons and creeks bordered by mangrove swamps. Forty miles south-east of the Gallinas the Windward Coast ended at the rocky headland of Cape Mount. Conditions for sailors off this fever inducing stretch of coast, especially during the six-month-long wet season, were as bad as its other name, the 'White Man's Grave', suggested.

The 200 miles of coastline from Cape Mount down to Cape Palmas was known as the Grain, or Pepper Coast. Trade in this region was carried out by a handful of Portuguese slavers based along the River Sesters and at the tiny port of Sanguin. The major headland of Cape Palmas, where the coastline changes direction and heads off to the east, was also the home of the Kroomen. Expert sailors, they were employed to great effect both by the slavers and the Royal Navy. There were only two major slaving areas on the Ivory Coast, situated on the rivers Cavally and St Andrews. Most of the remaining river mouths here were usually blocked by sand and were only navigable in the rainy season. Eastward of the Ivory Coast lay the Gold Coast, named, like all the other coasts in the region, after its principal export in the days before the West African slave trade. This was the home of the Ashantis and the Fantis, who spent as much time at war with one another as they did the British and Dutch slavers at the forts of Dixcove, Elmina, Cape Coast and Accra. Sixty miles east of Accra the headland of Cape St Paul's marked the western edge of the earliest and most important slave trading area in West Africa, the Bights of Benin and Biafra. This was the heart of the slave coast, a region estimated to have exported around two million slaves by the time the Trade was finally brought to an end in the late nineteenth century, more than half of them by the Portuguese. The Bight of Benin contained the Benin and Cameroon slaving rivers and was controlled by the notorious Dahomey tribe who sold their slaves through the Portuguese, English and French traders at Whydah. Thirty miles to the east of Whydah was Porto Novo and 18 miles further on lay Badagry, both of which were small trading stations. A further 45 miles to the east lay Lagos, the only harbour on the slave coast where vessels with draughts of up to 5ft could enter at high water during the dry season.

Eighty miles east of Lagos a network of rivers and creeks forms the delta of the River Niger. Here the shoreline turns first to the south-east then to the east as it enters the Bight of Biafra which contained another great slaving river, the Calabar, which had been a centre for English, French and Dutch slaving since the seventeenth century. Roughly 20 miles offshore sits the mountainous island of Fernando Po, under Spanish control since 1778, with the Portuguese islands of Princes and St Thomas lying a further 111 miles and 190 miles respectively to the south-west. The larger St Thomas, a centre for slave exports in the region until the seventeenth century, lies just a few miles north of the equator. Both these islands contained plentiful supplies of fresh water, fish, game, fruit and vegetables. They were also useful navigational aids in the Bights where constant attention to the lead was required as a vessel could quickly find itself on the breakers while her master still imagined her to be a mile out at sea.

Very little slave trading occurred along the 1,300 miles of coast south of the Bights from Cape Lopez down to Cape Frio in Angola, what there being centred around the River Congo and controlled by the Portuguese. The prevailing south-west trade winds in this region made sailing to Brazil faster and less expensive than from any of the rivers and creeks north of the equator and Angola's capital, St Paul de Loando, situated on the coast 700 miles south of the equator, had regularly exported 10,000 slaves a year to Brazil during the 1700s.

Prior to the turn of the nineteenth century the 3,300 miles of West African coastline had been of little interest to the hydrographers of the Royal Navy. However, the British government was quick to recognise that the Navy would require detailed and up-to-date charts of the region in order to carry out its new anti-slavery operations and in mid-August 1808 Castlereagh wrote to the Admiralty to explain that a commission had been appointed in Sierra Leone to survey the coast. The Navy was to supply a ship of 20 guns, fitted with instruments and stores for the survey and captained by an officer who would also act as third joint commissioner alongside the current governor of Sierra Leone, Thomas Ludlam, and his predecessor, William Dawes. In response to Castlereagh's letter Their Lordships replied that a ship would be provided as quickly as possible and recommended that Captain Edward Henry Columbine be appointed to the Commission.

A captain of six years' seniority on half pay, the 45-year-old Columbine was currently employed on temporary duty with the Hydrographer of the Navy in London. Within days of the receipt of Castlereagh's letter Columbine had been appointed as Commissioner (he would receive a salary of £1,500 per year) and on 6 September he travelled down to Spithead to take command of the 32-gun *Solebay*, an ageing frigate that Columbine quickly discovered was in urgent need of a refit. His new command was taken into dry dock at Portsmouth and by 6 October was back at Spithead, Whilst the Admiralty searched for a suitable vessel to accompany *Solebay* to Africa, Columbine ordered provisions and also requested the use of Portsmouth wherries which he though more suitable than his ship's boats for survey work.

On 9 April 1809 Columbine finally received orders to take a convoy of merchant ships under his protection and sail to Sierra Leone. Along with his orders Columbine also received two warrants from Castlereagh authorising and directing his actions off the coast of Africa. Three days later the gun-brig *Tigress*, Lieutenant Robert Bones, arrived at Spithead and Columbine, who was now taking his instructions directly from Castlereagh, was ordered to hoist a commodore's broad pendant upon leaving the English coast. On 5 May 1809 *Solebay* and *Tigress*, accompanied by eleven merchant ships, dropped down from Spithead to St Helen's and from there sailed to Africa.

Chapter 2

Early Operations:
November 1807–November 1814

Whilst *Solebay* was at anchor at Spithead, waiting for instructions, anti-slavery operations had in fact already begun off the West Coast of Africa. In November 1807 the newly-launched 18-gun brig-sloop *Derwent*, Commander Frederick Parker, had sailed from Spithead on a routine deployment to the colony at Sierra Leone. On 30 December the first arrest of the Royal Navy's six-decades-long suppression campaign was made when Parker's vessel, sailing off Freetown, detained the slave ship *Minerva*. More arrests were made in mid-March 1808 when *Derwent* captured two American-flagged slavers, *Baltimore* and *Eliza*, which she escorted into Freetown. Having appointed a storekeeper, Alexander Smith, as the judge of the newly-established Vice-Admiralty court, the Governor, Thomas Ludlam, requested that 127 of the newly-liberated slaves from these two vessels, eighteen men, fourteen women and ninety-five children, be sold to the settlers as 'apprentices' even though, as an experienced judge himself, he would have known that the sale of slaves for apprenticeship was illegal. On 23 August 1808 *Derwent* captured the French schooner *Marie Paul* with a cargo of sixty slaves and two weeks later she boarded the American slaver *Two Cousins*. Further captures were made in October when Parker seized the sloop *São Joaquim* and the schooner *São Domingo*, both carrying slaves and purporting to be Portuguese. *São Joaquim* sank soon after her capture, drowning a British officer and seventeen slaves. Her compatriot arrived in Freetown barely afloat. She was not carrying any papers and there was some confusion as to whether she was Portuguese or British in origin.

In late November 1808 *Derwent* sailed north to obtain supplies for the garrison at Goree. From there she set off on a three-month cruise down to the Bights. No arrests were made in either Benin or Biafra but on her return north *Derwent* seized two slavers, *Rapid* and *Africaan*, off Freetown. *Rapid* was released by the court but *Africaan* was eventually condemned.

Parker was due to return home the following spring but *Derwent* was on her maiden voyage and was not in need of a refit. Therefore the decision was made for her to remain on station with *Solebay* and *Tigress*.

Following their arrival at Sierra Leone in mid-June, *Solebay* and *Tigress* sailed north from Freetown accompanied by *Derwent*, the colonial schooner *George*, the transport *Agincourt* and several homeward-bound merchantmen. On 24 June this small convoy arrived at Goree where they stopped to water and provision. For the commandant of the Goree garrison, Major Charles Maxwell, the arrival of Columbine's small squadron was most opportune. Maxwell had been growing increasingly concerned at the damage being done to British shipping by French privateers operating on the River Senegal and was eager to put a stop to these attacks. An assault on the French colony at St Louis was deemed too risky as it would involve a 100-mile march through enemy territory but the arrival of Columbine and his ships opened up the possibility of an attack to seaward. Columbine was equally concerned over the possible disruption to his own anti-slavery work by the privateers and was also eager to take part in an operation that might improve his reputation at the Admiralty.

On 4 July *Solebay*, *Derwent*, *Tigress*, *George*, the transport *Agincourt* and several other smaller vessels sailed for St Louis with a contingent of 166 men of the Royal African Corps embarked on *Agincourt*. The squadron arrived off the mouth of the Senegal River on the evening of 7 July and anchored off the Senegal bar. The bar was a formidable obstacle with only one opening, the Passe de Gandiole, suitable for large, ocean-going vessels. Without detailed maps any attempt to enter the river was fraught with danger but the following morning 160 soldiers, 50 marines and 120 seamen were disembarked into boats under the command of command of Captain Parker. With two leadsmen in her chains calling out the depth, *George* carefully made her way through the Passe de Gandiole with *Solebay*, *Derwent* and *Tigress* following close behind. The operation to cross the bar had been progressing well when a large wave unexpectedly swept through the channel, capsizing one of *Derwent*'s boats and drowning Parker, Midshipman Francis Sealy and six other seamen. The remaining boats made it to the shore and the troops were landed in heavy surf. Sailing up the river *George* now ran ashore in sight of St Louis and two of the smaller vessels were also wrecked. Thankfully the French garrison, 160 regulars and 240 militia, had retreated on the arrival of the British and were now

10 miles further upstream of the bar at Babague. Whilst Maxwell's men took up defensive positions on the left bank of the river, attempts were made to re-float *George*. On 9 July the French marched out of Babague to attack the British, but they soon retreated when faced with sustained fire from Maxwell and his men. *George* was finally refloated on 10 July and that evening *Solebay* and *Derwent*, now commanded by Lieutenant Joseph Tetley, moved upriver to Babague where they found seven armed boats patrolling behind a chain boom stretched across the river. *Solebay* and *Derwent* opened fire and kept up a cannonade until nightfall. As she was attempting to shift her berth in a heavy swell *Solebay* first ran foul of *Derwent*, then ran ashore. Thankfully no lives were lost but *Solebay* was left a total wreck, forcing Columbine to shift his flag to *Derwent*. The following morning Maxwell and his men re-embarked and the flotilla proceeded upriver until they were within gunshot of Babague. Having received word that the French wished to surrender, the attack was postponed until the following morning when the British discovered that the boom had been broken and the French vessels guarding the river were now abandoned. Entering the French fort, Maxwell and his men captured twenty-eight long guns, four brass mortars and sixteen smaller guns. On 13 July terms were agreed for the surrender of Senegal to the British.

Derwent now sailed for home. On 22 August she dropped anchor at Weymouth and Columbine went ashore to prepare for his court martial following the loss of *Solebay*. Unbeknownst to him Castlereagh had already written to the Admiralty to request that another vessel should be made ready as quickly as possible to take the Commodore back to Sierra Leone and convey troops to Fort Louis in Senegal. At his court martial on 24 August Columbine was acquitted of all charges and was soon writing to the Admiralty offering his services once again. He was eventually offered the 22-gun *Crocodile* but in December the Foreign Secretary, Lord Liverpool, who had replaced Castlereagh three months earlier, informed the Admiralty that upon his arrival in Freetown Columbine was to assume the duties of temporary governor of Sierra Leone.

Columbine was to replace Governor Thomas Thompson who, having only been in the post for nine months, had been recalled to London following a series of very public complaints that he had made over the actions of his predecessors, Dawes and Ludlam, concerning their treatment of slaves and the selling of apprentices. Now, along with the command of

Crocodile, his commission for surveying the coast of Africa and his anti-slavery duties Columbine would also be in charge of the Vice-Admiralty court in Freetown and would have to fulfil the various time-consuming duties of colonial governorship.

Following the capture of Senegal *Tigress* had not returned home with *Derwent* but instead had remained off the Coast. Several suspicious vessels were stopped and boarded but no arrests were made. Bones's vessel was soon joined by the cutter *Tickler*, Lieutenant Richard Burton, which had sailed from Falmouth in July 1809 with instructions to assist *Solebay* with her survey work. Arriving at Goree in mid-August *Tickler* proceeded to cruise between Senegal and Sierra Leone, often in company with *Tigress*. On 4 October the brig-sloop *Hawke*, Commander Henry Bourchier, arrived off the Coast having escorted a large convoy out from Britain. Bourchier had orders to cruise off Cape Coast for two months before returning with any homeward-bound merchantmen requiring escort. Whilst off Cape St Paul's in early December the first cases of fever appeared on board ship. By the time *Hawke* sailed for home towards the end of the month Bourchier's ship had lost a midshipman and nine seamen and marines. The next arrival off the coast was the brig-sloop *Dauntless* which had stopped off at Cape Coast Castle on 25 December 1809 en route to Princes Island. Returning from two weeks ashore her commander, Josiah Whittman, fell sick and within days had died of fever.

On 13 January *Crocodile* sailed from Spithead, escorting a convoy of four merchant ships down to the West Coast of Africa. Conscious of his increased workload Liverpool had informed Columbine that he need not accompany the other commissioners on their survey but should assist in their joint report upon their return to Sierra Leone. *Crocodile* arrived at Goree on 3 February where she found *Tigress* at anchor. The two ships now dropped down to Freetown, during which passage *Tigress* lost her main topmast. Leaving Columbine to begin his duties as Governor, Bones headed back up north towards the Isles de Los, sending his ship's boats to investigate the Rio Pongas.

At midday on 24 March *Tigress*'s lookout spotted a strange sail emerging from the Pongas. Bones weighed, gave chase and had soon boarded the Spanish brig *Rayo* which he discovered to be loaded with 129 slaves. Suspecting her to be British in origin Bones put a prize crew aboard the vessel and sent her to Freetown. The court could not definitely state that the slaver was British and so she was eventually released. Two more unsuccessful boardings were made before the slaver *Lucia*, flying Spanish colours, was captured on 3 April and escorted to Freetown where she was eventually condemned. The prize crew from *Rayo* were re-embarked and on 3 May *Tigress*, which was now due a refit, sailed for home.

With Columbine now ashore concentrating on his duties as governor, his ship lay at anchor at Freetown until the end of March, her crew with little to do other than help fight a fire which destroyed thirty houses in the capital. On 30 March *Crocodile* departed Freetown for a short cruise north to the Isles de Los with her First Lieutenant, John Filmore, now in command. On 2 April Filmore sent the ship's barge to investigate the islands whilst *Crocodile* cruised inshore. No arrests were made and so *Crocodile* sailed the short distance to Matagong. There her barge discovered two abandoned American vessels, the sloop *Polly* and the schooner *Doris*, at anchor. Filmore put a prize crew on board *Doris* and took *Polly* in tow. Following their arrival at Freetown *Polly* was released by the court but *Doris* was carrying insufficient papers to prove her ownership and so was condemned. She was subsequently purchased by Columbine and employed as tender to *Crocodile*.

Columbine's ship remained at anchor at Freetown until mid–April when Commissioners Ludlam and Dawes boarded her to begin their long-delayed survey. All the rivers, forts and settlements between Goree and Gabon were to be visited in order to assess the state of the Coast in general and of the British settlements in particular. At the insistence of Wilberforce the commissioners had also been tasked with encouraging the various local chiefs and British settlers to abandon the trade in slaves and turn instead to legitimate trade in items such as ivory, gold and palm oil. On 17 April *Crocodile* sailed from Sierra Leone under the temporary command of Filmore and began slowly working her way down the coast, putting the commissioners ashore at each place she visited. Anchoring off the River Shebar on the evening of 22 April, Filmore sent the barge and cutter to investigate the river. The following day the boats returned carrying the master of the schooner *Esperanza*, a Portuguese vessel carrying ninety-one slaves. With a prize crew now on board the schooner she was taken to Freetown where, it having been proved that she was actually American in origin, she was condemned. In the meantime three of her crew had volunteered to join *Crocodile*. On 12 May a suspected slaver evaded capture off Cape Three Points, firing several muskets at *Crocodile* as she passed under the frigate's stern. Five days later a Spanish brig, *Ana*, was boarded without incident and escorted to Elmina. On 19 May *Crocodile* reached Cape Coast Castle. Three days later her barge was sent to investigate a brig flying Portuguese colours that had dropped anchor nearby. Documents found aboard the vessel, *Donna Mariana*, showed that she was in fact a slaver from Liverpool. Following her arrival at Freetown she was condemned as a British vessel under neutral colours.

After two weeks ashore at Cape Coast Castle the commissioners completed their survey and returned to *Crocodile*, ex-governor Ludlam now suffering the debilitating effects of dysentery. *Crocodile* set sail for Freetown but over the course of the next three weeks Ludlam's condition steadily worsened and he died on the morning of 23 June. His body was placed in a coffin but the ship was still making slow progress and by the beginning of July *Crocodile*'s surgeon had informed Lieutenant Filmore that if the corpse were to remain aboard ship any longer it would start affecting the health of the crew. Consequently, on 2 July Ludlam was buried at sea. Eleven days later *Crocodile* dropped anchor at Freetown.

On 19 February 1810 the Treaty of Friendship and Alliance was signed between Great Britain and Portugal. The act gave Britain a preferential tariff for her goods and Portugal promised her cooperation to secure the gradual abolition of the slave trade. Slaves would no longer be taken from regions of Africa not already under Portuguese influence or from any place formerly used for slaving that had now been abandoned. This meant that the Trade would be allowed to continue south of the equator at Loango, Angola, Mozambique and north of the Line at St Thomas, Princes and Whydah but not in Lagos. In effect the treaty had done little but maintain the status quo. Furthermore, the British goods now being brought in to Brazil under favourable tariffs could be traded in Africa for slaves. By the end of the year 18,677 slaves had been imported to Rio aboard forty-two ships.

The first slave ships condemned under the new treaty were from captures made, not by any of Columbine's cruisers, but by the privateer *Dart*, Captain James Wilkin, which had obtained a Letter of Marque to operate against slavers from the High Court of Admiralty. In March 1811 *Dart* brought the Portuguese slavers *Mariana*, *Santo Antonio Almos* and *Flor Deoclerin* into Freetown for adjudication by the court. *Dart* was one of a number of privateers operating along the Coast and Columbine had also received the unwelcome assistance of the colonial schooner *George*, converted into a cruiser without any legal authority by Lieutenant Moore of the Royal African Corps. Originally based at Goree, in August 1810 *George* had sailed south to cruise off Freetown against Columbine's orders. In response Columbine sent a party of marines to board the schooner and they returned with four seamen from *Solebay* and five from *Derwent* who had joined *George* following the attack on Senegal. By the end of the year the Vice-Admiralty court had adjudged eight cases brought in by *George*, five of which were condemned.

Columbine was now suffering repeated bouts of sickness and in the autumn of 1810 he requested permission to return home. Advised by his ship's doctor to leave the feverish airs of Sierra Leone, in October Columbine took *Crocodile* north to cruise off Goree and Senegal. During the vessel's absence her tender, the former slave schooner *Doris*, now renamed *St Jago*, captured three American slavers flying under Spanish and Swedish colours. This was the first example of a former slave vessel being employed in suppression duties on the Coast, and several more notable examples would eventually follow.

In May 1810 Wilberforce wrote to Liverpool regarding the island of Tenerife which was being used as a rendezvous for British and American slavers intending to sail to Havana under Spanish colours. Noting that this trade was being encouraged by the Spanish government and that the Governor of Tenerife was profiting greatly from the granting of Spanish papers, Wilberforce suggested that a British consul be appointed to the island and that the Navy should send a small squadron to cruise between Madeira, the Canaries and the coast of Africa. The Foreign Office acted quickly on Wilberforce's suggestions and on 8 August Captain Frederick Irby of the 38-gun frigate *Amelia* was ordered to sail from Spithead to Santa Cruz, Tenerife, where he was to examine all those ships flying British flags and arrest those clearly intending to engage in slaving. Following this he was to cruise between Tenerife and the Canaries for fourteen days before returning to Plymouth.

Amelia arrived at Santa Cruz from Spithead on 11 September where Irby discovered a large ship flying Spanish colours at anchor. An examination of her papers revealed that she had sailed from Liverpool bound for Buenos Aires. However, Irby suspected that she intended to sail to Africa and therefore decided to cruise offshore to intercept the vessel if she did indeed head eastwards. The following day *Amelia* boarded a ship, *Gallicia*, and a schooner, *Palafox*, flying Spanish colours and sailing in company towards Tenerife. Examining their papers Irby arrested both ships and sent them to Plymouth. It was later ascertained that they were both English vessels out of London and that *Gallicia*'s supercargo, Don Jorge Madresilva, was in fact an Englishman called George Woodbine. By 23 September *Amelia* had stopped and boarded twelve other vessels but she made no further arrests. Returning home in light winds, on 8 November Irby's ship fell in with the French privateer *Le Charles*, which was taken after a thirteen-hour chase. *Amelia* reached Plymouth on 16 November and Irby was soon offered the command of a brand-new frigate, *Crescent*, which he turned down, preferring to remain on board *Amelia* with her fine sailing qualities. Irby resumed his service with the Channel Fleet but the suppression campaign had not seen the last of this enterprising officer.

By the time *Crocodile* returned to Freetown towards the end of November 1810 the Admiralty had finally taken the decision to relieve Columbine the following spring. The overworked and ailing governor now ordered *Tigress*, which had returned to the Coast during his absence, to sail down to the Bights in company with the 12-gun brig *Protector*, Lieutenant George Mitchener, which had arrived at Freetown shortly after *Tigress*. As per his instructions from Liverpool, Columbine had been reviewing the survey reports of commissioners Ludlam and Dawes. Finding Ludlam's report to be lacking in detail and Dawes' report rather bizarrely to be concerned mainly with astronomy, Columbine, although still ill, determined to carry out his own brief survey of the Coast. In November he finally learned that he was to be relieved by Lieutenant-Colonel Maxwell as Governor of Sierra Leone and was to leave instructions for Bones and Mitchener prior to his return to Spithead on board *Crocodile*. Columbine's health deteriorated further over the winter and spring but there was still no sign of Maxwell. Now seriously ill, he could wait no longer and on 10 May Columbine handed over temporary command of the colony to Lieutenant Bones and *Crocodile*, briefly in company with *Protector*, sailed for home.

Columbine would not live to see England again. He died in the early hours of 19 June and his body was committed to the deep later that day.

Columbine had left Africa sick and disheartened. In his final report home he had written: 'I am sorry to acquaint Their Lordships that as far as I can judge the slave trade is carried on again to an extent nearly as great as ever, under the disguise of the Spanish or Portuguese flag. The nature of the coast in this neighbourhood renders it dangerous and generally impossible for a ship to go near the shore ... The only method therefore by which the Abolition Act can effectively be put in force is by means of small vessels.'[1] But Columbine had underestimated the successes of his small squadron. His ships had stopped around a third of the Trade between Cuba and the West African coast and the British Trade in the region had virtually been brought to an end. Through the capture of eight slaving vessels by his own ship *Crocodile*, Columbine was personally responsible for the liberation of around 600 slaves. However, the loss of Columbine left just two small gun-brigs to cruise the entire West Coast of Africa with Bones, an officer the rank of lieutenant, in command of the Squadron.

By mid-1811 it had come to the Government's attention that, following the Abolition Bill, British ships had begun using the subterfuge of sailing under foreign colours and that British firms were continuing to offer financial support and trade goods to other slaving nations. In response, in May 1811 Parliament introduced the Felonies Act. From that point on any involvement in the Trade would be punishable by transportation for up to fourteen years or three to five years' hard labour. The Act also allowed Royal Navy officers, authorised privateers, commanders-in-chiefs and colonial governors to seize slave ships and receive prize money from their captures.

This Act of Parliament had followed on closely from another important legal development in March of that year, this time regarding slave ships that were captured whilst still empty of their human cargoes. Adjudging the case of *Fortuna*, an American slaver captured off Madeira with false Portuguese papers as she attempted to sail to Africa, Sir William Scott, Judge of the High Court of Admiralty, declared that that 'the right of seizure was conferred not merely by the circumstance of a ship having actually traded in slaves, but by the manifestation of an intention to trade in slaves'.[2] Grounds for suspecting this intention included: chains or fetters, material for constructing a temporary deck, additional main deck gratings for ventilating the slave deck, more bulkheads than were necessary for the size of ship (used to confine slaves) and a disproportionately large amount of water casks or quantity of provisions for the size of crew. Surprisingly little effort was made by the Admiralty to transmit the details of this important legal development to those involved in the suppression campaign until Their Lordships were sent accounts of the *Fortuna* judgement by the African Institution. Finally spurred into action, in May the Admiralty sent copies of these accounts to Sierra Leone along with copies of the Felonies Act.

The Squadron was further strengthened by the arrival on 13 May of the 18-gun *Myrtle*, Captain Clement Sneyd, which was on a six-week deployment from Admiral Berkeley's Tagus squadron to the Cape Verde Islands with despatches. Within days of her arrival *Myrtle* had captured two British-owned slavers, *Roebuck* and *Gerona*, along with the Spanish vessel *Santa Rosa* and was headed south to Freetown when Sneyd decided to investigate the River Gambia, adding the schooner *Nusetro Señora de los Delores*, an American-owned vessel flying Spanish colours, to his tally of captures. *Myrtle* arrived at Freetown on 4 June with her four prizes in two. *Gerona* and *Nusetro Señora* were condemned but the court was as yet unaware of Sir William Scott's recent decree over the right of seizure and so *Roebuck* and *Santa Rosa* were released as there was insufficient evidence of their intention to trade slaves.

On 12 June the frigate *Thais*, Captain Edward Scobell, arrived at Goree from Portsmouth, dropping anchor just two days behind another frigate, *Arethusa*, Captain Holmes Coffin. Coffin held seniority over Scobell and so it was he who assumed command of the Squadron from Bones. On 19 June *Arethusa* sailed from Goree in company with *Thais* and the colonial schooner *George*. On 23 June, a day after taking two prizes, the schooner *Hawk* and the brig *Harriet*, the vessels parted company, *Thais* and *George* heading north for Senegal and Coffin's frigate heading south. Arriving off the Isles de Los on 29 June *Arethusa* grounded on a rock off Factory Island and was soon taking on 6½ft of water an hour, her men continually at the pumps. Alerted to her predicament by the arrival of *Arethusa*'s launch at Freetown on 3 July, *Tigress* and *Myrtle* put to sea to provide assistance to the stricken frigate. That same day *Protector* arrived at Freetown in company with the Spanish schooner *Palomo*, taken off Cape Mount a week earlier.

Having learned of *Arethusa*'s accident, Mitchener left his prize with the court before heading off to the Isles de Los. By 7 July Coffin's frigate had been patched up and made ready for sea and two days later she arrived at Freetown in company with *Myrtle*, *Tigress*, *Protector* and *Arethusa*'s two prizes, both of which were condemned by the court.

On 29 June the much-delayed Lieutenant Colonel Maxwell finally arrived in Freetown aboard *Thais*, bringing to an end Lieutenant Bones's temporary governorship of the colony. On 16 July *Thais* sailed from Freetown in company with *George*, headed for Cape Coast Castle. On 27 July she boarded *Havanna*, a British slaver under Spanish colours carrying 100 slaves off Trade Town. *Havanna* was dispatched to the court at Freetown where she would be condemned. *Thais* now began cruising the Bights, arresting the brig *Venus* off Badagry on 30 August and the brig *Calypso* off Lagos three days later. Following a brief cruise off St Thomas and Princes, on 26 September *Thais* headed back to Cape Coast Castle towing *Venus* which was proving to be a poor sailer. Having stopped at Cape Coast Castle and Accra to pick up ivory and gold dust *Thais* then continued north to Freetown.

On 3 August *Arethusa*, still under temporary repair, headed home to refit, sailing in company with *Myrtle*, whose return to the Tagus was now long overdue. On 12 August the two ships parted company off the River Gambia. *Myrtle* sailed to Goree to pick up the condemned slaver *Gerona* en route to the Tagus and *Arethusa* headed for Portsmouth, arriving there on 21 September. Reporting to Berkeley on 2 October, Sneyd noted that nearly 1,000 slaves were ready for transportation from the Gambia, mostly aboard American vessels sailing under Spanish and Portuguese colours. He had also been informed that there were another 100 such slaving vessels in the Bights. Furthermore Sneyd noted with some disquiet that many of the vessels condemned in Freetown were being resold for use in the Trade, which he considered to be have been unaffected by the introduction of Abolition Act.

On 21 July *Tigress* had left Freetown for a cruise south of the Line. Arriving in the Bights on 26 August she briefly stopped off at the tiny island of Annobon before sailing 700 nautical miles further south towards the Angolan coast. Working her way into Cabinda Bay she found two Portuguese slavers, *Paquette Volante* and *Urbano*, at anchor. According to the recent treaty these were vessels trading legitimately in slaves at a recognised Portuguese settlement but Bones still decided to arrest both ships, sailing the following day for Freetown via Annobon. Arriving back in Sierra Leone on 14 September both prizes were, unsurprisingly, restored on appeal after the ninety-seven slaves had been released, not emancipated.

Following his return to Freetown Bones was informed that the colonial schooner *George* had become stranded up the Rio Pongas and her crew imprisoned. Embarking an African pilot and a British trader, Mr Lawrence, who would assist in negotiations with the local chief, King Cutty, on 18 September *Tigress* put back to sea in company with the tender *St Jago*. Crossing the Rio Pongas bar on 22 September, with the cutter sounding ahead, *Tigress* carefully made her way upstream using warps and kedges. On 23 September King Cutty and his entourage boarded *Tigress*. The following morning *Tigress*'s boats were employed towing the brig alongside Cutty's settlement, situated a quarter of a mile from the local British factory where *George*'s crew had been imprisoned. Fortuitously, a boat from the factory was now captured and its crew of nineteen including several British slavers held hostage aboard *Tigress*. Discussions for the return of the colonial schooner having come to a successful conclusion, King Cutty and his men returned ashore, a number of the captured British slavers were released with the members of the boat crew and *Tigress* weighed anchor.

As agreed at the palaver, the following day the crew of *George* arrived aboard *Tigress* and were taken back to their own vessel. Delayed from sailing for a day by a full-blown storm which swept through the river, the following evening *Tigress* and *St Jago* began their journey back down the Rio Pongas, once again warping and kedging in light airs. On 28 September the remaining British slavers were released and Mr Lawrence was landed. Three days later *Tigress* crossed the bar at the entrance to the river and fourteen Kroomen were discharged from Bones's vessel. On 6 October *Tigress* attempted to enter the Rio Grande using sweeps and the men were back at the oars two weeks later when their vessel chased a strange sail which turned out to be an English brig on legitimate business. *Tigress* finally dropped anchor at Freetown on 25 October, where she would remain for the next month.

Whilst *Tigress* was making her way back from the Rio Pongas a decision was being reached back in London that would ultimately be of great benefit to the suppression campaign. On 5 October Captain Irby was ordered to hoist his broad pendant aboard *Amelia* and to take under convoy trade bound for Goree in company with the 16-gun ship-sloop *Kangaroo*, Commander John Lloyd. Entering the Navy aged 12, the Hon. Frederick Irby had initially served on the North American and West Indies stations and had fought at both the Glorious First of June in 1794 and the Battle of Camperdown in 1797. In February 1809 he had taken part in an action which resulted in three French frigates being driven ashore at Sables d'Olonne. *Amelia* sailed for Africa on 14 October, three weeks before *Kangaroo* departed Spithead in company with her five merchantmen. On 26 November *Amelia* dropped anchor in Freetown. When, after a week of waiting, there was still no sign of *Kangaroo* or her convoy Irby decided to sail to the Gold Coast in accordance with his original orders. Departing from Freetown on 6 December *Amelia* slowly made her way down the Coast. From passing trade Irby learned of several vessels on the Pepper Coast but it was not until 31 December before *Amelia* made her first arrest, boarding the Portuguese brig *Sao Joao* outside Portuguese territory. A prize crew was put aboard the brig and she was taken back to Freetown whilst *Amelia* continued on down the Coast. Four days later another Portuguese brig, *Bon Caminho*, was stopped and boarded. Although she was on legitimate trade to Whydah, Irby noted she had two canoes onboard, purchased from the British at Cape Coast. A legitimate trader in gold or ivory would have no need for these native canoes, a favourite of the slavers, so Irby wrote to the Governor of Cape Coast Castle, Edward White, reminding him that any participation in the slave trade was now a felony punishable by transportation. A copy of the letter was also sent to the Colonial Secretary, Lord Bathurst, and Irby soon received an apologetic letter from Governor White.

Having passed a number of Portuguese brigs openly trading for slaves in Whydah Roads, on 5 January 1812 *Amelia* dropped anchor off Porto Novo where she found three more Portuguese brigs this time trading outside Portuguese territory, in addition more canoes from Cape Coast were discovered aboard these vessels. *Destino*, *Dezanganos* and *Felis Americano* were all arrested and sent north to Freetown. Several days later *Protector* arrived at Porto Novo with news that six suspicious vessels had been spotted headed for Lagos. Irby immediately made sail, arriving off Lagos on 9 January to discover that three of these vessels had almost completed loading their cargoes of slaves. All three slavers were arrested. The remaining vessels were warned not to load slaves in any non-Portuguese port. *Amelia* took the schooner *Flor de Porto* in company, *Protector* took the brig *Prezares* and *George*, which had recently arrived at Lagos, took the brig *Lindeza* and all six vessels headed north, led by *Amelia*, which was the first to arrive back at Freetown on 21 February.

In mid-January *Tigress* had returned to Freetown from the Isles de Los. Bones, who was to be promoted, was now replaced by Lieutenant William Carnegie, the two men exchanging command on 20 February. *Tigress* now headed north and spent the next month cruising off Senegambia before returning to Freetown once again empty-handed. On 12 April *Tigress* left Freetown for Cape Coast where she loaded with ivory and gold dust, valuable cargoes rarely entrusted to merchantmen and a sure sign that Carnegie's vessel was about to return home. After a brief stop off at Princes to water and provision *Tigress* sailed for Plymouth on 31 May.

Prior to his departure from Freetown Irby had left instructions for *Kangaroo* to rendezvous with *Amelia* either at Cape Coast Castle or St Thomas. On 8 January *Kangaroo* weighed anchor and headed south. For several days she lay becalmed and it was 24 January before she arrived at Cape Coast Castle. There was no sign of Irby at the Castle so Lloyd continued south to St Thomas. Arriving at the island on 16 January one of the brigs previously released by *Amelia* was discovered at anchor. Having once again missed Irby who had already departed for Freetown, *Kangaroo* was watered and provisioned, then, at dawn of 21 January a suspicious-looking cutter was sighed further out to sea. Having anchored in the lee of the island there was not enough wind to get under sail and the strange sail almost disappeared from view before a fresh breeze blew up and *Kangaroo* was finally able to give chase. Firing both guns and muskets at the cutter, Lloyd eventually forced her to lower her sails, upon which it was discovered that she was a British vessel, *Vigilant*, out of Liverpool, whose master claimed to be headed for Brazil with a cargo of sixty-three slaves. It seemed unlikely to Lloyd that a small vessel such as a cutter would attempt a perilous crossing of the Atlantic. Instead he suspected that she was intending to rendezvous with the Portuguese brig then at anchor at St Thomas. *Vigilant* was therefore arrested and taken to Freetown where she was eventually condemned.

From St Thomas *Kangaroo* headed east along the Coast. There was no sign of any slavers at Cape Lopez so Lloyd continued on to the Gabon, arriving at the mouth of the river on 28 February. A boat was dispatched and soon returned with news of a brig in the process of loading slaves further upstream. Entering the river *Kangaroo* ran aground on the bar but she was soon got off and made her way into deeper water, riding at anchor whilst the boats went off in search of the slaver. The following day a prize crew brought a schooner out of the river and she moored alongside Lloyd's ship, but no connection with the slave trade could be established so she was released. After forty-eight hours of searching there had been no sign of the brig and Lloyd concluded that she was either hiding in one of the Gabon's numerous creeks or may even have slipped past them during the night. The search was abandoned and *Kangaroo* headed north back to Freetown. Whilst passing Cape Coast Castle on 28 March a strange sail was sighted and *Kangaroo* gave chase. Coming alongside the vessel Lloyd ordered her to heave to but she hoisted more sail and attempted to escape. However, *Kangaroo* was the superior sailer and it was a short-lived chase. The vessel proved to be a schooner out of London called *Quiz* that had been issued with a Letter of Marque from Governor Maxwell allowing her to hunt for slave ships. Having watered at Cape Coast *Kangaroo* now headed for Whydah, where *Quiz*'s master, George Neville, had informed Lloyd that there were a number of slavers at anchor. Arriving in Whydah Roads on 5 April Lloyd discovered six Portuguese brigs including one surrounded by boats. Upon seeing *Kangaroo* the crew of this vessel suddenly abandoned ship and made for the shore. Lloyd sent a boat across to the brig, *Uranus*, which discovered five sailors still on board the vessel, including one who was in irons. It was quickly ascertained that these men were a prize crew sent from *Quiz* who had been overpowered by the Portuguese. *Quiz*'s men admitted that they had entered Whydah Roads flying the skull and crossbones. Upon examination of the other vessels the brig *San Miguel Triumphante* was discovered to have a cargo of 136 slaves, half of them children, brought onboard with canoes purchased from Cape Coast. The remaining brigs were without papers, their masters claiming that they had been taken by *Quiz*. *San Miguel Triumphante* and *Uranus* were both escorted back to Freetown, *Kangaroo* and her prizes arriving in port on 15 May.

Having written an angry letter to the Admiralty regarding the *Quiz* affair, Irby now took action against the privateer in the Vice-Admiralty court at Freetown, accusing her of trading with the enemy, plundering vessels she had arrested and flying Royal Navy pendants and the Jolly Roger. However, the King's Proctor of the court also happened to be the purser of *Quiz* and Irby's action achieved little more than the seizure of the offending flags and pendants. *Amelia* was now due to sail to the Cape Verde Islands to replenish with bread and flour but prior to his departure Irby had been informed by Maxwell that there had been an English brig in the port which had sailed for Goree with several free Africans aboard but she had been diverted to the Cape Verde Islands by her master in order to sell her passengers as slaves. Most had subsequently been taken to Cayenne but one was said to remain in Porto Praya. Irby arrived in the port on 28 April and, after much negotiation, the Portuguese governor eventually agreed to release the African and *Amelia* returned to Freetown via Goree.

In early January 1812 the 18-gun ship-sloop *Sabrina*, Lieutenant James Tillard, arrived on the Coast from Admiral Berkeley's Tagus squadron in company with the schooner *Vesta*, Lieutenant George Miall. On 11 January the two vessels entered the River Gambia where *Sabrina* took possession of the Spanish slaver *Il Pepe*. Whilst awaiting for the adjudication of his prize, the newly-promoted Tillard began cruising between the Isles de Los and the Rio Grande to intercept slavers coming out of the Nunez and Pongas rivers. Having been charged by Maxwell with bringing out four British slavers known to be trading in the area, Tillard eventually found two of these men, Hickson and Samo, who were arrested under the Felonies Act. By now Tillard had been cruising off the Coast far longer than his instructions allowed and on 18 April the Admiralty wrote to Berkeley requesting that *Sabrina* immediately be sent home so that the conduct of her commanding officer could be looked into.

On 13 March *Protector*'s sister-ship *Daring*, Lieutenant William Pascoe, left Spithead with instructions to escort a convoy of merchantmen to Africa and rendezvous with Irby at St Thomas. Whilst off Sierra Leone on 30 June *Daring* captured the Spanish brig *Centinella*. Following this arrest Pascoe detained another Spanish slaver in Trade Town but her crew quickly overpowered *Daring*'s men and retook their vessel before setting the British sailors adrift. Luckily Pascoe was able to quickly recover his men. On 5 July *Daring* stopped another Spanish slaver off Trade Town, *San Carlos*, and was escorting her back to Freetown when she fell in with *Amelia*. The apparent freedom with which slavers were continuing to operate so close to the British at Freetown was a constant irritation to Irby and Pascoe was now ordered to head north and cruise between Cape Verde and Cape Palmas once his prize had been adjudicated. *Amelia* had been headed for Cape Coast Castle but Irby now began a fruitless search for the Spanish slaver that had escaped from *Daring*.

Upon his eventual arrival at Cape Coast in late July Irby was informed that the British fort at Winnebah had been attacked by locals. Taking on board a detachment of the Royal African Corps, *Amelia* sailed to Winnebah only for Irby to discover that the fort had been abandoned. To prevent further such incidents Irby now set about burning both the fort and the local town. Following a 1,300-mile detour to St Helena *Amelia* returned to the Coast and worked her way northwards from Benguela Bay to the River Congo, searching for any British slavers engaged in the trade to Brazil. At St Paul de Loando Irby found thirteen vessels slaving under Portuguese colours. Writing to the Secretary to the Admiralty, John Croker, later that year, Irby estimated that around 10,000 slaves were being exported annually from St Philip de Benguela and 20,000 more from Loando to Brazil, some of these in English or American vessels sailing under Portuguese flags. *Amelia* had briefly run aground on a spit of sand off Loando but was got off again with no great damage. She sailed on 5 October and five days later whilst in Ambriz Bay arrested a British vessel, *Andorinha*, sailing under Portuguese colours with 270 slaves onboard. Taking his ship into the River Congo Irby heard of another slaver further upstream at Embomma but he judged that stretch of water too dangerous either for *Amelia* or her boats and so he continued further north to St Thomas to water and provision. There was no word of any potential slavers operating in the region so Irby now headed back to Sierra Leone.

Whilst *Amelia* had been busy cruising to the south Irby had ordered *Kangaroo* to the Gambia, where on 11 July she fell in with the colonial schooner *Princess Charlotte* and learned that several of her crew had been injured in an encounter with locals whilst trying to arrest a suspected slaver further upstream. Entering the Gambia in company with the schooner, both vessels cautiously made their way up the river, anchoring at the village where the incident had taken place only to discover that the slaver had been moved into one of the Gambia's many creeks. It was only when Lloyd threatened to burn the village that the slaver, an American vessel, and her cargo of sixty-seven slaves was handed over. As *Kangaroo* left the Gambia the first cases of fever began appearing aboard ship and by the time of her arrival in Freetown nine sailors had died and of her remaining crew of 121 only sixteen were deemed fit for duty.

On 18 June 1812 America declared war on Britain, a result of increased tensions between the two countries over issues such as the impressments of American seamen by the Royal Navy, the boarding of American vessels to recover British deserters and the effects on American trade caused by the continued blockade of European ports by the Royal Navy. The war, which would last for the next eighteen months, would cause an additional strain on the resources of an already-stretched Royal Navy, detracting from her anti-slavery operations. Whilst the two countries were at war American-owned slavers could be seized as prizes of war, but the boarding of American vessels, regardless of whether they were sailing under false colours, would remain a bone of contention between the two countries long after the war was concluded.

On 10 June *Thais* arrived off the Coast from England, having departed Portsmouth on 30 April following her refit. Sailing to the south of Goree on 24 June she arrested the schooner *Dolphin*, an American vessel loaded with seventy-nine slaves and bound for Cuba. *Thais* now relocated to the Bights where Scobell disguised his vessel by lowering his fore and mizzen royal masts and hoisting a Portuguese ensign. On 14 August *Thais* arrested the Spanish brig *Carlotta* in Loango Bay. Returning from Cabinda, on 29 August Scobell arrested the Portuguese brig *Flor d'America*, also in Loango Bay. The conditions on this ship, with its cargo of 364 slaves, were so terrible that Scobell had to fumigate the slave deck and transfer two tons of water to her. The slaver's crew of seven were put in their boat with enough rations for the voyage to Cabinda and the brig taken under tow. On 5 September, whilst off Mayumba, *Thais* arrested the Portuguese schooner *Orizonte*, she then headed north up the coast towards St Thomas.

Upon his return to Freetown on 27 October 1812 Scobell discovered *Kangaroo* at anchor. During her recent cruise *Thais* had run short of rum so Lloyd sent a cask across to Scobell's frigate. The Squadron was reunited when, on 8 November, *Amelia* dropped anchor in Freetown harbour alongside *Kangaroo* and *Thais*. Upon discovering the condition of Lloyd's men, who had still not recovered from their recent expedition up the Gambia, Irby sent across a number of his own crew to *Kangaroo* and ordered

Lloyd's vessel home. Many of *Amelia*'s men were also suffering from fever and the ship, with her worn rigging, rotten sails and barnacle-encrusted hull, was due to return home for a refit. However, on 28 January Lieutenant Pascoe and his crew arrived in Freetown to report the loss of their brig *Daring*, burned following an encounter with two French frigates off the Isle de Los the previous day. Pascoe joined *Amelia* as a supernumerary and, exchanging his sick crew with men from *Daring*, on 3 February Irby weighed anchor and headed south.

In late November two French heavy frigates, *Arethuse* and *Rubis*, had escaped the blockade of Nantes and headed for the West Coast of Africa with the intention of attacking British trade in the region. Having captured several prizes upon their arrival, on 27 January the two ships were spotted by the British cruiser *Daring* off the Isles de Los. Vastly outgunned, Pascoe had run his brig ashore to prevent her capture. On the night of 5 February the French frigates encountered a storm and ran aground. *Rubis* became a total loss and her crew transferred to their Portuguese prize *Serra*. *Arethuse* was refloated, but with damage to her rudder. *Amelia* arrived at the Isles de Los from Freetown the following morning. *Arethuse*'s captain, Pierre Bouvet, immediately weighed anchor and on the evening of 7 February the two ships engaged one another. The action lasted almost four hours, the French gunners following their usual practice of aiming high at their opponent's masts and rigging whilst *Amelia*'s men aimed low at *Arethuse*'s hull. Twice Bouvet put his ship alongside *Amelia* and prepared to board her, but both times her boarders were repulsed by *Amelia*'s men, led by First Lieutenant John Simpson. Dreadfully exposed on her quarterdeck, all of *Amelia*'s officers were either killed or wounded with only the Sailing Master, De Mayne, left standing by the end of the battle. Low on powder, their gunners exhausted, both ships eventually fought themselves to a standstill and began to drift apart. *Arethuse* now turned and headed for the French coast but *Amelia*, her sails and rigging cut up by French fire, her masts wounded, was unable to give chase. Irby's ship had lost forty-six killed including Lieutenant Pascoe and two marines from *Daring*. One hundred more men were wounded, five of whom would later die from their injuries. *Arethuse* had suffered losses of twenty dead and eighty-eight wounded in the encounter. Whilst Bouvet returned to St Malo with his prizes, Irby headed north to Madeira for temporary repairs before sailing for Britain, arriving in Spithead in May 1813 where *Amelia* was paid off. Irby had returned to England with four

African children in tow, rescued by the Commodore from lives of servility. The children were baptised together on 30 May, one boy was named as Paulo Loando, another as Edward McKenzie. A 10-year-old girl taken from a slave ship bound for Brazil was baptised as Amelia Frederic Irby whilst another boy aged 14 discovered in irons at the Portuguese settlement at Benguela was renamed Charles Fortunatus Freeman.

On 17 March 1813, *Thais*, now the only cruiser left operating on the West African station, left Freetown for Cape Verde where Scobell had been informed that two American privateers had been spotted threatening trade in the region. Two weeks later, as *Thais* passed Cape Mesurado, a strange sail was spotted in the offing. Scobell gave chase and by midday was close enough to fire a shot across the brig's bows. Moments later the stranger hauled down her colours. As Scobell had suspected, she was one of the American privateers, *Rambler*. *Thais* escorted the vessel to Freetown where she was later condemned as a prize of war. On 28 May Scobell arrested the Spanish sloop *Juan* off Sierra Leone which was later proved to be an American-owned vessel. Two weeks later *Thais* sailed for the Pepper Coast in company with *Princess Charlotte* and *Juan* which Scobell had now converted into a tender for his frigate. On 25 June four of *Thais*'s boats, commanded by Lieutenant John Wilkins, were sent into the River Mesurado to arrest two well-known Liverpool traders, John Bostock and Thomas McQueen, who were reported to be operating further upstream. Early on the morning of 26 June musketry could be heard in the direction of Bostock's factory which was soon observed to be on fire. Scobell moved closer inshore and later that night the gig returned to Thais with two injured seamen, one of whom subsequently died, and news that Bostock and McQueen had evaded capture following the fire. However, three boats belonging to the slavers had been captured and over the next two days 233 slaves were taken on board *Thais* and *Princess Charlotte*. On 1 July Bostock and McQueen were captured by natives and brought onboard *Thais*. Both men were subsequently convicted under the Felonies Act and sentenced to fourteen years' transportation to Botany Bay.

Thais now returned to Freetown where Irby discovered the 16-gun ship-sloop *Albacore*, Commander Henry Davies, at anchor. Over the course of the next two weeks five of *Thais*'s men died from fever, most likely brought on board the ship by her boat crews following their excursion up the Mesurado. Scobell now decided a return to sea would help improve the health of his men and so *Thais* sailed for Cape Coast in company with *Albacore*. Unfortunately three more men died on the day *Thais* left Freetown. On her arrival at Cape Coast in August *Thais* met the frigate *Favorite*, Captain John Maxwell, which had arrived at Goree from England in mid-July. Following a stop off at Accra *Thais* headed for Annobon where, on 12 September, she rendezvoused with two merchantmen which she now escorted to Britain, arriving at Portsmouth in mid-November.

Prior to Irby's departure from the Coast the Admiralty had begun to shift its attention from the suppression campaign to the protection of trade, sending instructions for commanders to cruise off coasts that had little involvement in the slave trade. However, Captain Maxwell chose to ignore these instructions and began sailing as far south as the Bights. On 31 August *Favorite* captured the Portuguese brig *Providencia* at Porto Novo and the following day she took another Portuguese brig, *San Josef*, off Badagry. Following a search of the Old Calabar on 7 September the similarly-named Portuguese schooner *St Joseph* was discovered with fifty-nine slaves stowed so tightly aboard they barely had air to breathe. A week later *Favorite*'s boats were employed up the River Gabon, returning with another Portuguese schooner with fifty-five slaves onboard. On 10 November *Favorite*'s boats entered the Pongas where they burned nine slave factories. The English slavers retreated to a factory at the head of the river that was inaccessible to *Favorite*'s boats and no arrests could be made. Yet again a British cruiser paid the price for these incursions deep into the slave rivers, with sixteen of *Favorite*'s men dying from fever as the ship lay becalmed off Freetown. Maxwell sent an angry letter to the Governor, who had originally suggested the expedition to the Pongas, saying that it would have been better if he had sent his own native troops who would have been immune to the fever rather than risk the lives of British seamen.

By mid-1813 the Royal Navy's suppression campaign off the West Coast of Africa had caused such distress to Portuguese merchants that their government made a complaint to the Court of St James. Irby had possessed a copy of the 1810 treaty between Britain and Portugal and there was little evidence to suggest that its terms had been broken by the vessels under his command. In fact most of the slavers seized by Irby's cruisers had been Spanish vessels condemned for trading with British subjects. Nevertheless, on 6 May the Foreign Secretary, Castlereagh, wrote to the Lords Commissioners of the Admiralty requesting they inform 'His Majesty's cruisers not to molest Portuguese ships carrying Slaves *bona fide* on the account and risk of Portuguese subjects from the ports of Africa belonging to the crown of Portugal and the Brazils'.[3] Writing to Castlereagh for clarification of his orders, Irby, who had watched many men from the Squadron die of fever, and who himself had been injured in a battle against a French frigate, declared that it was 'not a light and easy service: on the contrary it was one of great and imminent peril, not only to health but also to life'.[4]

Chapter 3

Hagan Versus the Slavers:
December 1814–December 1819

ollowing his disastrous campaign in Russia, in April 1814 Napoleon
had been forced to abdicate and go into exile on Elba. The following
month hostilities between Britain and France were brought to an
end with the First Treaty of Paris. Britain, still at war with America, was
eager to resume its friendly relationship with an important trading partner
and, as the Navy no longer needed to blockade European ports nor take
seamen from American vessels to make up for a shortfall in manpower, the
two major grievances that had caused the war were now no longer an issue.
In the Treaty of Ghent, signed on 24 December 1814, Britain and America
agreed to a cessation of hostilities and the return of all captured territories.
The negotiations also included discussions over the slave trade and the
resulting treaty included a pledge that both Britain and the United States
would use 'their best endeavours'[1] to abolish the trade. 'Best endeavours'
was, of course, a highly subjective phrase and, having fought a lengthy war
over the issue, the United States was not inclined to begin allowing the
Royal Navy to board vessels flying the American flag, regardless of their
true country of origin.

The end of the American War also saw the emergence of the Navy's
greatest opponent in their long campaign against the slavers; the Baltimore
clipper. This fast, two-masted vessel had been developed during the war
for privateering and blockade-running but with the end of hostilities their
owners began seeking out new employment opportunities. The typical
design was a vessel 100ft in length and around 300 tons burthen, either
brig or schooner rigged. They had limited cargo space but their speed and
sailing abilities made them an ideal choice for use in the Trade. In contrast
the Navy had pressed into service whatever vessels it had at its disposal and
was in no position to develop a vessel specifically for use in the suppression
campaign. As the number of groundings had testified, frigates had proved
unsuitable for operations close inshore whilst the sloops and Sixth Rates

lacked the speed to keep up with the slavers in open sea. The best design to appear off the Coast in these early years was the gun-brig. Small and agile, they were well armed and could work inshore with ease. However, they were not designed for lengthy cruising and their small size made them uncomfortable to live and work in.

At the First Treaty of Paris King Louis XVIII had agreed to abolish the French slave trade within five years. There was further success for Britain in July 1814 when the Spanish government promised to prevent the use of its flag by foreign slavers. Then, in January 1815, Britain and Portugal signed a convention clarifying the wording of their 1810 treaty. The British government agreed to indemnify Portuguese merchants for property unlawfully seized and both sides also agreed they could arrest slavers belonging to the other country. Portugal also agreed to the signing of a second treaty, at a date as yet undecided, which would prohibit slavery in all Portuguese dominions. One month later, at the Congress of Vienna, Castlereagh obtained a declaration from the co-signatories of the general peace treaty – France, Austria, Russia, Prussia, Spain and Portugal – stating that, since 'the commerce known by the name of the African slave trade is repugnant to the principles of humanity and universal morality',[2] those powers with colonial possessions had a 'duty and necessity'[3] to abolish it as soon as possible. The Spanish representative, the Marquis of Labrador, had complained that the British colonies had already had twenty years to consider the abolition of the slave trade and that his country was not yet in any position to follow Britain's lead. The declaration concluded that no nation could be made to abolish the Trade 'without due regard to the interests, the habits and even the prejudices'[4] of its subjects. In France many had argued that the restocking of its recently-restored Caribbean colonies was in the national interest and whilst one arm of government argued for abolition, the other argued against it. The end of the war between Britain and France had meant an end to the blockade of her ports and in due course French slavers began appearing off the West Coast of Africa. British cruisers no longer had the right to detain, search or even stop any French-flagged vessel suspected of slaving and with the French government divided over the issue there was no sign of a treaty with Britain being signed any time soon.

In mid-October the 16-gun ship-sloop *Brisk*, Commander Henry Higman, arrived in Freetown from Britain and two weeks later she was joined by the 22-gun Sixth Rate *Porcupine*, Captain Booty Harvey. December 1814 saw the return of a commodore to the West Coast of Africa, following an absence of eighteen months. As a result of the Treaty of Paris Senegal and Goree were due to be returned to the French and in order to evacuate the British troops stationed there Captain Thomas Browne of the frigate *Ulysses* had been ordered to take under his command the ship-sloop *Comus*, Captain John Tailour, and sail for Goree in company with a store ship and a number of transports, hoisting a broad pendant in the Channel. An officer ten years older than Irby, this would not be Browne's first involvement in the suppression campaign, for in June 1814 *Ulysses* had captured a Portuguese vessel off Cuba with a cargo of 432 slaves, 130 of whom were dead at the time of her arrest. Browne had initially intended to send the slaver to the nearest Vice-Admiralty court at Jamaica but quickly realised that it would be far more humane to release her and let her continue to Havana.

Ulysses and *Comus* sailed from Portsmouth on 22 December, their arrival on the Coast bringing the strength of the Squadron back up to four vessels following the return home of *Albacore* and *Favorite*. In his instructions from the Admiralty Browne had been ordered to cruise between Cape Verde and the Gabon, visiting British settlements for as long as supplies and the health of his crew permitted, then proceed with one of the convoys from St Thomas back to Spithead. Arriving at Senegal and the Gambia in early February 1815, Browne left *Porcupine* in charge of the troopships then headed south to Sierra Leone. Harvey's vessel had been cruising off Senegambia for several months, her commanding officer providing his shore parties with cinchona bark, a proven remedy for malaria, thus ensuring that none of *Porcupine*'s men had yet fallen ill from fever. Soon after his arrival in Freetown Browne began receiving complaints from British palm-oil merchants operating along the Old Calabar who were suffering delays in the loading of cargoes due to the preference given to the many slavers also on the river. Browne was preparing to head south to investigate the slavers operating on the Grand Bassa River so he sent Tailour to investigate the problem on the Old Calabar.

On 16 March *Comus* was approaching the entrance to the river when she spotted two schooners to windward. Tailour sent a boat under the command of his First Lieutenant, Philip Graham, to board the nearest of these schooners whilst *Comus* set off in pursuit of the other vessel. As Graham's boat approached the schooner he fired several warning shots across her bows, but her only response was to hoist Portuguese colours. However, on the firing of the next warning shot the schooner suddenly bore up and fired her two starboard guns at Graham's boat. Graham returned fire and signalled *Comus* for assistance. Meanwhile the schooner fired her starboard guns for a second time then wore round and fired her larboard guns at Graham's vessel. As she attempted to tack to repeat the manoeuvre the wind suddenly died and she could not bring her starboard guns to bear, allowing Graham to approach and board the vessel, *Dos Amigos*. The schooner was found to be fully equipped for slaving and her crew informed Graham that the second schooner observed at the entrance to the river, the Spanish-flagged *Conception*, would be just as likely to resist arrest.

Having abandoned the chase of *Conception* when Graham had signalled for assistance, Tailour spent several fruitless days searching for the Spanish schooner to windward before proceeding to the Old Calabar as per his instructions from Browne. On 24 March *Comus* entered the estuary and dropped anchor. That night Tailour sent his boats, under the command of Lieutenants Graham and Pierce, to investigate further upriver. Arriving off Duke Town, Graham discovered five slavers at anchor. One of these proved to be *Conception*. As Graham had earlier been warned, her crew resisted the boarding with musketry and a ten-minute battle ensued before the British gained control of the schooner, by which time one of *Conception*'s crew lay dead and five more were seriously wounded. Thankfully British casualties were much lighter, with just one member of Graham's boat crews being wounded. Graham now went to the assistance of Pierce who was attempting to board the remaining slavers which were all eventually taken. There were two Spanish vessels, *Carmen* and *Intrepide*, carrying 365 slaves between them and two Portuguese vessels, *Bon Sorte* and *Estrella*, carrying a further 103 slaves. Writing to Browne later that day Tailour commended the actions of his First Lieutenant and the men under his command, declaring that he was 'proud to say that not an individual has failed to give me entire satisfaction'.[5]

On 19 February *Ulysses* weighed anchor and headed south from Freetown to investigate the slave trade along the Grand Bassa River. Three boats were dispatched into the river on 20 March but came back empty-handed. However, that evening a schooner was spotted in the neighbouring

St John's River. Upon the appearance of Browne's frigate the schooner relocated upriver and as *Ulysses*'s boats attempted to follow her they were fired on from the shore and forced to retreat. A native now appeared in a boat and informed Browne that the villagers had been told to fire on the boats by the British owner of a slave factory on the river. Browne sent his First Lieutenant, Phillips, with five ship's boats manned by marines to arrest the Englishman, Crewe, and burn his factory. However, due to the length of time it took for the boats to negotiate the river Crewe was able to send away his slaves and escape into the bush, but in his absence his factory was destroyed along with several of his buildings. Following a similar attack on another British-owned slave factory at Mesurado in late March *Ulysses* resumed her passage down to Cape Coast and St Thomas.

At Cape Coast *Ulysses* was joined by *Brisk*. During her six months off the Coast Higman's vessel had seized three slavers, the Spanish schooner *Union* and two Portuguese brigs, *Conceição* and *General Silveira*, these captures resulting in the emancipation of 239 slaves. Whilst at the Castle *Brisk* loaded 7,000 oz. of gold dust and 40 tons of ivory, a sure sign that she was about to depart for home. On 28 April *Ulysses* and *Brisk* arrived at St Thomas to water and provision. Whilst on the island Browne met with the Governor and raised the issue of the badly-provisioned slaver bound for Cuba that *Ulysses* had boarded the previous year. The Governor's only response was that he would have preferred it if the vessel had sailed with 1,000 slaves onboard as masters had to pay so much per head to him and the Royal Fund. On 6 May *Ulysses* and *Brisk* were joined by *Comus* and her clutch of prizes. Returning to sea from the Old Calabar on 3 April *Comus* had fallen in with and arrested the Portuguese brig *Santa Anna* fitted for slaving. There had been a further success for Tailour on 23 April when he had chased and boarded *Maria Madelena*, another Portuguese schooner fitted for slaving, off Princes Island. On 11 May *Brisk* departed St Thomas with a homeward-bound convoy of two merchantmen. The following day Higman chased and captured the Portuguese slaver *Dido*, carrying a cargo of 327 slaves. Towing his prize westwards, on 29 May Higman sent *Dido* into Freetown where she was eventually condemned. Following a lengthy passage home *Brisk* arrived at Portsmouth on 15 August and the following year was sold out of the Service.

Whilst waiting for the arrival of the French at Senegal and Goree *Porcupine* cruised as far south as the Gambia. For two weeks between

21 March and 3 April her boats, commanded by First Lieutenant Robert Hagan, were in constant use in the river, but they made just one arrest. On 23 March Hagan returned from the river escorting the Spanish slaver *Sophie*, one of two schooners that were reported to be trading along the river. *Porcupine* returned to Senegal from the Gambia and on 29 April the sloop *Ariel* arrived from Ireland with despatches announcing the alarming news that Napoleon had escaped from Elba and had arrived in Paris.

From St Thomas *Ulysses* headed south to St Helena where Browne found a convoy of eleven merchantmen carrying a cargo worth around £10 million. With the resumption of war following the escape of Napoleon the masters of these East Indiamen were eager for Royal Navy protection and asked Browne to escort them to England. As Browne was now ready to sail for home he agreed and the convoy left St Helena for Spithead on 15 June.

On 2 July *Comus* left Freetown for a cruise south. Shortly after her departure *Porcupine*, which was due to return home to be paid off, sailed with troops for Barbados, leaving *Comus* as the only cruiser operating off the Coast. At dawn on 15 July, whilst sailing off Cape Palmas, she arrested the Portuguese brigantine *Abismo*, fitted for slaving and headed for Elmina. A few hours later Tailour spotted another strange sail and after a six-hour chase boarded the Spanish slaver *Palafox*, also bound for Elmina for slaves. On 18 July *Comus* fell in with *Ulysses*'s tender, the ex-slaver *Dolores*, which had captured a Portuguese brig, *Nova Fragantinha*, off Anamabo. Tailour sent a prize crew across to the brig then sailed for St Thomas via Cape Coast. Having watered and provisioned, on 9 August *Comus* departed St Thomas for the final time, sailing for England with four merchantmen and *Dolores*'s prize which was sent into Freetown whilst the convoy continued on towards Spithead.

In June 1815 Governor Maxwell had resigned due to ill health. By the time his replacement, Lieutenant-Colonel Charles MacCarthy, arrived in Sierra Leone from Senegal to take over the administration of the colony in late July, the Chief Justice, Robert Thorpe, had been dismissed for misconduct. It was rainy season in Sierra Leone and as other members of the Vice-Admiralty court had fallen ill with fever, for the time being the court ceased to operate. There were now no cruisers operating on the Coast but the suppression campaign itself had not been completely abandoned. The colonial schooner *Princess Charlotte* continued to hunt slavers and had several notable successes including the Portuguese vessel *Nossa Senhora da Vitoria*, captured with 434 slaves aboard. However, in July 1815 her commander, Lieutenant Saunders of the Royal African Corps, fell ill and requested permission to return home. The new Governor of Sierra Leone had taken passage out to Senegal aboard *Porcupine* and so knew her First Lieutenant, Robert Hagan, well. When Hagan volunteered for the colonial schooner MacCarthy readily accepted. It would prove to be a very shrewd decision.

On 9 January 1816 the 20-gun Sixth Rate *Bann*, Captain William Fisher, arrived at Freetown via Madeira. The first cruiser to operate on the Coast for almost five months, *Bann* had been given the customary tasks of suppression and trade protection. Hagan had taken passage to Africa on board *Bann* and on 14 January he transferred to a small colonial sloop, *Mary*, to find his new command. Three days later *Mary* fell in with a suspicious-looking schooner off the Gallinas and gave chase. Having departed Freetown to hunt for several Spanish slavers said to be operating off the Gallinas, on 18 January *Bann* fell in with *Mary* and her chase. The boats commanded by *Bann*'s Lieutenant Tweed approached the Spanish-flagged schooner in a dead calm and were fired on with grapeshot and musketry. The British returned fire and fifteen minutes later had taken the schooner for the cost of two wounded. The prize proved to be *Rosa*, previously an American privateer named *Perry*, that was bound for Havana with 276 slaves. Whilst Hagan continued his search for *Princess Charlotte* Fisher took the prize to Freetown where she was condemned to both *Bann* and *Mary*. Once again Hagan's search for his new command was interrupted when, on 14 February, he seized the Spanish schooner *Guadeloupe*, empty but equipped for slaving, off Freetown. Having returned to port with his prize, Hagan now heard of two vessels slaving in the Pongas and, embarking a detachment of troops, set off to find them. Meanwhile MacCarthy had hired a condemned prize to re-supply *Princess Charlotte*, rather unhelpfully naming her *Queen Charlotte*. Having returned to Freetown with two prizes, *Eugenia* and *Juana*, both taken on 3 March. Hagan set off for a third time to find *Princess Charlotte*. His vessel, the hired prize and *Princess Charlotte* all met up on 9 March. Saunders had been hunting for *Compadore*, a slaver that was acting piratically, having seized two vessels the previous year. Hagan transferred to *Queen Charlotte* and both vessels headed down the Coast towards Trade Town. In the early hours of 11 March a vessel was spotted off Cape Mesurado. The three British vessels gave chase but only *Queen Charlotte*, using her sweeps, was able to keep in contact. By dawn Hagan's vessel had closed to within gunshot of what was now clearly not *Compadore* but a brig under French colours. There was a brief exchange of fire but then the wind died, forcing a temporary pause to the action. Eventually a fresh breeze blew up and by noon Hagan had closed to within grapeshot range of the chase. He fired a broadside with his larboard guns but there was no response from the brig. Thinking she had surrendered, Hagan sent the gig across to board her, at which point she opened fire. In attempting to respond all the breeching ropes of Hagan's larboard guns suddenly gave way. Fortuitously Lieutenant Saunders now arrived aboard *Princess Charlotte*'s cutter, which, along with *Queen Charlotte*'s barge and gig, attempted to board the brig whilst Hagan's vessel gave covering fire with her starboard guns. As the barge approached the brig she was met by a hail of grapeshot and musket fire and three-quarters of her crew were killed or wounded. With the other boats also taking casualties Saunders was forced to withdraw. Following another broadside from *Queen Charlotte*, the brig finally hauled down her colours. Upon boarding the prize she was discovered to be *Louis*, a French vessel clearly equipped for slaving that was sailing from Martinique to Bonny. Returning to Freetown, on 3 April the Vice-Admiralty court, now presided over by Dr Robert Hogan, condemned *Louis* jointly to *Queen Charlotte* and *Princess Charlotte*.

On 13 April *Bann* left Freetown and headed south towards the Bights. Fisher's instructions from the Admiralty had included the request to visit British forts and settlements as far south as the Gabon. Off Whydah on 5 March *Bann* captured the Spanish slaver *Temerario*, taken just as loading had begun with only five slaves aboard. Sending his prize back to Freetown, Fisher continued on down to Princes to water and provision. On 16 March *Bann* captured a Portuguese brig, *Santa Antonio Milagroso*, with 600 slaves aboard, twice the permitted number for a vessel that size. Entering the slaver's hold, *Bann*'s prize crew gagged at the stench which was beyond description. Thirty dead slaves had been thrown over the side of the slaver by her crew but another lay putrefying beneath the living, hidden from sight if not from smell. Another thirty Africans were discovered so near death that *Bann*'s surgeon considered them beyond saving. Three hundred slaves were taken aboard Fisher's vessel which took the slaver under tow and headed back to Freetown, sailing under light airs with a now depleted crew. On 23 March *Bann* encountered a storm, the water entering the ship's leaky timbers adding to the misery of the slaves crowded below deck. During the month-long journey a further forty-three slaves died and a third of Fisher's men fell ill. Following *Bann*'s return to Freetown seventy sick slaves were removed to hospital. The sick all eventually recovered and on 25 April *Bann* departed the Coast with troops for Barbados.

Just a few days after *Bann*'s departure a new commodore arrived in Sierra Leone aboard the 36-gun frigate *Inconstant*. Sir James Yeo had been ordered to visit British ports and settlements as far south as Benguela and enforce the abolition acts and the Portuguese treaty but was warned against interfering with merchant vessels of other nations. Entering the Navy in 1793, at the age of just 15, in 1805 Yeo had led an assault on the Spanish port of El Muros, bringing out every vessel in the port. For this success he was promoted commander aboard one of his prizes. Promoted captain in 1807, in 1809 he led an Anglo-Portuguese force that captured Cayenne, French Guiana, the grateful Prince Regent of Portugal conferring on him a knighthood of the Order of St Bento d'Avis.

Sailing south for the Bights Yeo began his tour by visiting Anamabo and Accra. On 21 May a schooner was observed at anchor off Quitta Fort to the north-east of Cape St Paul's. The vessel immediately weighed on the appearance of Yeo's frigate. *Inconstant* gave chase and within a couple of hours had drawn alongside the schooner and ordered her to heave to. Upon boarding, the schooner was discovered to be a Spanish vessel, *Carmen*, equipped for slaving. Continuing further east with the schooner in company, on 24 May Yeo arrested the Portuguese schooner *Caveira* off Lagos with ten slaves on board. *Carmen* was sent to Freetown where she was eventually condemned and Yeo headed for Princes to land the prisoners from *Caveira* before sailing east to look in at Corsico Bay. Having detected a vessel loading slaves, Yeo waited until dark on 27 June before sending his boats inshore. They returned in the early hours towing the Portuguese schooner *Dos Amigos* with 247 slaves on board. The Portuguese fort fired a couple of ineffectual shots but *Inconstant* soon had the schooner in tow and began her journey back to Sierra Leone. Whilst at anchor off Freetown on 28 July a strange sail was spotted out to sea and Yeo sent his boats to investigate. They soon returned with the brig *Monte de Carmo Testa*, empty but equipped for slaving. On 31 July *Inconstant* left Freetown for another cruise south to the Gold Coast forts.

Four weeks later she departed Africa for Barbados with troops prior to her return home.

Following her capture *Caveira* had been manned as a tender by Yeo but his remaining prizes were all condemned. However, according to the terms of the Portuguese treaty the capture of *Dos Amigos* had been illegal and the court appeared to have condemned the vessel simply because her crew failed to make an appearance. The court's decision was eventually reversed and Yeo received the Admiralty's 'decided disapprobation'[6] over the incident.

With the return home of *Inconstant* there was once again no cruiser on the Coast. The colonial schooner *Princess Charlotte* could make no further contribution to the suppression campaign for in April she had been declared unfit for service. Looking round for a suitable replacement, Governor MacCarthy eventually settled on the prize *Louis* which in April was renamed *Prince Regent* and placed under the command of Acting Lieutenant Hagan. On 20 April boats from *Bann* and *Prince Regent* were sent to investigate a Spanish-flagged schooner that had sprung a leak off Sierra Leone. Boarding the vessel, *La Neuve Aimable*, the British discovered a cargo of 388 slaves. She was brought into harbour and subsequently condemned. *Prince Regent* now left Freetown for a cruise south. On 5 May she encountered the piratical slaver *La Paz* off Cape Mesurado. The vessel was eventually captured following a chase of seven hours and a subsequent action lasting fifteen minutes. *La Paz*'s crew resisted arrest, Hagan being stabbed in the hand by the vessel's master who he then shot dead. On 30 September *Prince Regent* captured the Spanish-flagged brig *Triumphante*. She was taken in the Cameroons River by boats under the command of Hagan's First Lieutenant, Thompson, who was wounded in the head. On 7 November *Prince Regent* captured the Portuguese schooner *Santa Johanna* whilst disguised and sailing under foreign colours. Seventy-two slaves were discovered aboard this vessel, stowed in a space 40ft in length with just 2ft 9in of headroom. Hagan's final prize of the year was the Portuguese brig *Ceres*, taken in the Bight of Benin on 15 November with a cargo of eleven slaves.

In mid-July the new French Governor Designate of Senegal, Colonel Julien Schmaltz, had arrived on the coast in a boat following the loss of the frigate *Meduse* near Cape Blanco, a tragedy immortalised by the painter Théodore Géricault in his painting *The Raft of the Medusa*. MacCarthy had received little in the way of instructions regarding the handing over of Goree and Senegal to France from London and the British garrisons would not complete their evacuations of these settlements until early 1817.

On 19 December *Inconstant* departed Spithead for Africa. Arriving at Sierra Leone on 13 January 1817, she was soon joined by the 26-gun Sixth Rate *Cherub*, into which vessel Captain Fisher and his ship's company had transferred from *Bann*. Yeo departed Freetown and proceeded to cruise as far south as the Gabon. On 17 January *Cherub* captured a Portuguese ship, *Esperanza*, loaded with 413 slaves off Cape Lahou. Sending her prize to Freetown, *Cherub* proceeded to Cape Coast where Fisher had heard reports of several Spanish vessels acting piratically. Well manned 'by ruffians of all nations'[7] and heavily armed with up to twenty guns, these piratical vessels were becoming an increasing nuisance, seizing slaves from other vessels and determined to fight any vessel they might fall in with. Arriving at Cape Coast Castle Fisher was informed of a slaver in the area apparently operating under the directions of the Dutch governor of Elmina, Daendels. The vessel was spotted on 23 January but her superior sailing qualities kept her out of Fisher's reach.

Abandoning his hunt for pirates off Cape Coast, Fisher now turned his attention to the slavers operating out of Popo, a few miles east of Whydah. On 26 January *Cherub* gave chase to a suspicious-looking schooner but she evaded capture. Informed that the vessel had come from Princes, Fisher set course for the Bights in order to intercept his prey. After a brief sighting on 30 January *Cherub* finally fell in with the schooner the following day and Fisher sent in his boats under the command of Lieutenant James Henderson. As *Cherub*'s boats approached the schooner she opened fire on them with grape and musketry before hoisting her colours, indistinguishable in the calm airs. The schooner struck her colours as Henderson came alongside in the pinnace but then immediately fired two more rounds of grape and langrage into Henderson's boat and the gig, killing three men in the pinnace and wounding seven of the eight officers and crew in the gig. Firing a round of grape at the schooner's quarterdeck, Henderson boarded the vessel, which proved to be the French schooner *Louisa*, empty but fitted for slaving. Removing three officers and two crewmen to *Cherub*, Fisher dispatched *Louisa* to Freetown.

Following his arrival off Cape Coast Yeo had been informed of a piratical slaver of twenty-six guns that had asked the whereabouts of Yeo's ship, not in order to evade *Inconstant* but to find her and 'blow her out of the water'.[8] *Inconstant*'s boats searched for this Spanish-flagged vessel without success then sailed for St Thomas. Arriving off Annobon on 16 March, Yeo sent his cutter and barge inshore to rescue the crew of a prize belonging to *Cherub* which had been wrecked on the island. Five British sailors, three Kroomen and four prisoners were taken on board *Inconstant*. On the journey south to Ascension to water and provision four of the British prize crew and one Krooman died. On 1 May Yeo sailed for Barbados and home. When *Inconstant* finally arrived back in England in October she was discovered to be so far beyond repair that the Admiralty decided to break her up. Yeo, his officers and ship's company were transferred in to the 36-gun frigate *Semiramis*.

After watering at Princes Island *Cherub* sailed west via Whydah to Cape Coast. Here Fisher found the Dutch Government Secretary at Elmina, Herman Milet, who was seeking passage to Europe. Milet had obtained evidence that he wished to present to his government concerning Governor Daendels, who he claimed was trading with Spanish and Portuguese slavers, supplying them with trade goods and Africans. Fisher agreed to Milet's request and on 3 March *Cherub* sailed for England. Milet's claims against Daendels were never substantiated and the Governor died of an apoplectic fit in May 1818.

The capture of *Louisa* had brought a reminder from Castlereagh to Their Lordships that Royal Navy vessels had no right to arrest French-flagged vessels, regardless of whether or not they were involved in slaving. This resulted in a rebuke to Fisher from the Admiralty. In response Fisher replied that he had he known that *Louisa* was French he would have left her alone but he had chased the vessel for two days during which time she had declined to show her colours. In December 1817 Sir William Scott overturned the decision of the court in Freetown to condemn the similarly-named French vessel *Louis*, seized by Hagan in March 1816, declaring that British cruisers could not search or detain French vessels unless they suspected them of piracy and that, under the general law of nations, slavery could not be considered piracy. From now on British cruisers operating off the Coast would have to ignore French-flagged vessels, even if they were clearly involved in the Trade.

Whilst Scott's judgement over *Louis* was clearly a setback for the campaign against the resurgent French slavers, elsewhere significant progress was being made. In London on 28 July 1817 an Additional Convention to the Portuguese Treaty of 1815 was signed. This convention prohibited slaving by Portuguese vessels in any of the harbours covered by the 1815 treaty and by Portuguese vessels sailing for any port not in the Portuguese dominions. However, the slave trade would continue from Portuguese territories south of the equator and from between 5°12'S and 8°S. Portugal did, however, undertake to prohibit the importation of slaves into Brazil by non–Portuguese vessels. Vessels detained would now be brought before two Mixed Commissions, both with British and Portuguese officials. One of these Mixed Commissions would be set up at Freetown, the other in Rio de Janeiro. The convention also included Special Instructions covering the means of detention of vessels suspected of slaving. Boardings and captures were only to be made by cruisers of the British and Portuguese navies and only by vessels carrying copies of these Special Instructions. No vessel could be visited or detained whilst in the port of either signatory and searches could only be carried out by officers of at least lieutenant rank. Finally arrests south of the Equator could only be made if the pursuit had begun north of the Line. Following a recent Order in Council the amount of head money had now been reduced to a flat rate of £10 per slave. In 1816 the total sum paid in prize money and bounties had been £12,269, roughly a third of the money paid out in 1812.

On 23 September 1817 a treaty was signed in Madrid by which Spain promised to abolish the slave trade throughout her territories by May 1820. More immediately, the Spanish government agreed to abolish all Trade north of the Line on 22 November 1817, the date that the treaty was due to be ratified. As with the earlier Additional Convention between Britain and Portugal, the treaty also established Mixed Commissions (one in Freetown and one in Havana) and the Special Instructions for cruisers operating off the West Coast of Africa. London agreed to pay £40,000 as compensation for losses suffered by Spain during the suppression campaign, which the King of Spain used to purchase five warships from Russia.

Inevitably, the immediate effect of both these treaties was a sudden surge in the import of slaves into Spanish and Portuguese dominions and a rise in their price. In May 1818 the British Minister in Rio, Henry Chamberlain, reported that twenty-five slave ships had already arrived since the start of the year, importing around 10,000 slaves, and in the Caribbean the Commander-in-Chief of the Jamaica Station, Rear Admiral Home Popham, reported an increase of 25 per cent in the price of slaves with the cost of those arriving from north of the Line expected to double.

With the return home of Yeo and Fisher, Hagan, now confirmed as lieutenant, was once again left to continue the suppression campaign on his own. Prior to the departure of *Cherub* and *Inconstant*, his schooner *Prince Regent* had captured three slavers operating on the Rivers Nunez and Pongas; the Spanish vessel *Labertino* on 29 March, the Portuguese schooner *Gramachree* on 12 April and the Spanish brig *Esperanza*, which was discovered hiding in the Nunez, her masts wrapped in palm branches, on 18 April. It would be another six months before *Prince Regent* made her next capture, the English brig *Two Boats*, taken off the Pongas on 21 October. This vessel was discovered empty but Hagan's next prize, the Spanish brigantine *San Juan Nepomuceno*, was taken off the Pongas on 7 December with a cargo of 276 slaves. A week later the Portuguese schooner *Linde Africano* was taken from the same river as was the English schooner *Hannah*, captured on 21 January 1818 with five slaves on board. *Prince Regent*'s final capture was the Spanish schooner *Belle Machancho*, seized with a cargo of 130 slaves. After this Hagan's vessel fell foul of the recent Spanish and Portuguese treaties as he had not been provided with a copy of the Special Instructions, despite the efforts of Governor MacCarthy, and was restricted to revenue enforcement for the remainder of the year.

Following her return to Spithead in mid-July *Cherub* had undergone a refit and on 11 October had sailed again for Africa, this time under the command of Captain George Willes. On 29 November she chased a vessel off Grand Bassa which evaded capture, hoisting American, British then French colours. The following month *Cherub* cruised off the Gold Coast and whilst off Anamabo was run on board by a Spanish vessel which carried away her jib-booms and spritsail yard. Arriving at Princes Island on 27 December *Cherub* approached a schooner, *Concha*, which was wanted for piracy. In drawing alongside the vessel *Cherub* ran aground and Willes had to order his marines to fire at *Concha* to prevent the pirates manning her guns. *Concha* was boarded, her mate was killed and two seamen injured. The nearby fort fired several long-range shots at *Cherub* as Willes was kedging his vessel off the shoal and he then had to go ashore to enter into negotiations with the local governor before he was allowed to leave with his prize. On 8 January 1818 *Cherub* and *Concha* arrested two vessels off Porto Novo. A week later *Cherub* was cruising past Quitta Fort when she sighted and gave chase to a brig which only hove to after several broadsides from Willes's frigate. This vessel proved to be the Spanish-flagged *Descubridor* which had been accused of piracy against the Portuguese brig *Difforso*. Whilst *Cherub* sailed for Porto Novo to find a witness to the Spanish brig's piracy her prize *Descubridor* was sent to Cape Coast to await the return of Yeo.

On 17 January *Semiramis* arrived at Sierra Leone from Portsmouth. Proceeding on a cruise down to Cape Coast, she fell in with *Cherub* and her two prizes on 19 February. Yeo now ordered *Cherub*, *Concha* and *Descubridor* back to Freetown. Having watered and provisioned at St Thomas, *Cherub* and her prizes arrived at Sierra Leone on 15 April. The Vice-Admiralty court did not have the authority to try cases of piracy so Willes landed his slaves and awaited the return of Yeo. Having parted company with *Cherub* at Accra on 1 March, *Semiramis* sailed for Ascension via St Thomas, returning to Sierra Leone on 21 April. It was now agreed that, as *Semiramis* was due to sail to Jamaica, she should be accompanied by *Descubridor*, as the Vice-Admiralty court there could try the charges of piracy against the Spanish brig. *Semiramis* and *Descubridor* sailed for Jamaica on 24 April. *Cherub* was also due to sail to Jamaica but there was time for one last cruise down to the Gold Coast, having first dispatched *Concha* in *Semiramis* and *Descubridor*'s wake. *Cherub* sailed from Freetown on 29 April. Her Kroomen were landed at Cape Palmas and on 15 May she spotted and gave chase to a Spanish-flagged vessel off Cape Three Points. The chase lasted ten hours and after an exchange of fire the slaver, with damage to both her hull and rigging, hove to. Boarding the vessel she was discovered to be the packet *Josepha* with a cargo of thirty-five slaves. Sixteen male slaves were transferred to *Cherub* and Willes's prize was dispatched to Jamaica whilst *Cherub* continued on down to Accra before departing for the West Indies via Ascension.

On Willes's arrival at Jamaica he discovered that *Descubridor*'s master was now claiming to be merely a passenger aboard the vessel. Furthermore, the single witness of the brig's piracy had not been allowed to give evidence in court as he was an African. With the Attorney-General now deciding that there was not enough evidence to bring charges against *Descubridor*, her Cuban owners claimed restitution of both vessel and cargo. When Willes refused to pay he was arrested and bail was set at £6,000, a huge sum that *Cherub*'s commander had no possibility of paying. Willes was only released when he agreed to give up *Descubridor* and provide an account of the slaves and goods from the brig which had been landed at Freetown and Gold Coast. *Descubridor*'s owners now brought a case against Willes for wrongful arrest and in January 1820 he was ordered to pay £21,180. This sum was subsequently reduced to £6,507, most of which was met by the sale of perishable goods from the brig with the Treasury graciously agreeing to pay the remaining £62.11s.6d.

Unfortunately Willes was not the only officer to fall foul of the law. In October 1818 Captain Scobell learned that he had been summoned before the Court of King's Bench to answer a charge of false imprisonment and seizure of property brought by Robert Bostock and John McQueen, the slavers he had arrested in May 1813, who were now suddenly emboldened by the deaths of two key witnesses. Scobell was shocked that a decision of the Vice-Admiralty court could be challenged after so many years and wondered what officer who was simply following Admiralty orders would now be safe from the law. The Government eventually decided that the case should be handled by the Treasury Solicitor but it would be many years before a judgement was reached. There is unfortunately no record of the outcome of this case but in 1821 Bostock sailed for Australia with his wife and children as a free settler in the colony of New South Wales.

On 14 May 1818 an Anglo-Dutch treaty was signed at The Hague. It was agreed that within eight months of the ratification of the treaty Dutch subjects would be forbidden from taking any part in the slave trade. As with previous treaties, the co-signatories would have the right to detain vessels belonging to the other nation except in the Mediterranean and in waters outside the Straights of Gibraltar to the north of 37°N and east of 20°W. Mixed Commissions would also be set up at Freetown and Surinam. Later that year, at the first peacetime conference between the foreign ministers of Britain, France, Russia, Spain and Portugal, held at Aix-la-Chapelle, Castlereagh suggested that there be an international right of search, enforced by an international police force operating on the African coast. However, this idea was perceived as an effort by Britain to ensure supremacy at sea and was rejected.

Semiramis departed Jamaica for England on 26 July. Yeo had been ill for some months and during the long journey home his health grew steadily worse. On 16 August he took to his sickbed which he did not leave. He died on 21 August, aged just 35, of a 'general disability' or atrophy, whilst his ship was just south of the Grand Banks of Newfoundland; the second senior officer to fall victim to the maladies of the Slave Coast. *Semiramis* arrived back in Portsmouth on 7 September and Commodore Yeo's body was taken to the George Inn. The following morning Yeo was interred in the grounds of the Royal Garrison Chapel in a ceremony attended by all the off-duty officers of the local regiments and corps.

Following the Treaty of Ghent Britain had continued to press America to uphold its anti-slavery obligations. Emboldened by the recent Anglo-Spanish and Anglo-Portuguese treaties and the implementation of the Mixed Commissions, on 20 June 1818 Castlereagh had written to the American minister in London, Richard Rush, stating a need for the principal maritime powers to work in concert to prevent their flags being used as a cover for the slave trade. Referring to the recent treaties with Spain and Portugal, Castlereagh urged the American government to consider the advantages of a mutual right to search between Britain and America. When the Cabinet of President Monroe met to discuss the issue later that year, the main objection was the predicted abuse of the right of search by the British. A dispute over the right of search had already led to one war, and the Administration did not want it to be the cause of another. The Secretary of War, John Calhoun, noted his unease over any proposal that might 'allow a British officer to muster and pass under inspection the crew of every American vessel boarded by him. It would give rise to altercations and … would also be used as a weapon against the Administration.'[9] There were also concerns that the implementation of mixed courts of appeal would present constitutional problems. Rush was eventually ordered to reject the Mixed Commission proposal on two counts: firstly the United States had no colony or possession in Africa where a joint court could be established and secondly, the Constitution 'admitted no appointment of Judges who would not be amenable to impeachment'.[10] Frustratingly for the British it would take several changes of American administration before the two sides would finally come to an agreement over anti-slavery policies.

On 19 September 1818 Commodore Sir George Collier received instructions to sail with his frigate *Tartar* to Freetown. As with all previous instructions issued by the Admiralty, Collier was ordered to give assistance and protection to the various British forts and settlements along the coast and to pay particular attention to the slavers operating between Cape Verde and Benguela, at Whydah and the Bight of Benin, using the various acts of Parliament and 'every other means'[11] in his power to prevent a continuance of the Trade, although rather unhelpfully the Admiralty offered no advice as to what these 'other means' might be. Once again, Collier was ordered to depart the Coast before the rainy season set in, but for the first time the use of Ascension Island for recuperation was authorised.

Aged 44, Collier had first joined the Navy in 1787. Promoted lieutenant three years later, whilst en route to the East India station in 1792 his ship *Winchelsea* was wrecked off Mozambique and he spent the next two years as a prisoner in France. Collier made post in 1801 and in 1814 he had been given command of the 50-gun *Leander* and sent to North America to deal with the heavy American frigates harassing British merchant shipping, giving chase to but failing to bring to battle *Constitution*, just days before the cessation of hostilities. Appointed commander of the West Africa Squadron at a time when the Admiralty was beginning to refocus its attention on the suppression campaign, Collier would soon be in charge of one of the largest squadrons the Coast had seen for several years.

Tartar arrived at Freetown on 2 December. Four days later she left for a cruise down to the Gold Coast settlements. At Princes Collier spotted two suspicious-looking vessels in the harbour, the Portuguese schooner *Armistad* and the Spanish brig *Gavilan*. Collier questioned the Portuguese officials on the island but they did not know, or would not say, whether these were slave ships. However, Collier now learned of a Spanish schooner at St Thomas which claimed to have been stripped of her slaves by a vessel answering the description of *Gavilan*. Of more pressing concern to Collier were the reports of a piratical slaver operating off Cape Lopez and he now headed south to find her. On the passage down to Annobon *Tartar* fell in with and boarded a Spanish-flagged schooner with a cargo of 250 slaves. The Spanish members of the Mixed Commission had not yet arrived in Freetown so Collier released the schooner the following day. On his arrival at Annobon Collier was informed that the suspected pirate had sailed two days prior to *Tartar*'s arrival. Collier gave up the search and headed out towards Ascension before returning to Freetown, arriving in port on 18 February.

Tartar remained in Freetown for just ten days before setting off on another cruise south. Returning to Princes on 22 March Collier discovered that *Gavilan*, now repainted in different colours, was preparing to put to sea. As he weighed anchor on 24 March Collier was surprised to receive a 21-gun salute from the local fort. The real reason for this salute became clear, when, clearing Port Antonio, *Tartar* sighted two schooners heading out to sea and a large number of canoes making for the beach. During the night *Tartar* rounded the north end of Princes and the following morning Collier spotted the two schooners lying at anchor off a bay on the west coast of the island. Intending to catch the vessels in the act of landing slaves, Collier ordered *Tartar*'s cutter away but the boat capsized on lowering, throwing its crew into the water. Whilst they were being rescued Collier opened fire on the schooners. One, *Princessa*, remained at anchor but the second, *Armistad*, hoisted her Portuguese colours and made off to the north. Once *Tartar*'s boats were in the water and pulling for *Princessa* Collier set off in pursuit of *Armistad*. When the schooner was eventually stopped and boarded in the early hours of 26 March a licence from the Governor of Cabinda was discovered on board along with a log describing a slaving voyage to Bonny earlier that year. When questioned, *Armistad*'s crew admitted that both schooners had loaded with slaves at Bonny and had been attempting to rendezvous with *Gavilan* at Port Antonio. *Armistad*'s cargo of slaves was in such a debilitated state they required carrying to the boats, one 14-year-old boy weighing only 45lbs.

Tartar's boats had discovered *Princessa* abandoned. Six slaves were recovered from the beach and the schooner was taken to Port Antonio. She was fired on by the local batteries but successfully dropped anchor in the harbour. *Tartar* arrived on 27 March and Collier sent First Lieutenant Digby Marsh to examine *Princessa* and bring her out if she proved not to be Portuguese. The schooner's nationality could not be determined but when she attempted to sail she was fired on again by the local fort. Marsh went ashore to ask Governor Gomez if *Princessa* was being detained and in response Gomez angrily accused the British of murdering slaves. The six exhausted slaves rescued from *Princessa* were transferred to *Tartar* and Collier sent both prizes to Sierra Leone. However, as the court was still awaiting the arrival of the Portuguese and Spanish commissioners neither *Princessa* nor *Armistad* ever came to trial.

On 1 May *Tartar* returned to Freetown and three days later she sailed for Barbados and home. On 7 May the 22-gun ship-sloop *Pheasant*, Commander Benedictus Kelly, arrived at Sierra Leone from Cadiz where she had embarked the Spanish members of the Mixed Commission, the Judge, Don Francisco Le Fer, and the Arbitrator, Don Juan Campo. On 28 August the Dutch commissioners, Judge Dow van Sirtema and the Arbitrator, Mr Bonnouvrie, arrived in Sierra Leone aboard the Dutch sloop *Komet*. However, there was still no sign of the Portuguese commissioners, Lisbon explaining that it was having trouble finding suitable applicants willing to work in such a hostile environment for such poor remuneration.

On 9 June *Pheasant* left Freetown for a cruise south to the Bights. Three days later the ship-sloop *Morgiana*, Commander Charles Strong, arrived at Sierra Leone. The sloop *Erne* had been sailing a day astern of Strong's vessel but on 1 June was wrecked off Sal at the Cape Verde Islands due to incorrect Admiralty charts, thankfully without any loss of life. On 15 July the Admiralty sent Commanders Kelly and Strong copies of the recent treaty between Britain and the Netherlands, the new Act of Parliament carrying the treaty in to law and copies of the Special Instructions allowing them to board Dutch vessels suspected of slaving.

On 30 July *Pheasant* boarded the Portuguese schooner *Novo Felicidade* whilst cruising off the mouth of the River Campo. Seventy-one slaves were discovered on board this vessel of 11 tons. Seventeen men shackled together in pairs were discovered along with twenty boys in a space 17ft by 7ft 3in and just 1ft 8in high, one man's dysentery having caused 'an effluvion too dreadful for description'[12] amongst the yams the slaves had been stowed above. Thirty-four female slaves were discovered unshackled in a space barely half that allowed for the male slaves. Thankfully they appeared in a less distressed state than the male slaves, having presumably been allowed up on deck on occasions during the voyage. The schooner's master claimed he had loaded his slaves south of the Line but he had no papers for his journey and so Kelly arrested his vessel. Upon further questioning the master admitted that the slaves had been bought at Old Calabar and that the vessel belonged to Governor Gomez. Twenty-two male slaves were taken aboard *Pheasant* and Kelly returned to Freetown with his prize now under tow. Only one slave had been lost by the time *Novo Felicidade* arrived in

Sierra Leone on 17 August. Once there the British judge, Thomas Gregory, ordered the slaves to be removed ashore before adjudication. The court was, of course, still awaiting the arrival of the Portuguese commissioners but news eventually came through that the Portuguese Ambassador in London had agreed that the case might be heard by the British judge alone and *Novo Felicidade* was subsequently condemned.

On 10 August *Morgiana* captured the Spanish schooner *Nuestra Señora de Regla* off Little Bassa. The vessel had been forced to abort the loading of slaves due to deteriorating weather and was seized with just one slave on board and her master still ashore. Sailing off Grand Bassa in foul weather three days later, *Morgiana* chased another schooner which attempted to evade capture inside a rocky ledge but was driven ashore in heavy surf. Commander Strong sent a boat to stop canoes removing slaves from the wreck but she was fired on by the schooner. Within half an hour the slaver had been reduced to flotsam. Returning to Freetown on 18 August Strong reported that 'we have sailed well enough to convince them (for every vessel I have spoken to has been slaving) that there are Men-of-War upon the Coast with whose sailing they cannot trifle'.[13] Thankfully his crew were still in good health, despite it being the rainy season. *Morgiana*'s prize, *Nuestra Señora de Regla*, became the first vessel to be condemned by the Anglo–Spanish Mixed Commission, her solitary slave being emancipated on 13 September.

On 27 July the 12-gun brig *Thistle* departed Portsmouth for the Coast, stopping off at the Cape Verde Islands to pick up stores from the wreck of *Erne* prior to her arrival at Freetown on 23 September. *Thistle*'s new commander, Lieutenant Hagan, had been appointed in response to a recommendation from MacCarthy to the Colonial Office following the officer's earlier successes on the Coast. Recognising that the gun-brig's small size prevented adequate prize crews being sent across to any vessels that might be seized, the Admiralty had authorised Hagan to hire an additional twelve Kroomen for his vessel and he was also instructed to replace sick crew members when required at Ascension.

Having watered and replenished, *Thistle* set off for a cruise down to the Bights. On 9 October she spotted the Dutch schooner *Eliza* off St Eustatius. As *Thistle*'s boat pulled towards the slaver she began landing her slaves. Several children were also spotted being thrown into the water and were presumably drowned. By the time *Eliza* was boarded all but one of her remaining slaves had been put ashore. The following day another Dutch schooner, *Virginie*, was spotted at anchor off Rock Sesters. The crew attempted to run their vessel ashore but when this failed they abandoned ship with their cargo of thirty-one slaves still on board. Hagan escorted his two prizes back to Freetown where MacCarthy now requested passage in *Thistle* to the British settlement at Bathurst. However, Hagan was prevented from putting to sea whilst the Mixed Commission adjudicated on his two recent prizes.

It had been a long-standing tradition of the Vice-Admiralty court at Freetown to allow British officers to be represented by advocates, but the Spanish and Dutch judges now insisted that each officer present his case in person and then return when the court reached its decision. When the case of *Eliza* was eventually heard the Dutch judge, Dow van Sirtema, and the British judge, Thomas Gregory, disagreed again, this time over the wording of the treaty and whether the one slave found on board *Eliza* constituted a cargo. As per the rules of the Mixed Commission the two judges now drew straws to pick one of the arbitrators to break the tie. The Dutch arbitrator, Mr Bonnouvrie, was selected and thankfully for Hagan he sided with Gregory and agreed that *Eliza* was subject to condemnation under the treaties.

On 4 September a second gun-brig, *Snapper*, Lieutenant James Henderson, arrived at Sierra Leone from Portsmouth. Henderson's orders were identical to those of Hagan save for his instructions to cruise the Bights of Benin. Watering completed, *Snapper* headed south and on 30 September discovered the Spanish schooner *Juanita* in the middle of loading off the River Costa with a cargo of just nine slaves on board. Henderson dispatched the schooner to Freetown where she was condemned on 12 November. On 3 October *Snapper* fell in with *Pheasant* off Cape St Paul's and Kelly ordered Henderson to victual at Cape Coast Castle before rendezvousing with his sloop at Princes. Following her departure from Freetown in early September *Pheasant* had spent two weeks unsuccessfully chasing slavers off the Windward Coast before heading to Cape Coast to provision. Stationing his sloop west of Cape Formoso, on 6 October Kelly intercepted a Portuguese brig, *Vulcano do Sud*, headed south to St Salvador with a cargo of 270 slaves. A prize crew consisting of four British seamen, two Kroomen and two natives of Cape Coast commanded by Midshipman

Castles was put on board *Vulcano* and she was dispatched to Freetown. The brig was never seen again.

Towards the end of October *Pheasant* called at Accra and Whydah. By this time, the height of the rainy season, the sloop had lost her master, surgeon, gunner and acting pilot to fever. Having spent several weeks in the Bight of Benin, Kelly noted a decline in the activity of slavers in the region which he ascribed to the presence of his cruiser. As previously arranged, in late December *Pheasant* rendezvoused with *Snapper* at Princes. Henderson's gun-brig was now dispatched to Whydah whilst *Pheasant* remained at the island to renew her worn-out rigging. She returned to Freetown via Cape Coast in mid-January 1820.

On 27 November the 20-gun ship-sloop *Myrmidon*, Commander Henry Leeke, joined the Squadron from Gibraltar via Porto Praya. After just a few days at Freetown, *Myrmidon* set off on a cruise south to investigate the Gallinas and Sagary rivers where a number of slavers were rumoured to be operating. Anchoring just to the north of the Gallinas and out of sight of the suspected slavers, on 10 December Leeke dispatched his First Lieutenant, Richard Nash, with the pinnace and cutter to search along the river. The following evening six schooners were spotted at anchor. The boats were put alongside the largest of these vessels and after some resistance she was captured. She was found to be the Spaniard *Voladora* with a passport for slaving south of the Line but with a cargo of 122 slaves taken from the Gallinas. She was the only vessel with slaves still on board, the other schooners having landed their cargoes when they had seen the boats from *Myrmidon* approach. A prize crew was put on board *Voladora* but as she attempted to make her way out of the Gallinas she was fired on by the other schooners who each gave her three or four broadsides as they made their escape. Thankfully the British prize crew only suffered one man wounded, struck in the arm by a musket ball.

Four days later the Spanish schooner *Virgien* was arrested off Cape Mount on suspicion of piracy. *Myrmidon*'s Second Lieutenant, Edward Belcher, had just been placed in charge of a large prize crew of twenty-five men made up of British sailors and Kroomen when several more schooners appeared in the offing and Leeke set off in pursuit. Built in 1813 along the lines of a captured French corvette, *Myrmidon* was a fast sailer and by 11.00am had forced three of the schooners to heave to. Two had no slaves on board and were released but the third had a cargo of 140 slaves. Although she had papers suggesting she was a Spaniard, she was flying a French flag and Leeke was forced to release her. *Myrmidon* now set of in pursuit of another schooner, which after a three-hour chase was run ashore. Her cargo of slaves was landed before the vessel was wrecked and nine Africans were saved from drowning by *Myrmidon*. By this time Lieutenant Belcher had begun a pursuit of a large brig which hoisted Spanish colours and fired a broadside at *Virgien* before she too was run ashore to evade capture, her cargo of slaves jumping overboard before the vessel was wrecked.

On 23 December *Myrmidon*'s boats landed the Master's Mate, John Baker, and Leeke's clerk, John Evans, at Cape St Ann, Sherbro Island, to gain intelligence on the slavers operating in the region. Pretending to be from an American schooner trading for slaves, Baker and Evans met with an Irish trader named John Kearney who took them aboard his vessel, a small schooner. Kearney told Baker and Evans that he had just put 150 slaves on board a French vessel and was temporarily out of stock but he ought to be able to procure 800 slaves in two to three days. Kearney also boasted that he had embarked almost every slave bought between Cape St Ann and the Gallinas and claimed that no one suspected him of slavery as he had a deputation from MacCarthy to seize all persons and vessels involved in the Trade. Of course no such agreement existed and the governor was eager to arrest Kearney and send him for trial in England. MacCarthy knew the slave trader well. He had previously been a subaltern in the Royal African Corps and for a short while had also worked for the government in Freetown. Kearney told Baker and Evans that he had information on every Royal Navy vessel sailing from Freetown which he passed to other slavers to help them evade capture. Kearney added that the recent appearance of *Morgiana* had caused considerable alarm amongst his fellow slaver masters due to her superior sailing qualities. Their meeting with the unsuspecting Kearney over, *Myrmidon*'s warrant officers returned to their boat to report back to Leeke.

Having watered and provisioned at Freetown, *Morgiana* returned to the Pepper Coast and on 8 September encountered a schooner which ran herself ashore near Trade Town in an attempt to avoid capture. Within a quarter of an hour the schooner began breaking up, with, so Strong feared, a cargo hold full of slaves. On 17 September *Morgiana* gave chase to a schooner that was sighted off Cape Palmas. The chase continued into the night and by the following morning, it having fallen calm, Second Lieutenant Hugh Head was able to take three boats and board the schooner which was discovered to be a Spanish vessel, *Fabiana*, issued with a passport to trade south of the Line but with thirteen slaves already on board. Prior to her arrest her master had been ashore at Trade Town purchasing more slaves when it had blown a gale and the schooner had been driven almost 150 miles to the south-east. Discovered amongst *Fabiana*'s papers was a signed protest by her crew against their captain's conduct in trading slaves north of the Line.

Hoping to catch the slavers by surprise, on the night of 25 October Strong sent his boats inshore under the command of First Lieutenant George Ryves. At around 8.00pm Ryves boarded an English vessel off Cape Mount and was informed of the presence of another four slavers further north. After a short rest the boats set off again and soon found themselves pulling towards four schooners at anchor off Manna. Boarding the first vessel, they discovered her to be empty but the next vessel, the Portuguese schooner *Cintra*, had a cargo of twenty-six slaves and was waiting to complete her loading before sailing to Trinidad de Cuba. She had no passport to trade in slaves, even south of the Line. By now the other two schooners had weighed anchor and slipped away, but it was subsequently learned that neither had slaves on board.

On the morning of 10 December Strong's sloop was cruising off Little Bassa when two schooners were spotted heading out to sea. *Morgiana* gave chase and began gaining on the vessels but it then fell to a dead calm and so Strong dispatched his cutter and gig under Lieutenant Head to board the suspected slavers. On the approach of *Morgiana*'s boats one of the schooners hoisted French colours and so she was left alone. Approaching the second vessel she eventually hoisted Spanish colours and cleared for action. When Head's boats were within a cable's length either side of this schooner she opened fire with grape and canister. Head and another man were struck and the bowman was wounded as he hooked on. Midshipman Mansell, in command of the gig, was first on deck, fighting alongside a marine named Lord. Mansell was attacked by the schooner's master and two other men but was saved by a member of his boat crew, William Harris. Four British sailors received cutlass wounds in this brief action, and the schooner's master and three of his crew were wounded and two other men were killed before the remaining crew were driven below deck. The schooner proved to be *Esperanza*, a vessel bound for Puerto Rico with a cargo of forty-one slaves, one of whom died on the passage back to Freetown. The Spaniard was condemned on 27 December but there was still no Portuguese Mixed Commission to judge *Cintra*.

Chapter 4

The American Squadron:
January 1820–February 1822

On 23 November 1819 *Tartar* departed Portsmouth for the Coast, sailing via Sal to recover more stores from the wreckage of *Erne*. Dropping anchor at the Cape Verde Islands on 2 January 1820, Collier learned that Governor MacCarthy had recently arrived at the Gambia aboard *Thistle*. On 7 January *Tartar* arrived at Bathurst and Collier met with Hagan who discussed the recent problems he had encountered with the new Mixed Commission which had denied him his own counsel or access to papers. Hagan thought that the Dutch Judge van Sirtema was by no means impartial and indeed favoured the slavers. With the governor now aboard *Tartar*, Collier sailed for Sierra Leone in company with *Thistle*, arriving there on 13 January.

Upon his arrival in Freetown Collier found both *Morgiana* and *Myrmidon* lying at anchor and a brief inspection of the two ships showed their crews much debilitated by their recent cruises. Collier's solution was to send them both away from the harmful airs of Freetown and out into the Atlantic where, it was hoped, the men would feel the benefit of the Trade Winds. Following *Morgiana*'s return to Freetown Strong was promoted to captain and was replaced as commander of the sloop by Lieutenant Alexander Sandilands. On 20 January *Morgiana* and *Myrmidon* were dispatched to cruise between Cape St Ann and Cape Mount, and five days later *Tartar* and *Thistle* left Freetown and headed north along the Windward Coast.

Arriving at the Isles de Los, Hagan learned that the ex-master of *Louis*, seized by him in March 1816, was now in command of a slaving brig operating in the Pongas and was threatening retribution against *Thistle*. Undeterred by these threats Hagan crossed the bar and entered the river with three of *Tartar*'s boats commanded by Lieutenant Digby Marsh. On 30 January the Spanish schooner, *Francisco*, and a Dutch brig, *Marie*, were both captured whilst loading slaves. *Tartar*'s boats continued upriver to Kissing where two schooners were discovered awaiting slaves. The boats returned from the Pongas with their two prizes on 2 February.

Thistle and *Tartar* were both back at Freetown by 7 February. *Francisco* was quickly condemned but, as was earlier indicated with his discussion with Hagan, it took over a week for *Marie* to come to trial, with van Sirtema then refusing to allow Collier to be in court or to employ counsel. To add to the Commodore's anger, van Sirtema eventually declared that ten of the twelve slaves found aboard the Dutch vessel were in fact crew members. Further objections and obstructions over the coming months would lead a thoroughly frustrated Collier to complain to the Admiralty over the operations of the court.

On the evening of 25 January *Myrmidon* and *Morgiana* arrived off the Gallinas and Leeke and Sandilands despatched their boats to investigate the river. After a hard pull during the night the British discovered six schooners at anchor the following morning. Five were Spanish vessels with no slaves on board. The remaining schooner, *La Marie*, hoisted French colours but was boarded by *Morgiana*'s boats and they discovered a cargo of 106 slaves. An examination of her papers suggested that the slaves had been shipped by the British trader, Kearney, and Leeke and Sandilands therefore decided to send the schooner to Freetown. Later that day *Morgiana* and *Myrmidon* were cruising offshore when two more schooners were discovered at the mouth of the nearby River Manna. On the approach of *Myrmidon*'s cutter one of these schooners was observed hurriedly loading Africans into boats which then pulled for the shore. When *Myrmidon*'s cutter intercepted one of these vessels she was found to have had just one slave on board, the last of the 200 to be removed from the schooner. Leeke had encountered this Portuguese slaver, *San Salvador*, twice before, but on both occasions she had successfully offloaded her cargo before Leeke could reach her. This time, however, her master had mistimed the operation.

On the evening of 30 January, whilst *Myrmidon* and *Morgiana* lay becalmed off Cape Mount, firing was detected to the north. *Myrmidon*'s Lieutenant Nash was dispatched with both vessels' boats to investigate and discovered *L'Arrogante*, a piratical brigantine flying the flag of Artigas (the nomme de guerre of Simon Bolivar) with two Spanish prizes at the mouth of the River Manna. After a brief action, *L'Arrogante* was captured. The vessel was thought to have robbed a French schooner a few days earlier, imprisoning her crew. She was also believed to have attacked an American schooner whilst flying Spanish colours and was therefore arrested on suspicion of piracy along with her two prizes, *Anna Marie* and *El Carmen*.

Sailing north in company with her five prizes, *Myrmidon* arrived at Sierra Leone on 8 February. *Anna Marie* and *El Carmen* were both released as there were no slaves aboard either of these vessels and the case of *San Salvador* could not be heard as the Portuguese commissioners had still not arrived. It seemed increasingly unlikely that a case of piracy could be brought against the crew of *L'Arrogante* and as for *La Marie*, it was decided that the slaves had been purchased lawfully and were not liable for confiscation and that the vessel be escorted to either Senegal or Goree.

On the morning of 3 February *Morgiana* boarded the schooner *Prince of Orange* off Little Bassa. Like *L'Arrogante* she was a piratical slaver flying the flag of Artigas. *Morgiana* sent her prize to Sierra Leone and the following day boarded a French schooner, *La Jeune Estelle*, which Sandilands discovered had been plundered of seventy-three slaves by two piratical schooners on 3 February. The following morning *Morgiana* fell in with both these vessels, the American schooner *Swift* and the Spanish schooner *L'Invincible the Second*, which hoisted their Artigas colours and attempted to escape. *Morgiana*'s boats managed to come up alongside *L'Invincible the Second* but *Swift* used her sweeps to effect her escape. Having sent the Spanish vessel, discovered with twenty-eight slaves on board, to Freetown, *Morgiana* continued her cruise to leeward, arriving at Cape Coast on 15 February.

On 28 February *Tartar* arrived in the Gallinas where she fell in with *Thistle*. A French schooner, *La Catherine*, with a cargo of fifty slaves on board, was arrested at the entrance to the river and she was sent north to Goree under escort from *Thistle*. *Tartar* then boarded two Spanish schooners, *Esperanza* and *Anita*, both of which were clearly awaiting their cargoes of slaves. Collier decided to interrupt their operations by taking both vessels with him, intending to release them once past Cape Palmas. On 2 March *Tartar* abandoned *Esperanza* and *Anita* and gave chase to two French-flagged schooners spotted to the windward of Trade Town. During the chase one of the schooners was seen throwing casks over the side of the ship. *Tartar* was unable to catch either vessel but when a Spanish schooner was spotted running under a spread of sail to the south-west later that day Collier gave chase. The pursuit lasted most of the day and when the schooner, *Gazetta*, was finally brought to around sunset eighty-two wretched-looking slaves were discovered aboard the American-built vessel. Concerned by the aggressive behaviour of *Gazetta*'s crew, Collier removed sixteen of her men to *Tartar* and she was dispatched to Freetown.

Two days later *Tartar*'s tender, a vessel purchased by Collier and several of his officers and now commanded by Lieutenant William Finlayson, boarded the two French-flagged schooners, *La Jeune Estelle* and *Joseph*, that Collier had unsuccessfully chased on 2 March. *La Jeune Estelle*'s master, Olympe Sanguines, swore that he had no slaves on board but whilst examining the schooner's hold Finlayson noticed a cask carefully closed at the bung hole by canvas nailed over it. His suspicion aroused, Finlayson knocked the hoops off the cask to discover two African girls hidden inside, almost suffocated. Taken on board *Tartar* they were recognised by three of *Gazetta*'s crew who now revealed that they had previously sailed with the schooner *Swift* and claimed that Sanguines had taken by force fourteen slaves purchased by their own master at Trade Town. Questioned further, *La Jeune Estelle*'s master now revealed that a male slave was hidden between the casks under a deck plank and produced a receipt to provide his proof of purchase. With no sign of the remaining slaves it was now obvious to the British what had been hidden in the casks Sanguines had been so eager to dispose of two days earlier. The two girl slaves were removed to *Tartar* and were later taken into the care of missionaries at Sierra Leone. *La Jeune Estelle* was in such a deplorable state that Collier doubted she would make it to Goree now the rainy season had begun and both she and *Joseph*, discovered with twelve slaves on board, were released after the Commodore endorsed their papers.

Parting company with the two schooners off Cape Palmas, *Tartar* continued on towards Cape Coast. Here she found the gun-brig *Snapper* in a deplorable state, with many of her crew now sick and her commanding officer, Henderson, and her assistant surgeon both dead of fever. *Myrmidon*'s Lieutenant Richard Nash having been appointed her new commanding officer, *Snapper* was sent back to Sierra Leone and a midshipman from *Tartar* was promoted to second lieutenant aboard *Myrmidon*.

Arriving at Accra from Cape Coast, *Tartar* fell in with *Pheasant* and Collier sent Kelly's sloop to Ascension via Cape Coast to caulk before departing for Princes. Other than a vessel that had landed its cargo of slaves at the island just prior to *Tartar*'s arrival, there was no sign of any slavers in the Bights. Fever had now appeared aboard Collier's ship and he departed the Coast for the healthier airs of Ascension. By the time *Tartar* reached Ascension on 29 April the fever had abated. *Pheasant*, however, had been less fortunate and Collier ordered her to remain at Ascension for three weeks until the health of her crew improved. Having re-provisioned, on 2 May *Tartar* sailed for Sierra Leone where Collier had ordered all the ships in the Squadron to rendezvous prior to his return home.

In February 1820 the American frigate *Cyane*, Captain Edward Trenchard, sailed from New York, escorting the brig *Elizabeth* which was carrying eighty-six freed slaves back to Africa, where the United States was hoping to create her own colony along the lines of Sierra Leone. Convinced the place chosen for the new settlement, Sherbro, 60 miles north of Freetown, would prove to be too unhealthy, Governor MacCarthy had tried to deter the colonists from settling there following their arrival on 20 March. Unfortunately his predictions proved all to correct and twenty-five slaves soon died of fever. The remainder received a hostile reception from the local tribe and the slave traders operating in the area.

In the decade since Congress had abolished slavery the Trade to America had continued largely unchecked. When Royal Navy ships began arresting United States' ships American slavers simply began adopting the flags of other countries, most notably Spain. In 1816 the African Society estimated that of the 60,000 slaves taken annually from Africa, 15,000 were shipped by Americans. Having finally turned its attention to the long-ignored issue of slavery, in 1818 Congress introduced an Act to deter the purchase of slaves, but this proved largely ineffective so the following year another Act was introduced offering rewards to slavers who informed on their associates. Ships would be forfeit, with one-half of the sale going to the informer and the remainder to the US government. Any citizen found guilty of equipping a slaver, transporting or purchasing slaves could now be imprisoned for between three to seven years. The Act, which was passed on 3 March, also directed the President to employ armed cruisers on the coasts of the United States and Africa to suppress the Trade and allocated $100,000 for its enforcement. In a bill passed the following year slavery became an act punishable by death.

On 6 April 1820 the United States Navy finally entered the suppression campaign, *Cyane*'s boats boarding six vessels off the Gallinas River. Two schooners, *Endymion* and *Esperanza* (the same vessel encountered by *Tartar* the previous month), were sent back to New York but the remaining four vessels all had Spanish papers and, even though it was clear to Trenchard that they were in truth American vessels, he had no option but to release them. Four days later Trenchard sent one of *Cyane*'s boats to investigate two schooners sailing towards Cape Mount. The boat, commanded by *Cyane*'s Second Lieutenant, Silas Stingham, was fired on as she approached the nearest vessel, but both schooners were eventually boarded and discovered to be equipped for slaving. Their papers having confirmed to Stingham that they were American, *Plattsburg* from New York and *Science* from Baltimore, both schooners were arrested and sent to New York. Reporting back to the Secretary of the Navy on 10 April Trenchard declared: 'The slave trade is carried on to a very great extent. There are probably no less than three hundred vessels on the coast engaged in that traffic, each having two or three sets of papers.'[1]

In mid–April *Cyane* arrived at Cape Mesurado. Here the climate was much healthier than at Sherbro and Trenchard's First Lieutenant, Matthew Perry, recommended its possible use for a settlement. Following a meeting of the local tribal chiefs to discuss purchasing land for a colony, *Cyane* returned to Sherbro. In January 1822 the remaining American settlers relocated from Sherbro to Mesurado. Naming the new capital Monrovia in honour of President Monroe, the colony would eventually grow into the state of Liberia.

In early May USS *Alligator*, Lieutenant Robert Stockton, arrived in Freetown from Boston with another party of colonists. Between 17 May and 20 May Stockton's schooner arrested four French-flagged slavers, *Jeune Eugenie* and *Eliza* off the Gallinas and *La Daphne* and *Matilda* at Trade Town. A grand total of two slaves were found on board all these vessels and *Eliza*, *La Daphne* and *Matilda* never made it to court, having been recaptured from their prize crews. In mid–July *Alligator* was joined off the Coast by the schooner *Shark*, commanded by the newly-promoted Captain Perry. Off the Gallinas *Shark* chased a French-flagged vessel, *Caroline*. On board were discovered 164 emaciated slaves, naked and shaven to prevent lice. A cask of water was taken on board the slaver along with some bread and beef, but Perry had no authority to detain the ship and she had to be released. *Alligator*'s cruise was to be a brief one and following this boarding Stockton sailed for home, arriving in Boston harbour on 25 July, six weeks ahead of his prize *Jeune Eugenie*.

Upon his arrival at Freetown on 10 May Collier was greeted by the sight of all of the ships of the Squadron at anchor apart from *Pheasant*. There was a great deal of bustle and activity in the harbour as three companies of the 2nd West India Regiment, 150 men and four officers commanded by Captain James Chisholm, were embarking aboard *Myrmidon* and *Morgiana* for an expedition up the Rio Pongas.

A week earlier *Thistle* had been cruising off the Pongas. Learning from the British traders on the Isle de Los that a vessel belonging to a British merchant had been seized by pirates in the river, Hagan had decided to demand the release of this vessel from the leader of these pirates, a trader well known to the British called Thomas Curtis. With no pilot on board his ship *Thistle* could not pass over the bar into the river so on 6 May Hagan sent a boat under the command of Midshipman Robert Inman to deliver a letter to Curtis. Approaching the village of Boffa the British discovered Curtis's ship at anchor. Attempting to board the vessel Inman and his men came under fire from the riverbank. The young midshipman and several of his men were killed, others were wounded and Inman's remaining crew were all taken prisoner.

Hagan and his men could hear the sound of firing coming from the Pongas but, with his ship running low on provisions and incapable of passing over the bar, there was little *Thistle*'s commander could do but return to Freetown to report the incident to Leeke. Leeke and Hagan now met with MacCarthy who, although initially reluctant to act on what he saw as a purely naval matter, eventually agreed that a rescue attempt should be made and ordered three companies of the 2nd West India Regiment to join the expedition. It was at this point that Collier arrived on board *Tartar*. Whilst lamenting Hagan's initial lack of judgement, the Commodore gave his approval to the rescue effort and on the morning of 12 May *Thistle*, *Myrmidon*, *Morgiana* and *Snapper* sailed from Freetown for the Rio Pongas.

The British arrived off the Pongas at dawn on 15 May, anchoring within sight of the bar. The rest of the day was spent transferring the landing force, the 150 soldiers and 50 Royal Marines to the two smaller vessels, *Thistle* and *Snapper*. Early the next morning both vessels weighed anchor and headed for the river entrance, With Hagan leading the way *Thistle* and *Snapper* made it through a gap in the breakers and passed over the bar. The two gun-brigs now moved over to the eastern side of the river where the water was the deepest and around midday passed through a narrow channel between the bank and Big Island. Re-entering the main channel, the vessels anchored roughly a mile upstream of Big Island to enable contact to be made with the local tribal chiefs. Fortuitously a local canoe appeared on the river and its occupants were persuaded, with the aid of tobacco, to deliver a letter to a British trader, Wilson, who was known to be in Bangalong, close to where Curtis had his headquarters. The answer, received later that evening, came from another trader named John Ormond, who claimed to be guarding four British seamen who had escaped from Curtis. 'Mungo John' was a well-known slaver along the Pongas, the son of an Irish slaver from Liverpool and a local chief's daughter, Ormond had inherited a great deal of wealth and status through his mother. However, Leeke and Chisholm knew him by name only and, not knowing how far to trust him, suspected a trap.

By the following morning the British had still not heard from Wilson and so they decided to proceed upstream to the town where Curtis was based. The wind having died overnight, the boats were employed towing the brigs towards Curtis Town. After a three hour pull *Thistle* and *Snapper* dropped anchor on the east bank of the river. Carronades were lowered into the bows of the leading boats before the landing force embarked and headed for the shore under a white flag. A similar white flag was soon hoisted over the fort that stood above the town. However, as the boats approached the shore they came under fire from the fort and from men hidden in the mangroves. As the boats returned fire *Thistle* and *Snapper* joined the action, unleashing a series of broadsides at the fort. The landing force made it ashore without a single injury and advanced to the outskirts of Curtis Town where they discovered their approach blocked by a hastily-erected palisade. Rather than dig in, Chisholm decided to attack the enemy defences. Faced with a determined British attack Curtis's men turned and fled, abandoning both the fort and the town.

With the town now secure the palisade was destroyed and the fort and surrounding houses all burned down, once the fort's guns had been removed to the British ships. Leeke hoped this show of force would persuade Curtis to enter into talks but there was no sign of a response from the trader and so, with night drawing in, the British returned to their ships. The men had not been aboard their ships for long when a canoe came alongside *Snapper* carrying the British trader, Wilson, who now informed Leeke and Chisholm that it was in fact the local tribal chief, Mungo Brama, who had been responsible for the attack on *Thistle*'s boats, and not, as they had suspected, Curtis. Furthermore, Brama was holding the survivors from Inman's boats captive in his village roughly four miles further upstream from Curtis Town. It was too late in the evening to do anything with this information so Leeke and Curtis decided to sail to Mungo Brama's village first thing next morning.

At around midnight a severe storm hit the Rio Pongas. Following several hours of torrential rain, thunder and lightning, early morning revealed *Snapper* now aground on the mud. The boats were brought alongside and Chisholm and his men were transported across to the riverbank where they headed off into the mangroves. After a three-hour march in ankle-deep mud the British finally emerged into a wide clearing with a collection of huts that constituted Mungo Brama's town. The British launched their attack and Brama's men immediately fled into the surrounding bush. The houses were searched but there was no sign of the missing British sailors. The houses and a warehouse containing goods were all burned and the men returned to their boats.

The operations ashore had failed to secure the release of the British sailors but thankfully losses amongst Chisholm's men had been light. At times outnumbered twenty to one, only two soldiers and one marine had been injured. The only death, a corporal of marines, had been through heat exhaustion. Chisholm and his men returned to the ships and efforts to re-float Nash's gun-brig commenced. The boats were employed kedging *Snapper* off the mud and by early afternoon she was finally afloat. However, as *Snapper* was towed downstream by the boats she fouled *Thistle*'s hawsers, causing Hagan's brig to run aground. By now the tide was beginning to fall and after several attempts to re-float his vessel Hagan accepted defeat and a party of troops were sent ashore to set up defensive positions around *Thistle* whilst they waited for the next high tide, twelve hours away.

Early that evening a canoe appeared carrying two of *Thistle*'s missing seamen. Their release had been secured by a neighbour of Mungo Brama, King Yando Coney, who was anxious that the British did not visit his own town. To add to this welcome news, several hours later the trader Wilson arrived on board *Thistle* and reported that, together with the help of Ormond, he had secured the release of the remaining four British prisoners. A boat carrying Wilson and a party of marines was immediately despatched upstream, returning with the four seamen from *Thistle* just before midnight. An immediate attempt to get *Thistle* of the mud was made but this proved unsuccessful and it was not until 11.30am the following morning that she was finally refloated. Both ships now headed back out of the Pongas, crossing the bar to rejoin *Myrmidon* and *Morgiana* at the mouth of the river. Reunited, the squadron set sail for Freetown, arriving there on 23 May. In his report of the operation to Governor MacCarthy, Chisholm declared: 'I feel great pleasure in reporting to you that the behaviour of the troops has been highly satisfactory to me. The conquest of a large district of woody country, defended by an armed body of men, which … exceeded 3,500, and the destruction of several towns, with an inconsiderable loss on our side is to be ascribed to the resolute conduct of the conjoined forces in the attack on Curtis Town.'[2] Chisholm also commended Leeke for his support during the operation.

Pheasant quit Ascension on 16 May, cutting short the three-week period of recuperation ordered by Collier. Stopping off at Dixcove to replace a wounded topmast with one from *Erne*, she then headed east to Princes. Prior to his departure for the West Indies and home on 4 June Collier deployed his ships to avoid the worst of the rainy season. *Myrmidon* and *Thistle* were both sent north whilst *Morgiana* and *Snapper* were sent to Ascension. *Tartar* left Freetown with a number of Spanish sailors on board who had been arrested in various slaving vessels and who had subsequently requested passage to the Caribbean. In May the Anglo-Portuguese Mixed Commission finally opened following the recent arrival of the Portuguese judge Joao Altavilla and the Arbitrator, J. Cesar de la Figaniere e Morao. Thankfully, and rather surprisingly for the British, this court would prove to run more smoothly than either its Dutch or Spanish counterparts.

On 9 July *Pheasant* arrived off Corisco Island from the Gabon. One of her boats was sent inshore to take soundings close to a schooner at anchor off Cape Clara and was fired on by natives from the beach. *Pheasant*'s remaining boats were sent under the command of her one-handed First Lieutenant, Joseph Jellicoe, to capture the schooner or, if necessary, to burn her. By the time the boats reached the schooner she had been hauled onshore and secured by two anchors. Attempting to board the vessel Jellicoe and his men were rushed by more natives hiding in the bush. One seaman, Richard Thomas, was killed by musket fire and seven other men were wounded including Jellicoe who was injured in the throat by langrage. *Pheasant* tried to fire at the schooner but could not get close enough due to the shoals. Fearing that his ship might be grounded by the falling tide, Kelly called off the attack and stood out to sea.

In late July Governor MacCarthy went home for his first leave in more than eight years, having appointed the Governor of the Gambia, Major Alexander Grant, as his replacement. Grant had not been in post long when he learned that the British settlement at Bathurst was in imminent threat of attack by neighbouring chieftains on opposite sides of the river and so he sent *Morgiana* to investigate. Sandilands had been taken ill and when *Morgiana* sailed for the Gambia on 4 October it was under the command of *Tartar*'s Lieutenant William Finlayson. *Morgiana* anchored off Bathurst on 26 October and the local Commandant went on board Finlayson's vessel. The following day she sailed upriver for Fort St James where Finlayson held a meeting with the local chieftains. He then invited them on board *Morgiana* where he presented them with gifts. They were also treated to the firing of several guns and were informed that Royal Navy ships would be visiting the colony frequently. Her message having been well and truly received, *Morgiana* sailed from Bathurst with the thanks of the local merchants who had been greatly reassured by her visit.

Along with the loss of Sandilands, illness had also forced the return home of *Snapper*'s Lieutenant Nash, Commander Kelly taking it upon himself to place a midshipman from *Pheasant*, James Pratt, in temporary command of the gun-brig. *Morgiana* had similarly lost her First Lieutenant, George Ryves, invalided home together with a surgeon and a lieutenant from *Pheasant*. *Myrmidon*'s surgeon had also died and, following the loss of several other senior surgeons Collier had made a request prior to his return home that all the vessels in his squadron be allocated assistant surgeons to mitigate against the loss of any more of these valuable officers.

In mid-July *Thistle* had arrived at Goree, her crew badly debilitated by sickness. Returning from the Cape Verde Islands, on 12 September Hagan's brig arrived off the Rio Pongas and arrested the English sloop *Two Sisters* with fifteen slaves on board. Stopping off at Freetown to water and provision, Hagan continued on to Trade Town. On 16 October *Thistle*'s boats, under the command of her Sailing Master, captured the slaver *Nuestra Señora de Montserrate* up Little Cape Mount River. Eighty-five slaves were discovered on board the Spanish schooner which was escorted back to Sierra Leone. Soon after her return to Freetown *Thistle*'s Master died of fever, this left a midshipman as the only other officer on board the vessel besides Hagan.

By mid-October *Cyane* was preparing to return to America. On the 18th of that month she was cruising off Sierra Leone when she spotted two strange sails headed north. After an exchange of signals Trenchard discovered that one of these vessels was the frigate *John Adams*, Captain Alexander Wadsworth, newly arrived from America. In a rare example of Anglo-American cooperation she was sailing in company with *Snapper* en route to the Rio Pongas where several suspected slavers were said to be operating.

John Adams and *Snapper* arrived at the mouth of the Rio Pongas on 22 October. The following morning *John Adams*'s barge, manned by an Anglo-American force led by Lieutenant Nash and Wadsworth, crossed the bar and rowed upstream. After a long hard pull, two brigs and two schooners were spotted at anchor awaiting their cargoes of slaves. Whilst all four vessels were flying Spanish colours it was clear to both commanders that they were in reality Americans sailing under false flags. Nash thought they should all be arrested but Wadsworth insisted that he was only authorised to seize American-flagged slavers and therefore no action could be taken against them. The barge returned to *John Adams* empty-handed and Wadsworth continued to cruise off the river entrance. Within a few days ten of his crew had been struck down with fever and by the middle of November three of these men were dead. *John Adams*'s brief campaign against the slave trade came to an end on 21 November when she was recalled for duty in the Caribbean.

On 31 January 1821 *Tartar* returned to Sierra Leone where she found *Thistle* at anchor. The following day these two vessels were joined by *Myrmidon* and *Snapper*. Upon leaving the Pongas Nash had fallen ill and had been invalided home. His gun-brig was now under the temporary command of Midshipman James Pratt who had been taken out of *Pheasant* by Commander Kelly. *Pheasant* was still cruising the Bights in company with *Morgiana* and following a short chase on 14 February Finlayson's vessel captured the Portuguese schooner *Emilia* 180 miles south of Lagos. Three hundred and ninety-eight slaves were found aboard the dreadfully overcrowded vessel, 197 of whom were taken on board *Morgiana*. *Emilia*'s master, Severo Leonardo, insisted that he had come from Cabinda, south of the Line, but the newly-branded slaves and the state of water aboard the schooner, just four empty casks, told a different story.

Pausing briefly at Freetown, *Tartar* had then set off for a cruise down the Coast, examining the Gallinas and stopping off at the forts at Dixcove and Secondee. She arrived at Cape Coast on 2 March, a day behind *Morgiana* and her prize. Having landed eighteen slaves suffering from dysentery, Finlayson was now ordered to Freetown via Ascension. However, contrary winds prevented *Morgiana* from reaching the island so instead she headed for St Thomas. Upon his arrival there Finlayson learned that the Portuguese commissioner at Freetown had left due to poor health and that the court could therefore not adjudicate on *Emilia*. Instead he took his prize to the nearest Mixed Commission with sitting Portuguese members, Rio de Janeiro. *Morgiana* arrived at Bahia on 20 May, her provisions almost exhausted, and then continued on to Rio de Janeiro, arriving there on 7 July, 149 days after her prize had departed Lagos. *Emilia* was the first case to be heard by the newly-established Mixed Commission. She was condemned on 31 July and her surviving 354 slaves emancipated. Whilst at Bahia a native of Cape Coast who had served aboard *Pheasant*, Quashie Sam, had come onboard Finlayson's vessel to relate the loss of the slaver *Vulcano do Sud*, which had disappeared following her arrest nineteen months earlier. According to Quashie Sam, about a week into *Vulcano*'s passage to Freetown her prize crew of five British sailors and four Kroomen were overpowered by *Vulcano do Sud*'s men. Midshipman Castles was hacked to death and the four British sailors shot. Two Kroomen jumped over the side of the brig and Quashie Sam and another African were driven below and told they would be killed if *Vulcano* encountered a British cruiser. The vessel was subsequently taken to Brazil and the two Kroomen sold into slavery, Quashie Sam passed through the hands of several different masters before escaping back to Bahia where he had been in hiding for several weeks.

On 16 February *Myrmidon* was sitting at anchor off Cape Mount when she observed a schooner rounding the point. Upon sighting *Myrmidon* the schooner immediately made sail to evade Leeke's sloop. Leeke set off in pursuit, eventually boarding the Spanish schooner *Carlotta*, empty and without papers, around noon on 17 February. Her master was ashore with the vessel's trade goods and, suspecting her of hunting for slaves, Leeke arrested the schooner for piracy. Continuing her cruise to the south, *Myrmidon* fell in with *Tartar* and Leeke handed his prize over to Collier who eventually turned her loose. It was later learned that she had capsized in a gale whilst carrying a cargo of 270 slaves in early June.

From Cape Coast *Tartar* headed into the Bights in company with *Thistle*, Hagan's brig sailing further ahead and disguised as a Spanish slaver. Off Whydah a Portuguese vessel with a passport for a voyage to Cabinda was boarded. She was empty but was clearly preparing to take on board slaves. Continuing eastwards past the Niger Delta, on 23 March *Tartar* and *Thistle* arrived off the mouth of the River Bonny. Aware that *Tartar*'s tall masts would make her approach visible to the Spanish slavers working further up the river, Collier sent Hagan's smaller gun-brig, still flying her Spanish colours, on ahead. Hagan had soon navigated *Thistle* across the bar and was making his way up the river when a schooner was sighted at anchor. Hagan signalled *Tartar* and requested that she send in her boats to board the suspected slaver. Just then a canoe came alongside *Thistle* from the riverbank. Aboard was a local pilot who, clearly having mistaken Hagan's gun-brig for a slaver, offered to guide her to a safe anchorage from where Hagan would be able to procure slaves. To the surprise of the pilot, Hagan, a seaman and a Krooman now leapt into his canoe. Once seized, she was manned by thirty seamen led by Midshipman Charles Lyons, the British hiding from view as the native crew paddled for the slaver. The schooner hailed the canoe and, assured that all was well, the men on deck who had been manning the stern chaser returned to the cabin. The canoe came alongside the schooner and as the British commenced their boarding the schooner's crew began firing at them from the cabin. Lyons, a seaman and a marine were wounded but the Spaniards quickly surrendered their vessel. Unfortunately, fifty female slaves who had been on deck at the time threw themselves into the water to avoid the gunfire and were killed by sharks. The prize proved to be the 172-ton *Anna Maria* from Cuba. When questioned, her English-speaking supercargo, Matteo Sanches, who claimed to be a naturalised Spaniard, declared that he would have blown his vessel up if he had been able to reach the magazine. Discovered amongst her papers was proof that *Anna Maria* had been acting as a privateer sailing under the flag of Artigas. Entering the schooner's tiny hold, 491 slaves were discovered shackled together in pairs, many suffering from dysentery, others fighting one another for water or clinging to the gratings for a breath of fresh air. Seeing the British sailors they showed their parched tongues and pointed to their stomachs. One hundred and twelve slaves were removed for the immediate care of *Tartar*'s surgeon while her boats, commanded by Lieutenants Marsh and Graham, continued upriver. Approaching a Portuguese ship on 24 March *Tartar*'s boats received grape and musketry before the British boarders forced her crew below. The vessel was *Donna Eugenia*, another slaver with a passport to buy slaves at Cabinda which already had eighty-three slaves from the

Bonny on board. To relieve the suffering on board *Anna Maria* a further 125 slaves were removed from her to *Donna Eugenia*. *Anna Maria* was now sent to Freetown under the command of Lieutenant Christopher Knight, her crew in irons on the slave deck as a result of their cutting every piece of rigging they could lay their hands on during the boarding. Meanwhile *Tartar*, *Thistle* and *Donna Eugenia* proceeded to Fernando Po to water. On 5 April the prize departed the island for Freetown and *Tartar* and *Thistle* headed for the Old Calabar River.

With *Tartar* anchored offshore, on 6 April Collier sent his ships' boats into the river estuary, escorted by *Thistle*. When Hagan's brig had travelled as far as the river could be safely navigated his boats joined those of *Tartar*. Off Duke Town on 9 April the British discovered two Portuguese slavers at anchor. The 73-ton brigantine *Constantia* was boarded and was discovered to have a cargo of 250 slaves, which her master claimed had been loaded at Cabinda. Now alerted to the boats' presence, by the time the British moved on to the second slaver *Gavião* she had landed two of her cargo of ten slaves and a Portuguese crew member was discovered in the process of pulling trousers onto a third man.

On 13 April *Thistle* rejoined *Tartar* and Collier went aboard the prizes. Conditions on board *Constantia* were so appalling – a dead woman was discovered buried under the living, many of whom were suffering from dysentery and a skin condition known as craw-craw – that Collier decided to move all the male slaves to *Tartar* before they sailed for Fernando Po. Here the remaining slaves were distributed between *Gavião* and *Thistle* before Hagan's brig and the two prizes sailed for Freetown.

From the Old Calabar *Tartar* headed for Cape Coast where she was joined by *Pheasant*. Discovering Commander Kelly's crew much debilitated by sickness, Collier ordered *Pheasant* to sail for Ascension whilst *Tartar* continued on to Accra before she too headed south. Arriving at Ascension just a few days behind *Pheasant* Collier told Kelly he should remain at the island for at least a month before returning to the Gold Coast.

On his return to Freetown on 5 June Collier found *Thistle*, *Snapper* and *Myrmidon* at anchor. He now learned that *Anna Maria*, *Donna Eugenia* and *Constantia* had all been condemned, and that *Anna Maria* had already been sold and refitted. This last vessel had been condemned in the absence of her master, who was still on board *Tartar*, and the Spanish commissioner, Le Fer, who had travelled to the Gambia for the rainy season. Collier could only conclude that the British commissioner's unusual haste in dealing with the case was an attempt to hide any link between the vessel and British merchants. However, there was little he could do over the matter and on 17 June *Tartar* sailed for Barbados and home.

There would be more bad news for Collier following the trial of *Gavião*. Despite a letter from Duke Ephraim to the Commodore stating that he had sold three slaves to her Portuguese master, the Portuguese Judge, Altavilla decided that the remaining slaves were, in fact, free men employed to work the ship with the consent of the Governors of Princes and St Thomas. The British judge, Gregory, believed that the vessel should be condemned but the Arbitrator, Fitzgerald, sided with Altavilla and on 5 July Gavião was released. At a subsequent hearing on 28 July an award of £1,520 was made against Collier. When he finally learned of the court's decision at home in England Collier protested to the Admiralty but it remains unclear as to whether or not he ever paid the fine. In 1823 William James's multi-volume *Naval History* was published. In it the author stated that the escape of *Constitution* during the war of 1812 was due to incompetence on the part of Collier. Collier subsequently wrote to the Admiralty in an attempt to clear his name but this proved unsuccessful. On the morning of 24 March 1824 he took a razor to his throat and committed suicide.

The return home of Collier on 17 June had left Commander Kelly as senior officer on the Coast. On 23 June *Pheasant* sailed from Ascension for Cape Coast where she was joined by *Myrmidon*. From here the two vessels headed for Fernando Po for wood and water. Off Cape Formoso on 25 June *Pheasant* and *Myrmidon* chased the Portuguese schooner, *Adelaide*. When eventually boarded she was discovered to have a cargo of 232 slaves. Issued with a passport from Bahia for slaving at Malembo, *Adelaide* had actually loaded her cargo at Badagry. One of these slaves was a boy of 11 who was emancipated with his mother and two sisters following *Adelaide*'s condemnation on 17 September. Educated in Sierra Leone, the boy, Samuel Crowther, grew up to become the first Bishop of the Niger, credited with spreading Christianity through much of West Africa.

On 27 July Kelly and Leeke attempted to send their ships' boats into the Bonny River in rapidly deteriorating weather. As she crossed the bar *Myrmidon*'s cutter capsized, drowning five men. The boats turned back but there was no sign of *Pheasant*'s jolly boat. Both cruisers now headed for

Fernando Po. By now Kelly had caught a fever and his health had rapidly deteriorated, so whilst *Myrmidon* returned to the Bonny *Pheasant* departed the Bights for Freetown. On 10 August Leeke made another attempt to enter the Bonny. Commanded by Acting Lieutenant Parker Bingham, the boats successfully crossed the bar then entered a narrow, rarely-used channel known as Anthony River, arriving at Bonny Town unseen. Here they discovered six French vessels at anchor and in the process of landing slaves. Bingham could not interfere with French-flagged slavers but the master of one of these vessels told him about two Spanish slavers operating in one of the side creeks. Leaving his remaining boats at Bonny Town, Bingham took the pinnace and gig and set off in search of these vessels. The boats soon came across a brig and a schooner anchored in midstream. A few musket shots were fired in the air to announce the arrival of the British, but there was no response from either Spaniard, neither of which had their colours flying. As the boats drew nearer Bingham shouted a challenge which was immediately met with a volley of musketry and grapeshot from the slavers. Bingham and a midshipman, Deschamps, were both seriously wounded. Deschamps was struck in the head and Bingham received a chest wound that initially appeared fatal. Assuming command of the gig Deschamps ordered a withdrawal and the boats retreated back down the river.

When Leeke received word of events upstream he despatched reinforcements but by the time they joined Deschamps the Spanish had barricaded themselves aboard their vessels, making any further attack futile. The boats returned to *Myrmidon* and Leeke now decided to take his cruiser into the river. The boats began taking soundings and after several days' activity a channel deep enough for *Myrmidon* had been found and buoyed. Still worried that his sloop might run aground, Leeke decided to wait for the spring tide and a favourable wind. At dawn on 31 August *Myrmidon* finally weighed anchor and with men in the chains constantly taking soundings she cautiously made her way across the bar into Bonny Roads, anchoring in three and a half fathoms of water around sunset.

The following morning *Myrmidon* weighed and made her way upriver. As she approached Bonny Town a canoe appeared alongside carrying a letter from the captains of the two Spanish slavers. Startled by the appearance of *Myrmidon*'s tall masts above the trees the crews of both ships had fled ashore. In their letter the Spanish captains pleaded guilty to firing on Bingham's boats and offered their ships as prizes if Leeke did not charge them with piracy. When the two Spanish vessels were boarded it was discovered that the brig *La Caridad* had 153 slaves on board and that the schooner *El Neuve Virgen* had a cargo of 140 slaves. Men were sent ashore to round up the Spanish crews and *Pheasant*'s jolly boat was also recovered along with her crew who were being looked after by British merchants. There had been no deaths during the operation and the wounded, Bingham included, all eventually recovered from their injuries. *La Caridad* and *El Neuve Virgen* were condemned together on 7 November, a total of 242 slaves surviving to be emancipated. Their captains were both found guilty of piracy, for which the penalty was death by hanging.

In early June Lieutenant Christopher Knight had replaced Lieutenant Nash as commanding officer of *Snapper*. Later that month the gun-brig sailed to the Old Calabar River. On 1 August Knight stopped and boarded an English merchantman as she was leaving the river and from her master learned that there were three slavers off Duke Town loading cargoes purchased from Duke Ephraim. Removing the merchantman's pilot to *Snapper*, Knight crossed the bar and proceeded upriver before sending his boats on ahead to Duke Town under the command of his Acting Master, Mr Cowrie. When *Snapper* rejoined her boats Knight discovered that they had seized a Portuguese schooner, *Conceição*, with a cargo of fifty-six slaves. Of the remaining two vessels, one was a Spanish felucca that had no slaves on board and the other was a French brigantine which was left alone.

With Kelly remaining in Freetown to await the arrival of the new commodore, in late September he exchanged command of *Pheasant* with Douglas Clavering, Early the following month USS *Alligator* sailed from Boston for a second cruise along the Coast. On 5 November she encountered a vessel that, on sighting Stockton's schooner, hoisted signals, shortened sail and slowed. However, as *Alligator* approached she fired a cannon and when Stockton hoisted his colours she fired two more shots, one which fell short of *Alligator* and another which flew over her masts. As *Alligator* approached the stranger from astern she continued to fire her guns, cutting up Stockton's sails and rigging. Once in range Stockton fired a single, well directed broadside and the vessel finally hoisted her colours before surrendering. She was discovered to be the Portuguese privateer *Marianna Flora*, out of Lisbon. Stockton put a prize crew aboard her with orders to sail to Boston whilst *Alligator* continued on her way to Freetown before proceeding on a cruise down the coast to Cape Mesurado.

Returning from leave in late November, Governor MacCarthy had immediately despatched *Snapper* and *Thistle* to investigate reports of a Portuguese slaver operating in the Rio Pongas. On Christmas Eve boats commanded by Lieutenant Knight discovered the Spanish schooner *Rosalia* landing trade goods at Mungo John's factory. The vessel was not yet ready to load slaves so *Snapper* returned to Freetown whilst Hagan remained off the entrance to the river. On 7 January 1822 *Thistle* returned to Mungo John's factory where Hagan discovered that *Rosalia* was about to begin loading. Anxious to spend as little time as possible in the river with its feverish airs Hagan now took the extraordinary step of meeting with the local chiefs to encourage them to speed up the process. Fifty-nine slaves having been taken on board *Rosalia*, she was seized by Hagan on 11 January and taken to Freetown. Here, in the absence of the Spanish commissioner and any representatives of the Spanish schooner, she was condemned along with her cargo of slaves.

USS *Alligator* departed the Coast for Boston in early 1822 but Stockton left behind a tender under the command of Midshipman Harry Hunter. When *Snapper* returned to Freetown in early February to report that an American slaver had been sighted operating in the Pongas Hunter decided to head north to investigate but asked Kelly for assistance as his tender was short-handed. Kelly sent across twelve men under the command of Lieutenant James and the tender departed for the Pongas. On 16 February she returned to Freetown in company with the American slaver *Dolphin*. James later wrote in glowing terms of the cordiality which had existed between the British and American officers and their men during this brief expedition.

By early 1823 it seemed that Britain and America were moving into a period of co-operation against the slave trade. In February a committee of the House of Representatives had recommended that President Monroe enter into negotiations with Britain with the aim of denouncing the slave trade as piracy and to consider a limited Right of Search. Whilst personally opposed to American vessels being searched by vessels of foreign powers, the Secretary of State, John Quincy Adams, sent a draft treaty to London which would allow suspected British and American slave ships to be arrested by the navy of either country but to be tried under the national laws of the arresting vessel. The Foreign Secretary, Canning, agreed to the proposed treaty and in April 1824 President Monroe laid the draft treaty before the Senate. Numerous amendments, unacceptable to Britain, were now suggested, effectively wrecking the convention. These included refusing the right of search of vessels in the territorial waters of the United States and of vessels hired from a third nation. Efforts to re-open negotiations failed and the British minister in Washington, Stratford Canning, wrote to the Foreign Secretary to inform his cousin that he was engaged in what he considered to be a hopeless endeavour. For the next fifteen years Britain would continue her task without American assistance.

On 1 February the French brig *Huron*, Commodore Du Plessis, arrived at Freetown having completed a cruise to Grand Bassa in search of French slavers. MacCarthy was happy to provide Du Plessis with water and provisions prior to his departure for the Gallinas. However, France was yet to take its own suppression campaign seriously and it would be several more months before the Governor would see another French man-of-war off the Coast. The next cruiser to arrive at Freetown was the British frigate *Iphigenia* and she brought with her a new commodore to take command of the West Africa Squadron.

Chapter 5

The Equipment Clause:
February 1822–December 1824

Commodore Sir Robert Mends had joined the Navy in 1779, aged just 12. A battle-scarred veteran of the wars against America and France, he had lost his right arm whilst serving aboard *Guadeloupe* during the Siege of Yorktown in 1781 and in 1795 he had been badly burned by an explosion whilst serving as a lieutenant aboard *Colossus* during the Battle of Ile de Groix. During an action off Brest in April 1809 he received a head wound from a splinter that affected his eyesight for the rest of his life.

In his instructions from the Admiralty Mends had been told to support the British settlements in Africa and their commerce. Having been provided with copies of the various treaties dealing with the suppression of the slave trade, he was reminded that all Spanish slaving was now illegal and was ordered to watch the various bays and creeks from which slavers operated, particularly those in the Bights. He was also to support Ascension, which was now officially part of the West Africa Squadron infrastructure. At the end of his tour Mends was to return home via the West Indies with the Squadron's invalids, having replaced them with volunteers from his flagship *Iphigenia*.

As *Iphigenia* approached Sierra Leone on the night of 21 February 1822, Mends sent his boats under the command of his First Lieutenant, George St John Mildmay, into the anchorage at Bissau to board the Portuguese brigantine *Conde de Ville Flor*, which was seized with a cargo of 171 slaves. Arriving at Freetown the following day Mends discovered the rest of his squadron – *Thistle*, *Pheasant*, *Morgiana*, *Myrmidon* and *Snapper* – all at anchor there. Also in the harbour was the American-flagged schooner *Augusta*, left behind by USS *Shark* earlier that year to support the fledgling colony at Monrovia. Mends sent Lieutenant Clarkson and a small detachment of his men across to *Augusta* and she set off on a cruise to the Gallinas. The Commodore now ordered *Myrmidon* and *Thistle* to leeward and sent *Pheasant* and *Snapper* north before Governor MacCarthy embarked on board *Iphigenia* and she set off on a cruise to investigate the British settlements along the Gold Coast.

Thistle had arrived at Freetown a week ahead of *Iphigenia* following a cruise to leeward. At the Gallinas she had fallen in with two French vessels, the bark *Phoenix* and the brig *Espoir*, the latter vessel commanded by a frigate captain in the Marine Nationale who appeared aboard *Thistle* in full dress uniform and informed Hagan that a few evenings earlier he had met the French Commodore, du Plessis. Hagan also learned that two Spanish and two Dutch slavers had sailed from the Gallinas with full cargoes shortly before his arrival and that the river had recently been visited by two piratical schooners. From the Gallinas Hagan had sailed to Trade Town where he discovered that a Spanish schooner with 150 slaves on board had sailed for Havana just a few days previously.

Following *Augusta*'s arrival at the Gallinas, on 26 February Clarkson boarded the schooner *Joseph*, a Swedish-flagged vessel which, though clearly equipped for slaving, had no slaves on board. Her logbook revealed that she had been examined by *Huron* on 13 February but du Plessis had similarly discovered her empty of slaves. Suspecting her to be British, Clarkson detained the schooner and sent her to Freetown where the Mixed Commission concluded that she was part owned by an English resident of Cuba and ordered her to be condemned. Prompted by the Foreign Office, the Admiralty now wrote to Mends to remind him that only vessels carrying Special Instructions had the right to board and search suspected slavers.

Following the arrival of *Pheasant* and *Snapper* off the Rio Nunez Commander Clavering had sent one of *Snapper*'s boats across the bar and into the river. The boat, manned by men from both vessels and commanded by Acting Lieutenant John Helby, soon encountered a vessel showing no colours. Having previously heard of a Portuguese slaver loading in the river, Helby assumed it to be this vessel. However, when she was boarded she was discovered to be French and so Helby left her alone. When the French Chargé d'Affaires in London eventually heard of the boarding he complained of the misuse of the Right of Search and of plunder.

Command of *Snapper* had now passed from Christopher Knight to Thomas Rothery, with Knight moving to *Morgiana*. On 14 March Knight boarded a Spanish schooner, *Dichesa Estrella*, off Trade Town, another slaver previously stopped by *Huron*. As the schooner's cargo was still ashore waiting to be loaded, Knight decided to go ashore the following morning to speak to the local chief. However, that night a storm blew up, pushing the schooner further out to sea. The following morning Knight went ashore and arranged for twenty-nine of the slaves due to be loaded on board *Dichesa Estrella* to be sent to *Morgiana* instead. When five slaves were taken aboard the schooner from a canoe that had rowed out from the shore Midshipman Maclean was sent across to the Spaniard and she was arrested. Having boarded *Dichesa Estrella* with his prize crew MacLean discovered that her master was, in fact, a Frenchman by the name of Larose. The twenty-nine slaves on board *Morgiana* were now transferred to the schooner and Maclean anchored off Cape Mesurado to water. During the night *Dichesa Estrella* was wrecked, apparently due to some of the natives cutting her cables. Thankfully the prize crew and slaves all managed to reach the shore but nine slaves were then seized by the natives. The survivors were looked after by the American colonists at Mesurado and were eventually taken to Freetown by *Augusta* but Maclean died shortly after the American schooner's arrival in port. When the case of *Dichesa Estrella* eventually came to court in mid-June the vessel was condemned and her surviving twenty-five slaves emancipated.

Following her tour of the British settlements at Dixcove, Cape Coast, Anamabo and Accra *Iphigenia* was joined by *Myrmidon* and the two ships continued eastwards. On 1 April they stopped the Portuguese brig *Dies de Feverio*, empty but clearly equipped for slaving. On further investigation it was discovered that ten slaves had been landed on the approach of Mends' ships. A prize crew was put aboard the brig and she was sent to Freetown. Five days later the Portuguese schooner *Nymfa del Mar* was stopped off Whydah with a cargo of three slaves, all of whom who had been unshackled and dressed by the time the vessel was boarded. The remainder of her cargo of 250 slaves were waiting to be loaded and Mends intended to go ashore and demand them from the local chief but the high surf prevented his ship's boats reaching the shore. Lieutenant Mildmay was given command of the prize with orders to rendezvous with *Iphigenia* off Lagos. Arriving off that anchorage on 7 April Mildmay arrested the Portuguese schooner *Esperança Felix* loaded with 187 slaves.

On the afternoon of 14 April *Iphigenia*, *Myrmidon* and *Nymfa del Mar* anchored off the entrance to the Bonny. Having been briefed by Leeke on the resistance *Myrmidon*'s boats had received following her last visit to this infamous slaving river, Mends had decided that a strong show of force would be required to deal with the slavers said to be operating upstream. Early the next morning, whilst it was still dark, a force of 150 men led by Mildmay in six boats, several of which had guns mounted in their bows, crossed the bar and soon spotted a brigantine, four brigs and two schooners at anchor six miles further up the river. As they approached these vessels around 8.00am the two schooners began to swing round to bring their guns to bear on Mildmay's boats, opening fire with canister and grapeshot as soon as the British were within range and joined soon after by two of the brigs and the brigantine. The lead boats had to wait for the two slower boats which lagged behind, then opened fire when about three-quarters of a mile from the enemy. Having emerged from this twenty-minute onslaught with just two killed and seven wounded, the boats came alongside the nearest of the schooners which had still not hoisted her colours. She offered stiff resistance to the boarding and by the time she finally surrendered sixteen of her crew lay dead on the deck. Having watched this battle unfold, the crew of the second schooner abandoned their vessel, but not before setting a charge in her magazine, a lighted match that was discovered hanging over the open hatchway by a British seaman who calmly placed it in his hat. Both schooners were Spanish in identity whilst the remaining vessels were French. The first schooner boarded, *Icanam*, was discovered with a cargo of 380 slaves, whilst her compatriot, *Vecua*, had 325 slaves in her hold. A number of *Vecua*'s slaves had been armed following her boarding, forced to fire up though the open hatchways at the British. Four slaves had been killed and ten wounded in the battle. One girl had lost both legs and another her arm. A girl aged around 12 was discovered on the slave deck attached to a heavy iron chain around 10ft in length and Mildmay ordered this to be put on *Icanam*'s master. The British boats soon moved on to the two French brigs, *Petite Betsy* and *Vigilante*, and the brigantine *Ursule*, which were quickly boarded. Between them these vessels had a further 808 slaves on board. The remaining brig, *Theodore*, was discovered empty apart from some trading goods. As she had taken no part in the action she was left alone but *Petite Betsy*, *Vigilane* and *Ursule* were all arrested for piracy.

The three prizes were put in *Myrmidon*'s charge but prior to his departure from the Bights Leeke sent his boats into the Old Calabar under the command of Lieutenant Elliot and on 28 April they boarded the Portuguese schooner *Defensora da Patrie* with a cargo of 100 slaves. The schooner had a passport for Cabinda and her master used the excuse of his vessel being carried north by the current. Meeting with the English palm oil traders operating on the river, Elliot was informed that that there had been no other slavers in the Old Calabar for the past four months. *Defensora da Patrie* soon proved to be unseaworthy and so Elliot decided to scuttle her, having first transferred her slaves to *Vecua*.

Esperança Felix was also proving to be a poor sailer and Leeke, fearing that the majority of her cargo would die before they reached Sierra Leone, scuttled her and transferred her cargo to *Icanam* and *Vecua*. Then on 10 June, the ships were caught in a fierce storm and *Icanam* capsized, taking with her 400 slaves, sixteen seamen and two midshipmen. Seven of her seamen who were being towed astern of the schooner in *Iphigenia*'s pinnace were picked up in a distressed state by *Myrmidon* five days later. Soon after *Nympa del Mar* was wrecked just west of the Bonny and her three slaves were transferred to *Iphigenia*.

By the time of the arrival of the prizes at Freetown a further 150 slaves had died from sickness. *Esperança Felix* and *Defensora da Patrie* were both condemned by the Portuguese Mixed Commission on 4 July and their surviving 165 slaves emancipated. Their cargoes having been landed, the decision was now taken to send the French vessels for trial in the Admiralty courts. Lieutenant Mildmay was given command of *Vigilante*, *Petite Betsy* and *Ursule*, but upon their arrival in England in late July it was decided that the vessels should be dealt with in a French court and Mildmay, despite requests to the Admiralty for reimbursement, had to take them on to Cherbourg at his own expense.

Unaware of the fate of *Dichesa Estrella* and her prize crew, *Morgiana* had continued on to the Bights and on 15 April she boarded the Portuguese brig *Esperança Placido* at the mouth of the River Lagos. Her master and the majority of her crew had deserted ship upon sighting *Morgiana*, leaving behind a cargo of 149 slaves and her papers which included a passport for slaving at Malembo giving permission to call at St Thomas and Princes. From the Bights *Morgiana* returned to Sierra Leone, arriving there in mid-June to collect her prize crew before sailing for Ascension where Knight handed over what victuals he could spare to the local garrison prior to sailing for Brazil and home.

On 27 March *Bann*, recently converted from a frigate to a ship-sloop, departed Portsmouth for Africa under the command of Lieutenant Charles Phillips and in mid-April the 18-gun ship-sloop *Driver*, Commander

Thomas Wolrige, sailed for the Coast via Gibraltar. In mid-May *Pheasant* arrived at St Thomas to fish her foremast. From there she headed for Ascension and then home, having ended her three-year deployment off the West Coast of Africa. Adhering to his instructions to avoid the rainy season, on 26 June Mends sailed for England via Barbados. Three weeks later the 20-gun ship-sloop *Cyrene*, Commander Percy Grace, arrived on station. Meanwhile *Myrmidon* had sailed to the Cape Verde Islands to refit and whilst there she received orders to sail to Spithead. Now the senior officer on the Coast, Wolrige ordered his own vessel to head to the Bights in company with *Snapper*, *Cyrene* to the northern rivers and *Bann* to Ascension to deliver stores she and *Driver* had brought from England.

Thistle had been cruising the Bights since mid-April. At the Old Calabar on 23 June Hagan discovered the Portuguese schooner, *José Xalaça*, at anchor. A small vessel of just 7 tons, she was empty when boarded but Hagan soon discovered that a cargo of twenty slaves had been landed when she had sighted *Thistle*. Furthermore, upon questioning her crew it was revealed that the vessel had originally sailed from the river several days earlier with a cargo of thirty slaves stowed in a space just 17in in height. Intending to sail to Princes, the schooner had run out of water and provisions and ten of her slaves had died and a female slave, delirious with hunger, had been flogged to death before the vessel had returned to the Old Calabar. The schooner, one of several slavers owned by Donna Maria de Cruz, the daughter of the governor of Princes, was scuttled and the surviving slaves taken on board *Thistle*, which now headed for the Benin to investigate reports from the English palm oil traders of slavers operating in the river.

Three more slaves from *José Xalaça* died on *Thistle*'s passage west. Off Cape Formoso on 29 June Hagan chased and boarded the Portuguese brig *Estrella* which had a cargo of 296 slaves, several of whom were suffering from smallpox. This vessel had previously been boarded by *Thistle* and her papers endorsed whilst empty of slaves off Cape Coast Castle in April. With prize crews now on board two vessels Hagan had no more men to spare for two more slavers discovered in the River Benin and so *Thistle* returned to Freetown via Princes, arriving there on 19 July. Hagan's gun-brig anchored some distance away from the other vessels in the harbour and the sixteen slaves suffering from smallpox were sent to a hospital outside the town.

On 19 August *Driver* made her first capture, boarding the Spanish schooner *Josepha* (also known as *Maracayera*), following a 24-hour chase off the Bonny. Boats from *Driver* commanded by Lieutenant Saumarez had already stopped this vessel whilst empty during the sloop's first visit to the Bonny on 21 July but Wolrige now caught her putting to sea with a cargo of 216 slaves following his return from Princes. Three weeks later *Driver* arrived off the Cameroons and on 7 September Wolrige sent two boats under the command of Lieutenant John King upriver where he discovered the Portuguese brig *Commerciante* attempting to land her cargo of slaves. King met with the local chief who had sold the slaves and he agreed to reload them aboard the brig which King now arrested and brought back out of the river with her cargo of 179 slaves. The two prizes were sent back to Freetown but thirty-two of *Josepha*'s slaves died during the passage north. *Driver*'s prize was condemned on 28 September and her surviving 183 slaves emancipated, *Commerciante* was condemned on 7 December, thirteen slaves having died prior to her arrival at Freetown. *Driver* followed her prizes north, arriving in port on 19 October, three weeks behind *Josepha*. By the end of her first cruise Wolrige's sloop had stopped and examined twelve vessels, eight Portuguese, three French and one Spanish, just a fraction of the total number of slave vessels sailing from that part of the Coast.

Bann arrived in the Bights from Ascension in mid-August and on the 27th of that month Phillips arrested the Spanish schooner *San Raphael* at Whydah. The schooner, which was empty and waiting for her master who was ashore arranging her cargo, attempted to evade *Bann* but was eventually brought to by a round of grape and musket fire. When she came before the Spanish Mixed Commission in January 1823 the court judged that she had been seized illegally. However, as there was no claimant for her she was purchased by Phillips and for several months employed as a tender for *Bann*. On 29 September Phillips arrested the Portuguese schooner *Magdalena da Praca* 50 miles south-west of Princes, just one degree north of the Line and outside of Portuguese territory. Deeming the vessel to be unseaworthy, her cargo of thirty-three slaves were removed to *Bann* and the schooner taken to Princes. She was condemned by the Anglo-Portuguese Mixed Commission following *Bann*'s return to Freetown in January 1823.

Continuing her cruise, on 5 October *Bann* arrested the Portuguese brigantine *San Antonio de Lisboa* off Porto Novo. Having previously been stopped whilst empty by *Driver*, *Snapper* and Phillips' own vessel, he now caught her with a cargo of 355 slaves, a portion of which were put on board

San Raphael. On the last day of October *Bann* boarded *Juliana da Praca*, a Portuguese schooner with a cargo of 114 slaves which had just put to sea from Porto Novo. Finally, whilst off St Thomas on 13 November, *Bann* sent her boats to board the Portuguese schooner *Conceição* which was arrested with a cargo of 207 slaves. *San Antonio de Lisboa* was condemned by the Anglo-Portuguese Mixed Commission on 23 December, *Juliana da Praca* on 30 December and *Conceição* on 18 January 1823, a total of 568 slaves surviving to be emancipated.

On the morning of 23 October *Cyrene* was cruising off the Gallinas when her lookouts observed two schooners approaching from leeward. Spotting *Cyrene* both vessels quickly tacked away to the south and Grace set off in pursuit. The winds were light, resulting in a lengthy chase. Shortly before sunset the schooners parted company, the smaller one tacking to the north. Concentrating on the larger vessel, Grace held his course and with darkness setting in was close enough to open fire with musketry. Almost immediately the schooner hove to and awaited the boarding party from *Cyrene.* She proved to be the Dutch-flagged *Aurora* from St Thomas, empty but equipped for slaving. Once his prize was secure Grace resumed his pursuit of the second schooner. By 1.00am *Cyrene* was close enough to this vessel, the French-flagged *Hypolite*, to fire a warning shot across her bows, forcing her to heave to. A boarding party was sent across to *Hypolite* which was also empty but similarly equipped for slaving. An examination of their papers revealed that both vessels had cargoes waiting for them in the Gallinas, so Grace dispatched Lieutenant George Courtenay with the boats to meet with King Siacca to arrange the release of the slaves, either by diplomacy or force. Crossing the bar the cutter was swamped and most of her arms and ammunition lost in the surf. As the boats passed Lower Factory Island, struggling against a strong ebb tide, they came under fire from two 18-pounder long guns and an 8in howitzer and musketry from several hundred men lining both banks of the river. The boats ran aground several times but eventually the crews landed, took possession of the guns and turned them on their attackers. During the attack slaves were observed being taken from the factories, thrown into canoes and rowed upstream. Their ammunition running low, the British captured and burned the factories on Lower Factory Island and the adjacent island before spiking the enemy guns and returning to the boats. The tide, which was now in their favour, speeding them back down the river towards *Cyrene.*

The attack had cost the British one man killed and three wounded. Enemy losses were higher, four Europeans and several natives dead and many more injured. A few days later a messenger appeared on board *Cyrene* to explain that King Siacca had been visiting the interior and during his absence the masters of *Aurora* and *Hypolite*, Benjamin Liebray and Louis Gallon, had given rum and weapons to the natives and encouraged them to attack the British. Blaming these Frenchmen for the destruction of the factories, Siacca handed over the 180 slaves intended for the prizes which were now sent to Freetown on board *Aurora*. The schooner was condemned by the Anglo-Dutch Mixed Commission on 29 November and the surviving 179 slaves emancipated.

Whilst *Cyrene* was watering at Grand Bassa on 10 November Grace heard rumours of a schooner at Little Bassa that had variously flown the flags of France and Spain. Sailing further west *Cyrene* spotted this vessel which was now flying a French flag and gave chase. Upon boarding the schooner, *Caroline*, her master, Joseph Baron, claimed that she was empty and would be collecting her cargo at Trade Town. However, a search soon revealed five hidden slaves. Additional Spanish, Dutch and Portuguese colours were discovered in her cabin along with letters from a Dutch merchant in Surinam. Returning to Little Bassa, Grace received a message from King Wise informing him he would hand over *Caroline*'s cargo of slaves if Grace did not destroy his town.

With Grace's agreement eighty slaves were sent across to *Caroline* and the schooner sailed for Freetown under the command of *Cyrene*'s second master, William Hunter, who was now suffering the first effects of fever. During the voyage north Baron tried to poison Hunter and his prize crew and when this failed he attempted to destroy *Caroline* by setting off a small explosion. Baron was brought on deck for interrogation and Hunter shot *Caroline*'s drunken and abusive master dead in a fit of rage. Learning of this extraordinary turn of events, Canning ordered that both of Grace's French prizes, *Caroline* and *Hypolite*, should be released to French authorities and the Admiralty also ordered *Cyrene* to return to England with immediate effect. However, by the time these instructions reached Freetown Hunter had died of fever.

Following the arrest of *Rosalia* by Hagan in January 1822 slaving appeared to have all but ceased along the Pongas. However, disturbed by the circumstances surrounding the loading of slaves on board the schooner by *Thistle*'s commanding officer, in September the new Foreign Secretary, George Canning, wrote to the commissioners at Freetown to admonish them for establishing a precedent that might encourage other British officers to follow Hagan's example. The Admiralty also expressed its disapproval at Hagan's conduct and Canning asked the Treasury whether Hagan might be prevented from receiving any head money from his recent capture, a request of course that the Treasury was only too willing to agree to.

Canning had taken office following the death by suicide of an overworked and overwrought Castlereagh in August 1822. At the Congress of Verona, held in October 1822, the new Foreign Secretary, who was both a Pittite and an abolitionist, had recommended that slavery should hold the same status as piracy under the Law of Nations, but he found no agreement with this proposal from the representatives of France, Austria, Russia and Prussia. A further proposal that produce from Brazil should be boycotted was not taken seriously and led to suggestions of self-interest on the part of the British. Following these setbacks Canning soon resumed his predecessor's policy of direct negotiations with individual countries, which over the next four years would result in agreements with the governments of Spain, the Netherlands, Portugal, the United States and Brazil.

Having left the crews of *San Raphael* and *Conceição* at St Thomas, *Bann* headed out of the Bights and on 3 December arrested the Portuguese brigantine *Sinceridade* 430 miles south-west of Cape Palmas. The vessel, bound for Pernambuco, Brazil, had no royal passport but was discovered with a cargo of 123 slaves loaded at Cape Lopez. However, her arrest had taken place seven miles south of the Line, against the terms of the treaty with Portugal. Phillips escorted his prize back to Freetown where the British arbitrator, Fitzgerald, decreed that, as the chase had not begun north of the Line, her arrest was illegal and she should be restored. Fitzgerald also ruled against Lieutenant Rothery following the seizure of the Portuguese brigantine *Nova Sorte* by *Snapper* on 14 October. Rothery had first visited the vessel west of Little Popo on 12 October but found her to be empty. Having decided that the brigantine had hidden her cargo during his visit (her hatches had been covered by ropes, casks and bags) then unloaded them during the night, he had demanded the re-embarkation of the 122 slaves then proceeded to seize the vessel. Upon her arrival at Freetown Fitzgerald arbitrated and, having questioned the slaves, decided there had in fact been no earlier embarkation and ordered *Nova Sorte* to be restored.

On 1 December the Prince Regent of Portugal, Dom Pedro, was crowned Emperor of Brazil. His father, King John VI, had returned to Portugal in April 1821 to suppress revolts in Lisbon and Oporto, appointing Dom Pedro as regent in his absence. The Portuguese Cortes (Parliament) wanted to return Brazil to its former colonial status and ordered the Prince Regent home. However, Dom Pedro had remained in Rio and in September 1822 he declared Brazil independent and expelled all Portuguese troops. For the time being this new nation state had no treaty obligations with Britain and was therefore free to trade slaves south of the Line.

On a much more positive note for the suppression campaign, following intense diplomacy between Canning and Spanish ministers, on 10 December 1822 Britain and Spain signed additional articles to the treaty of September 1817 that now allowed cruisers to arrest slave ships even if their cargoes had been landed previous to being boarded. Later that month Britain and the Netherlands made an identical addition to the treaty of May 1818. In January 1823 these two countries signed an Additional Article that would be of huge importance to the suppression campaign. Known as the 'Equipment Clause', this article stipulated that a vessel could be detained even without slaves on board if specific alterations had been made to her outfit or equipment. These alterations included having gratings instead of solid hatches to improve ventilation below decks, extra bulkheads and spare planks for the construction of additional half decks in the hold, iron shackles, more mess tubs and cooking boilers than would be required by the crew and excessive quantities of food and water. Although not listed in the Equipment Clause, another indication that a vessel might be involved in slaving was the addition of several native canoes to her boats. These vessels were employed transporting slaves from the beaches to the waiting slave ships and also returning them to the shore quickly and safely upon the appearance of a British cruiser. As the officers on the Coast knew, they were rarely carried by vessels conducting legitimate trade.

Iphigenia arrived at Portsmouth from Havana on 13 October, on her return home from South America the ship had suffered an outbreak of yellow fever, recording 142 cases of the disease, sixteen of which proved fatal. The majority of those afflicted soon recovered once back in Britain and her officers and ship's company were eventually turned over to the 42-gun frigate *Owen Glendower*, which sailed from Spithead for Africa under Mends on 20 January 1823. Off Bissau on 4 March *Owen Glendower*'s boats, commanded by Lieutenant Edward Clerkson, boarded the schooner *L'Africain*, suspecting her to be a Portuguese slaver. Clerkson immediately left the vessel upon discovering her French nationality but the Foreign Office later received a complaint that *Owen Glendower*'s boarding party had plundered the ship of her ivory and tobacco along with various other items belonging to her crew, a claim strenuously denied by Clerkson.

On 20 March *Owen Glendower* arrived at Freetown where Mends found the whole Squadron now at anchor. *Cyrene* was ordered to Cape Coast and *Bann* and *Driver* to Ascension with stores. *Bann* was then to sail to Bahia to repair a broken rudder. *Snapper* was instructed to remain off Portendic to protect the British gum traders who had recently arrived there prior to her return home at the end of June. After three and a half years on the Coast *Thistle* was no longer fit for service and so she was ordered to return to Spithead to be broken up. Prior to his departure at the end of March Hagan, who had now spent almost seven years on the Coast and had been responsible for the capture of thirty-three slave ships and the release of around 3,100 slaves, was awarded a piece of plate by the Sierra Leone Council and the foreign judges and he was also given a hundred-guinea sword paid for by the officers and men of the Squadron.

A day prior to *Owen Glendower*'s arrival at Freetown the merchantman *Caroline* had appeared at the bar flying the white flag of distress. *Bann*'s pinnace was dispatched to give assistance, whereupon it was discovered that there had been an outbreak of fever on board the merchantman whilst loading timber on the Sierra Leone River. Fifteen of her crew were now dead and the three remaining seamen too ill to safely manage their vessel. *Bann*'s boat crew anchored the merchantman, landed her cargo and helped the sick ashore. *Bann*'s master, the master of *Snapper* and *Owen Glendower*'s carpenters then spent several hours on board *Caroline*, surveying the vessel. Following his return to the sloop *Bann*'s master fell ill with fever though he quickly recovered. A week later *Bann* departed Freetown for Ascension in company with her tender, *San Raphael*, and *Driver*. *San Raphael* had recently returned from Bunce Island to have her bottom cleaned and several of her crew were now ill with fever. Between 31 March and 3 April seven of *Bann*'s crew also fell ill, coughing up black bile and bleeding from their eyes and noses. The number of sick on board Phillips's sloop's increased rapidly, retarding her progress south, and when she finally arrived at Ascension on 25 April flying her yellow quarantine flag fifteen of her crew were dead and almost half her remaining men sick including Phillips, who had been relieved of command by *Driver*'s Lieutenant Thomas Saumarez. A shore-side hospital was set up some distance from the garrison at Ascension and *Bann*'s forty-five sick crew members landed. On 5 May *Driver* arrived at the island. When cases of fever began appearing on board his vessel Wolrige returned to sea. On her arrival at Cape Coast two months later thirty-one of *Driver*'s crew, almost a third of her complement, had been lost to the virulent disease. On 2 June *Bann* sailed for Bahia to repair her broken rudder and to rid herself once and for all of the yellow fever that by this time had claimed a further sixty-five of her crew.

Departing Freetown, *Owen Glendower* headed south to visit the British settlements along the Gold Coast, arriving there on 10 April. Amidst the backdrop of the ongoing war between the Ashantis and the British-backed Fanti, the execution of a sergeant of the Royal African Corps at Anamabo by the Ashantis had caused a rise in tensions in the area. MacCarthy had requested reinforcements and men began arriving from the Cape and Britain. Mends also agreed to station *Bann* on the Gold Coast as a deterrent against further Ashanti attacks following her return from Bahia, unaware that the sloop would not return to the Coast until early September.

Continuing her cruise to leeward, in mid-May *Owen Glendower* arrived off the Congo and Mends sent his boats to reconnoitre the river. On 13 May a Portuguese vessel was boarded. Her cargo of 320 sickly slaves were in such a wretched state that they were dying at a rate of ten to twelve a day but Portuguese trade was permitted south of the Line and Mends was forced to release the vessel. Continuing on towards the Bights, on 10 June the crew of the Spanish schooner *Maria la Luz* were seen abandoning their vessel in the New Calabar River on the approach of Mends' frigate, taking all but seven of her slaves with them. Seeing that *Maria la Luz* had been seized, the local chief sent her remaining 184 slaves back on board the schooner. She was subsequently lost on the bar as she attempted to leave the river but the slaves were successfully transferred to *Owen Glendower*. *Maria la Luz* had hoisted a French flag to avoid detention but was condemned in her absence by the Anglo-Spanish Mixed Commission on 8 September.

Hearing from several of *Maria la Luz*'s seamen of another Spanish slaver operating in the Old Calabar, Mends sent his boats under the command of Lieutenant Clarkson upriver. Following a lengthy search along the river's many creeks the schooner *Conchita* was finally discovered on 16 June. Upon the appearance of *Owen Glendower*'s boats *Conchita*'s crew and the slaves already on board the vessel were spotted jumping overboard and fleeing into the mangroves. When Clarkson and his men finally boarded the schooner they discovered her to be abandoned. Although she had been flying the Danish flag at the time of her capture her logbook had been written in Spanish. The vessel was clearly equipped for slaving and there was ample evidence that there had been slaves on board just prior to her capture. Clarkson took *Conchita* out into the river and the next day Duke Ephraim sent fifty-five slaves, mainly children, across to the schooner. By the time the boats set off downstream the rain had set in, reducing visibility to just a few yards. After several days the mist finally lifted and Clarkson finally spotted *Owen Glendower*, his men arriving on board ship soaking wet, covered in mosquito bites and many now suffering from fever.

Instructions for *Cyrene* to return home had not yet reached Freetown and, having embarked Governor MacCarthy at the Gold Coast she had sailed north to Bathurst, arriving there on 11 June. For a month she cruised offshore before re-embarking the governor and sailing to Freetown. Sierra Leone's capital had been in the grip of an epidemic of yellow fever since late April, her streets becoming almost deserted as 340 Africans and Europeans fell victim to the disease. Upon his return to Freetown after a four-month absence MacCarthy discovered that, along with the loss of numerous government administrators, the court at Freetown had lost the British Arbitrator, Fitzgerald, who had died on 3 June. MacCarthy now appointed the registrar, Daniel Molloy Hamilton, as Fitzgerald's replacement.

Owen Glendower arrived at Cape Coast on 31 July in an appalling condition. With nearly 200 naked, half starving and mostly sick slaves from their prize to feed, the ship's company had been placed first on half, then quarter rations. There had been no let-up in the heavy rains and many of *Owen Glendower*'s men had fallen ill with malaria and opthalmia. Having landed *Maria La Luz*'s surviving 183 slaves Mends attention once again turned to the Ashanti War. Promising to give Cape Coast Castle's

Commandant, Major Chisholm, any assistance he could, Mends sent instructions for *Cyrene* to join him from Sierra Leone with whatever other cruisers were available. At the same time *Snapper* was ordered home with despatches and the Squadron's invalids. She sailed for England on 1 September with the Portuguese judge, Altavilla, taking passage on board Rothery's ship for his return home on leave. Other members of the Mixed Commission having previously returned home due to ill health, the loss of Altavilla from the court and the recent death of Fitzgerald left the Dutch Arbitrator, Bonnouvrié, as the only surviving member of the original batch of commissioners to arrive in Freetown.

Following his arrival at Cape Coast Mends had sent his First Lieutenant, Pringle Stokes, to garrison a recently-completed Martello tower and *Driver*'s First Lieutenant, John King, had been placed in command of a large force of Fantis situated 12 miles from the castle. On 2 September Mends fell ill with gastroenteritis. By 4 September he seemed to have recovered and was walking from his cabin to the quarterdeck in conversation with his eldest son who was serving as a midshipman aboard *Owen Glendower* when he was suddenly seized by an apoplectic fit and died. Stokes was sent for and returned on board to assume temporary command of the frigate. The following day *Bann* arrived from Brazil and Stokes immediately ordered her to Ascension with despatches.

On 15 October the 12-gun brig *Swinger*, Lieutenant John Scott, arrived at Cape Coast from England. Her crew were very familiar with the Coast, having previously been turned over from *Thistle*. *Swinger* brought with her Lieutenant John Filmore who was due to take over command of *Bann*. However, following the death of Mends, Filmore was now the senior officer on station and so he appointed himself commodore, hoisting his broad pennant aboard *Owen Glendower* without proper authority and giving command of *Bann* to *Cyrene*'s Lieutenant George Courtenay. On 16 October *Driver* returned to Cape Coast from a cruise down to the Bights. Finding her in a much-dilapidated state Filmore now ordered her to Brazil via Ascension for repairs. *Bann* was told to remain at Cape Coast Castle unless Major Chisholm thought her services were not required. Finding the colony at Cape Coast in great want of provisions, Filmore now reluctantly sailed for Freetown prior to the arrival of MacCarthy and *Cyrene*, which arrived at Cape Coast to find her long-delayed orders to return to Spithead. On 28 November MacCarthy arrived at Cape Coast Castle aboard the colonial schooner *Prince Regent* and on 14 December *Bann* sailed for the Bights. That same day *Owen Glendower* arrived at Freetown, her crew on quarter rations and with a leak in her magazine. Midshipman Mends, the Commodore's eldest son, had fallen seriously ill and had died at sea on 5 December.

En route to the Bights from Cape Coast *Bann* boarded a large brig, *Cerquiera*, following a ten-hour chase off Lagos on 15 December. Her guns ready for action and her sides greased to prevent boarding, the Brazilian-flagged brig had no cargo but she was equipped for slaving and had been issued with a passport from the provisional government of Bahia for 761 slaves from Malembo. With twenty-five of his men on the sick list Courtenay could not spare enough men to put a prize crew on board *Cerquiera* so *Bann* continued on her way down to Biafra. On 25 December her boats discovered another Brazilian brig yet to have her slaves loaded in the River Formoso. Having investigated the Bonny and New Calabar *Bann* sailed to Fernando Po to water and provision. From there she sailed to the River Cameroons. Having sighted no slavers in any of these rivers *Bann* returned to the River Formoso but there was no sign of the brig encountered on Christmas Day, so *Bann* returned to Lagos. Arriving there on 30 January 1824 Courtenay discovered *Cerquiera* still at anchor but now joined by the ship *Minerva* and the schooner *Creola*, both of which were flying Brazilian colours. Noting that their passports were sealed with the Imperial Arms of Brazil and believing that the Portuguese treaty still applied to Brazilian vessels, Courtenay decided to board all three slavers. *Cerquiera* and *Creola* were both ready to sail but all three masters were on shore organising their slave cargoes. Courtenay waited twenty-four hours for these men to return to their ships then dispatched Lieutenants Armsink and Wilson with the pinnace, yawl and gig to bring the masters out together with their slave cargoes. Arriving at the village where the slaves were being held, the three masters refused to leave the river but the local chief agreed to hand over their cargoes, 700 slaves, the following day. After an uncomfortable night in the boats Armsink returned to the village at dawn. The chief attempted to detain Armsink and his men but they escaped and fled back to the boats, closely pursued by the slavers and around 3,000 armed natives. Arriving at the boats the British were opened fire on by three gun batteries. The pinnace and yawl returned fire with grape and canister, driving the enemy from one of the batteries, and Armsink went back ashore and spiked the guns. The boats returned to *Bann* with two men killed, one man, Lieutenant Wilson, severely wounded and five others with slight wounds.

Courtenay dispatched *Cerquiera*, *Creola* and *Minerva* to Freetown then headed for Cape Coast. *Creola* was boarded by a Spanish schooner en route to Freetown, her papers and some stores taken and the British prize crew plundered of all their possessions including their only quadrant, leaving Midshipman Miller to navigate the remainder of the passage back to Freetown by dead reckoning alone. *Creola* followed *Bann*'s two other prizes into port on 1 April. The Anglo-Portuguese court refused to adjudicate against any of the Brazilian prizes and they were all released, departing Freetown on 29 April to resume the loading of their slave cargoes at Lagos.

In early January 1824 Filmore had fallen ill and had returned to England, passing command of *Owen Glendower* over to his First Lieutenant, George Woollcombe. Soon after Filmore's departure word came through to Cape Coast that a large Ashanti army was on the march south. On 20 January MacCarthy left the Castle at the head of a force comprised of 250 men of the Royal African Corps and the Cape Coast Militia together with 240 Fanti under their local chiefs. The plan was to meet up with three other groups totalling 1,000 regulars and 11,000 Fanti tribesmen before engaging with the enemy. However, on 21 January MacCarthy's men were attacked by a large Ashanti army of around 10,000 men on the banks of the River Adumansu. Soon after fighting began the bearers bringing supplies of up from the rear fled the field and by 4.00pm the British had run out of ammunition. The Ashanti quickly broke through the British lines and MacCarthy, already wounded, chose to take his own life rather than be captured.

When reports of the battle first reached Cape Coast it was not clear whether or not MacCarthy was still alive and so Woollcombe decided to embark troops and sail to the fort at Sekondi in the hope of meeting up with the governor and the remainder of his forces. Upon his arrival at Sekondi in early February Woollcombe discovered that the locals were besieging the fort and he was refused entry. He returned with marines and sailors carrying small arms but in the ensuing skirmish two of his men were killed. Having made a failed attempt to burn the town, Woollcombe returned to Cape Coast Castle. Soon after his arrival the startling news came through that MacCarthy was dead and that only sixty-one men from the colonial militias had survived the battle.

On 16 February *Bann* arrived at Cape Coast, learning of Filmore's departure Courtenay, much to the annoyance of Woollcombe, appointed himself senior officer on the station, placing himself into *Owen Glendower* and appointing Woollcombe to *Bann*. Having been despatched to Princes to water prior to a return to Freetown, on 10 March *Bann* stopped and boarded a suspicious-looking vessel 560 miles west of the island. She was the Brazilian brig *Bom Caminho*, out of Bahia with a passport to Malembo but with a cargo of 334 slaves embarked at Badagry. Woollcombe had already boarded this vessel off Elmina the previous month whilst in command of *Owen Glendower* and had warned her against slaving in the Bights. *Bom Caminho* arrived in Freetown on 24 April, seven slaves having died on the passage north. She was condemned by the Mixed Commission on 15 May and her surviving 327 slaves emancipated. Having complained bitterly of his removal from *Owen Glendower*, *Bann*'s new commanding officer was now able to advise his parents that his share of the prize money from the condemned brig would amount to £1,200. On his arrival at Freetown in mid-April Woollcombe announced the death of MacCarthy to a shocked colony. The flag at Fort Thornton was lowered to half-mast and minute guns were fired sixty-five times to mark each year of MacCarthy's life. Officers were ordered to wear black armbands until further notice and for several weeks a black border appeared on the *Gazette*. Later that same month one of the survivors from Adumansu, MacCarthy's aide-de-camp, John Tasker Williams, appeared at Cape Coast Castle. For several months he and two other men had been locked in a hut together with several severed heads, including that of MacCarthy. The other two men had been executed and William's own life had only been spared because the Ashanti chief recognised him as someone who had earlier done him a small favour and he wanted a messenger to deliver the news of the death of MacCarthy to the British.

In early April the 18-gun ship-sloop *Victor*, Commander Thomas Prickett, arrived at Cape Coast from Ascension, where on 20 March she had dropped off the new commandant of the island's garrison, Lieutenant Colonel Nicholls. The arrival of Prickett, now the senior officer on station, brought yet another change at the head of the Squadron, Prickett appointing himself commander of *Owen Glendower*, moving Lieutenant John Scott from *Swinger* to *Victor* and taking First Lieutenant Herd out of *Victor* to replace Scott. This left Courtenay without a ship to command as *Bann*, still under Woollcombe, was off cruising in the Bights and from there she was due to head for Sierra Leone to refit.

On 17 April *Victor* sailed from Cape Coast to Ascension with stores for the garrison. Five days later Scott's new command spotted two brigs and a lugger off Lagos. All three vessels cut their anchors upon sighting *Victor*, but after a brief chase Scott's fast-sailing sloop came alongside the smaller brig, *El Vencador*, whereupon he learned that both she and the lugger had been seized by the larger brig, *Romano*, which had transferred part of *El Vencador*'s cargo into the lugger, intending to trade it for slaves. Returning to Lagos in order to apprehend the piratical *Romano*, Scott saw a fully-loaded boat leave the brig which was then run ashore, immediately breaking up in the heavy surf. *Victor* now headed for Princes in company with *El Vencador*.

As *Victor* lay at anchor at Port Antonio in the north-east of the island on 8 May a suspicious-looking schooner-boat, *Maria Piquena*, was seen entering the harbour. Scott sent a boat across to her and she was observed hurriedly landing six slaves. A further eleven slaves were discovered on board the vessel which was just five tons burthen, 22ft in length and filled to within 18in of her hatches with a cargo of ivory, beeswax and gum-copal. The slaves, purchased in the River Gabon 27 miles north of the Line, were all in such a state of severe starvation that six of her original cargo of twenty-three were discovered dead and another died soon after *Maria Piquena* was seized. The slaves that had been landed were eventually recovered from Governor Gomez and taken on board *El Vencador* along with the other eleven slaves from *Maria Piquena*, Scott leaving the schooner-boat with Gomez, having deemed it unsafe to make the passage north to Freetown. (In all likelihood it was the governor, or his daughter, Donna Maria da Cruz, who were the vessel's true owner.) *El Vencador* arrived in Freetown on 31 May and on 14 July she was condemned and the surviving sixteen slaves from *Maria Piquena* emancipated.

On 2 May the 36-gun frigate *Maidstone* arrived at Sierra Leone from Portsmouth, bringing with her a new commander for the West Africa Squadron, Commodore Charles Bullen CB. An old friend of Robert Mends, Bullen had first joined the Navy aged 10 in 1779. Promoted lieutenant in August 1791, he served aboard *Ramillies* at the Glorious First of June and as First Lieutenant of *Monmouth* had had a noose thrown over his head and narrowly escaped with his life during the Nore mutiny of 1797.

Promoted to commander in recognition of his bravery during the Battle of Camperdown later that same year, from 1801–2 Bullen commanded the sloop *Wasp* off the West Coast of Africa, protecting the newly-established Sierra Leone colony from attack. In recognition of this service he made post and was subsequently appointed flag captain to Lord Northesk, serving aboard *Britannia* at the Battle of Trafalgar. Following several years on half pay he had been appointed to *Maidstone* in December 1823. As with all previous orders issued to commanders of the West Africa Squadron, Bullen had been instructed to support the British settlements on the Coast and to send his cruisers to Ascension when necessary. However, rather than return to Britain during the rainy season Bullen had been ordered to remain on station until relieved unless sickness, damage or shortage of stores necessitated a return to England.

On 5 May *Maidstone* sailed for Cape Coast in company with a now-refitted *Bann*, arriving there on 24 May. On 31 May *Owen Glendower* sailed for England via Ascension, stopping off at the island on 2 July. As per Bullen's instructions a worn-out *Driver* also departed the Coast. Wolrige's sloop had brought Lieutenant Colonel Sutherland down from Freetown to take over command of the Cape Coast settlement and her men were subsequently employed repairing the castle's defences. Another battle with the Ashanti had been fought on 21 May and the enemy had been driven back but by now there were over 5,000 refugees crowded into the castle. The cemeteries were overflowing but with the Ashanti fires now visible from the castle the dead could not be taken outside for burial and so were left on the streets to rot. Supplies could not be brought in overland so the castle relied on ships coming down from Freetown to bring in food, medicine and ammunition.

Upon *Bann*'s arrival at Cape Coast Courtenay rejoined the frigate and took her north to support the British traders at Portendic. Woollcombe now replaced Herd in *Swinger*, his command lasting until early June when *Victor* returned to Cape Coast and he exchanged commands with Scott who went ashore to assist with the Castle's defences. Whilst *Swinger* remained off the Castle, *Victor* sailed for Accra and then for a cruise in the Bights. On 4 July *Thetis*, Captain Sir John Phillimore, arrived at Cape Coast bearing reinforcements for the Royal African Corps. The governor of the Danish fort at Accra also sent across a number of men and on 11 July another battle was fought with the Ashanti during which a shot grazed the Ashanti king in his palanquin and he fled the field, convinced the British knew his whereabouts. During the battle guns commanded by Scott fired several well-directed rounds at the enemy. Defeated and now ravaged by disease, the Ashanti finally retreated to their capital of Kumasi.

On 20 July *Maidstone* returned to Cape Coast from a six-week cruise down to the Bights. She had made no arrests and it had quickly become apparent to Bullen had that the Trade in Biafra was almost entirely in the hands of the French, and if not them then by slavers using the French flag as cover. Eight such vessels carrying an estimated 8,000 slaves were visited by *Maidstone* in just two days on the River Bonny. Another was boarded in the Old Calabar. Four Brazilian slavers, equally as untouchable, were also observed in the Bights, preparing to receive their cargoes. Watching these vessels operate with impunity, Bullen felt he was little more than an idle spectator. At the River Bonny *Maidstone*'s barge had capsized whilst trying to cross the bar, leading to the loss of eleven men including one of the Squadron's valuable assistant-surgeons. The survivors were looked after by the British palm oil traders operating along the river until they could be brought back on board Bullen's frigate.

Following his tour of the Bights Bullen had written a report to the Admiralty on the feasibility of using Fernando Po as a base for the Squadron. Bullen felt that this island, with its sheltered anchorage and abundant natural resources, was better placed than Freetown to monitor the Trade and catch slavers, the majority of whom operated in the Bights. On his return to Cape Coast Bullen discovered that the latest Navy Board transport had been delayed, depriving the Squadron of much-needed provisions and then, following *Maidstone*'s return to Freetown on 20 August, the Commodore discovered that the Squadron's main depot had been raided by the aptly-named frigate *Brazen* as she passed through Freetown and by the new colonial schooner *Prince Regent*, which had just completed her fitting out.

Since early August *Victor* had been maintaining a lonely vigil in the Bights and on 11 August she made her first capture under her new commanding officer, George Woollcombe. Following a lengthy chase beginning shortly after sunrise and ending around sunset the Brazilian brigantine *Diana* had been boarded 100 miles west of Princes. On board were 145 slaves loaded at the Rio Formoso. Nine slaves had already died from smallpox and another died from the disease just as *Victor*'s boat was drawing alongside the brigantine. The following morning Woollcombe had *Diana* cleaned and whitewashed, a procedure believed to prevent the spread of disease, and she was dispatched to Freetown to be condemned. On the journey north a further twenty-three slaves died of smallpox.

Victor followed up this success with the capture of another loaded Brazilian brigantine, *Dos Amigos Brazilieros*, taken on 18 September, 70 miles south-west of Princes with a cargo of 260 slaves from Badagry. This particular vessel had previously been boarded by *Maidstone* and *Bann* but neither cruiser could touch her as she was still to be loaded. By now fever had appeared on board Woollcombe's vessel and so he sailed to St Thomas in company with his prize to recuperate. *Maidstone* had also arrived at St Thomas, equally debilitated by fever. When Bullen went on board *Dos Amigos Brazilieros* he was shocked to discover that many of the female slaves were in advanced states of pregnancy and that several had babies varying in ages from 4 to 12 months old, all crowded together. Whilst at Fernando Po Woollcombe wrote to his parents to tell them he had suffered a brief attack of fever but was well. He also predicted the amount of head money he might be able to claim from his recent captures, but advised that the proceeds from their sales would hardly cover the expenses involved in condemning a vessel. Following their arrival at Freetown *Diana* and *Dos Amigos Brazilieros* were both condemned by the Anglo-Portuguese court on 15 November and their surviving slaves (the number is not known) emancipated.

From St Thomas *Victor* was ordered down to Ascension to recover the health of her crew before a cruise south of the Line. Meanwhile, having spent the last seven months in support of the British settlement at Cape Coast, *Swinger* sailed for Freetown to careen and refit. On 26 September, whilst still at sea, her commanding officer Lieutenant John Scott died of fever. That very same day *Maidstone* made her one and only capture of the year, chasing and boarding the Brazilian brig *Aviso* with a cargo of 465 slaves just south of Princes. Bullen took his prize to Annobon where he boarded another Brazilian brig loaded with slaves which he could not touch, her being discovered south of the Line. On 14 October a cleaned and whitewashed *Aviso* was despatched to Freetown whilst *Maidstone* made for Ascension. Despite the best efforts of her prize crew, by the time of her arrival in Sierra Leone *Aviso* had lost thirty-four slaves to dysentery. She was condemned by the Anglo-Portuguese Mixed Commission on 19 November. At Ascension Bullen met with Lieutenant Colonel Nicholls to discuss the supply arrangements from Freetown to Ascension. *Maidstone* landed a bull and a cow and Bullen noted the ample supplies of fresh meat and vegetables readily available on the island.

Having returned from a cruise along the coast up to the River Cameroons, *Bann* had joined *Maidstone* off St Thomas on 25 September. Courtenay's vessel had been the first to spot the slaver *Aviso*, some 10 to 12 miles distant on the morning of 26 September and had immediately signalled *Maidstone*. However, Bullen's frigate being a far superior sailer, she quickly overtook *Bann* and had taken possession of *Aviso* before dispatching *Bann* to St Thomas. When Courtenay later discovered that Bullen had claimed sole responsibility for the capture of the Brazilian brig he applied to the High Court of Admiralty, asking that he be considered a joint captor, arguing that *Bann* was sailing under Bullen's orders, she had been the first to sight *Aviso* and had also taken part in the chase. The court eventually found in Courtenay's favour, declaring that *Bann* should be awarded her share of the prize money.

Following the death in battle of MacCarthy, senior Sierra Leone Council member Daniel Molloy Hamilton had assumed temporary command of the colony whilst it awaited the arrival of the new Governor, Major General Charles Turner, from England. Turner had been appointed in June but appeared in no great haste to take up his new position, recruiting men for the Royal African Corps and arguing with the Colonial Office over various matters including his pay and accommodation. It would be another seven months before he finally made his appearance in Freetown.

In early November *Maidstone* returned to Sierra Leone to refit and re-provision. Concerned at news of a fast, well-armed piratical schooner operating in the rivers Nunez and Pongas, Bullen despatched his fastest sailing cruiser, *Victor*, northwards whilst he headed south to revisit the Bights, investigating the Sherbro and Gallinas en route. During their cruises *Victor* and *Maidstone* encountered a number of Spanish slavers that Bullen had received information about from the British judge in Havana, Henry Kilbee, but these were all empty. On his arrival at Cape Coast in January Bullen discovered that *Experiment*, a piratical schooner operating in the Rio Pongas, had been seized by the authorities and her crew arrested on suspicion of murder. Following a request from the Acting Commandant, Lieutenant Colonel Grant, they were taken on board *Maidstone* along with various witnesses for passage back to Freetown.

Chapter 6

Captain Owen's Island: January 1825–June 1827

oncerned at the number of British merchants still involved in the Trade, on 31 March 1824 Parliament had introduced an Act for the 'more Effectual Suppression of the African Slave Trade'. Under this legislation any British subject found to be involved in slaving would now be charged with 'felony, piracy and robbery, and should suffer death without the benefit of clergy and loss of lands, goods and chattels as pirates, felons and robbers on the seas ought to suffer'.[1] A subsequent Act redefined the various offences associated with the Trade and their penalties. It also adjusted the bounty for each man, woman or child emancipated to £10 and stated that a commodore should be entitled to an admiral's share of prize money.

On 14 January 1825, *Swinger*, now commanded by Edward Clerkson, formerly First Lieutenant on board *Maidstone*, captured the Brazilian schooner *Bom Fim*, with 149 slaves on board, roughly 100 miles north-west of Princes. All her slaves were in good health and she arrived at Freetown on 8 March having only lost one African who had either jumped or fallen over the side of the schooner. *Bom Fim* was condemned on 19 March and her surviving slaves emancipated. As she continued on her passage down to the Bights *Swinger* observed seven French vessels preparing to load their cargoes between the Sherbro and the Gallinas and at the Gallinas Clerkson boarded two empty Spanish brigs, both mounting 16 guns. At dusk on 9 February *Swinger* discovered four vessels at anchor off Lagos. Unable to determine which nation they belonged to in the gloom, Clerkson prepared to anchor alongside, with the intention of examining them once it was light. No sooner had *Swinger*'s anchor dropped than she was hailed by a large brig on her starboard beam which, moments later, fired a shot over her masts. Imagining her to be one of the piratical Spanish vessels in operation on this part of the coast, Clerkson fired four double-shotted guns in response. Shortly before midnight the brig's boat came alongside *Swinger* full of men clearly intent on boarding Clerkson's cruiser, but he quickly took them prisoner. The following morning *Swinger* weighed anchor and approached the brig. Recognising her as a vessel he had previously boarded in December, Clerkson now hailed the brig and advised her master to send his remaining crew below as he was about to open fire on her. After an hour's backing and filling *Swinger* fired four broadsides into the brig to dismantle her rigging then sent her boarders away. She proved to be *Alerto*, a Spanish-flagged pirate armed with sixteen long 12-pounders that had been harassing the British traders in the Bights for several months. As she was lacking any cargo Clerkson had no option but to release the vessel, but before he did so he threw all her long guns and other small arms overboard. When the Admiralty learned of this incident Clerkson was accused of 'unjustifiable aggression'[2] and of the illegal destruction of property. Bullen now came to Clerkson's defence, declaring that his actions would be of the greatest benefit to legitimate commerce, which lately had been disturbed by the many troublesome pirates operating on the Coast.

After much delay, on 5 February Colonel Turner finally arrived in Sierra Leone aboard a vessel hired especially to convey himself, his family and staff to Africa. This news, along with that of the arrival of the 28-gun ship-sloop *Atholl*, Captain James Murray, was conveyed to Bullen by *Victor* following her return to the Bights on 25 February. Leaving *Victor* and *Swinger* to patrol the Bights, Bullen now headed back to Freetown in order to meet with Turner. Upon his arrival at Freetown the Commodore discovered that *Atholl* had been joined by two more cruisers, the 22-gun ship-sloop *Esk*, Commander William Purchase, and the 12-gun brig *Conflict*, Lieutenant John Chrystie. Bullen also learned that *Atholl* had made her first capture, boarding the Spanish schooner *Espanola* with 270 slaves off the Gallinas on 7 May. There was, however, no sign of Turner who had left for Cape Coast four days prior to Bullen's arrival in Freetown.

With the return home of *Bann* in April after three years on the Coast the Squadron now consisted of a frigate, three sloops and two gun-brigs. *Maidstone* was a fast frigate but her deeper draught made her unsuited for inshore work and her tall masts were clearly visible to slavers working upriver. The two gun-brigs *Swinger* and *Conflict* were both dull sailers, as was the 'Seppings-built' ship-sloop *Esk* with her belt-and-braces construction. *Atholl* was also a slow sailer but the teak-built *Victor* had proven herself to be a fast vessel and was an eagerly sought-for command.

Sailing in company with *Esk* and *Conflict*, *Maidstone* left Freetown for a brief cruise to the north, leaving *Conflict* to protect the Portendic gum traders and the settlement at the Gambia before returning to Freetown in early May. Turner had also returned to Freetown but now refused to see Bullen. At Cape Coast a lieutenant on board the transport *Cato* had, in accordance with Bullen's instructions, declined an order to take a detachment of Turner's troops back to England in his already fully-laden vessel. His authority having been questioned, Turner had subsequently arrested the lieutenant, the transport's master and mate and had complained to the Colonial Office, arguing, wrongly, that the Navy Board transports were under his control, not Bullen's. The Admiralty gave its backing to Bullen and informed the Colonial Office that Turner clearly did not understand the full extent of his authority and that the officers whom he had clapped in irons would no doubt be seeking damages for their wrongful arrest. Lord Bathurst was advised to take steps to prevent Turner overstepping his authority again. Turner was quickly proving to be an unpopular Governor. At Freetown he had belittled the achievements of his predecessor, MacCarthy, and during his recent visit to Cape Coast he had complained about almost every aspect of its administration before dismissing the ailing Acting Commandant, Lieutenant Colonel Grant, from his post. Turner's humour was not improved following his return to Freetown when he learned that Daniel Molloy Hamilton, British judge since the death of Edward Gregory, had gone home on sick leave and that he would now have to act as judge due to a lack of other, more suitable candidates.

On 12 May *Maidstone* sailed in company with *Esk* for the Bights. Off the Gallinas various French slavers were spotted awaiting their cargoes. The two British cruisers spent several hours chasing a Spanish-flagged schooner only to discover that she too was empty. On 19 May Bullen seized a Dutch schooner at anchor off the Gallinas whose master was ashore purchasing slaves. Originally a Virginian pilot boat, *Bey* was manned mostly by Americans. Bullen seized her under the new Equipment Clause and sent her to Freetown where she was condemned later that month. Off the Pepper Coast Bullen discovered that the recently-arrived French Navy brig *Dragon* had arrested three slavers. However, these vessels were soon released by the court in Senegal and returned to the Coast to continue slaving.

Arriving at Cape Coast on 7 June Bullen found *Atholl* at anchor. Intending to restock his supplies of bread, sugar and cocoa, Bullen was alarmed to discover that these provisions, intended for the sole use of the Squadron, had been issued to troop transports on the orders of Turner. In consequence, rather than return to Freetown as originally planned *Maidstone*, now on two-thirds bread allowance, headed for Accra where Bullen found *Victor* and *Swinger* at anchor. Learning that Clerkson had died of fever on 2 April, Bullen now sent Lieutenant Poingdestre across to *Swinger* and the gun-brig headed to Freetown for a refit. Having ordered *Victor* home, on 19 June Bullen sailed from Accra for the Bights in company with *Esk* and *Atholl*. Off Lagos *Maidstone* chased, but could not catch, a rearmed *Alerto* and there were no more arrests until 17 July when *Esk* seized the Brazilian sumaca *Bom Jesus dos Navigantes* 100 miles south-west of Cape Formoso with a cargo of 283 slaves and barely a week's-worth of provisions. With seventy-three more slaves than his passport from Bahia to Malembo allowed, *Bom Jesus*'s master, Joao Pereiro, claimed, rather unconvincingly, that he thought Malembo was close to Benin. *Esk*'s prize was condemned by the Anglo-Portuguese Mixed Commission on 13 August, 267 slaves surviving to be emancipated.

Stopping off at St Thomas, where he was joined by *Conflict* following her return from the Gambia, on 31 July Bullen seized the Dutch brig *Z* off the River Sombrero. Empty, but equipped for slaving, *Maidstone* had been tailing the brig for two days prior to sending her boats across. *Z* was condemned by the court at Freetown and was subsequently employed as a colonial brig by Governor Turner. On 25 August whilst off Accra *Maidstone* was joined by the recently-arrived 18-gun ship-sloop *Redwing*, Commander Douglas Charles Clavering. Both vessel and commander had had previous experience of the suppression campaign, *Redwing* serving on the St Helena station in 1819, Clavering on the Coast as commander of *Pheasant* in 1822. On 4 September *Maidstone* spent eleven hours chasing a slaver, finally bringing her to with gunfire only to discover that she was an untouchable French-flagged vessel with a cargo of 698 slaves from the Old Calabar. On 1 September *Atholl* had arrested the Dutch schooner *Venus* off Cape Formoso. She had no slaves on board but was seized under the Equipment Clause and sent for adjudication. En route to Freetown she was fired at by a brig and a schooner sailing in company. *Venus*'s prize master was temporarily detained and ordered to keep his schooner between these two vessels. However, he managed to slip free during the night and continue on to Freetown where *Atholl*'s prize was condemned by the Anglo–Dutch court on 23 September.

On the way out from England *Redwing* had damaged her hull on a coral reef and was now a particularly poor sailer. On 8 September Clavering's sloop gave chase to a Brazilian schooner, *União*, which successfully evaded the British cruiser and slipped away during the night. However, the following morning *Redwing* spotted her quarry 130 miles south-west of Cape Formoso and resumed the chase. Quite fortuitously *Esk* and *Atholl* now hove into view ahead of *União*, preventing her escape. A prize crew led by *Redwing*'s Midshipman Rowe was sent across to *União* and, all three cruisers having claimed their part in the capture of the schooner with her cargo of 361 slaves, *Esk*, *Atholl* and *Redwing* now headed into the Bights, joining *Maidstone* and *Conflict* at Princes. *Atholl* was now despatched to Sierra Leone to replenish, *Esk* and *Conflict* were ordered to cruise the Bights and Bullen sent *Redwing* to look in on the Bonny, Old Calabar and Cameroons River. Having made his dispositions Bullen now sailed for the Bight of Benin. On 29 September *Maidstone* captured the Spanish schooner *Segunda Gallega*, with a cargo of 285 slaves bound for Havana, following a nine-hour chase off Lagos. The badly overcrowded *União* lost 112 slaves during her passage north to Freetown. She was condemned by the Anglo-Portuguese Mixed Commission on 21 October. Two days later *Maidstone*'s prize, *Segunda Gallega*, was condemned by the Anglo-Spanish court, 276 slaves surviving to be emancipated.

Arriving off the Old Calabar, *Redwing* sent her boats, under the command of First Lieutenant Robert Card, up the river. On the morning of 5 October Card discovered two slavers at anchor. Upon sighting *Redwing*'s boats the vessels, a schooner and a brigantine, hoisted Spanish colours and commenced a heavy fire of grape and musketry as the British made their approach. Sword in hand, Card led his boarding party up the side of the schooner and quickly took the vessel for the cost of two men wounded. By this time the crew of the brigantine had boarded their boats and escaped ashore with the vessel's papers. The prizes were the schooner *Teresa* and the brigantine *Isabella*, both from Santiago de Cuba, with cargoes of 248 and 273 slaves respectively. Learning of another slaver about to depart from the Cameroons, Clavering despatched *Isabella* to Freetown and set off for the Cameroons in company with *Teresa*.

On her passage north *Isabella* fell in with the Brazilian slaver *Disuniao*, which was quickly taken. *Isabella*'s prize master, Charles Jackson, now divided his crew of fourteen between the two vessels. When *Isabella* and *Disuniao* subsequently encountered the piratical Spanish brigantine *Gavilina*, neither prize crew were able to defend their vessel and both were taken. The British on board *Isabella* were all either killed in the action or subsequently murdered. She arrived at Cuba in late November sailing under the name of *Juanita*. Having been plundered of her cargo, *Disuniao* was allowed to continue on to Rio, arriving there with the five remaining members of her prize crew all badly mutilated.

On 11 October *Redwing*'s boats, once again commanded by Lieutenant Card, discovered a brigantine at anchor off the Cameroons. Upon sighting Card's boats the vessel fired several guns, slipped her cables and attempted to escape, but was caught after a chase of several hours by *Theresa*, now commanded by Lieutenant Wilson. The prize proved to be *Ana*, also of Santiago de Cuba, with a cargo of 106 slaves. Fifty of the slaves crowded on board *Theresa* were now moved to the brigantine. In the early hours of 19 October *Theresa* was caught in a heavy squall. Thrown on to her beam ends, she sank almost immediately, taking 193 slaves, four British seamen and one Spaniard with her. Lieutenant Wilson, her remaining prize crew and four slaves were able to escape from the brigantine and spent eight hours clinging on to floating spars. *Redwing*, sailing in company with *Teresa*, was not aware of the tragedy until first light the following morning when she spotted the survivors and was able to pull them from the water. *Ana* navigated her passage to Freetown without incident and was condemned on 3 January 1826, sixty-eight of her slaves having succumbed to disease.

In mid-October the 18-gun ship-sloop *Brazen*, Captain George Willes, arrived at Freetown from Portsmouth, bringing with her the government's new envoy to the Sultans of Sokoto and Borno, Captain Hugh Clapperton, fifty soldiers for the Royal African Corps and the explorer, Dickson Denham. Passing the Gambia *Brazen* had encountered *Swinger*, short of provisions and suffering from fever which had claimed six men including her commanding officer, Lieutenant Poingdestre. Upon his arrival at Freetown Wilkes found *Atholl* at anchor and before he set off in search of the Commodore with *Swinger*, now commanded by Acting Lieutenant Giles, he ordered Murray's ship to the Bights with several of the Squadron's prize crews who had recently arrived in port.

In a reminder that British merchants had not entirely abandoned the Trade, even in the face of new tougher legislation, on 17 October *Atholl* fell in with and arrested the English-flagged brig *George and James* off Whydah. Condemning the vessel in mid-October, the Vice-Admiralty court at Freetown surmised that the notorious slave trader Da Souza had been behind the purchase of the brig by her first mate, Ramsay, from her master, Dolland. *Atholl* continued to cruise the Bights and, responding to a report from the Dutch governor of Elmina, on 12 November she boarded the Dutch schooner *Aimable Claudina*, Murray ordering her cargo of thirty-four slaves waiting near Popo to be loaded on to the vessel before she was sent to Freetown where she was condemned and her cargo freed though not emancipated.

Atholl's next capture, taken on 28 November 130 miles off Cape St Paul's, was the Brazilian brig *São João Segunda Rosália* with a cargo of 250 slaves loaded at Lagos. Owing to a shortage of officers Murray entrusted command of this vessel to two inexperienced midshipmen, Kirby and Pipon, who, with no knowledge of local tides and winds, spent the next sixty-five days at sea, prize crew and slaves surviving for the last three weeks on a handful of farina beans and half a pint of water a day until *São João* was spotted headed out into the Atlantic by a Colombian privateer with an English commander. Re-provisioned and with accurate sailing instructions, she finally arrived at Freetown on 9 February 1826, having lost seventy-two of her slaves mostly through starvation. Bullen had already expressed his disapproval to the Admiralty over the number of floggings carried out on board *Atholl* by her commanding officer and this incident did little to improve the his opinion of Murray.

On 4 November *Brazen* seized the Spanish schooner *Clara* with a cargo of thirty-six slaves 50 miles south of Cape Mesurado. Regarded as one of the fastest and finest schooners out of Havana, Willes purchased the 50-ton vessel following her condemnation on 23 November, renamed her *Black Nymph* and employed her as a tender to *Brazen*. Arriving off Accra Willes discovered he had just missed Bullen. On 17 November the Spanish brigantine *Ninfa Habanera* was seized off the port with a cargo of just five slaves. When her master, José Morano, admitted he had another cargo waiting for him at Little Popo Willes sailed to this slaving station, a small collection of huts situated 45 miles west of Whydah. *Brazen*'s officers went ashore with Morano to meet with the local chief and demand that he hand the slaves over. When he refused the chieftain was informed that his town would be cannonaded and he and his sons taken prisoner. This ultimatum had the desired effect and 231 slaves were soon produced for loading on to the brigantine which, on her arrival at Freetown, was condemned for having taken fifty slaves from Accra to Little Popo.

Arriving off Cape Coast *Swinger* fell in with *Maidstone* and *Esk*. Off Accra on 22 November Giles captured the Brazilian brig *Paqueta de Bahia* with 386 slaves loaded at Whydah and sent her to Freetown where she was condemned by the Anglo-Portuguese court on 10 January 1826, having lost just one slave en route. Acting Lieutenant Giles was now replaced by *Esk*'s First Lieutenant, George Matson and as per Bullen's orders, *Swinger* headed to Ascension in order to recover the health of her crew. Arriving at the island the ship's company were looked after by the garrison who provided them with fresh vegetables and tents for accommodation whilst their brig was careened and her hull scrubbed clean.

Dropping the explorer Denham off at Whydah, home to the infamous slaver Da Souza, *Brazen* had continued on to Badagry where she landed Clapperton. On 13 December she arrived at Princes to find various vessels including the English ship *Malta* at anchor. Her crew complained to Willes over their ill treatment by the ship's master, Captain Thomas Young, and explained that the previous month whilst in the River Danger he had sold to a Spanish slave trader four female Africans he had been holding on board as hostages for part of a cargo his vessel had landed. When questioned, Young made no attempt to deny these allegations. On 17 December Willes took charge of the vessel and sent her to Freetown for adjudication. Young was sent to England to stand trial but was eventually acquitted of slaving.

In July Governor Turner had reported to the Colonial Office of an increase in slaving in the rivers adjacent to Sierra Leone. He then made the astounding claim that he would, at little or no expense and without the aid of the Royal Navy, eradicate slaving from the West Coast of Africa within the next six months. With the use of a steam vessel ordered from Britain and two French ex-slaver brigs Turner intended to persuade the chiefs and kings of the various rivers between Senegal and the Gold Coast to abandon slaving in exchange for British money and protection. Turner began his campaign in late September, sending troops to the Sherbro. By the end of the year Turner had concluded a treaty with Banka, King of the Sherbro, and Queen Ya Comba of the Gallinas which ceded control of territory covering 70 miles of land south of Sierra Leone to Turner. The treaty came with a British guarantee: if either tribal chief made an attack on their neighbour the other could call on British assistance. French traders operating in the Sherbro were soon forced to relocate to the Bolm River, a tributary of the Sherbro, and Turner began planning for an attack on their new base of operations.

On 19 December boats from *Conflict* had boarded a vessel in the Old Calabar purporting to be the French brig *Eugenie* with 265 slaves on board, which, upon discovery of papers concealed in her cabin, was revealed to be a Dutch vessel named *Charles*. Sent to Freetown for adjudication, she was condemned by the Anglo-Dutch court on 21 January 1826 and her surviving 243 slaves emancipated. On 27 December *Brazen* made the Squadron's final capture of the year, arresting the Spanish schooner *Iberia* with a cargo of 422 slaves following a 48-hour chase in the Bight of Benin. Boats from *Maidstone* had previously boarded this vessel whilst at anchor off Lagos in October awaiting her cargo. *Iberia* arrived in Freetown on 22 January 1826 and was condemned by the Anglo-Spanish court on 21 March, 417 slaves surviving to be emancipated. In mid-December *Maidstone* had returned to Freetown to refit before sailing for the Gallinas. On 3 January 1826 her boats, commanded by Lieutenant William Gray, boarded the empty Dutch schooner *Hoop* 20 miles off the Gallinas and seized her under the Equipment Clause. Following her condemnation in mid-February Bullen purchased the schooner for the shelter and comfort of prize crews awaiting the arrival of their parent ships at Freetown. The vessel, armed with a single 12-pounder long gun and four 18-pounder Govers (a long gun mounted on a sled like a carronade) was renamed *Hope* and provided with a crew of thirty-three men, including a midshipman, an assistant surgeon, five marines and eight Kroomen, commanded by Bullen's Second Lieutenant, William Tucker.

In late 1821, after nearly a decade and a half of anti-slavery operations, the Admiralty had, rather belatedly, decided it was time to properly map the coastline of Africa. The officer chosen to lead this most time-consuming and arduous expedition was Captain William Owen aboard the survey ship *Leven*, with support from the brig-sloop *Barracouta*, Captain William Cutfield. Owen was a vastly experienced surveyor who had mapped the Maldives, discovered the Seaflower Channel between the islands of Siberut and Sipora off the coast of Sumatra and surveyed the Canadian Great

Lakes. In his instructions from the Admiralty Owen had been told to survey the entire eastern coast of Africa, the western coast of Madagascar and the western coast of Africa from Zaire to Benin and from the Rio Grande to the Gambia. *Leven* and *Barracouta* sailed from Portsmouth in mid-February 1822. Stopping off at Rio de Janeiro to provision in May, around twenty seamen deserted, tempted by slavers promising better pay and an easier life. However, these men were quickly rounded up, brought back to their ships and flogged to prevent further desertions. Entering the east African port of Quelimane in July Owen witnessed the devastating effects of slavery first hand; the large warehouses filled with men, women and children awaiting transportation and the processions of shackled Africans being marched along the streets past those slaves too old or weak to work who had simply been abandoned to die. Returning to sea, once the survey work commenced scores of men from *Leven* and *Barracouta* began dying of fever, the surgeons from both vessels noting that the deaths seemed to be confined to those who had spent the night ashore or who were employed on boat service, investigating the myriad rivers and creeks along the coast. Between October 1822 and April 1823 thirty-six men aboard *Leven* and twenty-seven of *Barracouta*'s men succumbed to fever. In late November Captain Cutfield died and was replaced by *Leven*'s First Lieutenant, Alexander Vidal. Now a committed abolitionist, in February 1824 Owen began a one-man protectorate of Mombasa, created with the intention of disrupting the slave trade. This lasted for three years until the British government, eager to maintain friendly relations with the Sultan of Muscat and Zanzibar, with whom the inhabitants of Mombasa were now in open rebellion against, forced Owen to close it down. In total Owen spent four years mapping the coastline of Africa, his ships covering 30,000 miles of coastline and producing 300 new charts for the Admiralty. It had been an enormous undertaking which, by its conclusion had cost the lives of two-thirds of the officers and half the men employed upon the service.

In January 1826 *Leven* arrived off Freetown whilst *Barracouta* cruised to leeward. Bullen had been requested to give Owen as much support as he could to enable him to complete his survey before the rainy season set in and so he sent two midshipmen from *Maidstone*, Hutchinson and Bullen, across to Owen's sloop and sent instructions for *Conflict* to join *Leven* upon her return from the Bights. Impressed by Governor Turner's plan to crush the slave trade and by his acquisition of land which mirrored his one-man protectorate at Mombasa, Owen now temporarily abandoned his survey to join Turner in his expedition up the Bolm River. Sailing in company with Turner's cutter *Swift*, *Leven*'s boats set off up the river on 16 February. The slaving town was quickly destroyed but Owen lost three officers including Hutchinson and the Commodore's own relative, Bullen. Turner himself died of fever on 7 March. The Governor's treaty had never been ratified by London and was soon abandoned. The Colonial Office had no interest in expanding its territories in West Africa and as far as it was concerned British anti-slavery efforts should remain purely sea based. However, those in the front line of the endeavour would eventually come to realise that in order to end the Trade they would have to cut it off at the source, by means not so dissimilar to those attempted by Turner in 1825.

After a lengthy period of stability under MacCarthy the Sierra Leone administration was once again suffering from the effects of sickness, death and the demands of foreign governments. Following Turner's demise the senior member of the Sierra Leone Council, Kenneth Macaulay, had assumed temporary control of the government. The acting British judge, Daniel Molloy Hamilton, was still absent and the new Registrar, formerly the Colonial Secretary, Joseph Reffell, had also returned to England due to ill health, his position taken by William Smith, a civil servant who was the son of a Yorkshireman and a Fanti princess. On 5 January Molloy's replacement, John Tasker Williams, arrived in Freetown and on 10 January the various Courts of Mixed Commission were opened. The courts had only been in operation for four weeks when the Portuguese judge, Altavilla, was removed from his post for evidently having caused displeasure to his government.

On 22 January *Brazen*'s tender, *Black Nymph*, now commanded by Lieutenant Baldwin Walker, was en route from Sierra Leone with despatches for Bullen when she stopped and boarded the empty Dutch schooner *Vogel* off Grand Carrow on the Windward Coast. Equipped for slaving, she was discovered to be carrying French papers that gave the name of the vessel as *L'Oiseau*. As *Black Nymph* was regarded as *Brazen*'s boat the Anglo-Dutch court condemned the schooner to the parent vessel. Whilst off Cape Palmas *Black Nymph* chased another Dutch vessel, *Van Tromp*, but she escaped using her sweeps.

In January *Atholl* was ordered to India to reinforce the squadron of Admiral Gage. She departed from Freetown in mid-January and on 1

February stopped the Brazilian brig *Activo*, a vessel previously boarded off Elmina whilst empty but now with a cargo of 166 slaves. Claiming a hot pursuit, Murray arrested *Activo* 430 miles north-east of Ascension and 4° south of the Line. However, upon her arrival in Freetown the Anglo-Portuguese court decreed that although *Activo*'s slaves had been loaded at Badagry she should not be condemned as *Atholl* had arrested her well south of the Equator. Instead the court ordered her to be restored and awarded £258 against Murray for costs and damages. It was decided that a further £10,842 in compensation, including £9,983 for the loss of the 166 slaves awarded against Murray should be conditional on a final joint decision on the matter from London and Rio. Thankfully for Murray it appears that, as *Activo* had clearly broken the Anglo-Portuguese treaty, her owners request for compensation was eventually refused.

Having returned to the Bights from Freetown, on 28 January *Redwing* seized the empty Brazilian slaver *Pilar* off Whydah. She followed up this arrest with the seizure of the French brig *Cantabre* on 8 March and Clavering now removed half of *Pilar*'s prize crew, led by Lieutenant Wilson, to this vessel, leaving Master's Mate Samuel Falconer in command of *Pilar*. On 10 March *Redwing* and *Pilar* were separated in a squall and the following morning *Pilar* was boarded by the Brazilian imperial brigantine *Emprendedor* which stripped the ship of anything valuable then took her to Bahia where the British prize crew were imprisoned. When *Maidstone*'s boats subsequently fell in with *Emprendedor* off the Bonny the Brazilian commander reported that he had boarded *Pilar* and, having discovered no prize master or order (Clavering's orders were still with Wilson on board *Cantabre*), suspected that she had been retaken by her crew, most of whom appeared drunk, and had sent her to the British council in Rio. However, *Emprendedor*'s commanding officer failed to mention that he was holding three Kroomen from *Redwing* whom he subsequently attempted to sell to a slaver in the Old Calabar,

Although she had been flying a French flag, *Redwing*'s other prize *Cantabre* had been arrested on suspicion of being a Spanish vessel with false papers. During her passage north two of her prize crew managed to break into the spirit room and in a drunken state attempted to get the slaver's crew to retake their vessel. When *Cantabre* subsequently fell in with the French frigate *Flore*, her commanding officer, Commodore Massieu, removed her British prize crew and replaced them with his own men. However, before *Cantabre* departed for Goree *Brazen*, en route from Freetown to the Bights, appeared in the offing and Willes was surprised to see a French boat with British sailors on board pulling for his vessel. The drunken members of *Cantabre*'s prize crew were flogged upon rejoining their own vessel, one receiving six dozen lashes, his compatriot three dozen. When Bullen heard about the affair he wrote a letter of complaint to Massieu but the Commodore pointed out that, as there was nothing to prove that *Cantabre* was not French, her arrest had been illegal.

On 29 January *Esk* sailed from Freetown in company with *Maidstone*. Off Whydah on 22 February Purchas's sloop boarded and examined the papers of four schooners, three from Bahia and one from Bordeaux. Following visits to Badagry and Whydah, on 3 March *Esk*'s boats, under the command of Master's Mate Richard Crawford, entered the Benin River and the following day they arrested two Brazilian vessels, the sloop *Esperanza* and the brigantine *Netuno*. Upon sighting *Esk*'s boats both these vessels had attempted to land their slaves but Crawford managed to intercept a boat from each and take twenty slaves back to *Netuno* and four back to the empty *Esperanza*. A further fifty-eight slaves from *Netuno* managed to reach the shore and disappear into the mangroves. Upon boarding the brigantine seventy-two slaves were discovered still in her hold.

On 6 March *Netuno*, under a prize crew led by Crawford, began her journey back to Freetown in company with *Esperanza*, now commanded by Midshipman George Herbert. *Netuno*'s prize crew consisted of the 16-year-old Master's Assistant Finch, five British seamen, a 17-year-old boy called Olivine and four Portuguese seamen, including the brigantine's master, Jose Gomez. The vessel was armed with two 6-pounders, six cutlasses that had been used to keep the slaves under control and a brace of pistols brought over from *Esk*. *Netuno* was a poor sailer and during the night parted company with *Esperanza*. Travelling at an average of just 20 miles a day, a fortnight later *Netuno* had reached a point roughly 300 miles south of Whydah, still some 1,000 miles away from Freetown. At around 3.00pm on 20 March she found herself being quickly overhauled by a brig on her larboard quarter. Assuming her to be another British ship, possibly *Redwing*, Crawford shortened sail to allow her to catch up. Gomez, however was not so sure of the stranger's identity and repeatedly exclaimed 'Pirate, pirate!'

By 3.50pm the stranger was now two miles astern of *Netuno* but had still not hoisted her colours. Ten minutes later she fired two guns which Crawford took to be a recognition signal. Hoisting his own colours, Crawford took in more sail and stood towards the brig. As the two vessels converged, Crawford took a closer look at the stranger through his glass and grew concerned with her overall dirty appearance and the apparent lack of discipline of the men on her deck. With Gomez's words ringing in his ears he suddenly became very concerned and belatedly ordered all sail set. However, just as he did so the brig ran up French colours, opened her gun ports and fired several shots across *Netuno*'s bows. She then hailed the British prize and ordered her to heave to and to wait for a boat to come alongside. Crawford now ordered his 6-pounders to be loaded and made ready. When the boat came alongside *Netuno* the man at her tiller began shouting to Crawford in a mixture of Spanish and broken English and a heated argument now ensued, with neither side understanding the other until one of the other men in the boat, an Irishman, began acting as interpreter and Crawford realised that the man at the tiller, evidently the other ship's master, wanted him to go aboard his brig with *Netuno*'s papers. Pointing to his ensign, Crawford explained that his vessel was a British prize and that he suspected the other vessel not to be a French man-of-war. When the Spaniard replied menacingly that his vessel was the Havana brig *Caroline* and ordered his men to board *Netuno*, Crawford, warning against any such action, told *Caroline*'s master he would need to go below to fetch his vessel's papers. Returning to the gangway hiding the pistols brought over from *Esk* behind his back, Crawford asked several times if the Spanish master intended to leave without having him in the boat. Increasingly alarmed by his aggressive behaviour, Crawford shot the master and the bow-man, who had been holding on to *Netuno* with his boat-hook, dead. The remaining men in the boat were now ordered into the water. As the boat drifted away from *Netuno*, her crew clinging on to the gunwale, *Caroline* opened fire, raking *Netuno* from stem to stern. Most of the brigantine's crew quickly took cover, leaving just Crawford, Gomez, Olivine and a seaman named Frost on deck. Frost now took the wheel and Crawford and Olivine manned the 6-pounders whilst Gomez brought up powder and shot. The action continued for the next two hours. Most of *Caroline*'s gunfire was aimed high, cutting away *Netuno*'s sails and rigging and as *Netuno*'s guns pounded the piratical brig's hull the cries from below deck made it was clear that her cargo hold was full of slaves. A shot from *Caroline* smashed through *Netuno*'s bulwark, killing a woman on the slave deck and wounding another. Crawford was also scalped by a splinter and collapsed. Frost now left the wheel and took over the gun, firing a well-aimed shot at the brig, which proved to be the last of the battle, scattering the remaining crew members gathered on her forecastle. With twenty of her crew now dead and many more wounded, *Caroline* finally abandoned her fight with *Netuno* and hauled away on the wind, never to be seen again.

A battle-scarred *Netuno* finally arrived in Freetown on 5 May with fifty shot holes in her sails and several yards either damaged or shot away. There were just four cartridges left on board the vessel. For his gallantry in action Crawford was immediately promoted lieutenant but was invalided home with fever four months later. However, this would not be the last the Coast had seen of this enterprising young officer.

Following her return from Ascension in March *Maidstone* had visited Cape Coast, Accra, Princes and St Thomas. On 18 April she stopped the Brazilian brig *Perpetuo Defensor* south of the Line off Annobón. Bullen was certain that her 424 slaves had been loaded at Badagry, not Malembo as her master insisted, but was wary of his prize meeting the same fate as Murray's *Activo*. Luckily he discovered a British citizen named Cacow amongst the slaves who had been captured by the Ashanti and Bullen sent the prize to be tried by the Vice-Admiralty court on the charge of enslaving a British citizen. The slaves were very sickly and following her arrival in Freetown on 23 May *Perpetuo Defensor* was immediately placed under quarantine. Acting Governor Macaulay being away visiting the Gambia, the Council ordered the healthy slaves, just over half, to be put on board the colonial vessel *Susan*. In late June Macaulay returned from the Gambia and ordered *Perpetuo Defensor* to be released from quarantine and her now healthy slaves returned to the custody of the brig's Brazilian owners, who would now be responsible for their care. Concerned that the slaves still on board *Perpetuo Defensor* would be carried away, her prize master, Lieutenant Tollevey, requested habeas corpus but this was declined by the court who now ordered the slaves from *Susan* and *Perpetuo Defensor* on shore, Macaulay believing them to be free men once landed. However, the colony's Chief Justice, in a decision backed by London, ruled otherwise. Following the death of Cacow, *Perpetuo Defensor*'s case was eventually heard by the Mixed Commission which, as expected, released the Brazilian brig and also awarded costs of £351 against Bullen. However, as with *Activo*, the award for compensation was made conditional on the joint decision by the Portuguese and British governments and, as with Murray, it appears that the claim was eventually turned down.

Released from her survey work by Owen, *Swinger* had returned to the Bights to cruise between Cape St Paul's and Cape Formoso. Then, following a brief visit to the Gambia on 8 May, she sailed for home. During her three years on the Coast this little gun–brig had endured much hardship, losing a fifth of her crew to yellow fever soon after her arrival and suffering from the deaths of three commanding officers within a year. When *Swinger* was finally paid off in July 1826 the ship's company presented Lieutenant Matson with a dress sword and belt in token of their very great esteem for this popular officer.

Having rendezvoused with *Maidstone* at St Thomas *Brazen* remained in the Bights. On 17 May she arrested the Dutch schooner *La Fortuneé* with a cargo of 245 slaves following a ten-hour chase off Princes. On the approach of *Brazen*'s boats *La Fortuneé*'s master had thrown her Dutch papers overboard and raised a French ensign. The slaves were discovered in a very crowded and sickly state, with many cases of dysentery and opthalmia. Forty-six slaves died prior to her arrival in Freetown on 8 June and a further seventy-three died whist waiting for her case to come to trial, the Colonial Council taking the decision not to land the slaves following the events surrounding *Perpetuo Defensor*. The Dutch judge eventually declared that the vessel was French on account of none of the witnesses to the ditching of her Dutch papers being literate, but it came to drawing lots and the British Arbitrator decided to condemn her, just 126 slaves surviving to be emancipated.

Brazen's next arrest was the Brazilian ship *Benedicto*, boarded off Popo on 11 June. Discovered with twenty-five slaves on board, she was sent to Freetown for adjudication but the court accepted *Benedicto*'s master, Joao Sabino's, explanation that these Africans were canoemen and that he was sailing for Malembo for slaves and had only travelled north of the Line for provisions. The vessel was restored and costs of £32 were awarded. The court, however, did not grant any demurrage and its scepticism was well founded. The 'canoemen' were in fact Fantees sent to *Benedicto* as slaves by the tribal chiefs at Accra. In Freetown they were simply abandoned by the government and left to starve until Bullen put them on board *Conflict* and sent them home to Accra.

In June Owen finally completed his survey work and sailed for England with *Leven*, *Barracouta* and the schooner *Albatross*. Released from her duties with Owen's squadron, *Conflict* now sailed for the Bights via Accra. *Maidstone* had returned to Freetown via visits to Porto Praya, Portendic, the Gambia and Goree but her recently-acquired tender, *Hope*, remained in the Bights. Following a chase lasting twenty hours off Whydah she captured the Spanish schooner *Nicanor*, bound for Havana with a cargo of 174 slaves loaded at Little Popo. In condemning the schooner the Mixed Commission accepted that *Hope* was a *Maidstone* boat but asked for clarification of her status from London. Bullen was subsequently advised by Their Lordships that no vessels other than Royal Navy ships duly authorised by and carrying copies of the treaties could carry out search or seizure operations. In response Bullen argued that *Hope* was a *Maidstone* boat, purchased as a headquarters vessel for his boats on detached duty and that he was only following a practice carried out by previous Commodores Collier and Mends.

By 2 August *Hope* had carried out more than two dozen boardings but had made no further arrests. However, returning to Whydah she found the Brazilian brig *Principe de Guinea* preparing to load slaves. With a crew of seventy-two and armed with a traversing 24-pounder long gun, four 9-pounders, two 6-pounders and two swivels, the newly launched 280-ton brig was regarded as one of the fastest slavers on the Coast. Just a few days earlier she had been stopped and boarded by *Esk* whilst empty and her crew had boasted that no cruiser would ever catch her with slaves.

Learning from a merchantman that *Principe de Guinea* was shortly expected to complete her loading, Lieutenant Tucker began cruising across her expected track and early on 5 August spotted her putting to sea. Followed a chase lasting twenty–eight hours *Hope* eventually came up with the slaver the following morning and Tucker fired several shots across her bows to bring her to. *Principe de Guinea* returned fire, beginning an action lasting two hours and forty minutes, the last hour of which was spent at close quarters. With three of his guns out of action, Tucker, faint from the loss of blood caused by a wound to his foot, finally managed to run his bowsprit across *Principe de Guinea*'s quarter and the boarders were led away by Admiralty Mate Robert Pengelly and assistant surgeon George

Williams, who had just finished operating on three men below deck. The brig was quickly secured for the loss of just three British sailors wounded to *Principe de Guinea*'s eleven killed and fifteen wounded. Five hundred and ninety slaves were discovered on board the prize, two had been killed during the action and a further twelve wounded, sixteen others had drowned attempting to swim across to *Hope*. *Principe de Guinea* was condemned by the Anglo-Portuguese court on 2 September, 579 slaves surviving to be emancipated, including one new-born baby. The brig was briefly employed as a tender to *Maidstone*, but Bullen eventually sold her to the Portuguese Government's agent at the Cape Verde Islands and she inevitably found her way back in to the Trade.

On 3 August *Atholl*'s replacement, the 28-gun Sixth Rate *North Star*, Captain Septimus Arabin, arrived at Sierra Leone from Portsmouth. *North Star* was one of a particular class of vessel that had been converted from corvettes into frigates during their construction, earning them the unfortunate moniker 'Jackass' or 'donkey frigate' as it was said they could neither fight nor run. After a brief stop off in Freetown *North Star* headed down to Cape Coast and the Bights, where she would remain for the rest of the year, sailing to Ascension in December to refit and to collect rather than deliver provisions.

Still keeping an eye on *Maidstone*'s boats, on 10 August *Esk* captured the Spanish schooner *Intrepida* 80 miles north-west of Princes with a cargo of 290 slaves crammed on board a vessel of only 100 tons but armed with five 18-pounders. Bound from the Bonny to Havana, twenty slaves had already died and a further fifty-five slaves were lost prior to her condemnation on 26 September.

On 22 August the new Governor of Sierra Leone, Major General Sir Neil Campbell, arrived in Freetown on board the frigate *Lively*, Captain William Elliot. The Dutch judge, Bonnouvrié, had returned from leave just prior to the arrival of Campbell but on 10 August fever claimed the life of Judge John Tasker Williams. However, with trouble once again brewing with the Ashanti Campbell had little time to attend to matters in Sierra Leone and on 9 September sailed for Cape Coast on board *Lively*. Upon his arrival at the Castle the new Governor learned that on 7 August the British forces had defeated the Ashanti at Katamansu near Accra. Entering the abandoned Ashanti camp following the battle, the British had discovered

MacCarthy's skull which was being used by the king as a gold-rimmed drinking cup.

In mid-September Bullen arrived at Princes from Ascension to find *Esk*, *Redwing*, *Conflict* and *Brazen* all at anchor. Two surgeons from *Redwing* and *Conflict* had died of fever and a lieutenant, another surgeon and *Conflict*'s commanding officer, John Chrystie, had been invalided home. Bullen now appointed *Brazen*'s Lieutenant Arthur Wakefield as commander of *Conflict* and promoted *Maidstone*'s Midshipman Wingrove to Lieutenant on board Willes' vessel, he then ordered *Conflict* to investigate the Bonny, Calabar and Cameroons rivers. *Brazen* was sent to the Pepper Coast and *Redwing* was despatched to the River Benin where there had been reports of piratical attacks on British merchantmen. Leaving *Esk* to look after *Maidstone*'s boats, including *Hope*, Bullen now sailed for Cape Coast to meet the new governor, and to assist in the dismantling and evacuation of the fort at Dixcove, the Government having now decided to withdraw from its unprofitable Gold Coast settlements. From Cape Coast *Maidstone* headed into the Bights, boarding nine empty Brazilian and Spanish slavers off Whydah and four vessels at Badagry. At Badagry on 17 October she chased and boarded the empty Brazilian brigantine *Hiroina* with a passport for slaving south of the Line. Having by now received authorisation to seize Brazilian slavers discovered north of the equator, regardless of whether they were loaded or empty, Bullen sent *Hiroina* to Freetown for adjudication. The Anglo-Portuguese court, operating in the absence of the Portuguese commissioners, could find no legitimate reason for the brigantine to have been at Badagry and she was duly condemned on 11 November.

On 23 September *Brazen* captured the Dutch brigantine *Snelheid* with a cargo of twenty-three slaves off St Thomas. The brigantine was discovered to have been under the command of a prize master and crew belonging to the Spanish frigate *Atalanta* which had seized the brigantine off Trade Town. When the two vessels had subsequently separated *Snelheid*'s prize crew had turned piratical, plundering an American schooner's cargo to purchase slaves. *Snelheid* had initially given chase to *Brazen*, mistaking her for a Portuguese slaver and when Willes brought her to with gunfire he discovered Dutch, French and Spanish papers on board. Following her arrival at Freetown in late October the brigantine was condemned by the Anglo-Dutch court, her slaves were emancipated and her prize master and crew tried for piracy. On 22 October *Brazen* departed Freetown for home, ending a twelve-month deployment on the Coast that had seen the frigate capture seven slavers and emancipate 855 slaves. From May to September 1827 *Brazen* was fitted out at Chatham as an Anglican Floating Church for seamen visiting the Pool of London, spending the next eighteen years in this role before she was returned to the Navy and finally broken up in July 1848.

On 21 December *Esk*'s boats discovered the Brazilian ship *Invincival* at anchor in the Cameroons River with a recently loaded cargo of 440 slaves. A prize crew led by Lieutenant Tollevey took the overcrowded ship to Freetown but, having spent five days getting out of the river, *Invincival* was then struck twice by lightning which carried away her mainmast and split her mizzen-topmast. Four slaves were killed in these strikes and dysentery claimed the lives of further 176 during *Invincival*'s passage north, with eight more dying following her arrival at Freetown on 19 February. *Esk*'s prize was condemned by the Anglo-Portuguese court later that month and her surviving 250 slaves emancipated. Following her condemnation a sickly Lieutenant Tollevey had to be invalided home.

On 6 December *Hope* had made her third capture on behalf of her parent ship *Maidstone*, taking the Spanish schooner *Paulita* with a cargo of 221 slaves off Lagos following a chase of several hours. *Paulita* was believed to have been the same vessel that had committed several acts of piracy against vessels in the Benin River, from where she had loaded her cargo. Following her arrival in Freetown on 7 January 1827 the schooner was condemned by the Anglo-Spanish court and the 191 sickly and emaciated slaves that had survived the journey north emancipated. However, the Admiralty remained concerned about the possible illegalities surrounding the use of *Hope*.

In late December *Redwing* sailed for England to refit, arriving in Portsmouth on 27 January 1827. During her two years on the Coast Clavering's sloop had seized five vessels and released 130 slaves. It had been a hard deployment for the little brig-sloop, from her complement of 125, nine officers and fifty men had died from fever or been invalided home and one unfortunate sailor was taken by a shark whilst bathing just prior to the vessel departing the Coast.

The first three months of 1827 would prove to be a very fruitful time for *North Star*, *Esk* and *Maidstone*. Between 6 January and 22 March these three cruisers arrested thirteen vessels, freeing a total of 1,220 slaves. On 6 January *North Star* made her first arrest, boarding the empty Brazilian schooner *Eclipse* at Whydah. Her master, Joao Antonio de Fevia, claimed that he had been trading cloth at Elmina but there was no evidence of any such transaction having taken place. It being apparent that *Eclipse* had landed slaves at Whydah and Popo, Arabin arrested the schooner and sent her to Freetown. A precedent having now been set by the case of *Hiroina*, the Anglo-Portuguese court at Freetown had no hesitation in condemning *North Star*'s prize. Three days later *Esk* arrested the Dutch brig *Lynx* with a cargo of 265 slaves off Princes. The vessel was most likely French in origin but her decision to sail under Dutch colours proved to be her downfall and she was condemned by the Anglo-Dutch Mixed Commission, 251 slaves surviving to be emancipated.

On 31 January *North Star*'s boats seized the Spanish schooner *Emilia* with a cargo of 282 slaves in the Bonny. Prior to sending the vessel for condemnation Arabin removed three unsecured casks of spirits from the main deck to prevent the prize crew from getting drunk and he also removed a spare sail to provide somewhere for the eighteen members of *Emilia*'s crew that had been transferred to *North Star* to sleep on. *Emilia* was a very overcrowded and sickly vessel and 105 slaves died during the five-week voyage to Freetown. Arabin was subsequently accused of breaking bulk by the schooner's master, Manuel Prendez, but the Anglo-Spanish Mixed Commission took no further action against *North Star*'s commander who purchased *Emilia* as tender for his vessel following her condemnation, renaming her *Little Bear*.

On 6 February *Esk* intercepted the Brazilian schooner *Venus* roughly 200 miles south-west of Cape Formoso, discovering her to be carrying a cargo of 191 slaves loaded at Whydah, contrary to her passport for Malembo. The following day *North Star*'s boats arrested the Spanish schooner *Fama* in the Old Calabar. A vessel of just 33 tons, 100 slaves were discovered crowded together on her slave deck. Her crew of twelve were in an emaciated state and her master, Jose Miguel, asked to be transferred to the first passing Spanish vessel along with his men rather than remain on board the schooner for her journey back to Freetown. To remove a source of potential trouble and also to increase space in the vessel for the slaves, Arabin agreed to this request although it ran contrary to the requirements of the treaties. *Fama* was condemned by the Anglo-Spanish court on 16 March, a day after the condemnation of *Esk*'s prize *Venus* by the Anglo-Portuguese court, a total of 283 slaves survived to be emancipated from these prizes.

Continuing the Squadron's run of good fortune, on 8 February *Esk*, still cruising off Princes, boarded the Brazilian schooner *Dos Amigos* with a cargo of 317 slaves loaded at Badagry. As a result of his earlier captures Purchas had no officer left on board to perform the duties of prize master but his purser offered to act in this capacity and *Esk* followed her prize to Freetown prior to a visit to Portendic. *North Star* made two further captures in March, taking the Brazilian brigantine *Conceição de Marie* off Whydah on the fourth of the month and another Brazilian vessel, the brig *Silveirinha*, at the entrance to the Old Calabar on 12 March. *Conceição de Marie* had a cargo of 232 slaves that had only just been loaded and *Silveirinha*, a vessel boarded whilst empty by both *Maidstone* and *Esk* in late 1826, was discovered with a cargo of 266 slaves loaded a day previously. *Silveirinha*'s master died a day after her capture and the customary lengthy journey back to Freetown against the wind and tides cost the lives of fifty-seven of her slaves to dysentery. *Conceição de Marie*'s sickly master, de Souza, had asked to remain at Whydah and he had been landed on 5 March. The brigantine arrived in Freetown on 15 April having lost thirty-five of her slaves. She was condemned by the Anglo-Portuguese court on 15 May. *Silveirinha* arrived at Freetown on 31 May and was condemned by the Anglo-Portuguese court on 18 May. Four hundred and seven slaves survived to be emancipated from these two vessels.

Following visits the Cape Verde Islands and Bathurst at the start of the year *Maidstone* headed into the Bights via Cape Coast where Bullen now received a request from the Governor of Elmina to visit Accra where he alleged that both Dutch and British traders were openly slaving. Having looked in on Accra, *Maidstone* sailed from there on 11 March and in the space of four days she seized five empty Brazilian vessels operating in the Bights, all of which had previously been boarded by *North Star*. Her first capture was the brig *Trajano*, taken off Whydah. On 12 March another brig, *Venturosa*, and the schooner *Carlotta* were both taken off Badagry and the schooner *Tenterdora* was seized near Porto Novo. Arriving off Lagos the brigantine *Providencia* was arrested on 16 March. All five prizes were condemned by the Anglo-Portuguese court on 30 April following the precedent set by *Hiroina*. After this flurry of arrests *Maidstone* had to wait just under a week before her next capture, seizing the empty Brazilian sloop *Conceição Paquete do Rio* at the mouth of the Benin River on 22 March, Her master, Francisco d'Almeida, claimed she was there to plug a leak in her hull which, on examination by *Maidstone*'s carpenter, proved to be non-existent. She was condemned by the Anglo-Portuguese court on 15 May.

On 28 February *Conflict* had arrived at Accra from Freetown to find the Brazilian schooner *Independencia* at anchor in the roads. Although empty, the vessel had a passport to take 502 slaves from Malembo and apparently had been at Accra since 15 February, intending to purchase slaves from Dutch traders. Part of her trade cargo had already been landed and she was carrying a large amount of farina and jerked beef, well-known slave provisions. In passing its judgement on this vessel the Anglo-Portuguese court ignored the claims of her master, Jacinto Carniero, that his schooner had been at Accra to mend a leak and that her arrest was illegal because she was under the protection of the Dutch fort there. She was condemned on 15 May, the same day as *Conceição Paquete do Rio*.

Upon her return to Britain in July 1826 *Swinger*'s officers and company had been turned over to the 12-gun brig *Clinker* which arrived in Freetown in mid-February following a visit to Bathurst. Matson now took his new command to Ascension to deliver provisions before beginning an uneventful cruise of the Bights, having to wait over a month before making his one and only capture of the year, boarding the empty Brazilian brigantine *Copioba* at anchor near Awey on 15 May.

Following *Conflict*'s arrival at Freetown from the Gallinas in February her commanding officer received a request from the Governor to investigate the northern rivers. Wakefield's response was to inform Campbell that the Squadron received so many reports of slavers operating in these rivers that to act on every one would make the Commodore's dispositions useless. Having now been informed by Matson that his orders prevented him from investigating the Pongas prior to his departure for Ascension, Campbell wrote to the Colonial Office to complain of a general lack of naval cooperation and requested that a cruiser be stationed permanently between Sierra Leone and the Gambia.

In early April *North Star* had returned to Freetown from Ascension to collect her prize crews. Receiving information from the Governor that a vessel had recently left port with several slaves from St Paul de Loando concealed on board, Arabin sent his newly-acquired tender, now under the command of Lieutenant Thomas Crofton, to chase after her. On 19 April *Little Bear* boarded the Brazilian schooner *Tres Amigos* off the Cape Verde Islands and discovered three young female slaves hidden under the stove, close to suffocation. The schooner's master, Manoel dos Santos Pirez, offered Crofton his gold watch and £50 not to be detained, the boatswain declaring that Pirez would have thrown the girls overboard given half the chance. *Tres Amigos* was condemned to *Little Bear*'s parent vessel on 15 May.

On 10 April *Maidstone* sent her boats into the Old Calabar. As the frigate lay offshore she spotted a suspicious sail in the direction of Fernando Po and gave chase in light winds. Contact was lost after sunset around 7.00pm but was regained under moonlight three hours later at a distance of seven to eight miles. Bullen sent away his cutter and gig under the command of First Lieutenant Charles Morton, who, after several hours' hard pull, boarded the Brazilian brigantine *Creola* with a cargo of 308 slaves crammed into her slave deck. The brigantine had the usual passport from Brazil for a voyage to Cabinda, but in *Creola*'s case it only allowed for a cargo of 214 slaves. Having collected his boats from the Old Calabar, Bullen ordered Morton to wait for him at Princes whilst he sailed to Accra for provisions. Following their rendezvous at Princes on 6 May *Maidstone* sailed for Freetown with the extremely unseaworthy *Creola* now under tow, the brigantine losing nineteen of her slaves prior to her arrival at Freetown on 23 May.

The following day saw the arrival of the 38-gun frigate *Sybille*, Commodore Francis Augustus Collier CB, from Portsmouth. On 1 June Bullen handed over command of the Squadron to Collier and *Maidstone* and *Sybille* sailed in company for Cape Coast, arriving their on 26 June. From Cape Coast *Maidstone* called at Accra for repairs to her rigging and bowsprit then sailed for England via Ascension where, on 21 July, she picked up the Squadron's invalids, by which time Bullen himself was recovering from an attack of fever. *Maidstone* arrived at Portsmouth on 29 August and was paid off. Together with her tender, *Hope*, she had been responsible for the capture of seventeen vessels and the release of 2,485 slaves during her three-year, three-month deployment on the Coast. Under Bullen's command the Squadron had captured of a total of fifty-eight slave vessels, liberating around 4,500 slaves, still a drop in the ocean compared to the total number of Africans awaiting transportation from the Coast, estimated by one British officer to be around 30,000.

Chapter 7

The *Black Joke*: June 1827–December 1829

Thee son of Admiral Sir George Collier, Francis Augustus Collier had joined the Navy in 1794 aged just 11 and had served as a midshipman on board Nelson's flagship *Vanguard* at the Battle of the Nile. He made post in 1808 and ten years later joined the East Indies Station, taking command of a squadron tasked with destroying the pirate bases in the Persian Gulf that had been molesting British shipping in the region. This successful campaign resulted in the signing of a treaty that eliminated the pirates as a threat to the East India Company. Raising his flag on board *Sybille* at Portsmouth in December 1826, Collier's orders remained identical to those of his predecessor Bullen, namely to protect British settlements and trade and to carry out anti-slavery operations.

On 13 June 1827 *Redwing*, still with Douglas Clavering in command, returned to the Coast from her refit in England. Three days later she departed Freetown for Accra, never to be seen again. That same month *Conflict* sailed to Ascension for provisions, returning to the Bights in July to allow *Clinker* to sail to St Helena then Ascension. *Conflict* would remain in the Bights until the end of September when a badly sprung mainmast forced a return home. It was around this time that the Squadron began receiving reports that wreckage had been washed ashore at Matacong near the Isles de Los bearing *Redwing*'s name, although there was no definite news of the sloop's fate. In August *Esk* returned to the Bights from Ascension, having delivered invalids to the island, joining *Sybille* which was cruising to the north-west of Princes. *North Star* remained in Portendic until August when the last gum traders of the season had departed and, having been released from this duty, headed south to patrol the rivers between the Gambia and Cape Mount.

Whilst off the River Sesters Arabin learned that a brig out of Havana known to have previously robbed two American vessels at Mesurado was now at the Gallinas to buy slaves. Positioning his frigate off the mouth of the river, *North Star*'s commander waited for the brig which he finally spotted putting to sea on 31 October. The winds were too light for *North Star* to give chase so Arabin sent his boats away, commanded by Lieutenant Boultbee. The chase went on into the night and the boats lost sight of the brig but regained her the following morning. In the face of musket fire Boultbee led the boarding party over the brig's bows and quickly gained possession. The brig, *Gallo*, was sent to Mesurado, where it soon became clear that she was not the vessel that had plundered the Americans and so Arabin released her, having first given her master a certificate of the boarding and made a note of the incident in *Gallo*'s log.

Prior to Bullen's return home he had sold *Maidstone*'s tender *Hope* to a resident of Princes who had then sent her to Bahia where she obtained Brazilian papers. She would return to the Coast on a slaving voyage in April 1828, sailing under the name *Esperanza*. Governor Campbell had already voiced his concerns over vessels previously acting as tenders for the Squadron subsequently finding their way back in to the Trade and in late 1827 the Admiralty had instructed Collier to dissuade his officers from purchasing tenders and to ensure that existing vessels were only resold into the service. By this time Collier, impressed by *Hope*'s record, had already requested permission to purchase his own tender and had been informed by the Admiralty that if he could find one at a reasonable price the relevant papers authorising her to act against the slavers would be sent out to him.

On 6 September *Sybille* was cruising off Lagos, when, a little after midnight, she spotted a brig off her lee bow. Crowding sail she gave chase, and the stranger tried to cross in front of *Sybille*'s bows to get to windward of the frigate, putting her within range of Collier's bow chasers. After several well directed rounds the brig quickly surrendered. She proved to be the American-built, Brazilian-flagged vessel *Henriqueta*, one of the most notorious slavers operating on the Coast. Armed with one long 18-pounder mounted on a swivel and one long 18-pounder carronade, this graceful-looking vessel was on her tenth voyage in three years between Bahia and the Coast, having already transported over 3,000 Africans, earning her owner, Jose de Cerquiera Lima, a profit of £80,000. When she was boarded she was discovered to have a cargo of 569 slaves loaded just hours earlier at Lagos.

Henriqueta arrived in Freetown on 29 September under the command of Admiralty Mate Frederick Mather, having lost twenty-seven slaves during her journey north. By the time of her eventual condemnation on

29 October two of her prize crew had contracted fever, though one was saved by *Sybille*'s surgeon, Robert McKinnel, using large doses of quinine. A visitor to Freetown, James Holman, described conditions on board the slaver soon after her arrival in Freetown. 'The spectacle was humiliating in every sense and the immediate effect upon the olfactory nerves was excessively disagreeable and oppressive … the pressure of this dense mass of human beings was suffocating, and the crowd was so great that one poor slave girl who had fallen overboard during the night, on the voyage, was never missed until the following morning.'[1]

Sybille remained in the Bights and on 12 October captured the Brazilian schooner *Dianna* 180 miles west of Princes. During the chase the slaver had thrown some of her papers overboard but the Mixed Commission accepted that her eighty-seven slaves had been loaded at Benin and in early December she was condemned. *Sybille* sailed from the Bights towards the end of November, arriving at Sierra Leone on 12 December. Suitably impressed by his fast-sailing prize *Henriqueta*, on 31 December Collier wrote to the Admiralty to report that for £900 he had purchased her as tender for *Sybille*. In recognition of his capture of *Principe de Guinea*, Collier gave command of the brig to Lieutenant William Turner, manned her with fifty-five of his best men and on the advice of the commissioners at Freetown gave her one of *Sybille*'s boats so that any prizes she took would be condemned to her parent vessel. Renamed *Black Joke*, most likely after the song of the same name, she would soon earn a reputation as one of the most feared cruisers in the West Africa Squadron.

In September Captain Owen returned to the Coast on board the frigate *Eden*. Sailing in company with the transport *Diadem* he had been tasked with establishing a settlement at Fernando Po. Situated in the Bights with plentiful supplies of provisions and fresh water, this Spanish-owned island was considered a much more suitable base of operations for the Squadron than the distant, fever-ridden Freetown. Moving the Mixed Commission courts there would also spare captured vessels the long journey north, saving the lives of both British seamen and African slaves. Following his arrival at Freetown Owen embarked more artificers, labourers and troops and began discussing arrangements for the new colony with Acting Governor Lieutenant Colonel Hugh Lumley (Governor Campbell had died of fever in mid-August). With its excellent anchorage the most promising site on Fernando Po for a settlement was Maidstone Bay in the north-west of the island. Here Owen would build accommodation, court houses and facilities for the resettlement of Africans liberated by the Squadron. Following his arrival at Freetown Owen had discovered the steam vessel *African*, laid up and in a derelict state. Intending to use her as a transport vessel Owen had the vessel repaired, repainted and sent her to Fernando Po via Cape Coast Castle under the command of *Eden*'s Lieutenant Badgley with a complement of 300 soldiers, artisans, labourers and as much provisions as she could stow. *Eden* now sailed for Fernando Po in company with *Diadem*, arriving there in late October.

As he had done so with Bullen before, Owen would prove to be a thorn in the new commander-in-chief's side. The two men had been told not to interfere with each other's work but it remained unclear whether Owen was responsible to the Colonial Office or the Admiralty. He had been specifically ordered not to go after the slavers but had given *Eden*'s jolly boat to *African* and on 23 October Badgley detained the empty Brazilian sumaca *Soa João Voador* off Quitta Fort and the following day he arrested another empty Brazilian vessel, *Vencedora*, further east off Whydah. Both these vessels were equipped for slaving but Badgley failed to gain clear evidence of their illegal activities and were both released by the Mixed Commission with costs awarded against Owen. The court did, however, reject *Soa João Voador*'s master's claim for demurrage pointing out that if, as he insisted, his vessel was trading in palm oil, then it should not have been carrying slaving equipment.

Badgley arrived at Fernando Po on 31 October, four days after Owen, who had already bestowed royal names on several prominent features in the vicinity of Clarence Cove, Point William and Point Adelaide, and decided on a name, Clarence, for the capital he would build. Owen now requested that Collier send supplies down to the island. Reminding *Eden*'s captain of his instructions not to interfere with the operations of the Squadron, Collier informed Owen that *North Star* and *Esk* would deliver supplies in passing. Having purchased several plots of land from the local chiefs, on 25 December Owen took formal possession of the settlement in a ceremony that involved a march down to the flagstaff at Point William.

In December the 18-gun ship-sloop *Primrose*, Commander Thomas Griffinhoofe, and the 12-gun brig *Plumper*, Lieutenant Edward Medley, arrived on the Coast from England. Replacements for *Esk*, which was due to return home, and *Conflict*, *Plumper* had last been refitted in 1820 and appeared on the Coast in a most defective state, with many of her timbers rotten through and as a result was said to have sailed 'most wretchedly'.[2] Medley complained and found difficulties with everything and seemed unable to carry out his duties correctly, failing to water his vessel, perform regular gunnery practice or properly care for his sick. Collier, suffering from a bout of fever that did nothing to help his ill disposition towards *Plumper* and her commanding officer, thought her the 'most useless and inefficient vessel'[3] that he had ever encountered. The Commodore was further dismayed to discover that when Medley had left his previous ship in 1815 the Admiralty had been advised that he should not, for any reason, be taken off half-pay.

In early January 1828 as a very leaky *Esk* arrived in Freetown to be caulked, *Plumper* sailed for the Gambia and *Primrose* for the Pepper Coast. As per Collier's arrangement with Owen, on 25 January *North Star* stopped off at Fernando Po with stores en route to the Bights where she would join *Clinker*. On 9 February *Esk* and *Sybille* arrived at the island from Freetown with *Primrose* following shortly behind.

Collier's visit to Fernando Po proved to be a disaster, resulting as it did in a complete breakdown of relations between commodore and captain after Collier, a stickler for regulations, began interfering in the running of Owen's squadron. Owen, who by now had spent a great deal of time studying African culture, had encouraged all his officers to grow beards as they were worn both by village elders and by the Arabs who were greatly respected amongst the various African tribes. Collier had previously complained to Owen when one of *Eden*'s officers, Lieutenant Robinson, had appeared in Freetown on board a prize sporting a full beard. Now, confronted by another bearded officer, Lieutenant Woodman of *Diadem*, who had just returned from Cape Coast Castle 'in a state of tropical undress',[4] Collier announced that he would not receive the officer in 'Fernando Po costume'[5] and so Woodman was forced to remove his beard. Returning to Clarence clean-shaven, Woodman was now greeted with disdain by the previously friendly tribal chiefs who determined that the British officer must have committed some great crime to have lost his beard. An exasperated Owen wrote to Collier to explain that Woodman was just following the example of his superior officer who had worn a beard for the last six years, but Collier was not to be placated and there now followed a series of increasingly angry letters between the two men over the issue.

Following her departure from Fernando Po *Esk* had sailed for Ascension with provisions for the garrison then departed for home, arriving in Portsmouth on 1 May. During her three years on the Coast the sloop had been responsible for the capture of nine vessels and the release of around 2,250 slaves. Collier noted that she was a particularly healthy ship, invaliding fewer men than any other vessel on the Coast over a similar period and only burying four men. Her commanding officer, William Purchas, was highly regarded by both Bullen and Collier and in recognition of his service on the Coast was promoted captain just two weeks after his arrival back in Britain.

Issued with her with her own set of anti-slaving instructions, *Sybille*'s tender *Black Joke* had sailed from Freetown under in early January 1828 in company with *Sybille* and *Esk* and on 12 January she made her first arrest, seizing the Spanish schooner *Gertrudis* with a cargo of 155 slaves following a brief chase off the Gallinas. Following her condemnation by the Mixed Commission on 2 February *Gertrudis* was sold at public auction, re-entering the Trade as the Brazilian schooner *Ceres*. Departing the northern rivers, *Black Joke* now headed down towards the Squadron's usual hunting ground of the Bights, where she spent several uneventful months hunting for slavers but making no arrests.

Sailing from Fernando Po after just a few days at the island *Sybille* headed into the Bights and on 19 March she stopped the French schooner *Fanny* 115 miles south of Cape Formoso following a chase of six hours. The schooner, which did not hoist her colours until *Sybille*'s boats were nearly alongside, had a cargo of 280 slaves loaded just a few days earlier in the Calabar. Upon examination the British discovered that very few of the schooner's crew spoke French and that her real master and mate were in fact both Danish. Collier was aware that the Calabar had recently been visited by a French cruiser that had arrested a slaver flying the White Flag of France close to where *Fanny* lay at anchor and the Commodore concluded that on that occasion the schooner must have hoisted Dutch colours to avoid arrest. As predicted, upon searching the vessel a Dutch ensign and pendant were discovered hidden under the master's bunk. The Mixed Commission could find no other evidence to prove *Fanny*'s Dutch nationality and so decided to send her to Senegal, at which point her crew, seemingly not wishing to be tried by a French court, admitted that they had destroyed the vessel's genuine Dutch papers prior to her boarding. On this evidence the schooner was condemned by the court on 22 May and her surviving 252 slaves emancipated.

In the early hours of 2 April *Black Joke* gave chase to a suspicious-looking brig about 40 miles to the south-west of Princes. At first light Turner hoisted his colours and the brig responded by raising a British flag and coming within hailing distance of *Black Joke* on her weather beam. Changing her colours to Spanish, the brig gave her name as *Providentia*. A boat crew, led by Master's Mate Harvey, went across to the vessel to check her papers and were immediately taken prisoner, the boat returning with an officer and five seamen from the brig who demanded *Black Joke*'s papers, informing Turner his vessel was suspected of being a Colombian privateer. When Turner refused to produce his commission the Spanish officer demanded that he send across fifteen of his men in exchange for fifteen of *Providentia*'s crew and sail in company with the Spanish brig to Princes or he would open fire. Turner refused this second demand and detained the Spanish officer and his boat's crew. In retaliation *Providentia* opened fire on *Black Joke* with roundshot and grape. Turner manoeuvred his vessel to lie on *Providentia*'s bow so that he could fire at the Spanish brig with his pivot-mounted gun whilst she could not bring any of her guns to bear. The action continued for two hours until *Providentia*, her sails and rigging cut to pieces, hoisted a flag of truce and both vessels exchanged their prisoners, Harvey reporting back that *Providentia* had been boarded two days previously by *Sybille* and that Collier had endorsed her Letter of Marque from the King of Spain to hunt piratical vessels. She was next seen on the Coast sailing under the name *Fama de Cadiz* and was believed to have departed the Bonny with a cargo of slaves in June 1829.

On the morning of 13 April *Sybille* gave chase to a schooner off Lagos. Following a pursuit of three hours the vessel, *Esperanza*, finally showed Brazilian colours and hove to after *Sybille* drew close enough to fire two guns at her. The vessel was empty but equipped for slaving with a passport for Cabinda and her master, Jose da Silva Rios, claimed he had been forced north of the Line having spent three days being chased by a privateer and then encountering bad weather. *Sybille*'s prize was taken to Freetown by Admiralty Mate Samuel Richardson and condemned on 26 May. *Esperanza* was in fact *Maidstone*'s ex-tender *Hope*. Following her condemnation she had been sold at public auction and re-entered the Trade for a third time, departing the Coast for Bahia later that year with a cargo of 300 slaves.

Having dropped off provisions to Clarence in January, *North Star* had spent several fruitless months cruising the Bights. Finally on 20 April she arrested the empty Brazilian brig *Terceira Rosália*, lying at anchor off Little Popo with the customary passport for loading slaves at Cabinda. The brig was sent to Freetown, arriving there in mid-May but was not condemned until 17 June. This delay was due to the illness and subsequent death of the acting judge Lieutenant Colonel Dixon Denham just weeks after his arrival in Sierra Leone. With the colony still awaiting the arrival of John Tasker Williams' permanent replacement, George Jackson, who was due out in late August, *Terceira Rosália*'s case was heard by the Chief Justice, John William Bannister, who himself had only been in Sierra Leone since early April.

On 13 May *Sybille* returned to Freetown to find *Primrose*, *Clinker* and *Plumper* all at anchor. *North Star* arrived in harbour on 27 May and there the Squadron sat, unable to return to sea again because the storehouse was empty of provisions. In early June the Spanish schooner *Emprendedor* arrived in harbour. Taken by *Eden* on 11 June she had on board three Africans who had voluntarily embarked at Little Popo on the understanding they would be landed further along the coast. However, they were discovered by *Eden*'s boarding party under a nailed-down hatch in the hold, the vessel they had taken passage in now 450 miles from their intended destination. *Eden* arrived in Freetown a few days after her prize, Owen bringing with him the news that his new establishment on Fernando Po was ready to receive the Mixed Commissions. The Colonial Secretary, Joseph Reffell, now wrote to the acting governor, Hugh Lumley, to inform him that, as no instructions had been received from London regarding the removal of the Mixed Commissions from Freetown to Fernando Po, it would be 'quite impossible for the measure to be carried into effect'.[6]

Whilst the rest of the Squadron remained immobile at Freetown due to the lack of stores, *Black Joke* continued to cruise the Bights. On 16 May she gave chase to the Brazilian brig *Vengador* 70 miles south-east of Cape St Paul's. Armed with eight guns, the slaver offered no resistance and upon boarding she was discovered to have a huge cargo of 645 slaves loaded at Lagos two days earlier. Examination of her papers revealed that she was the renamed *Principe de Guinea*, taken by *Hope* two years earlier and subsequently sold at auction, so Collier suspected, to the agent of the American consul in Rio. The brig was taken to Sierra Leone in company with *Black Joke*, losing twenty-one of her slaves during the passage north prior to her condemnation by the court on 16 June.

The supply situation at Sierra Leone having been finally sorted out, *North Star* headed up to Bathurst and *Sybille* returned to the Bights. On 29 June Collier chased a Spanish schooner off Badagry which ran herself on shore to avoid capture. The surf was too heavy for either *Sybille* or her boats to get anywhere near the schooner and she quickly broke up with the loss of all her slaves. A chase five days later ended much more successfully when *Sybille* boarded the Brazilian schooner *Josephina* 120 miles south-west of Cape Formoso with a cargo of seventy-nine slaves. Two logbooks were discovered on board, one of which belonged to the Brazilian schooner *Voador*. *Josephina*, with her obligatory passport for Cabinda, was condemned by the court on 8 August and her surviving seventy-seven slaves emancipated.

Returning to Fernando Po from Freetown, on 11 August *Eden* boarded the French-flagged brig *Henrietta* just to the north of the island with a cargo of 425 sickly slaves loaded two days previously at the Old Calabar. Both French and Spanish papers were discovered on board the brig, her crew later admitting that her real Dutch papers had been thrown overboard on the approach of *Eden*'s boats. Fifty-nine of *Henrietta*'s sickest slaves were landed at Fernando Po before the brig departed for Freetown in company with *Eden*'s tender *Horatio*. Sixty slaves were lost on the journey north and a further fifteen died prior to the vessel's condemnation on 3 October. On his return to Fernando Po Owen decided to base himself ashore and he handed temporary command of *Eden* over to Acting Captain Harrison. He also purchased another tender, the schooner *Cornelia*, which he armed with one long 7-pounder swivel gun and two 6-pounders.

Having spent the last fifteen months without a single capture to her name, in August *Clinker* took two vessels in relatively quick succession. On 5 August Matson's cruiser arrested the Brazilian brig *Clementina* in the Cameroons River with a cargo of 271 slaves. The vessel had a passport for Cabinda and Malembo but upon questioning, her master, da Silva Guimarens, freely admitted that her slaves had been loaded in the Cameroons. The vessel was sent for adjudication but by the time of her condemnation on 18 September 115 slaves had died. On 20 August *Clinker* discovered the schooner *Voador* at anchor in the Bimia, adjacent to the Cameroons. The Brazilian did not give up without a fight and several of her men and *Clinker*'s boarding party were wounded in an exchange of small arms fire, *Voador*'s master was also killed. The vessel was empty but clearly equipped for slaving and was condemned on 17 November. The Brazilian government protested against the actions of Matson's men but the Foreign Office responded that the affray was due solely to the 'violent and premeditated'[7] attack made by *Voador*'s crew upon the British boats and their attacking the British officers and seamen after the boarding had been effected.

After more than seven months cruising without success, on 28 July *Primrose* made her first capture when she stopped and boarded the Brazilian schooner *Nova Virgem* off Lagos with a cargo of 354 slaves that her master insisted had been loaded at Malembo as per the ships passport. However, from the amount of water still on board ship it was obvious that the cargo had been loaded no more than three days earlier. *Nova Virgem* was condemned on 18 September and her surviving 320 slaves emancipated. Her case had begun in the Anglo-Portuguese court but had been withdrawn and restarted in the newly established Anglo-Brazilian court which opened on 29 August. The Brazilian Commissary Judge, Joseph de Paiva, who was still yet to arrive in Freetown, complained that the court should not have begun prior to the arrival of the Brazilian commissioners but Judge Jackson pointed out that the existing treaty between Britain and Portugal had agreed that cases could be heard in the absence of Portuguese commissioners and that the Brazilian government only had itself to blame for the late arrival of its officials in Freetown. Brazil had also refused to ratify a treaty amendment covering ships equipped for slaving but not yet loaded and this would cause numerous disagreements amongst the judges of the new court. However, due to the lengthy absences of Brazilian judges and arbitrators, the majority of these cases were heard by British officials who were able to put different interpretations on the existing treaties. Jackson also had his own complaint to make to the Foreign Office regarding the recent passports issued by the Brazilian government that were now giving permission for slavers to visit Princes, St Thomas and Elmina, an excuse to visit the Bights that was a clear violation of the treaty with Brazil.

On the afternoon of 27 August *Black Joke*, now armed with an additional 12-pounder carronade on a traversing carriage, was approaching Whydah when she saw a brig and two schooners weigh anchor and sail out to meet her. Presuming them to be slavers, Turner hoisted a Brazilian flag at his main topgallant masthead and closed on one of the vessels, a heavily-armed two-topsail schooner which signalled her consorts as she beat to windward. An hour later *Black Joke* was within half-gunshot of the schooner which hove to, still displaying no colours. Turner now raised the British ensign, set his main course and hailed the schooner. At this the schooner raised French colours and tacked inshore. Turner followed her and the schooner opened fire, at the same time exchanging French for Spanish colours. She fired another round at *Black Joke* and as the other two vessels joined in the action Turner's brig returned fire. Now just half a pistol shot from the schooner, *Black Joke* hailed her three times but her only response was a larboard broadside. Unwilling to fight three against one Turner broke off the engagement and stood away from the land in the hope that the schooner would give chase.

The two-topsail schooner that *Black Joke* had fallen in with was the notorious piratical vessel *Presidente* out of Buenos Aires. Sailing under a variety of flags and armed with six 12-pounder carronades and a long 12-pounder, she was captained by an Englishman with a crew of ninety-five men of different nationalities. The vessels sailing with her were two merchantmen she had taken as prizes, a Portuguese schooner, *Marianna*, and the brig *Jossé*. As expected *Presidente* now gave chase to *Black Joke*, the schooner using every scrap of canvas she could to close the distance with Turner's brig, the other two vessels quickly falling far behind. By 4.20am *Presidente* was close enough to fire a broadside at *Black Joke*. Turner returned fire, reloaded and fired a combination of roundshot, grape and canister together with musketry. One shot struck *Presidente*'s boom, brought rigging and several sails crashing down and left the man at her wheel dead. Turner immediately ordered his boarders away, leaving just one man and two boys on board *Black Joke*. In the brief fight *Presidente* lost six men including her captain, Prouting, for the loss of just one British sailor.

Using *Presidente*'s signal book, at first light Turner made the private signal for *Jossé* to close. Once boarded her original crew were discovered in irons below deck. By now *Marianna* had disappeared over the horizon and Turner could not give chase owing to the number of prisoners on board *Black Joke*, more than double the number of his own men, that now needed to be secured. Neither *Presidente* nor *Jossé* had any slaves on board and *Presidente* was wrecked off Sherbro Island en route to Freetown, thankfully without loss of life. *Black Joke* was later awarded salvage for the recapture of *Jossé*.

Having spent a week at Bathurst, *North Star* headed back down into the Bights and whilst roughly 100 miles north-west of Princes on 8 August she boarded the empty Brazilian schooner *Sociedade*. The schooner, furnished with a passport for Malembo, was condemned by the Anglo-Brazilian Mixed Commission on 3 October. By now severe rot had been discovered in both *North Star*'s main and foremast and so she headed to Fernando Po for repairs. With the assistance of *Eden*'s men the masts were lifted out and replacements installed and rigged. *North Star* returned to sea and on 27 September arrested the slaver *L'Aigle* with a cargo of 464 slaves loaded at the Old Calabar. The prize was dispatched to Freetown under the command of Lieutenant Blythe with a master's assistant, twelve seamen and twelve Kroomen but was never heard of again. On 17 October Arabin arrested the Brazilian schooner *Santa Effigenia* 50 miles south of Badagry. Her master, Matthias Baptista de Carvalho, admitted he had loaded his cargo of 218 slaves at Badagry and the vessel was condemned by the court in late November. Remarkably only one slave died on the journey to Freetown, an African already seriously ill at the time of the capture, and the court thanked the prize master, Mr Stone, for his strict observance of cleanliness on board the schooner.

In October the barely seaworthy *Plumper* somehow managed to make it into the Bights and on 18 October she boarded the Brazilian sloop *Minerva da Conceição* with a cargo of 105 slaves loaded at Lagos. The sloop's master, Manuel Francisco da Silva Araujo, had been in command of *Conceição Paquete do Rio*, boarded by *Maidstone* in March 1827 and it was subsequently concluded by the court in Freetown that both vessels had the same owner. Following *Minerva da Conceição*'s condemnation and the emancipation of her eighty-two surviving slaves in mid-December, Jackson wrote to the Foreign Office to complain that punishments for convicted slavers as prescribed in the anti-slaving treaties were being carried out far too rarely, leading to a large number of slaver masters returning to the Trade.

On 14 September *Primrose* seized the Brazilian schooner *Zepherina* with a cargo of 218 slaves 30 miles south of Lagos. The vessel, stopped by *North Star* whilst empty five weeks earlier, had a passport for Cabinda that allowed her to call at Elmina and the Bights Islands. *Black Joke* had been in company with *Primrose* at the time of the capture but the court saw *Zepherina* solely as Griffinhoofe's prize and condemned the schooner to his cruiser on 9 December.

On 30 October *North Star*'s tender *Little Bear* made two arrests whilst operating in the Cameroons River. The Brazilian vessel *Estrella do Mar* had no cargo on board and, although her master claimed she was in the river for repairs, her papers did not appear in order. Later that day *North Star*'s tender arrested the Brazilian schooner *Arcenia* with a cargo of 448 slaves, 179 of whom died on the passage north to Freetown. On 1 November *North Star* seized the Spanish schooner *Campeadora* which ran aground on the Bonny bar following a brief chase. She had a cargo of 381 slaves loaded just two days previously in the Bonny but most of her provisions had been thrown overboard during the chase and so Arabin took the schooner to Fernando Po instead of risking the lengthy journey north to Sierra Leone. Following her arrival at Clarence Cove Owen agreed to take 150 of *Campeadora*'s slaves and the schooner departed for Freetown where she was condemned on the same day as *Arcenia*, 18 December. *Little Bear*'s other prize, *Estrella do Mar*, was condemned to her parent ship the following day.

On 14 November a newly-promoted Commander Turner handed over command of *Black Joke* to *Sybille*'s Lieutenant Henry Downes and sailed for England on board *Plumper* along with the survivors from *Presidente* who were due to stand trial in Admiralty Courts on charges of piracy, robbery and plunder. *Presidente*'s men claimed they had been authorised by the government of Buenos Aires to seek out and attack Brazilian vessels and as Britain had recognised Buenos Aires' independence from Spain, *Presidente*'s letter of marque should be regarded as valid. The prisoners also claimed that they believed *Josée* to be a Brazilian vessel and her captain, Juan Maria Evangelista, unhelpfully refused to give evidence unless he was suitably remunerated. With no evidence to counter the defendant's claims, the charges were dropped and all thirty-eight men released.

On 26 August *Esk*'s replacement, the 22-gun ship-sloop *Medina*, Commander William Benjamin Suckling, had arrived in Freetown from the Cape Verde Islands, bringing with her the new British Commissary Judge, George Jackson. Ordered to sail for Ascension via Fernando Po, on 3 October *Medina* arrested the Brazilian schooner *Penha da Franca* with a cargo of 184 slaves just north of the Line. Her master, José Ferreira da

Maia, claimed his cargo had been loaded at Ambriz and that he had been forced north by adverse winds but this was soon disproved by papers found on board the schooner which stated that her slaves were purchased at Lagos. *Penha da Franca* was condemned by the Anglo-Brazilian Mixed Commission in mid-December and her surviving 169 slaves released.

Following her visit to Ascension *Medina* headed north and on 12 November she stopped the Spanish brig *El Juan* 180 miles south-west of Princes, discovering on board 407 slaves loaded two weeks earlier at the Bonny. During the chase the brig had heeled so far over that the frightened slaves had rushed the main hatchway, forcing the crew to fire at them through the grating, causing carnage on the slave deck. *El Juan* was condemned by the Anglo-Spanish court on 19 December and the 378 slaves who had survived the slaughter and the passage north emancipated.

There was yet more success for *Medina* later that month when on 23 November she stopped the schooner *Triumpho* about 90 miles south-east of Cape Formoso. Another Brazilian vessel with a passport for Cabinda, she was discovered with a cargo of 127 slaves. Whilst both *Triumpho*'s master and first mate insisted her cargo had been loaded at Cabinda, two of her crew members told a different story, explaining that the slaves had been taken from the River Benin. This was confirmed by the Overseer of Slaves at Freetown, a freed African from the Benin named Ogoo who spoke to the slaves when they were landed. *Triumpho* was condemned in mid-January 1829 and her surviving 122 slaves released.

Although he had been ordered not to interfere in the work of the Squadron, Owen continued to hunt for the slavers operating in the Bights, acquiring several vessels to act as tenders for *Eden*. On 16 October the schooner *Cornelia* had boarded a suspected pirate vessel in the Old Calabar but found her to be carrying French papers and so *Cornelia*'s commanding officer, Lieutenant Henry Kellet, took no action. The vessel, *Venus*, was well known to Owen and when, a month later, he heard that she was back in the Old Calabar, he sent *Cornelia*, now commanded by Acting Lieutenant Mercer, to arrest her. On 16 November Mercer spotted *Venus* at anchor, ran his ship close alongside her, sent his boarders away and within three minutes had taken possession of the vessel but not before her master and some of her officers had fled ashore. Seventeen of *Venus*'s crew were sent to England to stand trial. However, the court judged that their vessel was neither a slaver nor pirate and that the ten Africans found on board after her boarding were in fact crew members.

Another of Owen's tenders, *Portia*, commanded by *Eden*'s Master, Mr Simmons, had been sent to the Old Calabar to collect bullocks and was crossing the river bar on 18 December when she observed a brig which had been attempting to put to sea suddenly bear up and attempt to return to the river. Alerted by her suspicious behaviour, Simmons boarded the vessel, discovering her to be the Spanish brig *Bolivar*, her eight guns primed and ready for action. Simmons sent *Bolivar*'s master across to *Eden* and secured the remaining crew of forty-six below with her cargo of 426 slaves. Rather than send *Bolivar*'s master to Sierra Leone, Owen detained him at Clarence and landed the slaves until suitable transport became available to send them north.

It was around this time that the Admiralty received an anonymous letter alleging serious misconduct by Owen regarding the various seizures made by *Eden* and her tenders which, it was claimed, had been in contravention of the various treaties, as vessels were being condemned not by the Mixed Commissions but by Admiralty courts, which were only authorised to try vessels for acts of piracy. There were also complaints against the illegal landing of slaves and the flogging of black soldiers without due process. Defending his position, Owen claimed that certain members of the Freetown administration did not want the Mixed Commissions moved to Fernando Po and had set out to discredit him and he went on to publicly attack the Colonial Secretary, Reffell. By now Owen's behaviour and his often flagrant disregard for the orders of his immediate superiors had been made known to the Colonial Secretary and Owen was asked to explain himself. Soon after he was offered, but turned down, the position of Superintendent of Fernando Po at the Colonial Office.

In mid-September Collier, suffering from another bout of fever, had sailed to St Helena via Ascension, both to recover his own health and that of his men and to also allow his ship to undergo a refit. *Sybille* returned to Freetown on 30 November and from there sailed for her usual hunting ground of the Bights, where she remained until the end of the year, visiting Fernando Po in early January 1829. In the harbour at Clarence was *Clinker*, minus her mainmast which was being replaced. Also at anchor were two Dutch vessels seized by *Cornelia* off the Old Calabar on 6 January. The brig *Jules* had been discovered with a cargo of 220 slaves and the schooner

La Jeune Eugenie with fifty. *Jules* was a fast new vessel and Collier manned her from *Sybille*, intending to purchase her upon her arrival at Freetown. However, the prize masters appointed to these vessels by Owen for their passage north had not been present at their captures and were therefore unable to bear witness to their vessels arrests or to vouch for the authenticity of their papers. In consequence the commissioners at Freetown found they could not bring proceedings against either vessel and both were released. Unsuccessful in his attempt to acquire *Jules* as tender to *Sybille*, Collier now turned his attention to *Arcenia*, taken by *Little Bear* in October 1828, which he purchased and renamed *Paul Pry*, possibly after a play of the same name based on a nosy, interfering busybody (she was known on her lower deck as 'Peeping Tom' or 'Little Inquisitive'), placing her under the command of Lieutenant Edward Harvey.

During the course of 1828 the Squadron had arrested twenty-one slavers, with *Eden* and her tenders adding a further nine vessels to this total. With the assistance of Owen 4,476 slaves had been liberated. The Squadron had lost one vessel, *Redwing*, which was later discovered to have been destroyed by lightning during a thunderstorm whilst chasing slavers off the Isles de Los, resulting in the loss of her entire crew of 125. A further eighty-one men had died from disease out of a total Squadron strength of around 960, more than double the losses of the previous year. Collier began 1829 with five cruisers at his disposal. *Sybille*, *North Star* and *Medina* remained in the Bights with *Sybille*'s tender *Black Joke*. *Primrose* was off cruising to windward whilst *Clinker* was at Fernando Po having her mainmast replaced with the assistance of *Eden*'s carpenters.

Whilst cruising off Cape Formoso on 7 January *Medina* boarded the Brazilian schooner *Bella Eliza*, discovering a cargo of 232 slaves that her master, Gaspar dos Reis do Fonseca, freely admitted had been loaded at Lagos four days earlier. The schooner had the usual passport for Cabinda that also allowed her to touch at the Guinea Coast, Princes and St Thomas. Also discovered on board *Bella Eliza* was the mate from *Minerva da Conceição*, captured by *Plumper* off Lagos on 17 October. *Medina*'s prize was condemned on 27 February and her surviving 215 slaves emancipated

Anchoring off the Cacheau in early January, *Primrose* sent her boats, commanded by First Lieutenant Edward Parrey, to investigate the river. On 15 January Parrey seized the Portuguese brig *Vingador* with a cargo of

223 slaves loaded four days previously. The following day Parrey boarded the Portuguese galliot *Aurelia* whilst she was still loading her cargo. A further examination of the river revealed two schooners, one French, one Spanish, both awaiting their cargoes. Parrey's boats also discovered the English merchant brig *Lochiel*, her crew all dead from disease below deck. There was no pilot to put on board the brig but the merchantman and the two prizes were all successfully brought out of the river. *Vingador* was condemned by the Anglo-Portuguese court on 3 March and her surviving 220 slaves emancipated. Of the thirty-eight Africans discovered on board *Aurelia* it was eventually decided by the court that nine were bona fide servants. The remaining twenty-nine were declared to be slaves and were released. *Primrose* was also awarded salvage of £109 for *Lochiel*.

Returning from her cruise to windward *Primrose* sent her boats, once again commanded by Parrey, to look into the Rio Nunez. On 31 January they boarded the Cuban schooner *Favorite*, which was waiting to load a cargo of 120 slaves from the nearby factory. *Favorite*'s master, Antonio Belancent, casually informed Parrey he had been expecting *Primrose*'s arrival for the last fortnight, having been informed by a French schooner that she was off the coast. *Favorite*'s watering had been completed and her slave deck laid. However, as there was no Equipment Clause in the treaty with Spain she could not be detained. A further five schooners were discovered at anchor off the Gallinas, all awaiting their cargoes. This, along with *Primrose*'s recent captures in the Nunez and Cacheau and the capture of three slavers in the Pongas by a French cruiser, fed a growing concern in Freetown that slaving was once again breaking out in the north.

Arriving off Lagos on 15 January *Black Joke* discovered five Brazilian-flagged vessels at anchor. Learning that one of these was almost ready to load her cargo, Downes stood offshore waiting for her to put to sea. On the morning of 31 January a lookout on *Black Joke* reported that he had spotted a brig to the south on a bearing east-south-east. The chase began in light winds and by 9.30am Downes had ordered the sweeps out, the pursuit eventually lasting eight hours. By 5.45pm the brig, now flying Spanish colours, was finally in range and *Black Joke* fired a shot across her bows to force her to heave to. The brig responded with two broadsides from her guns, four long 9-pounders and ten 18-pounder Govers. With the light quickly fading Downes decided to break off the engagement until the following morning, the brig employing every tactic during the night to shake off her pursuer, all to no avail.

At dawn the two vessels were within one and a half miles of one another but both becalmed. It was not until 12.30pm that a fresh breeze blew up, enabling Downes to close within grapeshot range of the brig's weather bow. The Spaniard wore and fired at *Black Joke* with her larboard guns, *Black Joke* maintaining an accurate fire, trying her best to avoid the slaves that were chained in the brig's hold whilst the Spaniard's poorly-trained gunners wasted most of their shot. Attempting to board the brig, Downes closed on his opponent but once again the wind dropped and the slaver was able to bring her larboard guns to bear, firing at *Black Joke* with both roundshot and grape. The wind finally picked up at around 3.30pm and Downes managed to position his vessel on the slaver's larboard quarter, from where he was able to rake the brig fore and aft for the next twenty minutes. At 3.50pm, her guns silenced, the brig finally hauled down her colours. *Black Joke* run alongside her and Downes sent his boarders away. The slaver proved to be *El Almirante*, a vessel out of Havana that had been boarded on previous occasions whilst empty by *Black Joke* and several of the Squadron's cruisers. However, until now she had always avoided detention. The vessel had a crew of eighty, fifteen of whom now lay dead, with a further thirteen wounded. She was carrying a cargo of 466 slaves, eleven of whom had been killed during the action. *Black Joke*'s casualties amounted to six wounded, of whom two later died. *El Almirante* arrived in Freetown on 7 March, she was condemned on 20 March and her surviving 416 slaves emancipated. Examining the damage to the prize Collier declared it the best example of British gunnery he had ever seen. Following the action Downes was promoted to commander and Admiralty Mate Thomas le Hardy, who had been wounded in the engagement, received his full promotion to lieutenant.

By now the lack of petty officers and midshipmen to take command of prizes for their passage to Freetown was becoming an increasing concern for Collier, although he was unhelpfully informed by the Admiralty that the Squadron was sufficiently manned. When Collier, who had been on the Coast for almost two years, received word that the Admiralty intended to keep his ship on station for a further two years he wrote to inform to Their Lordships that *Sybille*'s hull was in need of cleaning and recaulking and that her bowsprit also needed replacing, all of which, in his opinion, necessitated a return home. Having spent a quiet couple of months patrolling the Bights, *Sybille*'s first capture of 1829 came on 6 February when she chased and boarded the Brazilian brigantine *União* roughly 90 miles south of Cape Formoso, discovering 405 slaves crammed in to her slave deck, thirty-five more than was allowed by her imperial passport to Cabinda. When questioned, her master, André Joaquim Ferreira, admitted the slaves had been loaded at Lagos four days earlier. Several papers that Ferreira had ditched during the chase were recovered and these revealed routes taken by slavers to Havana. The letters also revealed the difficulty slavers were having in evading the Squadron's cruisers and they advised the merchants in Cuba and Brazil to only send fast and well-armed vessels to the Coast. *União* arrived in Freetown on 1 March under the command of Admiralty Mate Mr Agassiz and her surviving 366 slaves were landed. Ferreira having died, the court heard statements from *União*'s cook and her cabin boy declaring that their vessel had collected her cargo at Lagos and had visited no other place on the Coast. *União* was condemned by the Anglo-Brazilian court on 20 March and her slaves emancipated.

At Lagos Roads on 19 February *Sybille* discovered a Brazilian vessel, two French vessels and a Swede all offloading their trade cargoes. The Brazilian brig *Andorinha*, which had the usual passport for Cabinda that allowed her to touch at Gold Coast, Princes and St Thomas, was arrested and sent to Freetown under the command of *Clinker*'s acting master, Mr Browne, a supernumerary on board *Sybille* chosen by Collier due to a lack of midshipmen. En route to Freetown *Andorinha* fell in with the Brazilian brig *Donna Barbera* with a cargo of 376 slaves loaded at Lagos. Browne seized the brig, although he had no Special Instructions and therefore no authority to do so. The two prizes arrived at Freetown on 14 March, anchoring alongside *Paul Pry*. Lieutenant Harvey now went across to *Donna Barbera* in one of *Sybille*'s boats and made her his prize. The Anglo-Brazilian court took little time to declare *Andorinha*'s passport illegal and she was condemned on 11 April. *Donna Barbera* was condemned to *Sybille* two days later and her surviving 351 slaves emancipated. *Andorinha* was subsequently purchased as a tender to *Sybille* and renamed *Dallas*.

When the Treasury heard of the capture of *Donna Barbera* it immediately questioned whether or not a vessel operating so far away from its parent ship (*Sybille* had been over 1,500 miles away in the Bights at the time) could be considered part of the squadron under Collier's command. The

Admiralty now showed its by now customary lack of support for the officers and men of the Squadron. Reviewing the case in July 1831 the Judge in the High Court of Admiralty, Sir Charles Robinson, ruled that *Paul Pry* was being used by Collier as a protection to the crew of *Sybille*[8] and was not empowered to make captures under the existing treaties, therefore any bounties due on vessels she detained should go to the Crown. Collier appealed against the decision, arguing that the seizure had been made not by *Paul Pry*, but by one of *Sybille*'s boats operating on detached service. The Commodore and his men would have to wait until January 1834 for the original verdict to be overturned.

On 15 February *Cornelia* seized the Brazilian schooner *Mensageira* on the bar of the Bonny with a cargo of 353 very sickly slaves suffering from dysentery and opthalmia. The prize was taken to Fernando Po where the slaves were landed to fumigate the vessel and prepare her for the journey north. When *Mensageira* eventually sailed for Freetown 127 slaves were left behind on the island. Of the remaining slaves only 177 survived to see emancipation, a further sixty-six dying prior to the Anglo-Brazilian court reaching its decision on 24 June. *Mensageira*'s case was one of the first to be heard by the Brazilian Commissary Judge, de Paiva, following his long delayed arrival at Freetown.

On 26 February *Cornelia*'s parent ship *Eden* seized the Dutch schooner *Hirondelle* at the mouth of the Old Calabar. The vessel had a cargo of 113 slaves and was carrying false French papers. Thirty-four slaves were landed at Fernando Po along with the schooner's cargo which was sold for £1,116. *Hirondelle* arrived at Freetown on 5 May and by the time of her condemnation on 24 June twenty-four of her remaining slaves had died. In July the Mixed Commission emancipated by decree the 161 slaves from *Mensageira* and *Hirondelle* still at Fernando Po.

On 11 February *North Star* departed the Coast for Brazil via Ascension and St Helena. Arabin's vessel had been ordered to Rio to pick up the British Ambassador, Viscount Strangford, who had helped negotiate the 1826 agreement whereby the Brazilian Emperor would agree to abolish slavery by 1830 in return for British recognition of Brazilian independence from Portugal. Also taking passage on *North Star* from Rio was the Reverend Robert Walsh who had spent the last three years employed as Strangford's chaplain. *North Star*'s crew were taking various exotic animals back home from the Coast to amuse and delight friends and family at home and embarking on the frigate Walsh discovered a vessel that did not so much resemble a British man-of-war as 'a perfect menagerie, with different kinds of monkeys, parrots and paroquets … and I was awoke in the morning by such a concert of chattering and screaming'.[9] The vessel also seemed to be infested with various insects including ants, cockroaches, centipedes and a colony of spiders which Arabin had brought on board to keep the other insects under control but which now seemed to have the run of the ship. Strangford kept to himself during the passage home and Walsh's conversations with Arabin inevitably turned to the various difficulties *North Star*'s commanding officer faced in trying to operate within the ambiguously-worded treaty with Brazil. Arabin also discussed an infamous slaver, *Veloz Passagera*, an old Spanish warship that occasionally acted piratically which the Squadron had been hunting for several months. Prior to his departure from the Coast Arabin had heard that *Veloz* was about ready to depart for Havana with a cargo of slaves so he had plotted his return course from Rio with the intention of intercepting the vessel as she crossed the Atlantic.

On the morning of 6 March *Sybille* was cruising off Princes when she spotted and gave chase to a large brigantine on her weather bow. Around 1.00pm both vessels were engulfed by a fierce storm which carried away *Sybille*'s main yard. When the storm finally blew itself out there was no sign of the brigantine, leading Collier to surmise that she must have capsized and sunk along with her cargo, which he estimated to be around 400 slaves. A French frigate cruising to leeward was hailed and closed on *Sybille* to offer assistance. The frigate, flying the broad pendant of Commodore Alexis Villaret de Joyeuse, supplied a grateful Collier with a spare spar of much greater quality to anything available at either Freetown or Ascension.

At almost exactly the same time that *Sybille* was being disabled by a tornado her tender was giving chase to a suspected slaver off Lagos. When *Black Joke* boarded the Brazilian brigantine *Carolina* on 6 March she was discovered to have a cargo of 420 slaves. Her master, João Alvez da Silva Porta, initially informed Lieutenant Downes that he was bound from Lagos to Bahia but that his cargo had been loaded at Malembo. However, upon further questioning he admitted that the slaves had been loaded at Lagos just nineteen hours prior to capture. *Carolina* was condemned by the Anglo-Brazilian court on 13 March and her surviving 399 slaves emancipated. Shortly after the capture of *Carolina* Downes had to be invalided home in poor health. On his arrival in England he received his promotion to Commander in recognition of his capture of the Spanish vessel *El Almirante*.

At dawn on 23 March *Sybille* seized the Portuguese brig *Jossé* off Whydah, from where she had loaded her cargo of 182 slaves the previous day. This was the same vessel recaptured by *Black Joke* following her encounter with the piratical *Presidente* eight months earlier. A vessel with a chequered history, she had been captured by *Maidstone* in March 1827 whilst sailing under the name *Trajano* and had then been sold at public auction following her condemnation. On 24 June *Jossé* was condemned for a second time, no doubt to re-enter the Trade once again. One hundred and sixty-six slaves survived to be emancipated.

On 29 April *Sybille* arrested the Spanish schooner *Panchita* with a cargo of 292 sickly slaves loaded in the Calabar four days earlier. A prize crew commanded by Midshipman Feltham was put on board the schooner and she was sent north. By the time of her arrival in Freetown on 18 May the capital was being ravaged by yet another fever epidemic and the Liberated African Department was filled with sick. On the recommendation of Dr Boyle, Surgeon to the Mixed Commissions, twenty diseased slaves from *Panchita* were landed but it was another eleven days before the remaining healthy slaves disembarked. By now Feltham and his men had all fallen ill. Due to sickness amongst the British commissioners it was not until 24 May that *Panchita*'s case was heard and the vessel condemned and her surviving 259 slaves emancipated. By then fever had claimed the life of Midshipman Feltham and all but one of his prize crew.

On the morning of 22 May Arabin and Walsh were breakfasting together aboard *North Star*, discussing the slaver *Veloz Passagera*, when a midshipman entered the great cabin and hurriedly announced that a sail was visible to the north-west on the frigate's larboard quarter. Breakfast was abandoned and as Arabin watched the stranger, a large three-masted ship, through his spyglass, she was observed to change direction and head directly for his frigate. She maintained this course for the next hour then suddenly changed direction, running before the wind as *North Star* crowded all sail in pursuit. Arabin knew *Veloz Passagera* well. Larger than any cruiser in the Squadron other than *Sybille*, he had fallen in with her on numerous occasions and was certain this was the ship he was now chasing after. For the next four hours *Veloz* continually changed course in an attempt to evade *North Star*. When only four miles separated the two vessels and his opponent's decks were clearly visible through Arabin's spyglass, he ordered the Union Jack to be hoisted and fired a signal gun to instruct the ship to heave to. This was ignored, as was a subsequent gun, so Arabin ordered one of *North Star*'s bow chasers to be fired at the ship. The ball fell short of her stern but induced her to raise a Brazilian flag. Two more shots were fired with little effect. By now it was evening and as the wind began to drop contact was lost. Arabin maintained his course during the night and there were occasional brief glimpses of the Brazilian from the mastheads. The following morning she was sighted on the distant horizon, a mere speck standing due north, and as the wind grew Arabin resumed the chase. By midday *North Star* was close enough to fire two shots at his opponent, now confirmed as *Veloz Passagera*, and she finally hove to, ending a thirty-hour, 300-mile chase. A boat was rowed across to the ship and her master, José Barbosa, brought on board Arabin's frigate. *Veloz Passagera*'s hatches were opened and her slave cargo, around 500 completely naked men, women and children, swarmed up from the slave deck, Walsh noted, 'like bees from a hive, till the whole deck was crowded to suffocation, from stem to stern, so that it was impossible to imagine where they could all have come from, or how they could have been stowed away'.[10] On board *North Star* Barbosa, his face scarred from a previous encounter with a British cruiser, paced the deck, informing Arabin that he had loaded his cargo south of the Line and had not heaved to when ordered as he thought *North Star* to be a pirate. *Veloz*'s papers were poured over in great detail but the British could find no fault with them. The slaves were counted and fell well within the tonnage rule. Upon examining *Veloz Passagera*'s and *North Star*'s own water casks it was realised that there was not enough water to keep the slaves alive for the three-week passage to Freetown. Nine hours had passed since the slaver had been boarded and it was now night. Arabin knew that he had no justification in detaining the vessel any longer so he reluctantly allowed Barbosa to return to his ship. After their all-too-brief taste of freedom the slaves were herded back down below and the hatches battened down. It was dark when the two ships separated. The last sounds the British heard, Walsh recalled 'were the cries and shrieks of the slaves'.[11]

When *Eden* arrived at Freetown on 1 May, dirty and badly in need of fumigating, the town was already in the grip of the recent fever epidemic. Having deposited her captured slaver crews she departed Freetown in haste. On the return voyage to Fernando Po, the ship lashed by incessant rains and frequent tornadoes, twenty-seven of her men succumbed to fever, the disease claiming the lives of the surgeon, two assistant surgeons and Lieutenant Badgley. When she dropped anchor in Clarence Bay on 11 June all but three of *Eden*'s officers were either dead or sick. For a month the ship was held in quarantine by Owen, who then ordered her stores to be removed so she could be fumigated and whitewashed. Having lost a further fifty men and with forty more still in quarantine at Clarence, on 9 July *Eden* sailed for St Helena under the command of a now sick Owen. By the time of her arrival at the island on 23 August her main deck was crowded with the sick, 'some dying, some dead, some delirious, some screaming for water to quench their parching tongues, and no one to attend their call'.[12]

Sybille arrived at Fernando Po on 21 June and, seeing the sickly state of *Eden*, Collier forbade any contact with Owen's frigate. However, the following day his own ship received eight marines from a vessel recently arrived from Freetown. The first case of fever appeared on board *Sybille* on 26 June and by the time she arrived off Princes on 2 July the epidemic had taken hold, killing twenty-two of the sixty-nine men it attacked. Collier began issuing his night watch-keepers with 'blanket dress', special clothing to keep the wet air from their skin and the seamen employed ashore were issued with Peruvian bark and wine. Thankfully, as the ship headed south the fever began to abate and she arrived at Ascension on 12 September having gone three days without any deaths and with no man on her sick list. By this time the fever had also spread to *Black Joke*. Contracted through a visit to Freetown, *Sybille*'s tender would eventually lose twenty-three out of her company of forty-five men to the disease. *Primrose* and *Clinker* escaped the worst of the outbreak, largely through their commanders' insistence on issuing their boat crews and the men serving ashore with measures of wine or rum mixed with bark.

The fever epidemic rampaging through Freetown had inevitably affected the running of the various Mixed Commissions, causing delays in several sitting cases. Judge Jackson fell ill and returned home in June, leaving an equally sickly Lieutenant-Governor Major Ricketts to act as temporary judge. The Acting Arbitrator, Samuel Smart, also returned home on sick leave but was replaced by the returning Arbitrator William Smith. In July the Registrar, Joseph Reffell, died and was replaced by Thomas Cole. The Anglo-Spanish Mixed Commission was still awaiting the arrival of its

Spanish judge and by mid-July the Brazilian judge, Joseph de Paiva, was the only foreign commissioner still at Freetown.

At dawn on 26 June *Paul Pry* had spotted and given chase to a suspected slaver in the Bight of Benin. By 4.00pm she was close enough to the vessel to fire a warning shot from her single 6-pounder and to prepare for boarding. However, under the imminent threat of a storm the men were ordered to trim the sails, placing their muskets on a hatchway to carry out this task. Sails having been shortened, the men returned to collect their weapons but one sailor inadvertently picked his up by the trigger, causing it to go off. The musket discharged in to a cartridge box which set off eight of the remaining muskets on the hatchway. The master, Joseph Allen, fell to the deck with both legs shattered below the knee. The Mate, Richard Nicholls, and three other able seamen, Rook, Harrington and Lewsy, were also wounded. There was no surgeon on board *Paul Pry* so her French cook undertook the task of operating on Allen. Both shattered legs were successfully removed but it took half an hour from the removal of his left leg before Allen could summon the strength to allow the cook to proceed with the amputation of his right. *Paul Pry* now proceeded to Fernando Po where on 30 July she fell in with *Plumper*. Allen and Nicholls had recovered sufficiently to be discharged to Medley's vessel but by the end of August the three remaining injured men still on board the tender had all died, Rook from fever, Harrington from tetanus and Lewsy from dysentery. Shortly after this incident Collier sold *Paul Pry* and wrote to the Admiralty to request that Their Lordships employ Allen as a clerk in a public office.

Having been forced to retreat south due to fever, Collier had left *Medina*, now under the command of Lieutenant Edward Webb, to cruise between Cape St Paul's and Whydah. On 7 August Webb arrested the Brazilian schooner *Santo Jago* with a cargo of 209 slaves, and on 17 August, whilst off the Gabon, he stopped and boarded the Spanish schooner *Clarita*, a vessel with an imperial passport for St Thomas that had loaded a cargo of 261 slaves at the Bonny. The following day *Medina* detained another Spanish schooner, *Atafa Primo*, which had on board six Africans held in irons. *Santo Jago* was condemned by the Anglo-Brazilian court on 30 September. She was a very sickly vessel and only 148 slaves survived to see emancipation. *Clarita* was suffering from an outbreak of smallpox and by the time she arrived at Freetown on 9 September thirty-five slaves had died from the disease. Dr Boyle advised that the sixty-three remaining slaves with the disease be landed and placed in quarantine. More slaves died whilst *Clarita* was awaiting trial and only 201 survived to be emancipated when the vessel was condemned on 19 September. There was not enough evidence to prove that *Atafa Primo* was involved in slavery, indeed the six Africans swore they had gone on board the vessel of their own free will. Therefore the court declared that her capture had been illegal and ordered Webb to pay £187 in damages to her master, José Mauri.

On 6 August a largely fever free *Plumper* captured the Brazilian schooner *Ceres*, 90 miles to the east of Princes. The majority of her cargo of 279 slaves who had been loaded in the Cameroons four days previously were suffering from dysentery, caused by her master taking brackish water from the river, and she arrived at Freetown on 10 September having lost 100 slaves to the disease. By the time of her condemnation on 22 September a further fifty-one had also died. The court discovered that *Ceres* had previously appeared before the Mixed Commission as the Spanish schooner *Gertrudis*, the vessel, *Black Joke*'s first arrest, re-entering the Trade following her condemnation and auction in February 1828. Shortly after this capture *Plumper* was beset by the fever epidemic afflicting the rest of the Squadron, although details of how badly the little gun-brig was affected are sparse.

On 16 August *Sybille*'s tender *Dallas* captured the Brazilian schooner *Emilia* off Lagos with a cargo of 486 slaves loaded just a few hours earlier. The schooner had a passport for Ambriz which allowed her to load no more than 402 slaves. *Sybille*'s prize arrived at Freetown on 12 September having lost fifty-one of her cargo on her passage north. She was condemned on 22 September and her surviving 435 slaves emancipated. On 18 September *Sybille* was joined at St Helena by *Medina*. Now refitted and caulked, Collier's frigate departed the island in company with *Medina* on 25 October, Webb's sloop heading north to Sierra Leone to collect stores for the Squadron whilst *Sybille* proceeded to Ascension where there were more stores waiting for Collier's cruisers. Provisioned for the next five months, *Sybille* then departed Ascension for Fernando Po. Prior to her arrival at the island on 19 November she boarded the French-flagged *Eliza*, with a cargo of 400 slaves. Collier was convinced *Eliza* was in reality a Dutch vessel but his instructions forbade him from interfering with her. Having previously advised the Admiralty of the advantages of using St Helena as a place of respite and refit for the Squadron, on his arrival at Fernando

Po Collier now received instructions from Their Lordships not to use the aforementioned island due to its extreme distance from the Coast.

On 1 August *Atholl*, now under the command of Captain Alexander Gordon, had departed Portsmouth for the Coast via Tangier where she was to deliver the new consul-general. Whilst 130 miles west of the Isles de Los on 1 October she seized the French-flagged *La Laure*, with a cargo of 249 slaves that had been taken off a Spanish schooner wrecked in the River Shebar. *Atholl* arrived at Freetown in company with *La Laure* on 4 October and the slaves were landed. Gordon attempted to bring proceedings against his prize in the Anglo-Spanish Mixed Commission but the British commissioners would not hear the case as they felt it would set a precedent that would allow cruiser commanders to search every French-flagged vessel in search of slaves belonging to other countries. Following this setback, Gordon decided to take *La Laure* north to Goree but had only just left port with his prize when her crew informed him that their vessel was actually Spanish and that they had thrown her real papers overboard prior to her boarding. *Atholl* and *La Laure* returned to port and on 13 October the Mixed Commission began proceedings against Gordon's prize. The slaves were eventually emancipated but the court was unable to determine whether *La Laure* was indeed Spanish. Her fate remains unclear as there are conflicting reports that she was both condemned by the Vice-Admiralty court and also restored as a French vessel. On 16 October *Atholl* sailed from Freetown for her rendezvous with the rest of the Squadron in the Bights and whilst 50 miles south of Lagos on 9 December she arrested the Brazilian brigantine *Emilia*, with a cargo of 187 slaves that her master, da Silva, admitted had been shipped at Whydah a day prior to her arrest. *Emilia* arrived at Freetown on 12 January 1830 having lost sixteen slaves on her passage north. A further forty-three would die prior her eventual condemnation on 1 May.

On 31 October *Clinker* made her sole capture of the year, boarding the Brazilian brig *Emilia* 80 miles north of Princes with a cargo of 157 slaves loaded at the Bonny a few days previously. *Emilia* was a very dull sailer and it took two months for her to reach Freetown. Rather remarkably, she lost only four slaves during her voyage north. Eighty-four of *Emilia*'s most sickly slaves, suffering from opthalmia and craw-craw, were disembarked on 1 January 1830 and a further five slaves died before her eventual emancipation on 14 January. On 1 November *Dallas* captured the Brazilian schooner *Tentadora*, with a cargo of 432 slaves loaded at Lagos. The schooner had left Bahia on 17 August with a passport for Malembo but had sailed straight for Lagos, arriving there on 14 September. She was captured by *Sybille*'s tender just a day out of port. Seventy-three of her cargo died on the passage up to Sierra Leone and thirty-nine more were lost following her arrival in Freetown. She was condemned on 1 May 1830 and her surviving 320 slaves emancipated.

Downes having now been invalided home, Lieutenant Edward Parrey of *Primrose* had assumed command of *Black Joke*. Cruising north of Freetown on 11 November Parrey discovered the Spanish brigantine *Cristina* stranded on the Scarcies Bank with a cargo of 348 slaves. Slaves and crew were successfully transferred across to *Black Joke* but the brigantine resisted every effort to refloat her and eventually filled with water and sank. Prior to her eventual condemnation on 27 November *Black Joke*'s prize lost 132 slaves, over a third of her cargo, principally to smallpox.

In late November Owen returned to Fernando Po from St Helena whereupon he discovered that command of the island had now passed to Lieutenant Colonel Nicholls. Sailing from Ascension with soldiers, marines and stores, Nicholls had arrived on the island unaware of the fever epidemic ravaging the colony. All construction work soon ground to a halt as those still fit enough to use a spade were now employed full time burying the dead. By the time of Owen's return to Clarence its white population had been reduced to just four officers and two women. Owen blamed the new governor for the collapse of his colony, convinced as he was that Nicholls was leading a conspiracy against the settlement. A heated argument between the two men ended in Nicholls barricading himself in his house and threatening to shoot Owen when he attempted to break down the door. Owen had already received word that he was to sail for Brazil and on 23 February 1830 he departed the Coast for the last time. His settlement at Fernando Po struggled on for another six months before finally being abandoned, the Foreign Office conceding that there was no possibility of moving the Mixed Commissions to the island and the Admiralty considering it of no use beyond that of a useful rendezvous for the Squadron.

On 10 December *Medina* seized the Brazilian schooner *Não Landia* 110 miles south-west of the Bonny. The vessel held a passport for Cabinda but her 184 slaves had been loaded at Lagos six days earlier. *Medina*'s prize was a relatively healthy ship and arrived at Freetown on 14 January having lost just twelve of her slaves to craw-craw. However, the ongoing disruption to the Mixed Commissions meant that it was 1 May 1830 before the schooner was condemned, by which time a further thirteen slaves had died.

The final capture of the year fell to *Atholl* when she chased and arrested the brig *Louise* off the River Gabon on 31 December. Sailing under the easy to forge White Flag of France, the brig had a cargo of 226 slaves loaded in the Old Calabar. Her master having admitted that his vessel held Dutch papers that had been ditched during the chase, Gordon dispatched her to Freetown under the command of Lieutenant Ramsay. On passage north, however, Ramsay began to suspect that *Louise* was in reality French and upon her arrival at Freetown on 21 January 1830 the brig's master and mate admitted that their previous statements had been false. To avoid the repercussions of having illegally detained a French vessel, on the evening of 23 January Ramsay took *Louise* back to sea under the cover of darkness and handed her back to her master along with her cargo of 226 slaves.

Chapter 8

The Brazilian Trade:
January 1830–November 1831

The convention of November 1826 for the abolition of the African slave trade signed between London and Rio had stated that the Brazilian Trade would become illegal on 1 January 1830 and that from that date slaving under the Brazilian flag would be considered an act of piracy. (Slave vessels sailing to Brazil under Portuguese colours had been liable to detention ever since Brazil had gained independence.) The knowledge that the Trade was due to end had inevitably led to a sharp increase in the number of slaves being exported to Brazil and as the deadline approached the Brazilian government employed every tactic to gain an extension. The last official clearances for slave ships were issued on 31 October 1829 but the Brazilian envoy in London then demanded that the Royal Navy not seize ships that might have been delayed by bad weather, poor tides, a lack of wind, a shortage of provisions, sickness amongst the crews etc. Finally the Foreign Office agreed to extend the deadline to 13 March 1830. Furthermore the Squadron was also instructed that any Brazilian-flagged slave vessel discovered at sea after this date should not be considered a pirate.

In January 1830 Major Ricketts returned home in ill health to be replaced both as temporary judge and governor of Sierra Leone by Captain A.W. Fraser. Fraser would himself be replaced in April by Lieutenant Colonel Alexander Findlay, then Governor of the Gambia. The Squadron's first arrest of the year was made by *Dallas*, Harvey's tender, seizing the Brazilian schooner *Nossa Senora da Guia* off Lagos on 7 January. Fifty-eight of her cargo of 310 slaves died of smallpox on the passage to Freetown and a further fourteen died prior to the schooner's condemnation on 13 May. Not for the first time it was discovered that a quantity of stores had been removed from the prize, in this instance a large amount of cable together with a new mainsail.

The next prize fell to *Dallas*'s parent ship, *Sybille* arresting the Brazilian schooner *Umbelina* on 15 January, 150 miles south of Porto Novo, her cargo of 377 slaves having been shipped at Lagos two days previously. There was terrible loss of life on board this vessel and by the time of her arrival at Freetown on 13 March she had lost a staggering 194 slaves. When asked why the slave losses on board *Umbelina* had been so fearsome, Dr Boyle stated that it was due to the general lack of understanding amongst prize officers in how to properly care for slaves and to treat their various diseases. On 23 January *Sybille* seized yet another Brazilian slaver, the brigantine *Primeira Rosália*, with a cargo of 282 Africans that had been loaded at Lagos on 19 January. *Primeira Rosália* arrived at Freetown on 26 February, having lost thirty-one slaves on her passage north. Both prizes were condemned on 13 May, by which date *Umbelina* had lost a further twenty slaves and nine more of *Primeira Rosália*'s cargo had also died.

On 2 February *Medina* arrested the Brazilian brigantine *Nova Resolução* south of Cape St Paul's with a cargo of forty-three slaves loaded at Awey. *Medina*'s prize was condemned on 13 May but was reported to be missing sails, rope, muskets and spirits. The Foreign Office sought an explanation via the Admiralty and the prize master, Mr Pearne, explained that the various missing sails had been used to repair other sails and to turn into clothes to make the slaves decent. The rope had been used to fish the prize's foremast, the muskets had been exchanged for provisions at Kroo Sesters and the spirits had been landed at Sierra Leone but misidentified during a muster. Judge Findlay requested that from now on prize masters deliver accounts of stores expended on passage along with the other ships' papers to court.

In March *Atholl* sailed north as part of the Squadron's continuing commitment to support the gum trade at Portendic. Gordon agreed to Acting Governor Fraser's request to take 150 liberated male slaves from Sierra Leone to the Gambia but declined to take fifty women on board his already crowded ship. Following the death of Thomas Griffinhoofe at Ascension on 10 February due to a pulmonary complaint command of *Primrose* had passed to *Black Joke*'s Edward Parrey. On 24 March *Primrose* captured the Spanish schooner *Maria de la Conception* in the River Pongas with a cargo of seventy-nine slaves. Following her condemnation on 11 May *Maria de la Conception* was purchased by Commander Webb as tender to *Medina* and renamed *Puss*.

On 27 March *Clinker* seized the Spanish schooner *Altimara* whilst cruising off Cape Formoso. The vessel had a cargo of 249 slaves loaded in the River Brass. However, by the time of her eventual condemnation on 11 May fifty-one slaves had succumbed to disease. Now suffering from severe rot and with a mainmast sprung in two places, *Clinker* was due to return to England, having spent almost three years on the Coast. In that time the little gun-brig had seized five vessels and emancipated 677 slaves. In May she transported the fifty liberated female slaves from Sierra Leone to the Gambia then departed for home via Princes.

On 1 April *Black Joke*, now under the command of Acting Lieutenant William Coyde, made her first arrest in almost five months when she seized the Spanish brigantine *Manzanarez* 200 miles west of Cape Mesurado following a chase of twelve hours. The prize had a cargo of 354 slaves shipped from the Gallinas five days earlier and, although armed with three guns, she was taken relatively easily. Following her seizure the slaves rose up against their captors, injuring both several of their own number and *Black Joke*'s assistant surgeon, Mr Lane, before order was restored. *Manzanarez* arrived at Sierra Leone on 5 April and on 11 May she was condemned and her surviving 349 slaves emancipated.

Since her return from St Helena in November 1829 *Sybille* had remained a relatively healthy vessel but in late January fever returned to Collier's flagship, possibly brought on board by a native boy at Princes. The frigate had returned to sea and by early February the outbreak had become quite serious. One of those to fall victim was the popular old sailing master, Tom Collins, whose sudden death within twelve hours of falling ill greatly upset the crew. His funeral produced the unnerving and macabre spectacle of his coffin bobbing to the surface of the water just yards from the boat that had performed the burial service. Whilst *Sybille*'s crew were convinced that the fever was contagious her surgeon, McKinnel, was certain that it was not. He tried hard to convince the men but to no avail. Finally he ordered his assistant surgeon, McKechnie, to collect a pint of black vomit from the next man to be attacked. Once this had been done McKinnel returned to the half-deck, filled a glass with the vomit and drank it in front of the men, remaining on the quarterdeck for several hours in plain sight of the crew before joining the other officers for dinner later that evening still in rude health. In contrast, the seaman from whom the vomit had been collected, Riley, had died several hours earlier.

With eighty-seven of his men sick with fever, Collier once again sailed for St Helena to restore the health of his crew but by the time *Sybille* arrived at the island twenty-six men were dead. A further six men died whilst at the island so Collier put to sea on 29 March to find healthier airs, removing the boats from the booms in the waist of the ship to provide better ventilation for the gun deck. Collier had by now decided that it was time for his ship to return to England and had already summoned his most senior officer, Captain Gordon of *Atholl*, to Ascension to take over command of the Squadron. *Dallas* rejoined her parent ship at St Helena where she was sold and a refitted *Sybille* now sailed for Ascension where Collier handed over to Gordon before sailing for home, arriving at Portsmouth on 26 June after three years on the Coast.

Gordon arrived at Princes from Ascension on 14 June to find *Black Joke*, inherited by *Atholl* from *Sybille*, hauled out of the water to undergo much-needed repairs to her hull. *Medina* and *Primrose* were also at the island and, having received intelligence that the elusive *Veloz Passagera* and nine other slavers were at Whydah awaiting cargoes, Gordon dispatched *Medina* to cruise off the port. He also sent *Primrose* to Ascension with the Squadron's sick and stationed his own vessel in *Sybille*'s old hunting ground north-west of Princes, where he expected to be joined by *Clinker* and *Plumper*.

After several years' hard service on the Coast both *Plumper* and *Clinker* were now due to return home. On 12 May *Plumper*'s boats had captured the Spanish schooner *Loreto* with a cargo of 186 slaves 25 miles off Trade Town. Three slaves were killed on the passage to Freetown, lost overboard during a storm, but the remainder survived to be emancipated. *Plumper* arrived at Princes in mid-May with her new commanding officer, Lieutenant John Adams, unwell and was ordered to Ascension. *Clinker*'s replacement, the gun-brig *Conflict*, Lieutenant George Smithers, arrived at Sierra Leone on 11 July following an absence from the Coast of three years. She immediately sailed for Ascension with several of *Sybille*'s men, prize crews stranded at Sierra Leone when their vessel had departed for England. From Ascension *Conflict* headed north to the Gambia.

Cruising south of the Line following her departure from Ascension, *Primrose* had discovered the Trade there decimated. The Spanish, Portuguese and Brazilians had all destroyed their forts along the coast and the King of Loango had been forced to kill around sixty slaves for whom he could find no buyers. On 3 September *Primrose* arrived back at Princes and Parrey, who was due to return home, handed over command of his sloop to Lieutenant William Broughton. *Primrose* returned to sea and on 6 September fell in with the infamous slaver *Veloz Passagera*.

At 4.00pm *Primrose* was headed for Badagry in poor weather when she spotted a sail on the horizon and gave chase. Broughton's sloop was fast but was still unable to overhaul the stranger and eventually lost sight of her in the failing light. Thankfully around 11.30pm the moon came through a break in the clouds and the chase, a large ship, was spotted directly ahead of *Primrose*. After another hour the distance between the two vessels had closed enough for Broughton to hoist his colours and fire a warning shot across the ship's bows. In response the stranger hove to and ran up her own Spanish colours. Broughton hailed her, demanding to know her name and where she was headed. The response, '*Veloz Passagera*, bound for St Thomas for wood and water,'[1] confirmed what Broughton had suspected and he sent away a boarding party led by his First Lieutenant, the recently promoted Edward Butterfield, to examine the Spaniard. When the boat arrived alongside *Veloz* Butterfield noticed that her gun ports were all open with lights in each and that her guns were all trained on *Primrose*. The ship's master was not on deck but eventually made an appearance, giving his name as Jose Antonio de la Vega and explaining that his ship was bound for Princes for wood and water (not St Thomas as was previously stated) but refusing several requests from *Primrose*'s First Lieutenant to examine his vessel. Butterfield recognised the stench of a loaded slaver well enough and decided to return to *Primrose* to report back to Broughton. Through a Spanish interpreter Broughton now hailed *Veloz Passagera* and informed her he would send another boat across to examine her. De la Vega replied that in the darkness he could not be certain who *Primrose* was and she might be a pirate, therefore he would not allow his vessel to be boarded.

With the weather fine and clear Broughton decided to keep company with *Veloz Passagera* throughout the night and to board her the following morning. At 5.45am, with her ensigns clearly displayed fore and aft, *Primrose* bore down on the Spanish vessel. Hailing *Veloz Passagera* and once again identifying his sloop as a Royal Navy cruiser, Broughton demanded that she heave to and permit a boat to board her within five minutes or he would open fire. De la Vega responded 'You can do as you please. If you fire, I will fire too.'[2]

By now both vessels were sailing broadside to broadside, almost touching one another. When the five minutes expired *Primrose* opened fire and *Veloz* immediately responded with a ragged broadside from her assorted guns. Upon firing his second broadside Broughton ordered his helm hard over to lay his vessel alongside *Veloz Passagera*'s starboard bow. Broughton now led the boarders across to the Spaniard. Her crew were slowly driven aft, and in the vicious fighting Broughton was struck in the abdomen by a pike and fell to the deck, his place taken by Acting Lieutenant Foley with Butterfield leading the boarders on. After battling for another ten minutes *Veloz Passagera*'s crew had been pushed back onto her poop deck and with nothing behind them but the sea they threw down their arms and surrendered their ship.

As anticipated, *Veloz Passagera* had a large cargo of slaves crammed into her hold, 556 Africans taken from Whydah, five of whom had been killed by the British broadsides. Forty-six of the Spaniard's crew of 150 had been killed in the battle and a further twenty wounded, including de la Vega who had lost an arm. *Primrose*, her rigging and boats severely damaged, had much lighter casualties, just three killed and twelve wounded. Acting Surgeon Lane had tended to the wounded even though he was sick with fever, his actions undoubtedly saving many lives.

Foley was given command of *Primrose* while Broughton recovered from his wound and Butterfield was made prize master of *Veloz Passagera* for her passage to Freetown. *Primrose*'s prize was condemned by the Anglo-Spanish court on 16 October and her surviving 551 slaves emancipated. Following her condemnation Governor Findlay ordered that twenty-four of *Veloz Passagera*'s crew be sent to England on board Broughton's sloop to stand trial for murder when it came time for *Primrose* to return home. However, Palmerston later informed the commissioners that the prisoners should be sent to Spain as the British courts had no jurisdiction over them.

In mid-September *Medina* had dispatched her tender, the ex-slaver *Puss*, to examine the Old Calabar. The schooner, commanded by Lieutenant Frederick Servante, had no warrant to arrest slave vessels and therefore Webb, still waiting at Princes for the return of *Primrose* from Ascension, intended to join her in order to make any seizures legal. On 24 September *Puss* arrested the Spanish brigantine *Pajarito* with a cargo of 293 sickly slaves loaded in the Old Calabar. Servante waited for three days, but, there still being no sign of *Medina*, decided to dispatch his prize to Freetown where she arrived on 24 October, sixty slaves having died on the passage north. *Atholl* arrived in port on the same day and Gordon was informed by the British commissioners that, as *Puss* was not authorised to make captures, they would have no option but to restore her prize. Gordon and the Captor's Proctor now met with *Pajarito*'s master, Fortunato Romero, who offered to manumit the surviving 233 slaves. They were landed on 27 October and sent to the Liberated African Hospital at Kissy. Three days later *Pajarito* departed Freetown for Havana.

Atholl had arrived at Freetown in company with her own prize, the Spanish schooner *Nueva Isabelita*, seized off Cape Mesurado on 17 October with a cargo of 144 slaves loaded at Little Bassa a week earlier. The schooner was quickly condemned and her surviving 139 slaves emancipated. Expecting the arrival of the new commodore, Gordon remained at Freetown for a week but then had to sail for the Bights to allow *Medina*, running short of provisions, to head for Ascension.

Learning that a Sierra Leone citizen had sent a vessel with a cargo of guns to the Pongas to sell to a slaver operating on the river, Gordon had dispatched *Plumper*, whose boats were still investigating the same river, back north to investigate. Entering the Pongas on 6 November *Plumper* hailed a schooner passing downstream and learned from her master, a Mr Smith, that he had sold guns to a French slaver. Smith was ordered to Freetown to explain his actions to Governor Findlay and *Plumper* pressed on upriver, anchoring close to the shore, her yards almost touching the overhanging trees. On 7 November *Plumper*'s boats arrested the Portuguese schooner *Maria* with a cargo of thirty-five slaves. The vessel, which had been abandoned by all of her crew save her master, was escorted back to Freetown by *Plumper* and condemned on 25 November. *Plumper*'s brief foray into the Pongas proved to be a costly one, for thirty-eight of her crew soon fell ill with fever and twenty-seven men subsequently died.

Cruising first off the Old Calabar and then Fernando Po, between 5 October and 3 November *Black Joke*, now sailing as tender to *Atholl* under her First Lieutenant William Ramsay, had boarded five vessels, *Duc de Bordeaux*, *L'Actif*, *Lynx*, *Bonne Aline* and *L'Hermoine*, carrying a total of 1,642 slaves, none of which she could touch as they were all sailing under the French flag. Moving to a new cruising ground off the Cameroons the brig had more success, seizing the Spanish brigantine *Dos Amigos* on 9 November. With *Black Joke* cruising offshore Ramsay had sent his gig and cutter in to the river where they encountered the fully-laden brigantine working her way downstream. The brigantine quickly turned and headed back up towards King Bell's Town chased by the two boats with *Black Joke* following close behind. By the time the boats had caught up with *Dos Amigos* her cargo of 563 slaves had been offloaded and had dispersed into the bush. Upon *Black Joke*'s arrival Ramsay went onboard the brigantine to demand the return of the slaves, threatening to set fire to the town. A handful of slaves were eventually handed over, but, discovering that the brigantine's coppers had been removed, Ramsay decided to send his prize back to Freetown empty. *Dos Amigos* was condemned on 5 February 1831 and Gordon, Ramsay's superior, charged £4.14 for missing stores.

Sailing from the Gambia in company with *Primrose*, on 24 November *Conflict* spotted a suspicious looking schooner off the River Pongas and immediately gave chase. It falling calm, Smithers sent his gig, commanded by the Sailing Master, Mr Rose, with six men to board the vessel. As the gig approached the schooner she came under fire from long guns and musketry and Rose, several of his men injured, signalled *Conflict* for assistance. Smithers dispatched his pinnace and she joined the gig in pursuit of the schooner which now had her sweeps out. The schooner fired a broadside of grape at the two boats which took away several of the pinnace's oars, damaged the hull and injured several men. Rose ordered the almost waterlogged pinnace to the opposite side of the schooner and commenced the boarding. Despite fierce resistance, the schooner was quickly taken for just nine British wounded. The prize proved to be the Portuguese vessel *Nympha* with a cargo of 169 slaves. Thirteen of her crew had been killed and a further seven wounded in the brief action. Four slaves had also been injured and these were taken on board *Conflict* for medical assistance. Upon her arrival at Freetown the master and crew of *Nympha* were imprisoned for firing on *Conflict*'s boats. The master, mate, second mate and a sailor were later sent to Lisbon to stand trial but three years later the British government was still waiting for proceedings against those men to commence. *Nympha* was condemned in the Anglo–Portuguese court on 9 December and her 169 slaves emancipated.

On 30 November the Squadron's new senior officer, Commodore John Hayes, arrived at Freetown on board his flagship, the 36-gun frigate *Dryad*. Known throughout the service as 'Magnificent' Hayes in honour of his brilliant handling of his ship *Magnificent* during a gale in December 1812,

Hayes, who had served several years apprentice to his uncle Adam Hayes, Master Shipbuilder at Deptford Dockyard, was also a skilled ship designer, responsible for the ship-sloop *Champion* and the recently-completed cutter *Seaflower* which accompanied *Dryad* to Africa, serving as her tender.

On 29 November, whilst still some 50 miles from Freetown, *Dryad* had spotted *Plumper* in pursuit of a brig which eventually hove to and hoisted the White Flag of France. The brig's master freely admitted to having a cargo of 300 slaves loaded at the Sherbro which he knew *Plumper* could not touch. Later that day Adams went on board *Dryad* to report to Hayes, briefing the Commodore on the current state of affairs on the Coast and at Freetown. He also informed Hayes of the sickness that had befallen his vessel following her recent visit to the Pongas. Of the thirty-eight men confined to hospital, fourteen had died the previous day and he did not expect the remaining twenty-four to survive for very much longer. Adams also informed Hayes of the recent captures of *Veloz Passagera* and *Nympha*, discussing the spirited defence of these vessels by their crews, no doubt a result of their pay largely depending on the success of their slaving voyages.

Following his arrival on station Hayes immediately ordered *Primrose* home, *Plumper* was sent back to the Pongas in what would turn out to be a fruitless search of a British citizen named Josiffe who was said to be trading slaves, *Seaflower* was despatched into the Bights to cruise between Cape Formoso and Fernando Po and *Conflict* was sent north to take Chief Justice Jeffcott to the Gambia. On 15 December *Conflict* fell in with the schooner *Caroline*, carrying French papers but flying a tablecloth instead of French colours. The vessel had a cargo of fifty-one slaves, four of whom called out in English to claim protection, explaining they had been abducted from Sierra Leone. Jeffcott advised Smithers to take the schooner back to Sierra Leone and from there she was escorted to Goree by *Medina*, recently returned from Ascension.

On 16 December *Primrose*'s replacement, the 18-gun ship sloop *Favourite*, Commander Joseph Harrison, arrived at Freetown from Gibraltar. Unusually for the Squadron she was a newly-launched vessel, only nineteen months old. However, she was just a slightly lengthened version of a design dating back to 1796. Having completed with stores and water, *Favourite* was ordered to cruise between Cape Mesurado and the Shoals of St Anne for the next ten weeks.

On their return to Freetown *Plumper* and *Conflict* received new instructions from Hayes. In October the Colonial Office had received a fresh complaint from Governor Findlay over the perennial problem of the Squadron's apparent lack of interest in the northern rivers and this had been passed on to the Admiralty. Hayes now instructed *Conflict* to remain at anchor at Freetown for three weeks to receive prize crews so that they need not go ashore. When relieved by *Plumper* she was to cruise off the Gallinas, Sherbro, Pongas and Nunez for another three weeks then return to Freetown. Both gun-brigs would continue to alternate between Freetown and the northern rivers every three weeks.

These were not the only new instructions Hayes had issued on his arrival at Freetown. He also ordered that Squadron's boats not be sent up rivers or even in chase if it meant losing sight of the parent vessel. Work on vessels at Freetown was to cease at 4.00pm every day and the Kroomen, twenty of whom had been taken on board *Dryad*, were not to be overworked. Hayes also ordered *Dryad*'s launch to be coppered and turned into a stores lighter so that crews need not go ashore and endure the unhealthy airs of Freetown. In response to the recent complaints from the commissioners at Freetown over several prizes recently arrived in port, Hayes also forbid improper use or removal of stores found in seized vessels and he requested that, whenever practicable, a surgeon be included in prize crews.

Following her return from the Pongas *Plumper* had been despatched in search of *Black Joke* which had not yet returned to Freetown from Ascension as expected. On 26 December Adams' gun-brig boarded the Spanish-flagged schooner *Maria* off Cape Mesurado, discovering a cargo of 505 slaves in her hold. Furnished with a passport for Princes and St Thomas but bound for Havana from the Gallinas, *Maria* was sent to Sierra Leone, losing eight of her slaves on the passage north. *Plumper*'s prize was condemned on 19 January 1831 and her surviving 497 slaves emancipated. During his cruise Adams failed to discover the whereabouts of *Black Joke* which eventually arrived at Freetown worn out and in need of repair. *Plumper* now proceeded to cruise off the Nunez and *Atholl* was ordered to leeward to investigate the state of the Trade along the Gold Coast. From Cape St Paul's *Atholl* was to sail to Princes and cruise to the west of the island until joined by *Dryad*. On 29 December Gordon's frigate struck Coley's Rock off Cape Palmas, suffering enough damage to her keel to affect her handling. Whilst off Popo in late January 1831 *Atholl* discovered the Spanish schooner *Mannelita* which had just returned to the Coast from a previous slaving voyage, during which she had also engaged in acts of piracy. Her master was ashore and her current crew had not been involved in her previous voyage and so, after holding the schooner for three days, Gordon was forced to release her after throwing her three guns overboard.

By mid-February *Black Joke* had completed her lengthy refit and was cruising off the Gallinas under the command of *Dryad*'s First Lieutenant, William Castle. On the morning of 22 February she spotted a suspicious looking schooner off Cape Mount and set off in pursuit. The chase continued throughout the day and it was night before *Black Joke* finally got close enough to the schooner to fire several blank cartridges, all of which were ignored, leaving Castle with little option but to fire a shot at the vessel her to bring her to. The schooner was found to be the Spaniard *Primeira* with a cargo of 311 slaves from the Gallinas, half of them children, crammed into her tiny hold. Two children had been killed by *Black Joke*'s shot and a further two injured. Castle escorted his prize back to Sierra Leone, both vessels arriving in Freetown on 3 March. The conditions on board *Primeira* were described by *Dryad*'s Lieutenant Peter Leonard: 'The small space in which these unfortunate beings are huddled together is almost incredible. The schooner is only one hundred and thirty tons burthen, and the slave deck only two feet two inches high, so that they can hardly even sit upright … The horrors of this infernal compartment – the want of air – the suffocating heat – the filth – the stench – may be easily imagined; although it is remarked that this ship is one of the cleanest that was ever brought to the colony.'[3] Over the course of two hours on 4 March the slaves, almost all of whom were completely naked, were ferried to the shore by canoe, the children singing on deck as they waited their turn to be landed, the adults becoming more sullen when the realisation dawned that they were not going to be released immediately. On 14 March *Primeira* was condemned and her surviving 310 slaves emancipated

Not long after his arrival on the Coast Hayes had received eight sets of Instructions for the Squadron's tenders signed by the outgoing First Lord, Melville. In anticipation of orders from the new Board of Admiralty, now led by Sir James Graham, prohibiting the purchase of tenders, Hayes wrote to inform Their Lordships that he intended to replace the now worn-out *Black Joke* with one of the two vessels due to be condemned at Freetown, *Dos Amigos* or *Maria*. In the meantime Hayes had *Black Joke* recaulked so she could spend her final days operating in the smooth, easy sailing waters off Sierra Leone. When *Dos Amigos* was condemned in late February Hayes purchased her for £609 as tender for *Dryad* and renamed her *Fair Rosamond*. In time she would become almost as feared by the slavers as *Black Joke*.

On 26 February, four days after the purchase of her replacement, *Black Joke* was in pursuit of a suspicious-looking schooner off Cape Mesurado when she spotted a strange frigate also in pursuit of the schooner. Coming under fire from both vessels the schooner turned towards the frigate which now hoisted American colours and identified herself as USS *Java* before she proceeded to board the schooner. Passing within hailing distance of the American, Castle requested permission to go aboard the schooner. This was refused but he was received courteously on board *Java* by her captain, Edmund Kennedy, who informed Castle he should treat any American slaver he encountered as a pirate.

On 24 March *Dryad* departed Sierra Leone in company with the freshly recaulked *Black Joke* and the Squadron's latest acquisition *Fair Rosamond* for a cruise down to Princes and Fernando Po. Arriving at Princes on 17 April, Lieutenant Castle was appointed in temporary command of *Medina* to replace the sickly Commander Webb and Ramsay returned to *Black Joke*. On the morning of 22 April Hayes received intelligence from a British merchantman of a heavily-armed slaver brig operating in the Old Calabar and he despatched *Black Joke* to investigate. For the next three days Ramsay's tender maintained a watch over the river, moving in close at night but moving further out to sea during the day to lie just below the horizon. Finally at 11.00am on the morning of 25 April the brig emerged from the mouth of the river. As the she headed off towards the south-east *Black Joke* gave chase but the brig proved to be an excellent sailer and it was 9.00pm before Ramsay was close enough to fire a shot across her bows. The brig responded to this attempt to bring her to by firing a broadside at *Black Joke*. The chase continued under light airs with both vessels using sweeps until the early hours of the 26th when a light breeze blew up. With *Black Joke* once again within range of the brig she shortened sail and the two vessels exchanged broadsides, *Black Joke*'s two guns to the brig's five. As the brig and *Black Joke* came together Ramsay changed to grapeshot to cause as much injury to the men on his opponent's deck before ordering his boarders away, Ramsay and Master's Mate Bosanquet leading sixteen men across to the brig moments before the two vessels drifted apart. There was vicious hand-to-hand fighting. Ramsay and Bosanquet were both injured and Midshipman Pearce, his hat already holed by pistol-shot, was knocked overboard by a cutlass-wielding Spaniard, hauling himself back on board with his sword clenched firmly between his teeth. In the meantime 15-year-old Midshipman Edwin Hinde used *Black Joke*'s starboard sweeps to bring her back alongside and have the two vessels lashed together before moving across to the brig where he was accosted by an angry parrot which bit his finger. Reinforced with men from the tender, Ramsay succeeded in taking the brig, which had now been identified as the Spanish vessel *Marinerito*. Fifteen feet longer than *Black Joke* and broader in the beam, she was an even finer-looking vessel than Ramsay's tender. On board she had a cargo of 496 slaves, twenty-six of whom had now died from suffocation as a result of the panic caused on the crowded slave deck during the engagement. Of her crew of seventy-seven *Marinerito* had lost thirteen killed and fifteen wounded. *Black Joke*'s losses were much lighter, just one man killed and four wounded. Assistant Surgeon Douglas was praised for his efforts attending to the injured during the engagement and was subsequently promoted to surgeon whilst Bosanquet was given his lieutenant's commission.

The slaves on board *Marinerito* were crying out for water and Ramsay ordered a large tub filled and placed on the deck. Mad with thirst, the slaves rushed the tub and so many tried to get at the water that they got their heads stuck in it and it was with some difficulty that the British extricated them. Upon reaching Fernando Po 107 of *Marinerito*'s most sickly slaves were landed before Ramsay's prize departed for Sierra Leone under the command of Bosanquet. On 3 June *Marinerito* was condemned and her surviving 373 slaves emancipated. Of the 107 slaves at Fernando Po, forty-one subsequently died either at the island or on passage to Sierra Leone, sixty-two arrived at Freetown on board *Plumper* and *Seaflower* in early June and the remaining four, too ill to travel, were emancipated by decree at Fernando Po.

Upon the arrival of *Atholl* at Princes in late April Hayes received a private note from Captain Gordon regarding an earlier instruction from the Commodore to sail to Fernando Po with a consignment of clothing for the soldiers on the island and to then offer assistance to Governor Nicholls. Gordon had taken this to mean he was to remain off Fernando Po instead of resuming his cruise and, already upset about the removal of

First Lieutenant Ramsay from *Atholl*, seemingly without his agreement, he now wrote to complain about an order which he felt had resulted in the loss from fever of several valuable lives. Furious at this letter, Hayes demanded to know the names of those who had died as a result of his orders. Gordon replied that he had been blaming himself for remaining at Fernando Po for too long and, now suffering from stomach and bowel complaints, asked permission to return to England. Hayes wasted little time having Gordon replaced as commander of *Atholl* with *Medina*'s Lieutenant Webb and, having appointing Lieutenant Castle to *Medina*, he now ordered an enquiry into Gordon's allegations which was to be led by these two officers. Their enquiry having concluded that no deaths had resulted from Hayes's orders the Commodore now applied for Gordon to be tried by court martial.

Gordon's court martial was held on board *Victory* at Portsmouth on 1 October 1832 with two flag officers and seven senior captains in attendance. Gordon faced five charges involving his not waiting on Hayes when he joined him at Princes, for negligently performing the Commodore's orders, an allegation that he had only agreed to be invalided home on condition he received money from Webb, his private letter to Hayes and a subsequent letter of complaint written to the Admiralty following his return from the Coast. The first three of these charges were found not proved (the only money Gordon had made was through selling his furniture to Webb) and the court felt unable to try the charge relating to the letter written to the Admiralty regarding the removal of Ramsay and a number of *Atholl*'s men to *Black Joke* and *Fair Rosamond* as it did not fall under the Articles of War, Gordon being on half pay at the time. The charge relating to the private note was judged to be partially proved. Whilst the court found that Gordon had been unguarded in his comments and had used an improper expression, it noted that he had immediately apologised on recognising the offence caused. Gordon was admonished by the court and told to be more circumspect in the future.

Following her departure from Princes on 24 April *Dryad* arrived at Fernando Po on 2 May where she found *Black Joke* refitting following her encounter with *Marinerito*. *Atholl* was also at the island and Hayes had the damage to her keel assessed. Deciding there was no immediate need for her to return home for a refit, she was dispatched to Princes to water and then to Ascension via Anobón, 150 miles off the coast, where

Marinerito's surviving crew had been deposited without provisions. (The Spanish bartered their clothing for food then built canoes to escape from the island.) From there she was to cruise between the Equator and 10° S. Having returned to the Bights from the Windward Coast, *Favourite* was despatched from Fernando Po in late July on a similar mission to *Atholl*'s.

Following a largely unsuccessful cruise in the Bights *Seaflower* had joined her parent vessel at Princes in April where her commanding officer, Lieutenant Henry Huntley, was transferred to *Fair Rosamond* following Ramsay's return to *Black Joke*. On the night of 20 July Huntley's new command was entering the anchorage at Lagos when she passed an outward-bound schooner. Huntley hoisted a Spanish ensign to avoid suspicion and the schooner, presuming *Fair Rosamond* to be a fellow slaver, maintained her course. Once out of sight Huntley hauled round in the schooner's wake and set off in pursuit under a fine breeze. The chase continued throughout the night and in to the morning. Huntley had promised eight dollars to the first man to spot a possible prize and as the early morning mist cleared at least four voices cried out 'sail ho!' as the schooner was observed on *Fair Rosamond*'s lee beam. The schooner appeared to be a fine sailer on a moderate breeze but no so when it freshened up. After a six-hour chase she finally came within range of *Fair Rosamond*'s single long gun and as Huntley sailed past barrels, spars and a boat jettisoned by the Spaniard in a desperate attempt to evade arrest, he fired a warning shot over her. Cutting away her anchors and wetting her sails, the slaver was able to pull away from *Fair Rosamond* but Huntley adjusted his vessel's trim and soon had his opponent back within range. Several well-aimed shots brought down her studdingsails and another aimed at the hull grazed her taffrail, killing the helmsman. Backing her fore topsail but keeping her other sails set, the schooner now lowered her colours and hove to. Experience had taught Huntley that the Spaniard meant to get under way once *Fair Rosamond*'s boat was in the water and so he hailed the vessel to lower all her sails. When the schooner answered that she did not understand English Huntley ordered her jib halliard cut away by his marines. The halliard having been brought down, the marines moved their fire to the peak halliard block at which point the schooner's master, Juan Baptista Arana, hailed in perfectly good English that he would come on board *Fair Rosamond*. His vessel proved to be the Spanish-flagged *Potosi* with a cargo of 192 slaves bound from Lagos to Havana. Arana's crew were removed to *Fair Rosamond* (they were eventually put on board a vessel at Lagos) and the slaves fed and watered before the prize was despatched to Freetown, arriving in port on 12 August. *Potosi* was condemned by the Anglo-Spanish court on 22 August and her surviving 183 slaves emancipated.

With Brazilian slavers now being treated as pirates, there was concern amongst the officers of the Squadron that they could no longer be adjudicated in the Anglo-Brazilian court. In March Hayes had sought clarification from the Mixed Commission of its role and was informed by the commissioners that the court had no authority to try Brazilian vessels for piracy under the existing treaty. Indeed the Brazilian Chargé d'Affaires in London, de Mello Mattos, had already demanded the dissolution of the court and the Brazilian judge, de Paiva, had received instructions to return home after the much-delayed trial of *Ismenia*. The Admiralty now sought instructions from the Foreign Office. Reminded of an almost-forgotten additional article in the treaty of 1817 that allowed it to remain in force for a further fifteen years in the absence of a further agreement, in mid-August Lord Palmerston informed de Mello Mattos that in his government's view the Anglo-Brazilian courts in Sierra Leone and Rio de Janeiro could continue to adjudicate on Brazilian-flagged vessels. Furthermore, as the Brazilian Trade was now entirely illegal the mutual right of search should no longer be restricted to the north of the Line.

Having spent several months in the Bights visiting St Thomas, Princes and the Bonny, in early July *Dryad* departed Fernando Po for Ascension, arriving at the island on 29 July to refit and provision. On 2 September *Conflict* arrived at the island suffering from an outbreak of fever with nine men dead and her commanding officer, Lieutenant Smithers, ill. Hayes ordered *Conflict*'s iron water tanks to be landed and her hold fumigated and whitewashed. During her stay on the island one-half of *Dryad*'s company were allowed on shore every day where they entertained themselves playing cricket, skittles and quoits. There were by now a number of fair-skinned African children on the island, a reminder of Ascension's other distractions. On 9 September a freshly painted and provisioned *Dryad* sailed for the islands of Princes and Fernando Po. Now restored to health, a similarly well provisioned *Conflict* departed Ascension in late September for a cruise to Accra via Princes.

Black Joke's damage from her encounter with *Marinerito* (both her larboard quarter and larboard forward bulwark had been stove in) having been repaired; in early May she departed Fernando Po for a cruise in the Bights of Biafra. On the afternoon of 8 September Ramsay arrived off the mouth of the Bonny to find *Fair Rosamond* at anchor. Apologising for encroaching upon Ramsay's station, Huntley explained that he had left his usual hunting grounds in the Bight of Benin upon learning from a British palm-oiler that two large, well-armed Spanish brigs, *Regulo* and *Rapido*, were at the Bonny loaded with slaves, intending to sail in company upon the next spring tide. As it happened Ramsay had sailed to the river upon hearing exactly the same information from a French slaver. The two men now agreed to work together against the powerful brigs, believed to be mounting fourteen long guns and four carronades between them.

On the morning of 10 September *Regulo* and *Rapido* were spotted emerging from the Bonny under a spread of sail. In order to avoid detection Ramsay and Huntley had left it as late as possible to hoist their sails and as they finally weighed and set sail around 9.30am the brigs, suddenly becalmed, anchored just inside the bar of the river. The two tenders headed inshore, *Black Joke*, which had been slow to weigh, quickly dropping astern of *Fair Rosamond*. At 1.00pm a fresh breeze finally reached the two brigs and they stood out to sea. When about three or four miles from *Fair Rosamond* the two slavers suddenly bore away for the river. Armed with one of Captain Owen's new charts Huntley headed into the maze of shoals at the mouth of the Bonny. By the time the two brigs had reached deeper water *Fair Rosamond* was just a mile and a half from the rearmost Spaniard, *Regulo*. The two tenders passed close by several British palm-oilers at anchor several miles upstream and a boat from one of these vessels managed to put eight volunteers armed with muskets on board *Fair Rosamond*. With a prize crew at Freetown and several men sick, the palm-oilers were a timely and welcome addition to Huntley's crew.

Regulo and *Rapido* now headed off into a tributary of the Bonny. *Fair Rosamond* was not far behind and when Huntley entered the tributary he found *Regulo* aground and surrounded by canoes which were being used to land her cargo of slaves. A shot fired over the slaver was enough to induce her to lower her colours. Leaving *Black Joke* to deal with this vessel, Huntley turned his attention to *Rapido* which, her canoes now all full, was in the process of throwing her remaining slaves, still shackled together in pairs, into the crocodile-infested water. Two slaves were pulled out of the water by their shared leg-chain using a boat-hook but the others were all lost. A boarding party made up of Huntley, *Fair Rosamond*'s mate, Mr Robinson, four marines and two seamen backed up by a volley of musketry quickly forced *Rapido*'s crew below, leaving her master alone on deck.

Rapido's compatriot *Regulo* was boarded by *Black Joke* with little resistance, most of the brig's crew of fifty-six having already abandoned ship. Two hundred and seven slaves remained on board and Ramsay was advised by his surgeon to land five infected with smallpox. The two tenders and their prizes now grounded on the mud as the tide went out and the British spent the next week lightening *Regulo* and kedging and warping both tenders and prizes back into the river. In this they were assisted by two palm-oilers, *Rolla* and *Huskinson*. These vessels, from London and Liverpool respectively, loaned men, boats, an anchor and a chain. With their help both tenders and prizes sailed ahead of the next spring tides, departing the river on 16 September.

Regulo was condemned on 22 October and her surviving 169 slaves emancipated (this included the five still in the Bonny). Twenty-eight slaves had died following the Spaniard's capture which left ten Africans that Ramsay was unable to account for. *Rapido* was condemned on 7 November on evidence given by the two slaves rescued from the water, the only survivors from her cargo of 150 slaves. One hundred or so mangled bodies, still shackled together in pairs, were later discovered washed up on the banks of the Bonny.

Expressing his approval of the conduct of all those involved in the capture of the two Spanish brigs, Hayes promoted *Fair Rosamond*'s mate, Mr Robinson, to command *Plumper* in place of the sickly Lieutenant Adams. However, when *Plumper* sailed for the Gambia on 5 September she was under the temporary command of Lieutenant Thomas Creser. On 21 November *Atholl* departed Fernando Po for England where, following her arrival back at Portsmouth on 14 February 1832, she was paid off. Responsible for the arrest of twelve vessels and the emancipation of 1,662 slaves over the course of the four years she had spent with the Squadron, *Atholl* would not be seen on the Coast again.

In December 1831 the colonial government at Sierra Leone received news that the British slaver Josiffe had returned to the Pongas. Mindful of his explicit instructions from Hayes, when *Favourite*'s Commander

Harrison was requested by Governor Findlay to arrest Josiffe, he wrote that he was under orders not to take his boats into any river for any reason and even if he were allowed to do so he doubted whether his search would be fruitful. Findlay now complained to the Admiralty over the matter and Their Lordships sought an explanation from Harrison, who repeated both the reasons given in his letter to the Governor and his orders from Hayes. The Admiralty appeared satisfied by his explanation and chose not to take any further action against *Favourite*'s commanding officer.

Having been a constant irritation to the Squadron during the previous year, 1831 had seen a significant reduction in the number of slavers operating under the French flag. During her summer cruise of the Bights *Atholl* had found no French slavers and there had been no recent French activity in the Bonny. In July 1830 the Anglophile French King, Louis-Philippe, had come to the throne and the abolitionist movement which had been steadily gaining momentum received a further boost when the new king agreed to a recommendation from Captain Villaret de Joyeuse, recently returned from the Coast, that slave trading be declared a crime punishable by imprisonment. Under a new law introduced in March 1831, slave merchants, supercargoes or captains were all liable to two to five years' imprisonment if their ships were seized in France. If their vessels were caught at sea the penalties would be much harsher, ten to twenty years in jail and ten years' hard labour if seized with a slave cargo. Freed slaves would be liberated in the colony for which they had been intended. The bill received overwhelming support and was carried by 190 votes to thirty-seven.

In early November 1831 Britain and France entered into negotiations regarding a convention for the suppression of the Trade. London initially proposed a treaty similar to those agreed with Portugal and Spain but Paris responded that Mixed Commissions were not possible under French law. The convention, signed on 30 November, agreed to a mutual Right of Search by vessels of war commanded by officers of the rank of lieutenant or above. The number of vessels issued with Special Instructions were to be fixed annually, lists of these vessels were to be exchanged and the number of cruisers operated by one nation could not exceed double that of the other. The regions covered by the convention included the West Coast of Africa, the islands of Cuba, Puerto Rico and Madagascar and the coast of Brazil. Vessels found to be slaving in these locations were to be handed over to the courts of whatever nation to which they belonged.

London proposed that courts be set up at Fernando Po, Rio de Janeiro, Jamaica and Martinique, but Paris, not unreasonably pointing out that Fernando Po belonged to neither Britain nor France, insisted that French vessels detained off the Coast be sent to Goree. In response the Admiralty argued that such a long passage from the Bights would result in an even greater loss of lives amongst the slaves than the already hazardous passage from the Bights to Freetown. The Admiralty nominated all its cruisers currently operating on the Coast for Special Instructions whilst the French Ministry of Marine nominated their four vessels currently in African waters.

Chapter 9

Commands Combined:
December 1831–September 1834

1832 saw the most significant change to the operations of the West Africa Squadron since its inception twenty-five years earlier. Following the recent signing of the Anglo-French Convention, slaving in the Bights was now at a low level. There was an expectation that Brazil would soon abolish the Trade but it was on the increase south of the Line. Therefore the Admiralty, with an ever-present eye on costs, decided to incorporate the Squadron into the Cape of Good Hope Station. An officer of flag rank would be needed to head this new enlarged command and in August 1831 Rear Admiral Frederick Warren was appointed the new Commander-in-Chief of the Cape and West Africa Station, replacing both Commodore Hayes on the Coast and Commodore Schomberg at the Cape. Entering the Navy in 1789 aged 14, Warren had first served on the North America station and then the Caribbean. He made post in May 1801 and was promoted rear admiral in July 1830. Placed in temporary command of a squadron formed as part of the failed expedition against the secessionist Kingdom of Belgium in the autumn of 1831, Warren did not depart for Africa until 24 December, sailing from Portsmouth aboard his flagship, the 58-gun *Isis*, in company with the gun-brigs *Brisk* (the namesake of a vessel that had served on the Coast almost twenty years earlier) and *Charybdis*. Both these vessels were uprated versions of the 'coffin brigs' designed by the Surveyor of the Navy, Robert Seppings, with upper works now lowered and shrouds attached to bulwark stanchions instead of the traditional channels. Their armament was also reduced to a long-gun on a pivot and two carronades. Unfortunately these changes had apparently done little to improve their sailing qualities and they were still much derided. Both gun-brigs were commanded by officers with great experienced of the Coast. *Brisk*'s Lieutenant Butterfield had been First Lieutenant on board *Primrose* during the capture of *Veloz Passagera* and *Charybdis*'s Lieutenant Crawford was famous amongst the Squadron for his defence of the Brazilian prize *Netuno* in 1826.

Sailing slightly astern of *Isis* and the two gun-brigs was *Pluto*, one of the new steam-powered vessels that were slowly entering service with the Navy. Commanded by Lieutenant George Buchanan with a crew of eighty and armed with two 18-pounders mounted on pivots fore and aft, the paddle steamer was powered by a 100-horsepower engine that gave her a maximum speed of between 7 and 8 knots. With just enough coal on board for ten days cruising Buchanan had been ordered not to raise steam unless in pursuit of suspicious vessels. Brig rigged and equipped with removable paddle boards, for the majority of the time *Pluto* would act as a traditional sailing vessel. With only one coaling depot at Fernando Po the Admiralty was concerned over *Pluto*'s fuel consumption and in addition to finding a location to procure wood for his boiler, Buchanan was asked to report on the quantities of fuel consumed, the occasions on which it was used and the length of time steam was kept up. Aware of the massive disparity in price that the Admiralty was paying for coal and the amount it was on offer for at Sierra Leone, Commodore Warren suggested that another station be opened there.

Whilst *Brisk* and *Pluto* continued on towards the Gambia, *Isis* and *Charybdis* stopped off at Tenerife to collect supplies. Arriving at Bathurst in mid-January Warren found *Plumper* and *Brisk* at anchor. Having discovered the settlement had narrowly survived a recent attack by the King of Barra, *Charybdis* was despatched to Sierra Leone with instructions for Hayes to remain there to await the arrival of Warren, who delayed his sailing to hold a meeting with the troublesome local king, informing him he would station a force on the coast to maintain the peace. Departing Bathurst in company with *Brisk*, Warren arrived at Sierra Leone on 27 January where he discovered *Charybdis*, *Seaflower* and the French frigate *Hermione* at anchor.

When *Dryad* finally arrived at Sierra Leone on 28 January to discover Warren's flagship at anchor, Hayes decided that, rather than remain on station under the new commander-in chief, he would sail for home with his broad pendant still flying. Protesting that he had been taken completely by surprise by the turn of events, having been given no intimation of the Admiralty's intentions to combine the Squadron and the Cape of Good Hope Station, Hayes now received permission from Warren to call at Fernando Po and Ascension prior to his return home.

In the autumn of 1831 the Admiralty had taken the decision to break up *Black Joke* as she now appeared worn out beyond the point of repair and on 31 January *Charybdis* departed Freetown to relieve the tender in order that she return to Sierra Leone to be paid off. However, on 1 February Hayes reported to Warren that *Black Joke* had been repaired at Fernando Po at 'trifling expense'[1] and now appeared in the same condition as when she was first built. Armed with this quite misleading report, Warren now asked that the brig be transferred to Governor Findlay for use as a colonial vessel to maintain communications with the Gambia. On the same day that *Charybdis* departed for the Bights the 18-gun brig-sloop *Pelorus*, Commander Richard Meredith, arrived from England.

On 2 February *Pluto* finally arrived at Freetown. *Isis* and *Brisk* now departed for a cruise down the Coast to visit the British settlements and the islands of Fernando Po and Princes before sailing to Ascension. *Seaflower* was despatched with stores for *Plumper* at the Gambia before heading for Ascension to await the arrival of Warren, falling in with *Dryad* prior to her return home. Dismayed by what he discovered upon his arrival at Fernando Po in late February, Warren recommended the shutting down of the island as a base and the removal of all stores to Ascension. In contrast he praised Princes for its usefulness as a watering place and its plentiful supplies of fruit, proposing that the Squadron rendezvous there instead of Fernando Po.

Although she was coming to the end of her career as a slave catcher, *Black Joke* was still a much sought-after command and, following Ramsay's promotion to commander, Lieutenant Huntley persuaded Warren to let him have the ageing vessel. Having been in a position to compare the two tenders, Huntley considered *Fair Rosamond* 'a fine schooner, though not equal to the sailing of the *Black Joke* by the wind, but she was certainly her superior when going well "free"'.[2] *Fair Rosamond*'s mate, Mr Robinson, was now made acting commander of the schooner just prior to a cruise to Ascension. Sailing off the Bonny on 15 February *Black Joke* made what would turn out to be her final arrest, seizing the Spanish schooner *Frasquita* with a cargo of 290 slaves and the customary passport for Princes and St Thomas. *Black Joke*'s prize arrived at Freetown on 10 March and ten days later she was condemned and her surviving 228 slaves emancipated.

On 25 February *Black Joke* was off the Bonny, lying in wait for her old adversary *El Almirante*, now sailing under the name *Cherouka*, when *Isis*,

Brisk and *Charybdis* hove into view. Warren now ordered an impromptu sailing competition between the three vessels. *Black Joke* reportedly ran rings round the two gun-brigs but Warren did not report this, instead sending his flag-captain, sailing master and two carpenter's mates across to the tender to survey Huntley's vessel. They concluded that her stem was decayed, her timbers rotten and the state of her deck so bad that she was no longer fit for service. Their report contained evidence of *Black Joke*'s poor condition in the form of various samples of her crumbling timbers that Warren sent to the Admiralty. *Black Joke* was ordered to Sierra Leone and instead of sailing for home as intended, Hayes was now instructed to make for Freetown from Ascension to attend the breaking-up of the tender.

On 19 March *Pelorus* made her first capture, arresting the Spanish brig *Segunda Teresa* 140 miles south of Badagry with a cargo of 459 slaves loaded at Whydah. On her arrival at Freetown and following consultation with Huntley, *Segunda Teresa*'s prize master Lieutenant Philip de Sausmarez had one of his prize crew, Francis Brown, punished with twenty-four lashes for neglect of duty. Flogging had been banned on board *Pelorus* and when de Sausmarez eventually rejoined the sloop Meredith placed him under arrest, sending him ashore to Simon's Town where he remained for eighteen months prior to his court martial at Portsmouth in June 1834. The court adjudged that de Sausmarez had been justified in his actions as Brown had shown clear signs of insubordination and he was therefore acquitted. *Segunda Teresa* was condemned on 21 April and her surviving 445 slaves emancipated. A fine-looking vessel, the Philadelphia-built clipper was eventually bought by Captain Greville, a member of the Royal Yacht Squadron, and renamed *Xarifa*.

Before departing the Coast for the Cape Warren ordered *Conflict* to Sierra Leone to be put out of commission, reduced to a hulk and turned into accommodation for the crews of prize vessels arriving at Freetown. With a crew consisting of a petty officer, four Kroomen and three landsmen, all on *Favourite*'s books, the gun-brig was placed under the charge of Governor Findlay. Passing command of the Squadron to the senior officer on station, *Favourite*'s Commander Harrison, Warren now sailed for the Cape via Ascension.

Whilst at Fernando Po Warren had been petitioned by a large number of free Africans who had learned that *Black Joke* was to be broken up. As

Warren was embarking on board *Isis* he was surrounded by a crowd of Africans who hugged and embraced the Admiral, pleading with him not to injure 'poor *Black Joke*',[3] reminding him of the great numbers she had rescued from slavery. But the Admiralty had made up its mind and there was nothing that could be done this late in the day to save the Squadron's most renowned slave catcher. On 29 April *Dryad* arrived at Freetown in company with *Fair Rosamond*, Hayes returning to Sierra Leone as requested to oversee the breaking up of *Black Joke*. The significance of the destruction of a vessel that had captured thirteen slavers and emancipated 3,692 slaves during the previous four and a half years was not lost on the officers of the Squadron, *Dryad*'s Lieutenant Peter Leonard writing:

> This favourite vessel – the terror of slave dealers and scourge of the oppressors of Africa, has done more towards putting an end to the vile traffic in slaves than all the ships on the station put together … It is to be regretted that she was not ordered to be so repaired as to endure whilst the traffic in slaves has an existence, for her very name serves as a check to it … Her demolition will, therefore, be hailed as the happiest piece of intelligence that has been received at Havannah, and wherever else the slave trade is carried on, for many years.[4]

Hayes had intended to break up the tender as was the normal practice but he was instead ordered to burn *Black Joke* by Warren as the Admiral thought there would be no demand for her rotten timbers, making the task of breaking her up a pointless and time-consuming exercise. Therefore, her masts, yards, rigging, guns and stores having been removed, on 3 May *Black Joke* was destroyed by fire on the shore of the Sierra Leone River, her remaining timbers visible for years to come at low tide.

On 9 May *Dryad*, *Fair Rosamond* and *Seaflower* sailed for England, escorting the brigantine *General Turner* to the Gambia with a cargo of 130 liberated slaves. With dysentery and opthalmia making heavy inroads amongst the Africans, the vessel arrived at the Gambia on 29 May with her cargo in as wretched and miserable a condition as any slaver captured on the Coast. *Dryad* sailed from Bathurst on 31 May and arrived back at Spithead on 26 July. Hayes hauled down his flag and went ashore. He would not serve at sea again, instead focussing his energies on naval architecture, rising to the rank of rear admiral a year prior to his death in 1838.

On 3 May, the same day that the Squadron's most renowned cruiser was being destroyed by fire at Freetown, the largely ineffectual sloop *Brisk* made her one and only contribution to the suppression campaign, seizing the Spanish schooner *Prueba*, with a cargo of 318 slaves, off the Bonny. *Brisk*'s prize was despatched to Sierra Leone, arriving there on 26 May. She was condemned by the Anglo-Spanish court on 5 June and her surviving 274 slaves emancipated. It would be another three months before the Squadron made its next seizure but the commissioners at Freetown dismissed any suggestion that this was due to a reduction in the level of slaving on the Coast and requested that the Squadron's size be increased to at least ten vessels. They also restated their desire that an Equipment Clause be introduced to all the treaties.

In early June *Pelorus* arrived at Ascension from Sierra Leone, returning to the island a month later before sailing for the Cape. In August *Brisk* sailed for Ascension where the recently-promoted Butterfield exchanged command of the brig with Lieutenant Josiah Thompson. The Squadron's sole capture in the latter half of 1832 fell to *Favourite* when, on 15 August, she fell in with the Spanish brig *Carolina* off Fernando Po with a cargo of 426 slaves loaded at the Nunez. *Carolina* was sent to Sierra Leone and on 11 September was condemned and her surviving 369 slaves emancipated. This would prove to be *Favourite*'s sole capture during that year's deployment.

In November the Foreign Office announced that the settlement at Fernando Po was to be evacuated. Having failed in its attempts to obtain permission from Spain for a base on the island, the Colonial Office had already asked the Admiralty to remove all non-essential supplies and persons from the settlement and in October the Government withdrew its proposals regarding the island. Following the announcement by the Foreign Office that all Spanish vessels discovered trafficking slaves were liable to condemnation regardless of whether they had been seized north or south of the Equator, in December Lord Palmerston called on all the signatories to the various treaties to agree to the destruction of condemned vessels to stop them falling back in to the hands of the slavers.

Having been absent from the Coast for much of 1832, on 11 January 1833 Warren hoisted his flag on board the frigate *Undaunted* and sailed from Simon's Bay at the Cape in company with the 10-gun brig-sloop

Curlew, Commander Henry Trotter, to visit the Bights and the settlements along the Coast as far north as the Gambia. It was a brief visit. Warren was back at the Cape by the end of April, but the commander-in-chief had seen enough to agree with the commissioners' assessment on the state of the Trade and was now convinced that the slavers were simply avoiding the areas in which previous arrests had been made. Warren also believed that the size of the Squadron should be increased, with eight or nine cruisers stationed off the major slave rivers and he considered the cut-down brigs much more suited to this task than the larger ship-sloops and ships.

On 17 February *Undaunted* and *Curlew* sailed together from Sierra Leone. Three days later the vessels parted company, *Curlew* heading for Accra whilst *Undaunted* continued on towards the Cape via Fernando Po. On 11 March *Undaunted* fell in with *Favourite*. Trotter having now superseded Harrison as Senior Officer on the Coast, *Favourite* was ordered to inspect the forts at Cape Coast and Accra before sailing for Fernando Po to refit and to assist in the evacuation of the British settlement there. On 6 April *Undaunted* arrived at Ascension and found the 16-gun brig-sloop *Trinculo*, Commander James Booth, recently arrived from the Cape, at anchor. On 9 April Warren's flagship sailed for the Cape and Booth took *Trinculo* onward to Fernando Po. Booth did not remain in command of the ageing vessel (she was now a quarter of a century old) for long and was invalided back home in May, *Brisk*'s Lieutenant Josiah Thompson eventually taking command of *Trinculo* in time for her first arrest in July.

Having spent over a year on the Coast without any captures to her name, on 22 February *Charybdis* finally made a contribution to the suppression campaign with the arrest of the Spanish schooner *Desengano* as she emerged from the mouth of the Bonny. Furnished with the usual passport for St Thomas, she had sailed directly for the Bonny and was bound for Cuba with a cargo of 220 slaves when she was detained. *Desengano* was condemned by the Anglo-Spanish court on 11 April and her surviving 209 slaves emancipated.

There was a further addition to the Squadron that spring with the arrival at Freetown in late April of the 3-gun brigantine *Griffon*, Lieutenant James Parlby, following a long-delayed departure from England. Having originally departed Plymouth in company with fellow 'Coffin' class brigantine *Forester*, Lieutenant William Quin, in mid-January, both vessels had been caught in a fierce gale in the Channel approaches. *Griffon* had returned to

Plymouth whilst *Forester* had sought shelter in St Mary's Roads, the Scilly Isles. Unfortunately on 13 February Quin's vessel had run aground off St Martin's. She was eventually got off and towed back to Plymouth where she underwent repairs. Quin, his officers and crew were transferred to the 10-gun brig *Britomart* and in early May sailed from Portsmouth for Africa.

On 23 April *Curlew* made her first arrest, seizing the Spanish schooner *Veloz Mariana* with a passport for Princes and St Thomas but bound for Havana with a cargo of 290 slaves that the schooner's master, Fortunato Romero, had purchased from the King of the Old Calabar. Twenty-five slaves died between *Veloz Mariana*'s capture and condemnation on 31 May. The vessel proved to be a valuable prize, realising £479 at auction.

Following her arrival from England *Pluto* had spent a quiet sixteen months on the Coast. Supplies of coal were limited and despite her novel propulsion the steamer had spent most of her time under sail. In late March Buchanan died and command of the steamer passed to *Favourite*'s Lieutenant Thomas Ross Sullivan. Finally, on 5 May the little steamer made her first contribution to the suppression campaign, seizing the Spanish brig *Josefa* 50 miles south-east of the Bonny. *Pluto*'s prize was bound for Santiago de Cuba and had a cargo of 278 slaves loaded at the river the previous day. Eighty-five slaves died on the passage north to Freetown. The vessel was condemned on 22 June and her surviving slaves emancipated.

Having assisted in the evacuation of the settlement at Fernando Po, on 6 May *Favourite* sailed from Clarence Cove and on the 13th she fell in with the Spanish sloop *Indio*, furnished with a similar passport to *Veloz Mariana* but bound for Santiago de Cuba with a cargo of 117 slaves loaded at the Bonny four days earlier. *Indio* was condemned on 22 June and her surviving 108 slaves emancipated. With her deployment on the Coast now coming to an end, *Favourite* stopped off at Ascension in June before sailing for home, dropping anchor at Portsmouth on 19 August.

Fresh from her success against *Josefa*, in mid-May *Pluto* sailed for Ascension for a long-overdue refit. By early August her machinery was back in full working order and she departed the island for Princes. On 8 June *Britomart* arrived off the Gambia and on 14 June she sailed in company with *Trinculo* for Sierra Leone. The following month *Charybdis* arrived at the Cape to refit. Having examined *Charybdis*'s logbooks Warren now interrogated Crawford over several questionable purchases of provisions made at Sierra Leone and during a cruise to the Gambia and the Cape

Verde Islands. When the vessel's second master, Charles Caseley, came forward with a series of serious allegations against Crawford, Warren had little option but to order *Charybdis*'s commanding officer home to face a trial by court martial.

Sailing from the Cape in mid-September and calling at St Helena and Ascension, *Charybdis* arrived at Portsmouth on 23 November. Crawford's court martial was held on board *Victory* on 9 December. He originally faced nine charges but the last of these, that he acted in a cruel and oppressive manner to Caseley during *Charybdis*'s return journey home, was soon abandoned. The remaining eight charges accused Crawford of the unauthorised disposal of various stores, of locking Caseley in a cabin and ordering him to make a false log, of authorising fictitious expenditures, of causing two able seamen to abandon ship and of striking another able seaman, William Halse, on the head with a telescope, using such force that several fragments of bone eventually passed out through the sailor's nose. After three days of often confusing and contradictory evidence the various charges regarding unauthorised disposal of stores were found not proved, the charges regarding the assaults on Caseley and Halse were proved in part and the charges regarding the authorising of fictitious expenditures and causing two sailors to desert ship were both proved. The court ordered Crawford to be dismissed from the service but in consideration of the various glowing testimonials he had produced during the trial, recommended him to the favourable consideration of the Admiralty. The sentence was later revoked and Crawford was placed on half pay.

In May *Curlew* visited Princes. Whilst at the island Commander Trotter heard of an attack on an American merchantman *Mexican*, carrying around 20,000 silver dollars. She had been boarded in mid-Atlantic by a party of knife-wielding sailors from a piratical schooner and her crew forced below. The brig had been thoroughly looted, her compasses smashed, her rigging cut to pieces and a fire lit in her galley before the boarding party abandoned her to her fate. Thankfully *Mexican*'s crew managed to escape through an unsecured skylight, extinguish the fire and navigate the brig to her home port of Salem. Discovering that a vessel matching the description of the schooner that attacked *Mexican* was in the River Nazareth, south of Cape Lopez, Trotter decided to investigate.

On the evening of 3 June *Curlew* anchored at the mouth of the river and the following morning Trotter sent three boats upriver. Their progress proved to be slow and by the time they reached the schooner smoke was seen coming from her decks and her boats were spotted disappeared toward the riverbank. Boarding the vessel *Curlew*'s men realised that the smoke was coming from the magazine which was now on fire. Thankfully they managed to extinguish the flames before they reached the powder. Searching the vessel they discovered a large selection of foreign ensigns and papers that revealed she was a Havana schooner called *Panda*. The prize having been sent down river to anchor alongside *Curlew*, Trotter now entered into negotiations with the local king, Passall, for the rest of *Panda*'s crew to be handed over. When Passall rather unconvincingly claimed that the men had disappeared into the bush, Trotter decided to deliver an ultimatum to the king. His own vessel was too big to pass over the bar so he sent *Panda* back into the river. The message was delivered and the British waited for a response but none came. Firing a shot to indicate that the ultimatum had expired, a spark ignited some loose powder on the schooner's deck from when the pirate crew had tried to destroy their vessel. This time the powder reached the magazine and the stern of the vessel was blown off. The purser, the gunner and a marine were killed and several others wounded in the explosion and *Panda* rapidly filled with water and sank. The survivors managed to cling to her starboard rail until they were rescued by *Curlew*'s boats.

Five of *Panda*'s crew were now brought on board *Curlew* by some natives. Having interrogated these men, who had joined the schooner after her act of piracy against *Mexican*, on 20 June Trotter headed for the Gabon, where he had been informed *Panda*'s second mate could be found. However, the mate had already left for Cuba and so Trotter departed the Gabon for Princes where he learned that two of *Panda*'s crew were now at Whydah. After calling at Cape Coast and Accra, *Curlew* proceeded to Whydah. Thirteen slavers at that anchorage were boarded but there was no sign of the two Spanish sailors. Trotter went ashore to seek information from an influential local resident, Mr de Souza, and was told that one of the Spaniards from *Panda* had gone to Bahia and the other was now under the protection of the King of Dahomey. On 17 August *Curlew* anchored at Clarence Cove and Trotter went ashore seriously ill with fever.

On 31 July, whilst to the windward of Accra, *Trinculo* boarded the Spanish schooner *Rosa*, equipped for slaving but still awaiting her cargo. With Warren's son, Richard Laird Warren, now in temporary command of the brig-sloop, she headed down into the Bight of Biafra and whilst off Cape St John on 18 September she seized the Spanish schooner *Caridad* with a cargo of 112 slaves, mainly children, bound for Cuba. *Trinculo* headed for the Cape via Ascension and *Caridad* was dispatched to Freetown, arriving in harbour on the evening of 10 October. The slaves were generally healthy, with just a few cases of dysentery, opthalmia and craw-craw. *Caridad* was condemned on 19 October and her surviving 107 slaves emancipated.

Whilst Trotter and the other sick members of *Curlew*'s crew were at Fernando Po convalescing, five Spanish sailors who claimed to have been shipwrecked at Bimia arrived on the island. However, they were soon identified by the Portuguese prisoners from *Panda* as members of her crew and the youngest, Jose Perez, agreed to turn King's evidence. Perez admitted to *Panda*'s piracy and declared that after her crew had gone ashore they had divided their plunder then gone their separate ways, with their captain, Don Pedro Gilbert, remaining at Nazareth under the protection of Passall. Twelve of *Curlew*'s men commanded by the Mate, Henry Matson, now embarked on the English merchantmen *Princess Elizabeth* and sailed for Nazareth with *Curlew*, disguised as a Portuguese trader, following close behind.

The plan was for *Princess Elizabeth* to moor alongside the other merchantmen and when King Passall went on board to inspect her according to the usual custom he would be seized and held as a prisoner until the arrival of *Curlew*. Unfortunately, upon his arrival at Nazareth Matson discovered that Passall was now at Cape Lopez and he was forced to take a boat and four men and row 20 miles upstream to that anchorage. Arriving at Cape Lopez at dawn Matson bumped into *Panda*'s master, Don Pedro Gilbert. The two men greeted each other cordially but something in Matson's demeanour immediately aroused Gilbert's suspicions. However, he let *Curlew*'s mate pass and Matson met with Passall, persuading the king that he had come to trade for ivory and had many dollars to spend. Leaving the king's residence, the British were accosted by Gilbert and several of his men and marched to a nearby house for questioning. Again Matson's nerve held and he was allowed to return to *Princess Elizabeth*. Shortly after midnight *Curlew* arrived at Cape Lopez flying the Brazilian flag. The following afternoon Passall's son, Prince Nazeen, went on board Trotter's cruiser to inspect the new arrival and was taken prisoner along with several members of his entourage. After a day of negotiations Gilbert and three members of *Panda*'s crew were handed over in exchange for the prisoners on board *Curlew* who left Trotter's sloop bearing gifts from the British which, in Nazeen's case, included a full naval uniform.

Having received information from an American merchantman that the mate and a number of men from *Panda* had arrived at St Thomas on board the schooner *Esperanza*, Trotter headed back into the Bights, arriving at the island on 4 October. There was no sign of the schooner but Trotter was informed that the Spanish pirates were still on St Thomas and had purchased a boat from the Governor, hoping to rejoin *Esperanza* which had relocated to the far side of the island. The schooner was found and seized by Matson at which point the Governor, who had previously denied all knowledge of the Spaniards, suddenly declared that he had been hunting the pirates all along. Sailing in company with *Esperanza*, *Curlew* now departed St Thomas for Princes.

In mid-July *Isis*, no longer flying the flag of the commander-in-chief, had headed north from the Cape for a rare foray into the Bights. On 28 October the frigate, commanded by Captain James Polkinghorne, arrested the Spanish brig *El Primo* 60 miles north-west of Princes with a cargo of 343 slaves loaded in the Bonny. Her passenger list included an African boy who had been purchased by the brig's master, Don Ignacio Calvet, at the Bonny. On 10 December *El Primo* was condemned by the Anglo-Spanish Mixed Commission and her surviving 335 slaves, Don Calvet's boy included, emancipated.

Once again sailing under the command of Lieutenant Josiah Thompson, on 23 October *Brisk* arrested the Portuguese brigantine *Virtude* as she emerged from the mouth of the Old Calabar with a cargo of 350 slaves. Fitted out at Bahia and bound for Cuba, *Virtude* was condemned by the Anglo-Portuguese Mixed Commission on 21 November, 314 slaves surviving to be emancipated.

Departing the Cape towards the end of November, *Pelorus* arrived in the Bights where Meredith relieved Trotter as Senior Officer on the Coast. A repaired *Forester* had sailed from Plymouth for the Coast in October under the command of Lieutenant George Miall. *Trinculo*'s former commanding officer, James Booth, had taken passage in the refitted brigantine but *Forester* arrived at Sierra Leone on 21 November needing repairs to a sprung mainmast and Booth was therefore unable to rejoin his sloop which on 2 December was ordered to cruise between Cape St John and

Ambriz Bay, situated almost 600 miles south of the Line. Cruising off St Thomas on 27 December, *Trinculo* seized the Portuguese schooner *Apta*, with a cargo of fifty-four slaves, which was headed from Cape Lopez, just one degree south of the Line, to St Thomas. At only 30ft in length and 11ft in beam, Lieutenant Warren decided that the schooner was unfit for the passage to Sierra Leone and instead landed the slaves and stores at Fernando Po. The following day *Trinculo* seized an even smaller schooner, *Santissimo Rosario e Bon Jesus*, with a cargo of fifty-four slaves which were also landed at Fernando Po. Both vessels had identical papers, written in the same hand and signed by the same persons and both had embarked exactly the same number of slaves, on the same day and at the same place. It would be another six months before both sets of papers arrived in Freetown on board *Forester* and the prizes could come to court. Fittingly, both schooners were condemned together on 25 June 1834 and their surviving slaves emancipated by decree.

Having now succeeded in rounding up fifteen of *Panda*'s crew, in January 1834 Trotter learned that one more pirate was still at Nazareth and so *Curlew* and *Esperanza*, with Matson in command, sailed for Cape Lopez. *Curlew* had been back to Nazareth since her initial visit and Trotter, confined to his cot through sickness, did not anticipate any trouble. However, when Matson went ashore with a small party he and his men were seized by the drunken King Passall who declared that Trotter had made war against him. The prisoners were stripped naked apart from Matson who had the protection of Prince Nazeen. Passall now demanded a ransom of 3,000 dollars for the hostages. After two days of negotiations between Trotter and Passall goods worth £100 were sent onshore only for Passall to increase his demands. Fortunately the arrival of *Fair Rosamond* induced Passall to hand over his prisoners. Determined to recover his ransom and his men's clothes and personal items, Trotter sent Matson to Princes to find *Trinculo*. On *Esperanza*'s return in company with the sloop Trotter launched an attack that involved eleven boats loaded with sailors. Muskets, rockets and carronades were used to destroy the village and drive Passall's men out into the bush where they assembled in such large numbers that Trotter had to abandon his plan to burn the town. Instead, with a large number of his men now sick, he withdrew and sailed for Ascension in company with *Esperanza*, arriving there in early March.

Following her arrival at Portsmouth in late July 1832, *Fair Rosamond* had been laid up in ordinary until January 1833 when the decision was taken to refit her for a return to the Coast, not as a tender but as a commissioned man-of-war. Her sail plan was changed to that of a brigantine but this thankfully did not affect her superior sailing qualities. Refit completed, *Fair Rosamond* departed Spithead for Lisbon in July 1833 under the command of Lieutenant George Rose, arriving off the Coast in early January 1834. January also saw the return to the Coast of Lieutenant Henry Huntley in the newly-launched 3-gun brigantine *Lynx*.

On the morning of 8 January *Pluto* was lying at anchor off the Bonny when she spotted a sail to the north-west. Having recognised the vessel as the Spanish brig *Vengador*, boarded twice by his cruiser, Lieutenant Sullivan weighed, raised steam and set off in pursuit of the brig, which was now headed off to the south-west under a full press of sail. Within an hour of having raised steam *Pluto* was close enough to the brig to fire a gun to bring her to. However, *Vengador* responded by firing two of her guns, aiming roundshot, grape and canister at *Pluto*'s paddle-wheels and jettisoning her anchors and boats as Sullivan's vessel closed in on her leeward beam and quarter. *Vengador* eventually lowered her colours and came to but from his vantage point on the paddle-box Sullivan could see that the brig's crew were preparing her guns for a starboard broadside. He lay *Pluto* across *Vengador*'s larboard quarter and ordered the boarders to the starboard bow. Rather than stand and fight the brig's crew abandoned their posts and retreated below deck. The first slaver to have been captured by a cruiser under steam power, 406 slaves were discovered in *Vengador*'s hold. In accordance with the treaty, her master, the slaver Pedro Badia, and two of her crew of forty-seven remained on board the brig with the prize crew for her passage to Sierra Leone whilst the remainder were landed at Princes. *Pluto*'s prize was condemned on 21 February, 376 slaves surviving to be emancipated, seventeen of those lost having jumped overboard during her journey north.

With Warren's flag now flying on board *Forester* at Simon's Bay, on 16 February *Isis* made her second capture in the Bights, seizing the Spanish brigantine *Carolina* with a cargo of 350 slaves loaded at the River Lagos. Twenty-seven of her sickly slaves died on the vessel's passage north and a further 100 were removed to the Liberated African Hospital following *Carolina*'s arrival at Freetown on 12 March. The brigantine was condemned on 22 March and her surviving 320 slaves emancipated. Following this arrest *Isis* sailed to Ascension to refit, arriving at the island on 2 April.

As *Isis* was dropping anchor at Ascension *Curlew* was departing the Coast for England in company with her prize *Esperanza*, the two vessels arriving at Plymouth on 5 June. *Panda*'s piratical crew were transferred to the brig-sloop *Savage* to stand trial in America and *Esperanza* sailed for Lisbon where she was returned to her original owner. When *Savage* arrived at Boston the brig *Mexican* happened to be at anchor in Salem Harbour. Her master and mate now gave evidence of the act of piracy against their vessel two years earlier and in June 1835 Don Pedro and five of his crew were found guilty of piracy and hanged. Warren had written to the Admiralty to express his disapproval of Trotter's obsessive hunt for *Panda*'s crew but Washington was delighted that Don Pedro and his men had received American justice and, Their Lordships having conveyed to Trotter the personal thanks of President Jackson, in September 1835 he was promoted captain.

Following watering and provisioning at Ascension, *Fair Rosamond* proceeded to her cruising grounds in the Bights and on the night of 26 April arrived off the Old Calabar. The following morning a Spanish-flagged schooner was discovered close by, preparing to weigh anchor. A rocket fired over the vessel by *Fair Rosamond* quickly induced her to strike her colours. Upon boarding she was discovered to be the schooner *La Pantica* with a cargo of 317 slaves. Rose sent a prize crew across to the slaver but, concerned that her crew might smuggle liquor to his men and retake their vessel, he had them all removed, leaving just the master, Jozé Carbo, on board ship. An official at Sierra Leone, Francis Harrison Rankin, described the arrival of *La Pantica* in port the following month.

> One fine day in May the signal gun told of the approach of a vessel, which the lookers-out on the signal hill announced, by the usual method of hoisting a coloured ball to the top of the staff, to be a schooner or brig from the south. A sharp-built schooner with crowded canvas glanced up the estuary like lightning. She was a prize … We easily leapt on board as she lay low in the water. The first hasty glance around caused a sudden sickness and faintness, followed by indignation more intense than discreet. Before us, lying in a heap, huddled together at the foot of the foremast on the bare and filthy

deck, lay several human beings in the last stages of emancipation – dying. The ship, fore and aft, was thronged with men, women and children, all entirely naked, and disgusting with disease. The stench was nearly insupportable, cleanliness being impossible. I stepped to the hatchway; it was secured by iron bars and crossbars, and pressed against them were the heads of the slaves below.[5]

The rainy season had now set in and over 100 slaves, many barely alive, had to endure a night exposed on the deck whilst the slave master slept undisturbed in his cot. On 2 June *La Pantica* was condemned and her surviving 270 slaves emancipated. The commissioners expressed their displeasure at Rose having only sent one witness to Freetown, which was contrary to the terms of the treaty and they also questioned *Fair Rosamond*'s commander over a missing boat. The boat, which had been used to land *La Pantica*'s officers at the Old Calabar, was eventually returned to Rose at Fernando Po and disposed of as per the commissioners' instructions.

Following the court martial of Richard Crawford, *Charybdis* departed Portsmouth for the Coast on 10 March under the command of Lieutenant Samuel Mercer, an officer who had previously served as a midshipman on board *Eden*. Calling at Lisbon and the Cape, *Charybdis* arrived in the Bight of Benin in early June. On the 14th she was cruising 50 miles south-west of Lagos when she spotted and gave chase to a strange sail. There then followed a lengthy pursuit in which Mercer was forced to fire fourteen rounds of grape and canister at the vessel to bring her to. At around 4.00pm *Charybdis* boarded the Portuguese brig *Tamega* with a cargo of 444 slaves. The vessel did not possess a royal passport but instead had papers for a voyage from Gibraltar to Lisbon via Bahia and the Coast. However, following her arrival at Bahia *Tamega* had then sailed to Lagos where she had shipped her cargo of slaves. *Charybdis*'s prize was condemned on 12 July and her surviving 434 slaves emancipated. A question now arose over some hams, a cheese, a log line and a barrel of wine which had gone missing from the brig. The wine, it transpired, had been taken ashore at the request of *Tamega*'s master, Jose Lopez Ferreira, who now came to Mercer's defence by declaring that the remaining articles had been stolen by his own men.

The Squadron's next arrest was made under highly irregular circumstances. Having waited for several days at the mouth of the

Cameroons River for a Spanish schooner that was known to be awaiting her cargo of slaves, on the evening of 30 June *Pelorus* sent her pinnace and cutter upriver under the command of First Lieutenant Thomas Barrow. Landing at the barracoon where the slaver's cargo was being held, Barrow removed three African boys, then boarded the schooner as it lay at anchor. Driving the Spaniards aft, Barrow put the three children into the hold then arrested the vessel, *Pepita*, for having slaves on board. The following morning a further 176 slaves from the barracoon were exchanged for the trade goods still on board *Pepita* and sent across to the slaver by Barrow. These trade goods were also used to pay for fresh provisions and pilotage for *Pepita*'s voyage back to Freetown. Having grounded on leaving the river, *Pepita* was taken to Fernando Po for repairs and further provisioning before her journey north in company with *Pelorus*. None of the officers in charge of the schooner's prize crew had been present at her capture which caused a delay in her case being seen by the Mixed Commission. When Meredith's illegal actions came to light the commissioner had no option but to restore *Pepita* to her owner and award damages of £1,091 against *Pelorus*'s commanding officer. The surviving 153 Africans who had arrived at Freetown on board the schooner could not be emancipated as they had not been shipped for the purposes of the slave trade but were handed over to the Colonial Government to be employed as servants and free labourers.

On 5 August *Fair Rosamond* captured the Spanish schooner *Maria Isabel* following an hour long chase off Princes. The schooner was carrying a provisional passport from the Havana Navy Board that allowed her to carry goods to Princes but had sailed directly from Santiago de Cuba for the Benin where she had loaded 146 slaves. *Fair Rosamond* returned to Freetown in company with her prize, arriving in harbour on 1 September. On 9 September *Maria Isabel* was condemned and her 131 surviving slaves emancipated. Her master, José Mauri, had appeared before the Mixed Commission twice before, sailing on board the slavers *Gazetta* in 1820 and *Atafa Primo* in 1830. He was also suspected to have served on board the piratical vessel *Pelicano* which had murdered *Redwing*'s prize crew in 1825 but the court lacked sufficient evidence to prosecute him for this crime.

Following her refit *Isis* had arrived at the Cape from Ascension on 2 May. With the commander-in-chief's flag once again flying on board the frigate, on 17 July she had departed Simon's Bay for the Gambia where Warren was to hand over command of the Cape and West Africa Station to his replacement, Rear Admiral Patrick Campbell. Arriving at Ascension in early September *Isis* fell in with *Pluto*, *Lynx* and the brigantine *Griffon* which was undergoing a refit. Following the departure of *Isis* from the island on 10 September, *Lynx* sailed for Princes and *Pluto* headed home. On 17 September Huntley's brig fell in with and gave chase to a Spanish-flagged vessel, boarding her several hours later 330 miles off Ascension and 4° south of the Line. She proved to be the schooner *Arogante Mayaguesana*, bound from Loango to Puerto Rico with a cargo of 350 slaves, mainly children, loaded a fortnight earlier. *Lynx*'s prize arrived in Freetown on 30 September, forty-one slaves having died on the passage north. This was the first slaver brought to the Anglo-Spanish Mixed Commission to have been arrested south of the Line and the court hoped that her successful condemnation on 9 October would lead to greater activity by British cruisers in those latitudes.

Chapter 10

The Spanish Equipment Clause:
September 1834–December 1836

In late December 1831 a large-scale slave revolt had broken out in Jamaica, led by the Baptist minister Samuel Sharpe. Largely peaceful in nature, by early 1832 the rebellion had been forcibly put down by the militia of the local plantocracy with the assistance of the British garrison on the island. In the reprisals that followed missionaries were arrested, chapels destroyed and around 500 slaves either killed or executed. The Government subsequently held two enquiries into the revolt and these, together with public revulsion over the actions of the plantation owners, were instrumental in the introduction of the Slavery Abolition Act. The Act, which outlawed slavery in the British Empire, affecting around 800,000 black men, women and children, had its third and final reading in the House of Commons on 26 July 1833, just three days before the death of William Wilberforce. It received Royal Assent the following month and came in to force on 1 August 1834. Slaves below the age of six were now freed in the colonies, former slaves older than six were redesignated 'apprentices' and these apprenticeships were scheduled to end by 1 August 1840. The Act also put aside £20 million to provide compensation for slave owners, approximately 5 per cent of British GDP (around £100 billion today).

In March 1833 Britain and France had signed a supplementary convention to the Treaty of November 1831 establishing the procedure for dealing with slaving vessels that were discovered in convoy and vessels that were equipped for slaving but detained without slaves. In late 1833 Britain and France simultaneously invited the United States to agree to this convention. The US Secretary of State, Louis McLane, deferred answering this proposal until Congress had met, then postponed negotiations through fear of upsetting the southern states. Britain had proposed a reciprocal right of search of ships suspected of slaving within certain geographical limits but these limits would extend to the coast of the United States. In exchange Britain offered to include the British West Indies. Concerned over the Right of Search by British cruisers in American coastal waters, Washington refused the proposal in March 1834. Britain offered to drop the offending clause and in September the French urged the United States to join the convention. However, on 4 October the new Secretary of State, John Forsyth, wrote to Palmerston to explain that a determination had been made not to make the United States a party to any convention on the Slave Trade. Forsyth declared that the United States would best perform its anti-slavery duties by employing its own means of detecting and punishing American citizens employed in the Trade. The American refusal was so definite that Palmerston realised any further negotiations at that time would be pointless. In a further blow to the abolitionist cause, a change in government the following month saw Palmerston replaced as Foreign Secretary by the Duke of Wellington.

On 6 September Rear Admiral Patrick Campbell hoisted his flag on board the 46-gun frigate *Thalia*, Captain Robert Wauchope, at Spithead and sailed for the Gambia. Famous for his cutting-out of the French frigate *Désirée* from Dunkirk Roads in July 1800 whilst in command of the experimental sloop *Dart*, Campbell had held several commands in the Mediterranean between 1811 and 1827 before being promoted rear admiral in 1830.

On 24 September *Isis* arrived at Bathurst from Ascension to find *Buzzard* and *Lynx* both at anchor. Following the arrival of *Thalia* on 10 October Warren handed over command of the Squadron to Campbell then sailed for home that same day, arriving at Portsmouth on 21 November. Discovering that the health of *Buzzard*'s commanding officer, Lieutenant Jeremiah McNamara, was broken, Campbell offered command of the brigantine to his senior lieutenants. For unexplained reasons his First and Second both turned the position down, but his Third, Clement Milward, accepted and moved into *Buzzard*. On 12 October *Thalia* departed Bathurst for the Cape, Campbell intending to visit Sierra Leone, Cape Coast, Accra, Princes, St Helena and Ascension en route.

Following her refit at Ascension *Griffon* had departed the island to cruise in the Bights. On the morning of 31 October Parlby's brigantine was 75 miles south-west of St Thomas, headed for Princes, when a schooner was spotted to leeward. *Griffon* immediately gave chase and within several hours was close enough to fire two shots which induced the stranger to heave to and surrender without resistance. The vessel proved to be the

Spanish schooner *Indagadora*, bound from New Calabar for Havana with a cargo of 375 slaves. *Griffon*'s second master, Mr Noddall, was sent on board the schooner for her passage to Freetown. At 10.00am on 3 November *Griffon* was 40 miles south-east of Princes when a strange sail was seen from her masthead. Parlby ordered all sail and following a hard chase of seven and a half hours put a shot close up under the stranger's stern. The vessel raised a Spanish ensign and hove to. Twice the size of *Indagadora*, the brigantine *Clemente* had departed the Bonny for Havana with a cargo of 415 slaves around ten days earlier. On board were papers revealing that she was the same vessel that had been detained by the sloop *Pylades*, Commander Edward Blanckley, in mid-Atlantic and sent to Portsmouth before being released and allowed to proceed to her original destination. Mr Gammon and a prize crew of nine men were sent across to the brigantine. She arrived in Freetown on 19 November to find *Griffon*'s other prize, *Indagadora*, already in harbour. *Indagadora* had lost twelve of her slaves on her passage north and *Clemente* just seven. In total 764 slaves were emancipated from these two prizes. Following their condemnation in December the commissioners took the unusual step of praising Parlby, the prize masters and their crews, not only for the care and attention they had paid to the slaves on board their vessels but also for ensuring that the papers presented to court were all in order, a reminder that this was not always the case for vessels seized by the Squadron.

After nearly six months without any capture to her name, on 17 December *Pelorus* fell in with the Spanish schooner *Sutil* to the north-east of Princes. Following a chase of several hours the schooner was boarded and was discovered to have a cargo of 307 slaves loaded at the Old Calabar. The schooner had already lost twenty-seven slaves, crushed to death in the scramble for space the night she had departed the river. *Sutil*'s drinking water was now discovered to be foul, having been taken from alongside the river, and a further seventy-nine slaves died during her passage north. Her prize master, Mr Judd, died a few days after her arrival at Freetown on 23 January 1835 and by the time of *Sutil*'s condemnation on 31 January twelve more slaves had perished.

On the same day that *Sutil* was being arrested *Buzzard* boarded the Spanish brig *Formidable*, also from the Old Calabar, following a chase of seven hours. A large vessel armed with two long 16-pounders and six 18-pounder Govers, *Formidable* had recently been boarded by *Pelorus* and her master, Manuel Mateu, had expressed a determination not to be taken by any of the Squadron's smaller cruisers. With light winds Milward's brigantine employed her sweeps to keep pace with *Formidable* which threw overboard her stores, casks and spare masts to avoid capture. She then cut loose her stern-boat, ran out her stern guns and hoisted her Spanish ensign. Finally within pistol shot, *Buzzard* opened fire with her small arms and *Formidable* replied with her stern guns. Milward fired his long guns and attempted to run the brig on board. At 4.30pm *Formidable* finally lowered her colours but when Milward hailed her to confirm whether she had in fact surrendered she fired her stern guns, shooting away *Buzzard*'s flying jib-boom. Ten minutes later *Buzzard* was close enough to put her larboard bow alongside *Formidable*'s starboard quarter and Milward sent his boarders away. Cutting their way through the side netting, *Buzzard*'s men were met by the brig's crew and a number of armed Africans. After a brief struggle in which six of *Buzzard*'s men were wounded, *Formidable* was taken. Upon examination 712 slaves were discovered packed in her hold. Milward had no senior officers to spare so his acting second master was placed in command of the slaver for her passage to Sierra Leone. During her journey north *Formidable* was struck by lightning and ten slaves and two of her prize crew were killed. Before her arrival in port on 28 January 1835 a further six slaves had jumped overboard through the rips in *Formidable*'s side netting, preferring death to further confinement on board the overcrowded vessel. Having arrived at the Old Calabar in company with *Sutil*, which was most likely acting as her tender, *Formidable* had also filled her water barrels from alongside the river, so by the time of her condemnation on 6 February sickness had further reduced her cargo to 418 slaves. Milward, who was later promoted to commander, was commended by the Senior Officer on the Coast, Meredith, for his 'coolness and gallantry'[1] during the action, Meredith writing: 'The *Formidable* was the crack vessel here, and I trust that I may be permitted to add, that in no action on the coast has the disparity of force been greater, the resistance more determinedly kept up, or more coolly and gallantly overcome, than in this instance.'[2] *Buzzard* had ended the action with her forestay cut through and damage to bowsprit, sails and rigging. The slaver had received damage to her rigging and sails. Six of her crew had been killed and sixteen wounded, including the master and three of the armed slaves.

On 20 December *Lynx* boarded fifteen slavers at Whydah Roads, two of which, the Portuguese brigs *Atrevido* and *Fortuna*, were almost ready to load their cargoes. *Lynx* departed the anchorage, retreating to just below the horizon to wait for the brigs to put to sea. At dawn on 22 December two vessels were sighted from *Lynx*'s masthead, one on her weather bow, the other on her weather quarter. Huntley decided to give chase to the vessel furthest to seaward, gaining slowly on her during the course of the day. As night fell Huntley briefly lost sight of the brig but she was sighed again as the moon rose. Now within range, a shot was fired through her boom mainsail head and she came to. Huntley sent a boat to board her but she was discovered to be the empty *Fortuna*, sent out as a decoy for the now-loaded *Atrevido*, a ploy often employed by the slavers on the Coast.

Lynx returned to Whydah, hiding below the horizon to wait for *Atrevido*. On 24 December a brig was sighted headed in the direction of Huntley's cruiser. When she finally spotted *Lynx* she tacked and steered to the north-west. *Lynx* hauled sail and gave chase in a fresh breeze. The chase lasted all day, *Lynx* losing sight of the brig when darkness fell. However, Huntley correctly guessed that she would alter course to the south-east and at dawn on 25 December *Atrevido* was spotted on *Lynx*'s lee bow. The chase was resumed and *Lynx* was almost in gun range when the two vessels were engulfed by a storm and lost sight of one another for the next two hours. Certain that *Atrevido* would alter course again, Huntley brought *Lynx* about on the starboard tack and when the sky finally cleared *Atrevido* was spotted becalmed and within range of *Lynx*'s guns. A shot fired over her induced her to lower her colours and surrender without further resistance. Upon boarding she was discovered to have a cargo of 494 slaves bound for Montevideo. *Lynx* took her prize to Princes to water and provision before she departed for Freetown where, on 31 January 1835 *Atrevido* was condemned and her surviving 482 slaves emancipated.

Having spent four months cruising without any success, the first arrest of 1835 fell to *Fair Rosamond* when, following a nine-hour chase in light and variable winds off the River Gabon on 3 January, she seized the Portuguese schooner *Maria*, headed from Mayumba Bay, 200 miles south of the Line, to Princes with a cargo of forty-eight slaves. Towing her prize to Fernando Po, Rose's brigantine arrived at the island with just one day's water remaining. Forty-four of *Maria*'s slaves were landed at West Bay before the prize was sent to Freetown where she was condemned on 28

February. The commissioners noted that *Maria* was typical of the small vessels employed to ship slaves from the mainland to Princes, from where she had obtained her papers.

Learning that a Spanish slaver was about to depart from Duke's Town, on 12 January Commander Meredith dispatched First Lieutenant Barrow with three of *Pelorus*'s boats up the Old Calabar to investigate. Discovering from the master of an English merchantman that the slaver was loaded and ready to sail, on the night of the 15th Barrow positioned his boats at the narrowest point of the river and lay in wait until the vessel came abreast under the tow of several canoes. As the boats pushed off, the marines provided covering fire, receiving a hail of musketry from the slaver until the boats were alongside. The vessel had side netting set up so the boarders climbed in through the gun ports and quickly forced her surrender, thankfully with no loss of life on either side. The vessel proved to be the Spanish polacca barque *Minerva* with a cargo of 650 slaves. Her master, Andres Puig, was absent but returned an hour later, unaware his vessel had been seized, with a further twenty-five slaves in a canoe who were put on board the slaver by Barrow. Meredith was in the fortunate position of having two surgeons on board *Pelorus* so he was able to send Assistant Surgeon Stevenson across to *Minerva*. The slaver arrived at Freetown on 20 February and was condemned eight days later. Four hundred and forty-four slaves survived to be emancipated but this number did not include the twenty-five brought on board after her capture who were handed over to the Colonial Government. Stevenson now sent a report on the care of slaves on board prizes to the commissioners and this was forwarded to the Foreign Office. His report recommended that all cruisers carry two surgeons, additional medical supplies to treat the common diseases found on board slavers – dysentery, diarrhoea and opthalmia – and at least eight blankets per slave due to fouling. Stevenson also recommended that the sick and healthy be separated. The Admiralty eventually decided that most of the report's suggestions were impracticable but the Squadron did receive an additional supply of blankets.

On 4 January *Britomart* departed Sierra Leone for the Bights, carrying despatches for Governor George Maclean at Cape Coast Castle. On his arrival at Cape Coast Quin was informed that Maclean was now besieged at Axim, having been defeated in battle by the King of Apollonia who had been plundering native British subjects and vessels landing at the Castle.

Britomart now sailed for Axim and with her assistance on 1 February the Governor began a march along the coast to the nearby fort of Apollonia with his remaining expeditionary force, 400 men including a number of Dutch soldiers from Elmina. Attacked from the bush, most of Maclean's men quickly deserted but Quin brought his cruiser close enough to the shore to provide covering fire and clear the beach of the enemy. When Maclean camped that night *Britomart* anchored close inshore and resupplied the Governor with ammunition, provisions and water. The following morning Quin sent his cutter with marines to give Maclean musketry support, once again keeping *Britomart* close to the shore as the governor recommenced his march. With the enemy once again massing, Quin landed his marines and opened fire with a starboard broadside. The enemy scattered, allowing Maclean to reach the British fort at Apollonia. Whilst Maclean's wounded were taken on board *Britomart*, the governor entered discussions with the King of Apollonia who agreed to release thirty-seven prisoners, renounce human sacrifice and deposit 300 ounces of gold at the Castle. For his invaluable assistance Quin received the thanks of Maclean, the Council and merchants of Cape Coast and was awarded a piece of plate worth 100 guineas. In early April *Britomart* departed Cape Coast for Accra to replenish her supplies of ball cartridge then headed for Princes to rendezvous with *Pelorus*.

On the evening of 2 February *Buzzard* arrested the Spanish schooner *Iberia* off the Bonny, the schooner only surrendering as *Buzzard*'s men were boarding the vessel following a chase of nearly four hours. Sailing from Havana and furnished with a passport for St Thomas, *Iberia* had made directly for the Bonny where, on the morning of her capture, she had loaded a cargo of 313 slaves. As the drunken Spanish prisoners were being removed to Milward's brigantine her gig capsized, drowning two men. Short-handed, with a prize crew still on board *Formidable*, Milward decided to escort *Iberia* to Freetown, arriving there on 3 March. The schooner was condemned on 11 March and her surviving 303 slaves emancipated.

In late February the 10-gun brig *Curlew*, Lieutenant Joseph Denman, and the 18-gun brig-sloop *Pelican*, Commander Brunswick Popham, departed Portsmouth for the Coast, having been ordered to relieve *Pelorus* and *Brisk*. Meanwhile Commander Booth had requested permission to return home and was temporarily replaced as commander of *Trinculo* by the First Lieutenant of *Thalia*, Henry Puget. In mid-February Major

Henry Dundas Campbell arrived at Sierra Leone to take over the duties of Lieutenant-Governor from the Acting Governor, Thomas Cole, who resumed his duties as Secretary of the Colony.

On 23 February *Forester* made her first arrest in fifteen months following a seven-hour chase of a suspicious-looking vessel off Cape Formoso. The Spanish brigantine *El Manuel* had a cargo of 387 slaves loaded five days earlier at the Bonny and her master, Jose Curbo, had been in command of *La Pantica*, seized by *Fair Rosamond* in April 1834. Lieutenant Miall despatched his prize to Freetown and on 24 March she was condemned and her surviving 375 slaves were emancipated. Sailing off Cape St Paul's, on 20 March Miall's brigantine fell in with the Portuguese schooner *Legitimo Africano* with a cargo of 190 slaves loaded at Whydah by her owner, Da Souza, five days earlier. *Forester*'s prize was condemned on 9 May, 186 slaves surviving to be emancipated. In adjudicating on the case the commissioners ignored the rather implausible claim of her master, José Manuel de Lima, that his cargo were Africans being taken to Bahia to be educated.

On 28 March *Buzzard* fell in with the Spanish schooner *Bienvenida* whilst en route to Sierra Leone, arresting the vessel 300 miles south of Cape Coast Castle. Along with a cargo of 430 slaves loaded at the Gabon, *Bienvenida* also had twenty-five passengers, the crews of condemned vessels who were returning to Havana. Forty-five slaves died during *Bienvenida*'s passage north and a further eighteen were lost following her arrival in port on 15 April. The schooner was condemned on 23 April and her surviving 367 slaves emancipated.

On 21 March the 10-gun brig *Rolla*, Lieutenant Frederick Glasse, departed Sheerness for the Coast. Campbell had still not received any official notification of the arrival of *Pelican* and *Curlew* and prior to *Rolla*'s appearance at Freetown on 30 April he had written to the Admiralty requesting that he be informed of new arrivals on the Coast and that they be directed to the Cape, not Sierra Leone so that he could make the proper disposition of his forces and order relieved vessels home.

In April the Commissary Judge, William Smith, retired and was replaced by the Arbitrator, H.W. Macaulay, Macaulay's position as arbitrator being filled by the Registrar, Walter Lewis. That same month Lord Palmerston drew the commissioners attention to the case of *Conchita*, a vessel fully equipped for slaving but discovered deserted that had been arrested by

Owen Glendower in June 1823. The original case had been postponed due to lack of evidence but Palmerston now informed the Anglo-Spanish Mixed Commission that the condemnation of the vessel would have been justified and he requested that the case be re-opened. *Conchita* was finally condemned on 20 July 1835, twelve years after her original capture.

On 15 June *Forester*, cruising off the Bonny in company with *Britomart*, arrested the Spanish schooner *Numero Dos* as she emerged from the river with a cargo of 154 slaves. The schooner, furnished with a passport for Princes and bound for Santiago de Cuba, tried to turn back towards the river when she spotted *Forester* but offered no resistance to her boarding. She arrived at Freetown on 12 July and was condemned on the 28th, 141 slaves surviving to be emancipated.

With the resumption of duties of *Buzzard*'s Lieutenant McNamara her acting commander, Lieutenant Milward, had returned to *Thalia*. However, in July Commander Puget reported McNamara's death and appointed *Trinculo*'s First Lieutenant, Thomas Roberts, as acting commander of *Buzzard*, unaware that the commander-in-chief had already appointed his flag lieutenant and nephew, Patrick Campbell, to the position. In early July *Pelican* arrived at Simon's Bay from Freetown. Having received orders to return home, on 18 July *Pelorus* departed Ascension, where she had been refitting, for Portsmouth, arriving there on 9 September. On 22 July *Charybdis* joined *Thalia* at St Helena before departing for a cruise along the coast from Benguela to Princes, looking into the various rivers along that stretch of coast. Meanwhile the commander-in-chief had arrived at Ascension on 13 August to find *Brisk* and *Britomart* at anchor. *Thalia* now sailed for the Cape and *Brisk* for England, the brigantine arriving at Spithead on 4 October.

On 27 July *Fair Rosamond* sailed from Princes where she had watered and provisioned. At 9.30am on the 29th a vessel was observed sitting low in the water to the north-east, scarcely visible from the mast head. Rose gave chase in light winds and the stranger was soon observed discarding her boat. At 5.30pm with the stranger, a fully-laden brigantine, still two miles distant *Fair Rosamond* fired several rockets which, falling short, the slaver ignored. Rose's vessel closed a little and as dusk fell he fired his single long gun but her shot also fell short. At 8.30pm the stranger was finally within range and the 9-pounder was once again brought into action along with several volleys of musketry and the brigantine, *Volador*, finally hauled down her colours and surrendered. Boarded without any resistance, she was discovered to have a cargo of 487 slaves loaded a day previously at the Bonny. Her master, Angel de Aguirre, claimed that his vessel, one of the fastest sailers out of Havana, had often been chased by cruisers on both sides of the Atlantic but had always escaped capture. *Volador*'s pivot-mounted long 18-pounder was discovered loaded with shot and a length of chain cable but de Aguirre had thankfully been unable to force his crew of forty-four to stand and fight. Forty-six slaves died during a passage of just seventeen days from the Bights to Sierra Leone (the average passage being twenty-eight days). A further thirteen died following the brigantine's arrival at Freetown. On 25 August *Volador* was condemned and her surviving 428 slaves emancipated.

In April the suppression campaign had received fresh impetus with the return of Palmerston as Foreign Secretary and on 28 June a new Anglo-Spanish treaty that included the long sought-for Equipment Clause was signed at Madrid. The treaty, which was ratified on 27 August, granted a mutual right of search of vessels engaged in and equipped for the slave trade. The criteria demonstrating that a vessel had been equipped for slaving were identical to those used in the Anglo-Netherlands treaty of 1823. The two existing Anglo-Spanish Mixed Commissions would continue to hear cases until new Mixed Courts of Justice had been set up. A provision of the treaty was that condemned vessels were to be broken up and their fittings sold to prevent them returning to the Trade. Inexplicably, considering the importance of this treaty, Palmerston did not make the commissioners at Freetown aware of its signing until late October. He then failed to clarify that, whilst legislation had to be passed in London before British vessels could be brought before the courts, Spanish vessels could be judged immediately.

On 2 September *Buzzard* seized the Spanish schooner *Semiramis* with a cargo of 477 slaves loaded at the Bonny earlier that same day. The schooner had tried to re-enter the river upon spotting Robert's brigantine, but with insufficient depth of water beneath her keel to make it back over the bar she had surrendered without a fight. *Buzzard*'s prize arrived at Freetown on 5 October and was condemned on 12 October. The schooner was rife with the usual slave diseases of smallpox, opthalmia and dysentery and fifty-one slaves died prior to emancipation. The day after her condemnation *Semiramis*'s prize crew departed Freetown for the Bights on board *Rolla*.

Arriving off St Paul de Loando in early August *Charybdis* discovered thirty-two slavers at anchor, all flying Portuguese colours. At Ambriz Mercer boarded a Spanish brigantine waiting to load a cargo of 500 slaves and was dismayed to learn from a British merchantman that another Spanish vessel had departed two days earlier with a cargo of 450 slaves. *Charybdis* now entered the Congo where she discovered more Portuguese and Spanish vessels awaiting their slave cargoes. Arriving at Loango on 16 August Mercer boarded several more vessels and discovered that a Spanish brig had departed the bay with a cargo of 500 slaves the previous morning. *Charybdis* immediately set off in pursuit but with no sign of the brig had to give up the chase forty-eight hours later. On 23 August Mercer's brigantine anchored in the River Gabon, where she discovered two empty Spanish schooners. From what he had seen Mercer estimated that the annual trade between St Paul de Loando and Camma Bay was upwards of 47,000 slaves carried in around 130 vessels. Sailing to Fernando Po to replenish, on 6 September *Charybdis* arrived at Princes where Mercer reported his findings to the Senior Officer, Commander Puget.

Having returned to sea, at 2.40pm on 8 October *Charybdis* spotted a suspicious-looking brig off the River Gabon and gave chase, but eventually lost sight of her prey as darkness set in. Spotted again two days later, the brig was once again able to evade capture under the cover of darkness. The game of cat and mouse finally ended on the morning of 11 October when the brig was sighted six miles to leeward of *Charybdis*, now sailing off Cape Lopez. By 7.45am the slaver had hauled down her colours and surrendered. She proved to be the Spanish vessel *Argos*, bound for Havana with a cargo of 429 slaves loaded at the Bonny on 3 October. Her papers showed that she had originally loaded 500 slaves and when questioned her master, Narciso Estiva, claimed that the missing seventy-one had died, the river being very sickly. He later admitted to throwing the ten sickliest slaves overboard just prior to capture but his crew informed Mercer that most of the other missing slaves had been disposed of the same way. Forty-six more slaves died during *Argos*'s five-week passage to Freetown and with another seventeen dying following her arrival in port on 15 November, only 366 of her cargo survived to see emancipation later the following day. Seemingly of more concern to the commissioners, however, was the fact that Mercer had forced Estiva to sign a document stating that nothing had been taken from the vessel, even though *Argos* was in fact missing several jars of sperm oil and candles for use in her binnacle. An offer to pay for these articles by the prize master was refused but they were later replaced by the Captor's Agent prior to *Argos*'s sale.

At dawn on 16 October *Britomart* spotted a schooner off the Rio Nunez and set off in pursuit, beginning a two-day chase that ended at dawn on 18 October with the fully-laden Spanish-flagged schooner *Conde de Los Andes* surrendering to *Britomart* without resistance. Lieutenant Quin took his prize to Fernando Po to water and provision before she was dispatched to Freetown, arriving there on 21 November. She was a very overcrowded vessel but thankfully only thirteen of her 282 slaves died on the passage north. Commending her prize master, Mr Burslem, the commissioners condemned *Conde* and emancipated her surviving 269 slaves.

On 16 November *Britomart* arrested the Portuguese schooner *Theresa*, 30 miles west of Lagos from where she had loaded a cargo of 214 slaves. Quin's prize was condemned on 31 December and her surviving 202 slaves emancipated. The schooner, armed with two guns but boarded without resistance, was owned by Joaquim Telles de Menezes, the son-in-law of Da Souza, and had sailed from Princes with papers for Montevideo. All the Portuguese vessels that had come before the Mixed Commission during the year had cleared out from Princes and three of the four that had been condemned had proceeded directly from that island to Whydah where Da Souza had overseen their loading of slaves.

Learning from a British merchantman that a treaty which included an Equipment Clause had been signed between Britain and Spain, on 17 November Denman arrested the empty Spanish schooners *Victorina* and *Josepha* off Cape Mesurado, even though he lacked the proper authority to do so. The following day he arrested the Spanish brigantine *General Manso* off the Gallinas. As a young lieutenant aboard the ship-sloop *Snake*, in January 1834 Joseph Denman had been placed in command of the barque *Maria da Gloria*, a Portuguese vessel with a cargo of 423 slaves seized off Brazil that had been sent to Sierra Leone for condemnation. The suffering he had witnessed first-hand on board that vessel during her 46-day passage, the deaths of fifty-five slaves, followed by her eventual restoration due to lack of evidence, had left an indelible impression on the young officer and he was now intent on doing everything in his power to help bring the Trade to an end. Upon Denman's arrival at Freetown on 23 November with his three prizes the commissioners denied all knowledge of the new treaty and declined to pass judgement on *Curlew*'s prizes. Realising that the seizures were illegal and could not be supported, on 2 December Denman made a deal with the Spanish masters in which they would be allowed to return to their original point of capture so long as they did not to press any claim on him regarding their illegal seizure and detention. The following day the 10-gun brig *Leveret*, Lieutenant Charles Bosanquet, arrived from England with a copy of the 1835 Treaty. Taking passage on board *Leveret* was Denman's replacement in *Curlew*, Lieutenant Edmund Norcott, Denman having now been promoted. On 4 December *General Manso* and *Victorina* sailed from Freetown, still under the charge of their prize masters. *Leveret*, with Norcott still on board, now gave chase and arrested both vessels. Meanwhile a British officer had gone on board *Josepha*, which was riding at anchor, and declared that she was being arrested by *Curlew* and *Leveret*. The officer demanded *Josepha*'s papers along with the recent agreement signed between her master, Miguel Calvet, and Denman. Proceedings against the captured slavers were quickly dismissed by the commissioners, who declared that they had received no authority from the Government to carry into effect the treaty or confirmation that it was now in force. Norcott sent a copy of the treaty to the court but the commissioners pointed to the fact that there had been no accompanying letter from the Admiralty and the treaty had not been signed. Furthermore, there was no evidence that it had been ratified and to their knowledge there had been no Act of Parliament to bring it into effect. Denman, alarmed by the actions of his fellow officers, assured the Spanish masters that the arrests by *Curlew* and *Leveret* had been done without his knowledge or agreement.

General Manso's master now sent the Mixed Commission a petition explaining the agreement made with Denman and claiming that £2,900 worth of Spanish doubloons had been taken from his vessel. He asked that the brigantine be restored and the money returned. The petition was rejected because the case had not been adjudicated by the Commission. Proceedings against the three captured slavers would not begin until mid-1836 whilst the commissioners waited for confirmation that the treaty had come into effect.

In mid-October the 18-gun ship-sloop *Pylades*, Commander William Castle, arrived at Freetown from Plymouth. On the 28th she departed for a cruise along the Windward Coast. On the morning of 27 November *Buzzard* seized the Spanish schooner *Norma* off the mouth of the River Bonny, from where she had loaded 234 slaves earlier that day. On the passage to Sierra Leone four slaves jumped overboard, forcing the prize master to put the remaining male slaves in irons to prevent them from taking their own lives the same way. A further eleven slaves died of disease prior to *Norma*'s arrival at Freetown on 28 December. Proceedings were begun under the 1817 Treaty but were interrupted by the arrival of copies of the new treaty which caused some confusion. *Norma* was eventually condemned on 6 January 1836 under the earlier treaty and her surviving 218 slaves emancipated.

On 19 December *Curlew* seized the Spanish cutter *Tres Tomasas* 130 miles south-west of Freetown. According to her master, Nicholas Echeandia, the vessel, empty but equipped for slaving, was en route to the Cape Verde Islands to repair her masts, but Norcott suspected she was headed there to obtain Portuguese papers and colours. Proceedings against the cutter were begun on 4 January but then suspended until mid-July when she was condemned.

Although the Squadron's cruisers had now begun scooping up Spanish prizes under the Equipment Clause, the Mixed Commission had delayed beginning proceedings against these vessels until it received formal notification that the treaty had been passed by Parliament. In fact legislation was only required to bring British vessels before the court but confirmation of this took several months to reach Freetown. Thankfully, the next two Spanish vessels to arrive at Freetown proved much simpler for the Mixed Commission to adjudicate on as they were both loaded slavers.

On 22 December *Trinculo*'s boats seized the Spanish brigantine *Isabella Segunda* at anchor on the Bonny Bar. The vessel, bound for Santiago de Cuba, had a cargo of 347 slaves loaded from the river a day prior to her arrest. Following the brigantine's arrival at Freetown her master, Isidro Reynals, complained that 6,000 cigars had been taken from his vessel before she had met *Trinculo* outside the bar. Puget, however, informed the court his boats had all been searched, with no sign of the missing cigars and that Reynals had declared, in front of *Trinculo*'s officers, that his own 'rascally crew had not only robbed him of everything but threatened and would have murdered him had not His Majesty's Sloop's boats come up with her as quickly as they did'.[3] Thirteen deaths from dysentery between

Isabella Segunda's seizure and her condemnation on 3 February resulted in 334 slaves surviving to see emancipation. Having been condemned under the older 1817 Treaty, the vessel was sold instead of being broken up.

On 24 December *Buzzard* seized the Spanish schooner *Ligera* 40 miles south-east of Cape Formoso. The vessel, bound for Santiago de Cuba and carrying a cargo of 198 slaves loaded at the River Nun a day previously, was taken without resistance following a six-hour chase. Deeming her to be unseaworthy, Lieutenant Roberts took *Ligera* to Princes, intending to caulk her. However, with the schooner taking on 3ft of water an hour while at anchor, she was handed over to the Portuguese authorities and her slaves were taken on board *Buzzard*. Roberts arrived at Freetown on 26 January and proceedings were immediately begun against *Ligera*. On 3 February the schooner was condemned in her absence and her surviving 192 slaves emancipated.

Still cruising off the Windward Coast, on 25 December *Pylades* arrested the Spanish brig *Tersicore*, 100 miles west of Sierra Leone. Proceedings were begun against the brig under the Equipment Clause. However, following a survey of the vessel's fittings a joint petition from the Captor's Proctor and the Claimant was presented to the court requesting that she be returned to her owner, as the evidence in the case did not warrant her original arrest. Therefore, on 27 January *Tersicore* was restored to her master, Juan Maynoldi, and immediately departed Freetown.

On 28 December *Fair Rosamond* arrested the Spanish schooner *Segunda Iberia* 160 miles south-east of Cape Formoso. The schooner, bound for Santiago de Cuba from the Nun where she had loaded a cargo of 260 slaves, was armed with a pivot-mounted long 9-pounder but was taken without resistance. Sixteen of *Segunda Iberia*'s cargo died on her passage to Sierra Leone and a further six following her arrival in port. On 3 February the vessel was condemned and her surviving 238 slaves emancipated. Upon the schooner's arrival at Freetown her master, Mariano Caias, had accused several of *Fair Rosamond*'s crew of having plundered his personal possessions. The court recommended the Claimant's Proctor make suitable remuneration to the master for the losses he had sustained but the Proctor declined this request, considering it an indication of guilt. He moved that the case be delayed until *Fair Rosamond*'s arrival at Sierra Leone but the court, having already censured Rose, referred the matter to the Admiralty. When he learned of the allegations against his crew Rose explained that he had searched the accused men, their bags and *Segunda Iberia*'s lower deck with no sign of the missing articles. It was only when he had searched the bags of the Spanish crew that several of these articles had finally come to light. Caias had then agreed to sign a document stating that Rose had done all in his power to recover the missing property. Rose, however, now believed that Caias never possessed the majority of items he claimed that had been stolen, having given different accounts on different occasions. From the records, there appears to have been no satisfactory resolution to the allegations of theft made against Rose's men.

The first arrest of 1836 fell to *Curlew* when Norcott's brig seized the Spanish brigantine *Rosarito* at anchor in Accra Roads on 2 January. Equipped for slaving, *Rosarito*'s master, José Maria Tarreguerra, claimed that the slave irons found on board his vessel were part of her cargo bound for Lagos, but the court declared that under no circumstances could shackles, bolts or handcuffs be considered articles of lawful commerce and on 23 July the vessel was condemned and ordered to be broken up.

On 2 January the commissioners at Freetown finally received twelve copies of the 1835 Treaty and accompanying Special Instructions from London. Four days later *Thalia* arrived at Freetown from the Cape. Finding *Pylades* at anchor, Campbell learned from Castle that *Rolla* had relieved *Griffon* at the Gambia and that *Curlew* had headed south with the copies of the new treaty and Instructions for distribution amongst the cruiser commanders. *Trinculo* was due to return home and so, having ordered Castle to the Bights to relive Puget as Senior Officer, Campbell departed Freetown for Accra where *Thalia* fell in with *Leveret* and the newly-arrived 10-gun brig *Waterwitch*, Lieutenant John Adams. *Leveret* was sent to the Cape with dispatches and *Waterwitch* was ordered down into the Bights.

The Squadron's next seizure was of a fully-loaded schooner with a cargo of 225 slaves taken from the New Sesters. The vessel was first spotted by *Pylades* at midday on 13 January as she cruised off Cape Mount. The chase lasted until the following evening when the Spanish schooner, *Gaceta*, was boarded without resistance. The prize arrived at Sierra Leone on 24 January but the usual delay in hearing cases under the new treaty meant that she was not condemned until 5 July, by which time her cargo had been reduced to 169 slaves due to a smallpox epidemic sweeping through the colony. Eight days later *Lynx*, cruising off the Bonny, seized the Spanish brig *Vandolero* following a nine-hour chase. The vessel, with a cargo of 377 slaves loaded in the New Calabar, had thrown her guns, anchors and boats overboard in an effort to avoid capture. She arrived at Sierra Leone on 29 February, five days behind *Gaceta*. However, as she was heard under the 1817 Treaty she was condemned almost four months ahead of *Pylades*'s prize on 8 March, 343 of her slaves surviving to be emancipated.

On the evening of 22 January Commander Puget sent *Trinculo*'s boats into the Bonny River under the command of Lieutenant Robert Tyron. On the 28th Tyron discovered and arrested four Spanish vessels, the schooners *Feliz Vascongada* and *Eliza*, the brigantine *Diligensia* and the brig *Maria Manuela*, all awaiting their cargoes. In retaliation for the seizures, King Pepple of the Bonny declared he would cease all trade with the British merchantmen then in the river. The masters of these vessels persuaded Tyron to go ashore with them and confer with the king. However, once ashore the men were seized by natives led by the Spanish and were stripped naked, put in irons and chained by their necks to a log of wood. Tyron managed to bribe one of the locals into sending a message back to Puget who then took *Trinculo* into the river to rescue the prisoners. *Lynx* now arrived from Ascension and Puget was able to transfer provisions, spare spars, cables and most of his shot across to Huntley's brigantine, reducing his own vessel's draught by 2ft, enabling *Trinculo* to enter the river using the South Channel. The sloop struck the bottom hard three times, but made it over the bar and anchored close to King Pepple's town, where Puget fired four blank rounds using his remaining ammunition. Faced with this show of force, Pepple released his prisoners and on 30 January *Trinculo* headed back out of the river followed by her four prizes. Puget now headed for Princes, arriving at the island on 13 February, and *Lynx* escorted *Trinculo*'s prizes to Sierra Leone, all four vessels having to wait until September to be condemned.

On 25 January *Leveret* arrested two empty Spanish schooners 20 miles south east of Sanguin on the Pepper Coast, both under the Equipment Clause. *Atafa Primo* had already appeared before the Mixed Commission in August 1830 and would be condemned for a second time on 23 July. Her compatriot, *Zema*, was condemned six days later. The last of the eight Spanish Equipment Clause captures to take place in January fell to *Fair Rosamond* when she seized the brig *Esplorador* 120 miles south-east of Cape St Paul's on 29 January. Her master being ashore, the slaver was under the command of her first mate, who professed ignorance of where the brig had come from or where she was bound. A week after the seizure of this vessel *Charybdis* arrested the Spanish schooner *Matilde* close to St Thomas, discovering amongst her equipment a normal-looking cooking stove which could be expanded for feeding slaves. One day later, on 6 February, *Britomart*'s boats seized another Spanish schooner, *Mosca*, in Whydah Roads. *Matilde* was condemned on 29 July, *Esplorador* on 10 August and *Mosca* on 7 September. Questioned over the loss of two anchors and cables from *Mosca*, her prize master, *Britomart*'s Mate, Henry Cox, explained that two suspicious vessels had been spotted standing towards the schooner. Wishing to rejoin his vessel with all possible haste and there being a heavy swell, Cox had ordered the cables to be slipped.

On 6 February *Waterwitch* made her first contribution to the suppression campaign, seizing the Spanish brig *El Casador Santurzano* under the Equipment Clause whilst her master, Angel de Elloriaga, was ashore at Whydah arranging his shipment of slaves. Following the usual delay in adjudging empty Spanish vessels, *Waterwitch*'s prize, the first of many, was condemned by the Mixed Commission on 23 August. Commissioned by the Earl of Belfast and designed by the celebrated yacht designer Joseph White, *Waterwitch* had been purchased by the Admiralty in October 1834 when nearly complete and had begun fitting out as a 10-gun brig. Lieutenant Adams had been appointed commander of the vessel in November 1835, departing Plymouth for the Coast the following month.

With *Waterwitch* in sight, on 8 February *Thalia* seized the Spanish brigantine *Seis Hermanos*, 140 miles south-east of Cape Palmas. The vessel was bound for Cuba from the New Calabar with her cargo of 189 slaves. Twelve slaves died of dysentery and a further four threw themselves overboard prior to the brigantine's arrival at Freetown on 3 March. *Seis Hermanos* was condemned on 12 March and her surviving 171 slaves emancipated.

Following a rare visit to Loango Bay from one of the Squadron's cruisers, on 9 February *Forester* seized two empty Spanish vessels, the schooner *Golondrina* and the brig *Luisa*. *Forester*'s prizes arrived at Sierra Leone in early March but were not condemned until 10 August. On 19 February *Charybdis* seized the Spanish brig *Tridente* under the Equipment Clause whilst cruising in the same bay. The brig arrived at Freetown on 18 March and proceedings were begun against her the following day but she was not condemned until 23 August.

On 15 February *Thalia* departed Princes for the Cape. En route she stopped off at Ascension on 2 February where Campbell received an unsettling letter from *Buzzard*'s Lieutenant Milward regarding a rumour circulating his brigantine suggesting cowardice on his part during the capture of *Formidable* in December 1834. Campbell ordered an enquiry and the two sailors who had started the unfounded rumour were discharged from the Service along with Mr Bickford who had overheard the rumour being discussed but had let the slur against Milward pass unchallenged. The warrant officer was sent home in *Trinculo* when she departed the coast in late March.

On 6 March *Britomart*'s boats seized two Spanish schooners, *General Mina* and *Dos Hermanos*, under the Equipment Clause in the River Nun, both vessels having more water casks than were required for use by the crew along with loose slave decks. *Britomart*'s boats had entered the river without a copy of the Special Instructions so the schooners had to be re-arrested by Quin upon leaving the river. Then, following their arrival at Freetown, it was discovered that neither vessel had the relevant declarations describing the circumstances of their capture as required by the treaty. However, these documents were brought to Freetown by *Britomart* in time for their adjudication on 3 October.

On 10 March *Fair Rosamond*'s boats seized the schooner *La Mariposa* at anchor in the Old Calabar. Having been warned of the arrival of a British cruiser, *La Mariposa*'s master, Pedro March Oliver, was in the process of destroying his vessel, having already landed his cargo and sails the previous night. However, when *Fair Rosamond*'s boats arrived off Duke Town there was still enough evidence on board the schooner to seize her under the Equipment Clause. A very leaky vessel, when she arrived at Freetown *La Mariposa* was hauled ashore to await adjudication but began to fall apart and was sold at public auction a month later, what remained of the schooner being condemned by the court on 27 September.

On 13 March *Waterwitch* seized the empty Spanish schooner *Galanta Josepha* off Little Popo and the following day she took the schooner *Joven Maria* whilst 25 miles off Whydah. Also on 14 March *Charybdis* took the Spanish brig *El Mismo*, south of the Line off Ambriz. After a flurry of arrests, this would prove be the Squadron's last capture under the Spanish Equipment Clause for almost four months. *Galenta Josepha* was condemned in September and *Joven Maria* and *El Mismo* in October.

On 23 March *Thalia* arrived at the Cape and Campbell shifted his flag to the mooring vessel *Badger* before ordering *Thalia* to return north. Following his arrival in the Bights Wauchope assumed the duties of Senior Officer and he ordered *Forester*, then at Freetown, to take charge of the prizes awaiting adjudication in the various courts. Miall gave the Acting Judge, Governor Campbell, a copy of the recent Act of Parliament that brought the 1835 Treaty into effect but the commissioners refused to begin hearing Equipment Clause cases until they received formal notification of the new legislation from London. Having been ordered home, on 28 March *Trinculo* departed Sierra Leone for England, arriving at Portsmouth on 14 May with a cargo of 2,300 ounces of gold dust and 309 elephant tusks. *Trinculo* reported that, on the day she had sailed from Freetown, there were nineteen Spanish vessels at anchor in the Sierra Leone River still awaiting adjudication.

On 4 May *Buzzard*, now under the command of Lieutenant Campbell, seized the Portuguese brigantine *Mindello* to the south-east of Fernando Po. Having obtained a passport at St Paul de Loando for Montevideo, the Brazilian owned vessel had visited Ambriz, Cape Lopez and the Cameroons River, from where she had loaded a cargo of 267 slaves the previous evening. Dispatched north, the vessel lost four slaves prior to her arrival at Freetown on 2 June. On 14 June *Mindello* was condemned and her surviving 257 slaves emancipated. In their judgement the commissioners noted that the Customs Houses of Rio and St Paul were either very neglectful of their duties or, more damningly, complicit in illegal acts.

On 3 June *Britomart* and *Pylades* were both reported to be at Ascension. *Curlew* was ordered to cruise the Bights and on her way down from Freetown she handed out copies of the new Act of Parliament to the Squadron's cruisers. The newly-arrived 18-gun ship-sloop *Scout*, Commander Robert Craigie, departed the Cape for the Coast on 15 June and *Britomart* was ordered home. Having received information of a loaded slaver in the Bonny that was about to sail, on 30 June Lieutenant Campbell sent *Buzzard*'s boats to wait off the bar. Two days later a vessel was spotted heading out of the river. The boats set off in pursuit and caught her after a pull of more than 20 miles. The prize proved to be the Spanish brigantine *Felicia*, bound for Havana with a cargo of 395 slaves. Her master had deserted his vessel on the approach of *Buzzard*'s boats, taking most of *Felicia*'s papers and twenty-four of her slaves with him. The brigantine arrived at Freetown on 25 July and was condemned on 2 August, 355 slaves surviving to be emancipated. During the hearing it was revealed that *Felicia*'s Havana Customs House papers had stated that her water casks were for palm-oil use and that her rice and farina were entered in her manifest as cargo. Her cooking boiler was also of a type that could be easily disposed of over the side in the event of an interception by a British cruiser.

On 5 July the much-delayed Anglo-Spanish Mixed Court of Justice finally opened at Freetown with Macaulay appointed as British Judge, Lewis as Arbitrator and Melville as Registrar. However, Macaulay was on sick leave and so Lewis assumed the duties of Judge with the Lieutenant-Governor taking on the responsibilities of Arbitrator. On the same day that the court opened, *Gaceta*, seized by *Pylades* on 13 January, was condemned and ordered to be broken up. She was cut athwart amidships once all her stores, masts, rigging and boats had been landed, with both halves being sold separately.

On 13 July the slaver *Tres Tomasas*, seized by *Curlew* on 19 December 1835, was finally adjudged by the Mixed Court to have been equipped for slaving and was condemned. On 18 July *General Manso*, arrested by Denman in November 1835, was restored to her owner, the court ruling that the seizure had been an unlawful act. *Josepha* and *Victorina* were also restored. *Victorina*'s master had reported a deficiency in her stores amounting to £125 and the court, having declared that this was due to the neglect of her prize master, Mr Reid, ruled that the captor should not bear the cost of these deficiencies. However, the court did not have sufficient funds with which to make the repayment so the matter was referred to the Foreign Office who agreed to remunerate *Josepha*'s owner.

At dawn on 6 July *Buzzard* was cruising off the Bonny when she spotted a schooner leaving the nearby St Bartolomeo River. The Spanish vessel, *Famosa Primeira*, was quickly seized under the Equipment Clause, offering no resistance. At her adjudication in October it was revealed that her master and alleged owner, Mateo Moya, had been second mate of the schooner *Nympha*, responsible for firing on *Conflict*'s boats in November 1830. Handed over to the authorities in Lisbon, Moya spent the next four years in jail before returning directly to the Trade.

Learning of a Portuguese slaver in the Old Calabar, on 22 July Campbell sent *Buzzard*'s gig, under the command of Samuel Woolridge, a mate from *Thalia*, to look in to the river. The gig was helpfully given a tow 20 miles upstream by the steamer *Quorra* which happened to be in the river. Upon reaching the Panot Islands the tow was cast off and almost immediately *Buzzard*'s gig fell in with the suspected slaver, the brigantine *Joven Carolina*. Boarding the vessel, Woolridge discovered her to have a cargo of 421 slaves along with eight Spanish passengers. Woolridge put sixteen of the slaver's crew of twenty-three in her boat before taking *Joven Carolina* out of the river, meeting up with *Buzzard* almost twelve hours after the brigantine's capture. The vessel was condemned on 23 August and her surviving 383 slaves emancipated. Learning of the seizure, Palmerston sent his thanks to Commander Beecroft of the steamer *Quorra* for the assistance he had given to *Buzzard*'s gig. In a separate note Palmerston also informed the commissioners that they ought to have begun hearing Equipment Clause cases once they had been handed a copy of the new Act of Parliament by Miall rather than waiting for advice from the Foreign Office.

On 17 September *Pylades* seized the Portuguese-flagged brigantine *Esperança*, with a cargo of 477 slaves, following a chase of several hours off the Bonny. The brigantine, which had begun her voyage as a Spanish vessel named *Isabelita* prior to obtaining Portuguese papers and colours at the Cape Verdes in June, was condemned on 22 October and her surviving 417 slaves emancipated. Sold to an English master, *Esperança* eventually found her way into the hands of the well-known slave trader Pedro Blanco. The day following *Esperança*'s arrest *Thalia* gave chase to a Portuguese brig, *Felix*, as she was leaving the Bonny with a cargo of 591 slaves bound for Havana. Boarded without resistance the brig, which had similarly changed identities at the Cape Verdes, in this instance beginning her voyage as a Spanish vessel named *Recluta*, was also condemned on 22 October, 481 slaves surviving to be emancipated.

The next seizure was a joint capture by *Thalia* and *Buzzard*. The Spanish schooner *Atalya* had left the Bonny about the same time as *Felix* with a cargo of 118 slaves, *Thalia* gave chase and was joined by Campbell's brigantine. The schooner was eventually seized on the morning of 19 September, eighty-eight slaves surviving to see emancipation in late October. Having visited Ascension to load stores for the cruisers in the Bights, *Thalia* now departed the Bights for Simon's Bay, leaving Commander Cragie of *Scout* as Senior Officer on the Coast.

Following the departure of *Trinculo* and *Britomart* from the Coast, late September saw the first of two welcome additions to the Squadron. On

31 September the 3-gun brig *Bonetta*, Lieutenant Henry Deschamps, arrived at the Cape from England. Designed by the Surveyor of the Navy, William Symonds, and launched just six months earlier, *Bonetta* was armed with three 32-pounders but pierced for twelve, the guns mounted in such a way as to be easily moved around the deck as required. She was followed a day later by another Symonds design, the well-regarded 18-gun *Columbine*, Commander Tom Henderson, her sailing much improved through a recent conversion from a barque to a brig, After several weeks without any arrests, the first capture of October fell to *Curlew* when she seized a loaded Portuguese slaver following a five-hour chase off the Bonny. Norcott's brig had arrived off the river on the evening of 30 September, relieving *Pylades* which had been cruising off the river for the previous six weeks. On the afternoon of 3 October a brig was observed on *Curlew*'s starboard bow. Making all sail Norcott gave chase, firing his long guns at the stranger to bring her to. Instead the vessel headed for the Balem Bank near the entrance to the Bonny. *Curlew* followed the slaver over the bank, with the depth beneath her keel dropping to as little as two and a quarter fathoms before she thankfully found deeper water. Rapidly closing on the brig, a broadside of grape and roundshot together with a volley of musketry from *Curlew*'s forecastle finally brought her to. *Curlew*'s prize proved to be *Esperança*, a vessel pierced for ten guns but only mounting two, with a cargo of 438 slaves. *Curlew*'s prize arrived at Freetown on 26 October and was condemned on 2 November, 396 slaves surviving to be emancipated. Learning of a slaver preparing to load her cargo at Lagos, Norcott departed the Bonny on 7 October and following a seven-hour chase on 19 October seized the Portuguese ship *Quatro de Abril* 50 miles south of the port. This vessel, bound for Havana, had a cargo of 478 slaves embarked at Whydah a day previously. Also on board were ten Kroomen who had been seized whilst attempting to return home from the Benin Roads. Twenty of *Quatro de Abril*'s slaves died prior to her condemnation on 25 November.

Having returned to the Bights from Sierra Leone, on 20 October *Forester* arrested the Portuguese schooner *Victoria*, bound for Havana with a cargo of 380 slaves loaded at the New Calabar. The schooner attempted to avoid capture but was boarded without resistance. As with *Esperança* and *Felix*, prior to a visit to the Cape Verde Islands *Forester*'s prize was originally a Spanish vessel, *Iberia*, and had made one successful slaving voyage under her new Portuguese colours prior to seizure. *Victoria* was condemned on 20 October and her surviving 316 slaves emancipated.

Following a brief chase, on 21 October *Charybdis* seized the empty Spanish schooner *Cantabra* off Grand Bassa. The schooner's master, Pedro Miguel Delesquent, had fled ashore upon sighting the British cruiser, which resulted in some difficulty establishing *Cantabra*'s Spanish identity prior to her condemnation in early November. A week later *Buzzard* took the first of two prizes whilst cruising in the eastern end of the Bights of Biafra. On 28 October she arrested the Portuguese schooner *Olimpia* with a cargo of 282 slaves loaded at the River Cameroons. Then on 12 November Campbell arrested the schooner *Serea*, one of the small vessels operating between Princes and the mainland. Carrying a suspiciously large amount of timber for a small vessel, twenty-two slaves were discovered hidden in a space beneath her cargo. Having sent *Olimpia* north with a prize crew, *Buzzard* accompanied her second prize to Freetown, arriving in port on 9 December. Two hundred and fifty-two slaves from *Olimpia* and twenty-one from *Serea* survived to see emancipation in mid-December.

Following *Columbine*'s arrival in the Bights on 10 November, Commander Henderson learned of the recent failure of *Charybdis* to catch a suspicious looking brig following a chase lasting forty-eight hours. Confident in the sailing abilities of his own vessel, Henderson calculated a course to intercept the slaver and set off in pursuit. The brig was first spotted on 13 November and following a chase of three hours was boarded without incident 40 miles north-west of Princes. She proved to be the Portuguese *Veloz* with a cargo of 508 slaves loaded at Whydah and Lagos. *Columbine*'s prize arrived at Freetown on 3 December, she was condemned on the 16th and her 460 surviving slaves emancipated.

Having ended her stint as the Gambia guardship, in November *Rolla* visited the Cape Verde Islands where she discovered a Spanish schooner, *Luisita*, whose master, Manuel Tort y Esclus, had failed in his attempt to change his vessel's nationality. Glasse followed *Luisita* to the River Sherbro and on 21 November arrested her under the Equipment Clause. Eleven days later, whilst still in the same river, *Rolla* arrested the Spanish brig *San Nicholas*, which was also equipped for slaving. *Luisita* was condemned on 16 December, *San Nicholas* on 10 January 1837. The Squadron's next Spanish prize fell to *Scout*. On the night of 5 December her boats seized the schooner *Gata* as she attempted to cross the Bonny bar with a cargo of 111 slaves. Boarded without resistance, she was discovered to have a large number of water casks which, according to her Manifest of Cargo issued by the Havana Customs House, were intended for storing castor oil, a substance the commissioners noted with some incredulity that was not even available on the West Coast of Africa. *Gata* arrived at Freetown on 4 January and the following day fifty of her sickest slaves were landed. On 12 January the schooner was condemned and her surviving 101 slaves emancipated.

On 14 December the newly-launched 3-gun brig *Dolphin*, Lieutenant Thomas Roberts, arrived at Ascension from Britain. Designed by Joseph White's great rival, William Symonds, *Dolphin* was a fast sailer, outperforming *Waterwitch* in trials. Her commanding officer had been First Lieutenant of *Trinculo* and had briefly been in command of *Buzzard*, as a result he had great experience of the Coast. En route to Ascension on 10 December Roberts's vessel had fallen in with the Portuguese ship *Incomprehensivel* which surrendered following a chase of seven hours when fired on by the British cruiser. On board the ship were 696 slaves taken from various ports in Mozambique, the largest cargo yet seized by the Squadron. It was also the first slaver headed for Brazil that had been captured south of the Line for over nine years. *Incomprehensivel* was despatched to Freetown but her original arrest being so far south, by the time she arrived in the Sierra Leone River six weeks later 190 slaves had succumbed to disease. On 17 February *Incomprehensivel* was condemned and her surviving 506 slaves emancipated.

Returning to the Coast from the Cape Verde Islands, on 27 December *Rolla* seized two more Spanish vessels in the Rio Pongas. The first, *Lechuguino*, was a pilot boat with a cargo of forty-nine slaves. The second vessel, and the Squadron's final prize of the year, was the schooner *Esperimento*, seized off the village of Saraby under the Equipment Clause. *Lechuguino* was condemned on 10 January 1837 and her forty-nine slaves emancipated. *Esperimento* was condemned two days later.

Chapter 11

The Fever Coast: January 1837–December 1838

In recognition of British assistance in ending six years of civil war over the royal succession, in 1835 the Portuguese government had promised London that efforts would be made to strengthen the country's existing anti-slavery policies, offering to declare the Trade illegal and instructing colonial governors in Africa not to grant passports to ships transporting slaves to countries where slavery was prohibited. Mounting political instability within the country led to a revolution in September 1836 and the new government, headed by the abolitionist Sa da Bandiera, quickly forced a new abolition bill through the legislature. The bill, which became law on 10 December 1836, prohibited the import and export of slaves throughout Portugal's dominions, both north and south of the Equator, although slaves could be imported into its territories in Africa by land. It also authorised severe penalties for Portuguese subjects who engaged in the slave trade and colonial officials who failed to take action against or connived in it. In the event, the governors of Mozambique and Angola both suspended the law as they felt it would be ruinous to their economies and impossible to enforce. There was still no mention of an Equipment Clause and Portuguese colours would increasingly be used by ships of other nations, covering most of the trade to Brazil and, following the Anglo-Spanish Treaty of 1835, that to Cuba as well.

On 1 January 1837 *Fair Rosamond* departed Ascension for England, arriving at Portsmouth in mid-February. On 11 January *Thalia*, once again flying Campbell's flag, arrived at Ascension from the Cape and the following day *Pylades*, travelling in the opposite direction, arrived at the island en route to Simon's Bay. The Squadron's first three arrests of the year fell to *Scout*, which, since her capture of *Gata* in December 1836 had remained off the Bonny, waiting for the departure of two Portuguese brigs from the river. *Scout*'s pinnace and gig had been sent into the river under the command of Lieutenant John Price and at 9.00am on 11 January one of the brigs was observed standing directly for the boats under a full spread of canvas. Price ordered the gig, which was armed with rockets, to a position lower down the river in case the brig slipped past his pinnace then waited for the slaver's approach. When she was within 100 yards Price rowed across to the brig and managed to hook on to her main chainwale with grapnels. A well-aimed round of shot and grape from the pinnace's carronade cleared the brig's main deck, allowing her to be boarded. Leaving *Scout*'s mate, Arthur Barrow, in charge of the prize with four men, Price set off in pursuit of the second brig which was now observed surrounded by canoes offloading her cargo of slaves. However, the pinnace was soon alongside and this vessel was also boarded. It had taken Price less than half an hour to capture the two brigs. The first, *Paquete de Cabo Verde*, had a cargo of 576 slaves, her compatriot *Esperanca* 108, 500 having been landed in the canoes. *Esperanca*'s crew had attempted to escape ashore with the brig's papers but returned to their vessel when fired on by Price. Four days later *Scout* seized the empty Spanish schooner *Descubierta* as she approached the Bonny. The vessel was clearly equipped for slaving, having extra planking and water casks and a cooking boiler hidden in her hold. However, her regular-sized hatches, whilst perfectly fine for a legitimate merchantman, were far too small to provide adequate ventilation for a cargo of slaves. *Paquete de Cabo* arrived at Freetown on 20 February, 106 slaves having died on the passage north, all from dysentery apart from three slaves who took their own lives. The vessel was condemned on 2 March and her surviving slaves emancipated. *Esperanca* arrived at Freetown four days after *Paquete de Cabo* and was condemned on 4 March, eighty-nine slaves surviving to be emancipated. *Scout*'s third prize, *Descubierta*, arrived at Freetown on 29 March following an unusually slow passage north. She was condemned on 20 April.

The last seizure of January fell to *Bonetta* when Deschamps's gun-brig arrested a vessel flying newly-purchased Portuguese colours off the Bonny on 20 January. The brig, *Temeraria*, had a cargo of 349 slaves, many members of rival tribes who were discovered quarrelling amongst themselves and attempting to beat and strangle one another, forcing the British to fit iron gratings to the slave deck. During her passage north a large number of Africans attempted to gain control of the vessel, leaving the prize master, Mr Roberts, with no option but to flog twenty slaves and place a further forty in irons to maintain the safety of the vessel and his crew. Four other slaves were discovered hanging by ropes from the main hatchway. *Temerario* arrived at Freetown on 22 February, followed closely by *Bonetta*. She was condemned on 1 March and her surviving 236 slaves emancipated, 111 having been lost to dysentery.

There were just two seizures in February, both made by *Columbine* under similar circumstances. The first prize was a Portuguese schooner, *Latona*, bound for Havana with a cargo of 325 slaves that was seized by Henderson's brig off Whydah following a five-hour chase on 4 February. The second prize was the schooner *Josephina*, arrested on 10 February with a cargo of 350 slaves loaded at Lagos a few days previously. She too was taken after a five-hour chase that ended in calm airs, the arrest being made by *Columbine*'s boats. *Josephina* was a successful slaver, having made no less than three visits to Bahia prior to her arrest. She arrived at Freetown on 8 March and was followed a day later by *Latona*. Both vessels were condemned on 17 March, 320 slaves from *Latona* and 346 from *Josephina* surviving to be emancipated.

Passing through the Bights from Cape Coast Castle in mid-March, *Thalia* fell in with *Scout* and *Columbine*, providing stores for these two vessels prior to her arrival at Princes on 14 March. Whilst there had been no signs of slaving on the Gold Coast it was clear to Campbell that it was still flourishing in the Bights, mostly carried out by Spanish-owned vessels that were now flying Portuguese colours, the Spanish flag having all but disappeared from the Coast. Satisfied that his instructions were being carried out as intended, Campbell returned to the Cape via Ascension, arriving at Simon's Bay on 22 April.

During his tour of the Coast Campbell had written to the commissioners to reassure them following the usual complaints that not enough was being done to police the northern rivers. Another issue exercising the commissioners' minds was the financial implications of the introduction of the Equipment Clause. Whilst seizors were responsible for provisioning the crews of detained vessels, the costs of bringing a vessel to adjudication, including the maintenance of the vessel and care of the slaves, were paid from the funds that arose from the vessel's sale. However, vessels with no slave bounties payable were now being destroyed and the proceeds of their sale was failing to cover the cost of their condemnation, the shortfall being made up from the Sierra Leone military chest. In late March the Foreign Office informed the commissioners that the Government was considering establishing a bounty based on the tonnage of a vessel condemned without slaves. However, no indication was given of when this bounty might come into effect.

On 30 March *Bonetta* seized the Spanish schooner *Cinco Amigos* off New Sesters. This vessel, like *Descubierta*, was equipped with regular-sized hatches although she was clearly engaged in the Trade, having additional water casks and planks for a slave deck. Her galley was also large enough to fit a slave cooker, although this item had been landed prior to her boarding. *Bonetta*'s prize arrived at Freetown on 8 April and was condemned twelve days later. It would be another three weeks following this solitary success in March before the Squadron's next arrest. On 19 April *Dolphin* arrested the Spanish schooner *Dolores* off the entrance to the Old Calabar. The schooner, which was bound for Cuba, had on board a cargo of 314 slaves, many of whom were suffering from dysentery. She was condemned on 23 May, having lost twenty-eight slaves prior to the adjudication.

On 9 April a Convention of Amenity and Commerce was signed at Grand Bonny between Great Britain and the King of Bonny. The British signatories included Commander Craigie and Lieutenant Acland of *Scout*, Lieutenant Huntley of *Lynx* and Lieutenant Roberts of *Dolphin*. The convention ratified a treaty of January 1836, the articles of which stipulated that no British subjects would be detained or harassed onshore and that merchantmen entering the Bonny would pay customs in proportion to the size of the vessel. The convention was intended to encourage the legitimate trade in palm oil and discourage slaving. As the British took their fight against the slavers inland, local treaties such as this would become more and more common, an important additional diplomatic weapon in the Squadron's arsenal.

Since 1830 the Squadron had remained relatively healthy, with on average eighteen deaths a year from disease, but in the spring of 1837 there were outbreaks of fever at the Gambia, Sierra Leone and Fernando Po, which, by the end of the year had claimed the lives of 105 officers and men. At Sierra Leone, where there was especially high mortality, Judge Macaulay was absent on extended leave, with Walter Lewis continuing his role as acting judge and Lieutenant-Governor Campbell acting as Arbitrator until he was replaced in June by Colonel Richard Docherty. On 1 April Lieutenant Campbell had voluntarily exchanged command of *Buzzard* with *Thalia*'s Lieutenant John Stoll. On 29 April Lieutenant Roberts died of fever at Fernando Po. With *Dolphin*'s other senior officers having been taken ill, the vessel's second master, Mr Pike, was given command of the brig for her journey south to Ascension. Following her departure from the Bonny *Scout* was also hit by fever, losing Lieutenant Acland, her mate, her gunner and ten men before sailing for the recuperative airs of Ascension. At the Gambia Lieutenant Norcott had hired a vessel to accommodate *Curlew*'s seventy-five sick, the second master, assistant surgeon, purser and twenty of her crew eventually succumbing to disease. By June there were eight cases of fever on board *Columbine*, most likely brought on board the vessel from the boats that had been operating in the Cameroons and Bimia Rivers. With the master and two sailors dead she was ordered to Ascension to recover the health of her crew. In June fever claimed the lives of *Buzzard*'s master, assistant surgeon and three of her sailors whilst she was hauled up on the beach at Fernando Po for repair work to be carried out on her hull. Her boat crews, also working in the Cameroons, were similarly struck by fever, three men succumbing to the disease. With forty-six of *Buzzard*'s crew incapacitated, for several weeks Lieutenant Stoll and the purser, Mr Sidall, were the only officers capable of carrying out their duties, assisted by just six British seamen and several Kroomen.

There were just two seizures by the Squadron in May. On the 11th *Charybdis*, thankfully largely unaffected by fever, arrested the Portuguese schooner *Lafayette* 50 miles south-east of Lagos. The vessel, armed with two guns, was carrying a cargo of 448 slaves loaded a day previously at that same port. Her master, Manoel Nogueira, initially stated that his vessel was sailing for Bahia but later admitted that she was bound for Havana. *Charybdis*'s prize arrived at Freetown on 6 June and was condemned ten days later, 441 of her slaves surviving to be emancipated. On 27 May *Dolphin*, now under the temporary command of Lieutenant Joseph Bates, seized the Portuguese schooner *Cobra de Africa* off Bimia Island. Another vessel that had most probably changed identities at the Cape Verde Islands, she was captured en route to Havana with a cargo of 162 slaves loaded at the River Bimia. Her slaves were in a very poor condition, having spent three months confined to the barracoons prior to their embarkation and sixty-one died on the passage north. Following *Cobra de Africa*'s arrival at Freetown on 14 June forty-four of her sickest remaining slaves were immediately landed and taken to hospital. On 22 June the schooner was condemned and her surviving 101 slaves emancipated.

On 1 June *Dolphin* fell in with the schooner *Providencia* whilst cruising off the Old Calabar. The schooner, flying colours newly purchased from Princes, was bound for Bahia from Lagos with a cargo of 198 slaves, one-third of whom had been bought by twenty-seven residents of Lagos. *Providencia* arrived at Sierra Leone on 1 July and was condemned on 10 July, just five slaves dying on her passage north. Following this capture command of *Dolphin* passed to Lieutenant Campbell.

On 3 June *Pelican* arrived at Ascension from a six-month cruise in the Indian Ocean. Discovering *Scout* at anchor, Commander Popham ordered Craigie's vessel, which now requiring new rigging, to the Cape to refit. She arrived there on 10 July having largely recovered the health of her crew but with six men now dead. Leaving the healthy airs of Ascension behind, *Pelican* sailed for the Bights where Popham would assume the duties of Senior Officer on the Coast. Arriving at Fernando Po on 5 July *Pelican* spent two days at the island before departing for the Bonny. Within the next three weeks there were thirteen cases of fever on board Popham's brig, though thankfully resulting in just two deaths.

Following the signing of the Bonny trade convention, in mid-April *Lynx* had been ordered home with copies of the agreement by Craigie. Having departed the Bights in May under the command of Lieutenant Thomas Birch, on 1 June the brigantine arrived at Simon's Bay via Ascension. Four days later she sailed for England, calling at Freetown to drop off her Kroomen before departing the Coast. On 26 June the largely fever-free *Charybdis* boarded the Spanish-flagged brig *General Ricafort* off Accra. In addition to her slave irons and additional planking for a slave deck, the brig also had a trade cargo of tobacco, rum and muskets. She was condemned on 25 August, her cargo and fittings being sold for £3,137. In mid-July *Charybdis* sailed for England, dropping anchor at Portsmouth on 10 September, five days after *Rolla* arrived at Plymouth from the Coast.

Having seized just two vessels in June the Squadron, debilitated by disease, would have to wait a further six weeks for the next arrest. On 6 August *Waterwitch*, under the temporary command of Lieutenant John Marsh following the promotion of Adams, seized the Portuguese brig *Amelia* 60 miles south-east of Lagos, from where she had loaded a cargo of 359 slaves that same day. *Amelia* was condemned on 30 August and her surviving 345 slaves emancipated. With just one solitary arrest in August it would be late September before the rate of seizures began to improve, beginning with the arrest of the Portuguese brig *Velos* by *Fair Rosamond* on the 23rd. The brigantine, now under the command of Lieutenant William Oliver, had returned to Sierra Leone from England in mid-July, discovering the colony much recovered from the recent fever epidemic. Upon her arrival at the River Benin on 18 September *Fair Rosamond* had fallen in with *Velos* as she attempted to leave the river. The brig had then fled back into the river to offload her cargo of slaves, firing at a boat from *Fair Rosamond* as it attempted a boarding, killing one seaman. On 23 September Oliver took his schooner into the river, firing on *Velos* before boarding. Some of *Velos*'s crew attempted to swim to another Portuguese vessel, *Camoes*, awaiting her cargo of slaves, so Oliver also boarded and arrested this vessel before placing *Velos*'s crew in irons on board *Fair Rosamond*. After thirty-six hours *Camoes* was released but Oliver then arranged for her to be loaded with 138 slaves from *Velos* before she was re-arrested on 28 September. Neap tides now prevented *Fair Rosamond* from crossing the bar until 2 October, during which time there were three deaths from fever. When *Camoes* arrived at Freetown on 10 November under the command of *Fair Rosamond*'s drunken master's assistant, George Boys, she was in a deplorable state, twenty-two slaves having died of dysentery during the passage north. The Surgeon to the Courts reported a further eighteen cases of dysentery and forty-four of craw-craw amongst the surviving slaves. Drawing comparisons to the case of *Pepita*, seized by *Pelorus* in June 1834, the Mixed Commission found that Oliver had placed the slaves on board *Camoes* as a pretext for seizing her and therefore on 22 January sentenced the vessel to be restored to her master, Antonio da Silva, ordering costs of £1,734 against Oliver. A further forty-five slaves having died subsequent to *Camoes*'s arrival at Freetown, just seventy-one slaves survived to be freed, not emancipated by the court. Following several delays to her case being heard, *Camoes*'s compatriot *Velos* was finally condemned on 5 May 1838.

On 25 September *Waterwitch*, now under the command of Lieutenant William Dickey, seized a loaded Portuguese schooner off Fernando Po. The vessel's papers gave her name as *Vibora de Cabo Verde* but it seems most likely that she had been the American-flagged *Viper* prior to her arrival at the Cape Verdes. She had been bound for Rio with a cargo of 269 slaves loaded at the River Cameroons when boarded by Dickey's schooner on 25 September, her master, Joaquim Antonio, claiming to have served on board *Maidstone* during the American War. *Waterwitch*'s prize arrived at Freetown on 4 November, forty-eight slaves having died during her passage north, mostly due to dysentery. She was condemned on 30 November and her surviving 221 slaves emancipated.

On the same day that *Vibora de Cabo Verde* was being arrested, *Dolphin*, cruising off Princes under the command of Lieutenant Campbell, seized the Portuguese schooner *Primoroza* with a cargo of 182 slaves loaded at the Bonny. Losses on board this slaver were similarly high during her passage north, forty-six slaves dying prior to her arrival in the Sierra Leone River on 19 October. Nevertheless, the commissioners acknowledged the efforts of her prize master, Mr Burslem, in maintaining the clean and orderly state of the schooner prior to her condemnation and the emancipation of her surviving 136 slaves on 28 October.

On 24 September the 18-gun brig-sloop *Childers*, Commander Henry Keppel, arrived at Sierra Leone from Gibraltar via the Gambia where she had briefly operated in support of the Portendic gum trade. Having provisioned and received her allocation of twenty-four Kroomen, *Childers* proceeded south to her cruising grounds in the Bights. Arriving off Cape St Paul's she boarded one Portuguese vessel awaiting her cargo before spotting another vessel, a smart-looking brig towing two native canoes. Keppel went on board the vessel, *Dos Amigos*, but was unable to ascertain her nationality. Finding her master, Fernando Jose Canieras, to be an 'obliging, civil fellow', Keppel accepted an invitation to dinner on board his vessel. He would later write 'Most of the captains of these slavers are superior men; some belong to good Spanish and Portuguese families; generally young. I believe that many of them take command of these vessels for the excitement of the service.'[1] It was not unusual for British officers to fraternise with slave-ship masters or those involved in the Trade: indeed they were frequent visitors to West Bay, the residence of the Governor-General of Princes, Don José Ferreira Gomez, whose portly wife Maria, the daughter of a Brazilian major and a native woman, was herself both a prominent slave trader and owner. Campbell had even gone so far as ordering Captain Craigie to round up a number of Madame Ferreira's slaves who had fled to Freetown and Fernando Po and return them, an issue over which her husband and Governor Nicolls had previously clashed. As he headed down along the Coast towards the Bights, Keppel encountered a number of empty slavers but made no arrests. Upon her arrival in the Bight of Benin *Childers* fell in with *Waterwitch* and two recently-arrived vessels from England, the 6-gun schooner *Viper*, Commander William Winniett, and the 10-gun brig-sloop *Saracen*, Lieutenant Henry Hill.

On the morning of 29 October the French-flagged schooner *Africaine* arrived off British Accra where *Childers* was lying at anchor and Keppel sent a boat, commanded by his trusted master, Jonas Coaker, across to board the vessel. There are competing British and French versions over what happened next. According to Coaker, upon boarding the vessel he had discovered her main hatch covered, immediately arousing his suspicions. His request for the schooner's papers was refused by her master, Monsieur Fabre, and when he attempted to look down the companionway to the cabin the cover was slammed shut in his face. Fabre then called his crew aft and Coaker was hit by two men. With a third man poised to strike him with a large billet of wood, *Childers*' boat crew leapt on board the schooner to come to his defence. Fabre, who had gone below, now returned with a tin box containing *Africaine*'s papers, which Coaker seized and took to *Childers*, returning with three marines to remove the two men who had struck him and place them in irons aboard *Childers* overnight.

In Fabre's account of events, on the morning of 29 October he had anchored off Dutch Accra alongside *Childers* and the merchantman *Robert Heddle*. When Coaker, dressed in a blue jacket and gold-laced cap, had come on board *Africaine* he had acted boorishly. In response Fabre had refused to let the British officer examine *Africaine*'s hold without first producing his warrant. Coaker had then grabbed Fabre and attempted to drag him into the gig when two of Fabre's officers had come to his assistance. According to Fabre, in order to avoid further confrontation he had gone below to fetch the box containing his vessel's papers and this was taken back to *Childers* by Coaker. Half an hour later Coaker returned with three marines to arrest *Africaine*'s two officers. The Foreign Office received an official complaint over the matter from the captain of the French corvette *Triomphante* but Keppel thoroughly refuted Fabre's statement. The crew of *Robert Heddle* also backed up Coaker's version of events, having witnessed the altercation on *Africaine*, and they pointed out that she had been anchored off British Accra at the time of the incident, not the Dutch fort as claimed by Fabre.

Two weeks following *Childers*' boarding of *Africaine*, *Bonetta* seized the Portuguese schooner *Ligeira* 70 miles south of Cape Formoso with a cargo of 313 slaves loaded at the Rio Bento (or Brass River). The vessel, which had purchased a passport at the Cape Verde Islands, was en route to Havana when arrested by *Bonetta* on 15 November. Amongst her papers there was a certificate from the Havana Customs House for the shipment of extra planks and beams, a large boiler and staves and hoops for forming casks for the storage of palm oil. *Ligeira* arrived at Freetown on 15 December and her cargo landed. On 28 December she was condemned and her surviving 280 slaves emancipated.

Cruising off Lagos on 20 November *Scout* arrested the Portuguese brigantine *Deixa Falar* with a cargo of 205 slaves bound for Bahia. Three days later Craigie's sloop seized the brig *Gratidao*, another Portuguese vessel, with a cargo of 452 slaves similarly loaded at Lagos and bound for Bahia. By the time of *Deixa Falar*'s arrival at Freetown on 1 January 1838 she had lost nineteen of her cargo, mostly to dysentery, with at least thirty more cases of the same disease on board the vessel. She was condemned on 10 January 1838 and her surviving 186 slaves emancipated. *Scout*'s second prize *Gratidao* arrived at Freetown the following day. An even more sickly vessel, she had lost fifty-six of her slaves to dysentery and there were a further sixty-four cases of the disease still on board. She was condemned on 19 January, 380 slaves surviving to be emancipated.

On 6 December *Leveret* arrived at the Cape from Ascension, departing for Mozambique ten days later. The day following *Leveret*'s arrival at Simon's Bay *Forester* returned to the Coast from England, now under the command of Lieutenant George Rosenberg. On 13 December *Waterwitch*'s boats spotted a Portuguese schooner attempting to work her way out of the Bonny. The cutter, commanded by Mr J. Pritchard, exchanged fire with the schooner, whilst the gig, commanded by Midshipman Voules, managed to latch on. A musketoon fired into the gig killed one British sailor and wounded another. With just two uninjured men left on board his boat and the cutter dropping astern, Voules reluctantly cast off and rejoined Pritchard. It was later discovered that schooner, *Donna Maria*, had a cargo of 350 slaves and that several of her crew had been injured in the encounter.

The final arrest of the year took place on 26 December, *Curlew*'s boats seizing the Portuguese-flagged schooner *Princéza Africana* as she left the River Sherbro with a cargo of 222 slaves bound for Puerto Rico. Another vessel that had more than likely undergone a recent change of identity, the schooner's logbook was suspiciously missing twenty-six pages covering the period prior to her arrival at the Cape Verde Islands. Quite remarkably all

222 of *Princéza Africana*'s slaves survived to be emancipated following her condemnation on 10 January 1838.

On 5 January *Forester* arrived in the Bights, relieving *Columbine* which had been ordered to Plymouth. Rosenberg's brigantine was carrying the prize crews from Freetown for redistribution around the Squadron but yellow fever had re-appeared in the colony and Popham, the Senior Officer on the Coast, was distressed to learn that *Waterwitch* and *Bonetta* had both lost four out of seven men and that *Fair Rosamond*'s prize crews from *Velos* and *Camoes* had all died. *Forester* had not escaped the epidemic, having lost five men on passage from Freetown, and when she fell in with *Waterwitch* off the Bonny Lieutenant Dickey immediately ordered her to Ascension. Rosenberg never made it to the island, dying of fever on 23 January and by the time *Forester* dropped anchor on 7 February she had buried a further fifteen of her crew. An equally sickly *Bonetta* had arrived at Ascension a week earlier, having lost eight men, including her assistant surgeon, Mr Jolley. A further thirty-one of her complement including her commanding officer, master and purser lay about the deck close to death, three with black vomit. Under the instructions of *Buzzard*'s assistant surgeon, Mr Elliot, only recently recovered from fever himself, the brig's company were landed, but despite Elliot's best efforts he could not prevent a further eleven men from falling ill and there were eight more deaths including that of Lieutenant Deschamps on 8 February. Temporary command of *Bonetta* was given to her only officer fit for duty, her mate, Benjamin Fox, and on 13 March she sailed for the Cape.

Having examined the various anchorages along the Coast, observing several vessels preparing to load their cargoes, on 16 January 1838 *Childers* arrived off Quitta where she re-encountered the slaver *Dos Amigos*. Canieras now lent Keppel his native canoes to enable his sloop to re-provision before inviting Keppel and his officers to spend the night on board his much more spacious vessel. From Quitta *Childers* proceeded to Little Popo, where Keppel had been informed that a Spanish schooner under Portuguese colours was preparing to sail with a cargo of up to 300 slaves. Keppel lay in wait off the coast for several hours until the schooner, *Dulcinea*, finally made an appearance. Hoisting all sail *Childers* gave chase, but the schooner disappeared from view as night set in. Keppel now stood out to sea in hopes of cutting the slaver off but she was never seen again. Early the following month *Childers* called at Whydah where she fell in with *Fortuna*, whose one-armed captain, Don José Barbosa, invited Keppel to breakfast and recounted the infamous battle between his slaver *Veloz Passagera* and the gun-brig *Primrose* in September 1830. Over cigars a clearly delighted Barbosa informed Keppel he had recently helped a loaded slaver escape *Saracen*, having made a private signal upon sighting the British cruiser.

In November 1837 Don José Ferreira Gomez, Governor-General of Princes, had died. The news had been withheld by a self-appointed junta and the islanders had stopped paying his widow their rents, forcing her to write to Popham for assistance. Worried that Madame Ferreira might lose her property at West Bay and his cruisers the ability to wood and water there, Popham headed to Princes on board *Pelican*, sailing in company with *Fair Rosamond* and *Scout*, with *Dolphin* following a day behind. Dropping anchor in Port Antonio on 27 January, Popham went ashore to meet with the new junta and, although he regarded them as entirely untrustworthy, they eventually agreed to the election of a new lieutenant-governor.

On 2 March *Saracen* made her first arrest whilst en route to Freetown, seizing the Portuguese-flagged schooner *Montana* 160 miles south-west of Sherbro Island. *Montana*'s logbook showed that she had called at the Cape Verde Islands after sailing from Havana and her master admitted that her Portuguese papers had been purchased at the island for 400 dollars. *Saracen* continued on to Freetown in company with her prize but on 7 March fell in with *Buzzard* which was departing the Coast for England under the acting command of Lieutenant Benjamin Fox. Having met with Fox to discuss his prize, Hill now decided not to take *Montana* for adjudication, later explaining that he expected a low probability of condemnation. On 11 March *Saracen* arrived at Freetown to pick up the prize crews waiting there. Finding *Waterwitch* at anchor, Hill learned that Dickey had recently boarded an empty slaver flying Russian colours, her crew mainly consisting of Spaniards, and there had also been a recent sighting of another vessel flying Austrian colours.

On 8 March *Scout* made the largest seizure of her suppression campaign, arresting the Portuguese brig *Felicidades* off the Old Calabar with a cargo of 559 slaves loaded from the river three days earlier. Another vessel out of Havana, this fine-looking brig had been one of the first to use the subterfuge of a fictitious transfer and a nominal flag, having acquired a Portuguese passport at the Cape Verde Islands as early as December 1835, although her employment from that date to October 1837 remained a mystery. There were many cases of dysentery and opthalmia on board the brig and 134 slaves died prior to her arrival at Freetown on 6 April. Her remaining slaves were landed the following day and proceedings were begun against her. Prior to *Felicidades*'s condemnation and the emancipation of her remaining 408 slaves on 17 April a further fourteen Africans had died and three more had run away.

Following what had been a brief deployment on the Coast, on 2 April *Childers* departed Ascension for Portsmouth. On 7 March the 74-gun Third Rate *Melville* arrived at Simon's Bay flying the flag of Rear Admiral George Elliot. Having issued instructions to Lieutenants Colin Campbell and John Stoll, the newly-promoted commanders of *Forester* and *Bonetta*, on 12 March Rear Admiral Campbell passed command of the Cape and West Africa Squadron to Elliot and *Thalia* departed the Cape for Ascension and home, dropping anchor at Portsmouth on 19 May, the same day that *Childers* arrived at that port from the Coast. On her going into dock it was discovered that 7ft of *Childers* false keel was partly athwartships, explaining to Keppel why his sloop had always seemed to sail better on one tack than the other.

During the first few weeks of April both *Waterwitch* and *Fair Rosamond* sought the recuperative airs of Ascension and were there as *Thalia* passed through on her return to England. Unfortunately the normally healthy island was in the grip of a fever epidemic, brought to it by *Forester* and *Bonetta* earlier in the year. The outbreak claimed thirty men including the island's Commandant, Captain Bate of the Royal Marines, who died on 15 April. *Waterwitch* departed the island on 3 May and headed for her usual cruising ground in the Bights. Fever appeared on board the vessel later that month, claiming the life of Lieutenant Dickey as she arrived off Princes on 29 May. By 4 June sixty of her complement were sick and fifteen were dead. For the next couple of days there were just three members of crew fit enough to man the vessel. Her mate, William Austen, took temporary command of the brig and made for Ascension, arriving there on 9 June. Once he had enough men fit to work his vessel Austen sailed for England, taking his Kroomen with him.

Following her departure from Ascension *Fair Rosamond* had headed north to Freetown, embarking Lieutenant-Governor Docherty and sailing for the Gambia on 5 May. By the time of her return to Freetown in early June there were eleven cases of fever on board the vessel and five men had died. *Fair Rosamond* now embarked the survivors of the prize crews waiting at Freetown; an officer and three men from *Scout*, the same number from *Forester* and one man from *Bonetta*, leaving six more men from *Scout* sick in the hospital. Four of the prize crews embarked on Oliver's brigantine would subsequently die from fever.

In mid-April *Saracen* arrived at Princes and the Senior Officer on the Coast, Commander Popham, went on board Hill's brig along with Craigie and Castle to inspect the vessel and read the Printed Instructions out the assembled crew. The insolent behaviour of several of *Saracen*'s officers towards Lieutenant Hill, a 'combined determination to oppose and to break him',[2] had been concerning Popham for some time. Midshipman Holmes had already been placed under arrest and removed to *Scout* to be taken to Simon's Bay and he now ordered Hill to the Cape. Following the arrival of *Saracen* at Simon's Bay in June Elliot ordered Holmes and the purser, John Angelly, to be dismissed from Hill's brig and sent home. Although Elliot expressed his disapproval at two instances of excessively harsh punishments meted out to his crew, Hill clung on to his command, no doubt partly so that those conspiring against *Saracen*'s commander would not be seen to have succeeded in their actions against him.

On 2 April *Childers* departed Ascension for England, arriving at Portsmouth on 19 May where she was paid off. Keppel then entered into correspondence with the Admiralty regarding the incident over the French vessel *Africaine* at Dutch Accra in October 1837. On 3 April the 10-gun brig *Nautilus*, Lieutenant George Beaufoy, departed Portsmouth for the Coast to relive Keppel's vessel. On 2 April, *Forester*, now under the temporary command of Lieutenant Francis Nott, seized the schooner *Dous Irmaos* off the River Bonny. The schooner, which had departed the river a day earlier with a cargo of 305 slaves, was on her fourth visit to the Coast since 1836. She was flying Portuguese colours but her papers included clearance from the Havana Customs House for a cargo of staves, hoops, twelve casks and 3,000ft of planking. *Forester*'s prize was condemned 19 May and her surviving 241 slaves emancipated, fifty-five having died of dysentery and a further six committing suicide by throwing themselves over the side of the vessel prior to her arrival at Freetown on 11 May.

On 17 April *Pylades* boarded a suspicious-looking brig only to discover she was a genuine French palm-oiler en route to Gabon. Castle provided the master with a certificate of the boarding and the incident passed off without further complaint. There were no captures at all by the Squadron in May but, following his arrival off the Old Calabar, Castle sent his gig into the river under the command of Lieutenant John Price and on 3 May she seized the Portuguese-flagged schooner *Prova*, which was about to get underway with a cargo of 225 slaves. Yet another vessel with papers procured from the Cape Verdes and with a cargo of casks and planking cleared from Havana, *Prova* was condemned by the court at Freetown on 2 July and her surviving 194 slaves emancipated.

On 4 May the 16-gun brig-sloop *Lily*, Commander John Reeve, departed Portsmouth for Rio, where she was to convey the newly-appointed British Secretary of Legation to the Court of Brazil, Sir Gore Ousley, prior to sailing for the Cape. On 15 May *Brisk*, now under the command of Lieutenant Arthur Kellett, arrived at Simon's Bay from Portsmouth. The following day *Scout* departed St Helena for Ascension en route to relieve *Leveret* in the Indian Ocean. Her replacement was *Lynx*, returning to the Coast from Plymouth, now under the command of Lieutenant Henry Broadhead. In late June the recently cut-down 3-gun brig *Termagant*, Commander Woodford Williams, sailed from Portsmouth for the Cape. Taking passage on the brigantine was Lieutenant George Napier who had been appointed to *Forester* in the room of Campbell who was to join *Melville*. *Termagant* also carried notice of Popham's promotion to captain.

Following the capture of the schooner *Prova* in the Old Calabar *Pylades* was once again attacked by fever, brought on board the sloop by the boat crews working in the river. With six men falling ill and one man dying, Castle thought it prudent to retreat to St Helena to recover the health of his vessel before returning to cruise off the Bonny. On 30 June a sickly *Forester*, en route to the Bights from Sierra Leone, fell in with *Fair Rosamond* and recovered her prize crew. With her purser and two seamen sick and her assistant surgeon close to death, *Forester* now headed for Ascension in company with *Pylades*.

On 13 July *Fair Rosamond* seized the Portuguese brigantine *Paquete Felis* about 10 miles south of the Bonny from where she had loaded her cargo of 195 slaves three days earlier. The brigantine had sailed from Havana under the name of *Ceres* but at the Cape Verde Islands she had purchased a change of identity and was placed under the nominal command of a Portuguese citizen, Manuel de Brito Lima, whilst her real master, Pedro Tudela, remained on board to direct the voyage, having obtained a document from the Governor of the Cape Verde Islands stating that he was a shipwrecked Spanish sailor. *Paquete Felis* arrived at Freetown on 1 August and was condemned a week later, 187 slaves surviving to be emancipated.

To compensate for the loss of head money payable for empty vessels condemned under the Equipment Clause, on 27 July 1838 Parliament introduced the Tonnage Act. For vessels seized and condemned without slaves an additional bounty of £4 per ton would be paid to the captor. For vessels seized with slaves on board and broken up after condemnation a further bounty of £1 10s per ton would be paid on top of the £5 per slave. (This head money was reduced to £2 10s if the slave was dead by the time the prize reached port.) The tonnage of vessels would be ascertained using the British system of measurement. For vessels condemned with slaves on board, if the head money calculated on the number of slaves was less than the bounty calculated on the tonnage, the captor could choose to take the latter.

Perhaps as a solution to Hill's poor leadership qualities, following *Saracen*'s arrival at Simon's Bay Elliot ordered her home to re-fit and she departed the Cape on 23 July. However, a week prior to *Saracen*'s arrival at Mauritius on 19 August a serious incident had taken place on board *Lily* requiring her to be ordered home too. On the morning of 12 August First Lieutenant Richard Inman was discovered in bed with his boy, John Payne. He had then gone absent from his vessel for a week. The seriousness of this offence meant a court martial for Inman and so both he and Payne were sent home to England on board *Lily*. Having decided to replace Popham as Senior Officer on the Coast with Craigie, the Commander-in-Chief now dispatched *Nautilus* to Madagascar to relieve *Scout* which was to rendezvous with *Melville* at Simon's Bay. *Lily* arrived at Portsmouth on 14 October and Inman's court martial was held on board *Royal Adelaide* five days later. He claimed that a drunken Payne had entered his cabin during the night and had laid down in his cot unbeknownst to him. Inman had then been informed that he had been ordered home on board *Pelican* and should go ashore until that time. The court declared that Inman had not been conscious of Payne being in bed with him and the charge of desertion was not proved. However, he was dismissed from the service for behaviour irregular and unbecoming that of an officer.

Following her return from England *Brisk* had been cruising off the Windward Coast. Over the course of the next two months Kellett's new command would take the majority of the Squadron's seizures, seven vessels, with only two other arrests by cruisers during this period. On 15 August *Brisk* seized the brig *Diligente* as she lay at anchor in the Gallinas under Portuguese colours. The following day Kellett arrested the Portuguese-flagged schooner *Ligeira* and dispatched her to Sierra Leone. *Diligente* was condemned on 12 October. From her papers it was shown that she had originally been *Paqueta de Cabo Verde*, condemned by the court in March 1837, then purchased by an Englishman and resold to a Spanish slave dealer in the Gallinas who had taken her to Cadiz via Havana where she had been sold yet again. *Diligente*'s poorly-forged papers erroneously stated that her sale at Cadiz had occurred before her sale at Freetown. *Brisk*'s second prize *Ligeira* arrived at Freetown on 23 August. She had the usual passport from the Cape Verdes, but, it being proved that she was fully equipped for slaving and that her owner was a merchant from Havana, she was condemned on 4 October.

Brisk's run of arrests was interrupted by *Fair Rosamond*, the brigantine boarding a suspicious-looking schooner lying at anchor in Accra Roads on 21 October. Clearly equipped for slaving, the Portuguese-flagged vessel *Constitução* was also armed with an 18-pounder on a pivot, two other long 18-pounders, six blunderbusses, twenty muskets and an equal number of cutlasses. Grape, chain and bar-shot had also been placed on deck, suggesting to Oliver that she was intending to carry out acts of piracy once at sea. In addition to the now-customary passport from the Cape Verde Islands there were also blank clearance papers that had been issued by the American Consul in Havana, Nicholas Trist. Unfortunately this was not the first time Trist's name had been attached to such documents. When *Brisk* had been at the Gambia in early August she had boarded the Portuguese schooner *Senhora de Bom Viagem* out of Havana, an examination of her papers had revealed that they had been signed by the American consul, apparently in the absence of a Portuguese official. *Fair Rosamond*'s prize was condemned on 12 October. Following the removal of articles from several vessels waiting adjudication it was now ordered that the Marshal to the Court make an inventory of a prize's tackle and stores immediately upon her arrival in the Sierra Leone River, that her prize crew transfer to the accommodation vessel *Conflict* and that the Portuguese or Spanish sailors be landed and remain on shore until their vessel was either condemned or restored.

On 21 September *Brisk* boarded the Portuguese-flagged schooner *Eliza* in the River Sesters. Her papers included the usual passport from the Cape Verde Islands and a clearance from the Havana Customs House. The discovery of a Spanish ensign led to her master, Manoel Muniz, admitting to Kellett that he was a resident of Havana, that he was the sole owner of the schooner and that he was trading for slaves. Seven out of ten infringements of the Equipment Clause being discovered on board *Brisk*'s prize, she was condemned on 12 October.

Still cruising off the Sesters, on 30 October *Brisk* seized another Portuguese-flagged schooner, *Constitução*, as she was preparing to load her cargo of slaves. The schooner's nominal master, Joaquim da Souza Pinto, and mate were both dangerously ill by the time of her arrival at Freetown on 8 October, causing her case to be delayed, her mate dying before he could be examined. When the court finally sat on 10 November it was determined from a letter found on board the schooner that *Constitução* was owned by a company out of Havana and that her actual master and supercargo, Don Juan Batalla, was a Spaniard masquerading as a passenger, whilst da Souza Pinto was in fact the carpenter. The contract with Messieurs Rorosa Marino and Company stipulated that the crew would not be paid if *Constitução* was captured by a vessel of equal or even greater force unless determined resistance was put up and that the wages of those who did not fight would be forfeited and shared amongst the other members of the crew. *Constitução* was condemned on 10 November.

Arriving off Trade Town from the Sesters, *Brisk* boarded *Mary Hooper*, an American-flagged vessel with a cargo of goods consigned to a slave trader at the Gallinas. The schooner's master, Charles Bergstiand, had twice been arrested for slaving and Kellett's suspicions regarding the nationality of the vessel were aroused by the fact that her supercargo was a Spaniard and her nine passengers either Spanish or Portuguese. The vessel had Portuguese papers obtained at the Cape Verde Islands, presumably as a precaution should she be stopped by an American cruiser in the West Indies and Kellett also noted that her papers from Havana had been signed by Trist. Kellett, of course, had no authority to detain a vessel flying American colours so he reluctantly allowed her on her way.

Brisk's series of seizures was next interrupted by *Termagant* when William's brigantine captured the schooner *Prova* off the River Bonny on 9 October. The vessel was flying Portuguese colours but was en route to Havana with a cargo of 326 slaves loaded at the Bonny. Amongst the master's papers was a declaration by Trist that he was a resident of the Cape Verde Islands, but the master, Lourenço Viadomonte, subsequently admitted that he had been living in Havana for the last six years. *Prova* arrived at Freetown on 17 November and was condemned nine days later, 295 slaves surviving to be emancipated.

In mid-October *Columbine* had returned to the Coast from Portsmouth under the command of Lieutenant George Elliot, an officer who had previous anti-slavery experience, commanding the cruisers *Nimble* and *Firefly* in the West Indies a decade previously. Taking passage on *Columbine* along with the Kroomen from *Waterwitch* was Lieutenant Edward Holland who was to assume command of *Dolphin*. This perhaps explains why *Columbine* had been ordered to sail directly to the Bights rather than Freetown which was the normal routine for cruisers arriving from England. The Kroomen returning home on board *Columbine* all resided in a district of Freetown known as Krootown and so Elliot, who was due to sail south to the Cape from the Bights, had to leave the men at Princes with a month's subsistence money until they could find passage north.

On 17 October *Brisk* made two arrests on the same day under almost identical circumstances. The first was the schooner *Veloz*, empty but equipped for slaving and flying Portuguese colours, which was discovered by Kellett just off the Gallinas. She had undergone a change of identity at the Cape Verde Islands and her real Spanish master was masquerading as a passenger. The second arrest was the Spanish schooner *Josephina*, lying in the Gallinas under Portuguese colours and also equipped for slaving. Amongst her papers, which her master was discovered attempting to destroy, there was a document signed by Trist certifying that *Josephina* was a Portuguese vessel bound for St Paul de Loando. *Brisk* arrived at Freetown on 25 October with her two prizes in company. *Josephina* was condemned by the Anglo-Spanish court on 10 November and her compatriot *Veloz* two weeks later.

Returning to sea, *Brisk* boarded *Mary Anne Cassard*, a schooner flying American colours which was discovered just off Freetown on 27 October. Clearly equipped for slaving, the only American on board the vessel was her master John Bacon, whilst her five passengers were all Spanish. (Bacon was in reality Edward Graham, an English sailor who had previously served on board *Lynx* and was recognised by a seaman who had transferred from that vessel to Kellett's brigantine.) Rather than allow *Mary Anne Cassard* on her way Kellett arrested the schooner under the Equipment Clause and despatched her to Freetown. The Mixed Court, however, felt unable to bring a vessel with an American passport and flying the Stars and Stripes to trial, regardless of the irrefutable evidence that she was a Spaniard engaged in slaving, and ordered her to be restored to her owner, a decision for which they would later receive a rebuke from Palmerston.

The next two slavers taken by the squadron were both fully laden. On 31 October *Pelican* seized the Portuguese-flagged schooner *Dolcinea* with a cargo of 253 slaves off Lagos and the following day *Lynx* arrested the Portuguese brig *Liberal* with a cargo of 591 slaves off Whydah. *Dolcinea* was another vessel armed with papers signed by Trist. She was condemned by the court on 3 December and her surviving 249 slaves emancipated. *Liberal* had been furnished with false papers by the provisional government of Princes stating that she was owned by a resident of the Cape Verde Islands. She was condemned on 7 December and her surviving 583 slaves emancipated. The court commended *Liberal*'s prize master, Mr Slade, for the attention paid to the slaves under his care.

Heading north from Freetown, in early November *Brisk* arrived off the Guinea Coast. Kellett had been tasked with protecting British merchants on the rivers Nunez and Pongas from warring tribes and he went ashore to demand the local chief release several British subjects that had recently been seized. On 8 November his cruiser, now under the temporary command of her second master, seized the Portuguese-flagged schooner *Maria* as she awaited her cargo of slaves in the Pongas. Kellett returned from his meeting with the local chief having been unable to effect the release on the hostages and he strongly suspected they had already been sold into slavery. *Maria* arrived at Freetown on 12 November and, it being proven that she was a Spanish vessel, was condemned a week later.

A change of commanding officer brought a change in fortune for *Dolphin* which, having gone a year without making any arrests, took four prizes in one day in mid-November. Looking into Lagos Roads on 16 November Holland's brigantine found four vessels waiting for their cargo of slaves. Three were under what Holland assumed were false Portuguese colours whilst the last was flying no flag at all. Holland sent his mate, Mr Rowlatt, to take possession of all four slavers and to remove their crews to the other vessels lying at anchor. One prize departed for Freetown but a storm was coming on and Holland delayed the sailing of the remainder until the following morning, bringing them all in close to his cruiser.

In early November *Buzzard* returned to the Coast from Plymouth under the command of Lieutenant Charles Fitzgerald. Cruising off Freetown on 17 November Fitzgerald arrested *Sirse*, a Portuguese schooner clearly equipped for slaving. Lacking the evidence to establish beyond doubt that *Sirse* was owned by a resident of Havana, the Mixed Commission employed the 'course of trade' test, recently introduced to determine the national character of a vessel. Having been adjudged to be involved in the Cuban slave trade, *Sirse* was condemned as a Spanish vessel on 21 December.

On 18 November *Brisk* arrested the Portuguese-flagged *Veterano* whilst cruising off the Gallinas. The brig, which was equipped for slaving, had arrived at the Coast from Falmouth via Cadiz and Cuba and the court regarded the papers she had obtained from her new master in England, John White, and the Portuguese consul-general at Cadiz as fraudulent. Her true owner was discovered to be Pedro Martinez & Company of Havana and her real master, Carlos Sassetti, was listed as a passenger on board the vessel, as were her Spanish crew. *Veterano* was condemned under the Equipment Clause on 11 December.

On the night of 27 November *Buzzard*, also cruising off the Gallinas, spotted a suspicious-looking vessel about 35 miles to the west of the river mouth and sent her boats to board her. She proved to be the Portuguese brig *Emprendedor* with a cargo of 467 emaciated and diseased slaves that had been loaded from overcrowded barracoons in the Gallinas six days earlier. *Emprendedor*, a vessel which had been condemned ten years earlier as a Spanish slaver with the same name and master, was now claiming a Portuguese identity with papers purchased from the Portuguese consul-general at Cadiz. She was condemned by the court on 11 December and her surviving 458 slaves emancipated.

Sailing from the Bights to the Windward Coast, on 3 December *Bonetta* arrested the schooner *Isabel*, equipped for slaving and flying a Portuguese flag. The vessel was boarded to the west of St Thomas where she had changed her identity, having begun her voyage at Havana under the name of *Hyperion*. She was condemned by the Anglo-Spanish court as a Cuban-owned vessel equipped for slaving on 8 February 1839.

Whilst at Freetown Kellett had been asked by the Governor to visit the British territory of Bolama, one of the Bissagos Islands, where the Portuguese had reportedly gone ashore. Arriving off the island on 9 December *Brisk* found the Portuguese schooner *Aurelia Felix* at anchor and arrested her for having a solitary slave on board. Transferring a prize crew of twenty-five seamen and marines led by *Brisk*'s senior mate, William White, to his prize, Kellett took two armed boats in tow and set off for Bolama, where he discovered a recently-erected Portuguese slave factory with a garrison of sixteen soldiers. The barracoons were burned, 211 slaves who had been driven into the bush were rounded up and the Portuguese ordered to leave the island. The Union Flag having been hoisted in place of the Portuguese Bandiera, *Brisk* departed the island. Upon her arrival at Freetown it was discovered that *Aurelia Felix*'s solitary slave had in fact been entered in the ship's muster as a cabin boy and the court subsequently ordered the schooner to be restored to her owner and also awarded damages of £109.3s 10d against Kellett.

Pelican was now due to return home and on 15 December she departed Princes for Ascension. On the morning of 17 December, whilst roughly 50 miles north-west of St Thomas, she spotted a suspicious-looking vessel which immediately tacked upon sighting Popham's brig. Following a short chase *Pelican* arrested the Portuguese schooner *Magdalena* with a cargo of 320 slaves loaded three days earlier at the River Brass. On board the vessel, which had flown Spanish colours prior to her arrival at the Cape Verde Islands, was an American shipowner, Eleazer Huntington, whom Popham discovered had recently sold his vessel, the schooner *Ontario*, to a Spaniard, Jose Maria Mendez of the River Nun. From a discussion with *Magdalena*'s master, Jozé Cordozo, Popham learned that both she and *Ontario* had been in company on 16 December and so Popham set a course to intercept this second slaver. Spotted at daybreak on 18 December through heavy rain, Popham waited until the weather cleared before dispatching Lieutenant Marsh with two gigs to take possession of *Ontario*, which was discovered to have a cargo of 219 slaves loaded at the River Nun four days earlier. The schooners were condemned together on 17 January 1839, 302 slaves from *Magdalena* and 219 slaves from *Ontario* surviving to be emancipated.

A week after these arrests *Lynx* seized the Portuguese-flagged schooner *Victoria* off Princes Island on 24 December. Empty but fully equipped for slaving, there was not enough evidence for the court to prove that Broadhead's prize was a Spanish vessel, but it seemed most likely and, having employed the 'course of trade' test, *Victoria* was condemned by the Mixed Commission under the Equipment Clause and ordered to be broken up. By this time the court had negotiated a contract with the Clerk of Ordnance Works for a fee for breaking up vessels of four shillings per Spanish ton for the first 50 tons of a vessel and two shillings per ton thereafter.

By 22 December *Dolphin* and three of her prizes taken off Lagos in mid-November had arrived at Freetown. The fourth prize, *Astran*, arrived in port on 26 December along with another vessel seized by Rowlatt off the Gallinas, the schooner *Amalia*. Rowlatt had no authority to arrest suspected slavers and so the Portuguese-flagged vessel was immediately rearrested by Holland. Her Spanish ownership having been ascertained, *Amalia* was condemned under the Equipment Clause. The two brigs, *Victoria* and *Dos Amigos*, and the brigantine *Ligeiro* were all condemned by the Mixed Commission on 28 January 1839. The fate of *Astran* remains a mystery and it is reasonable to assume that the court restored her to her owners, being unable to prove either Spanish or Dutch ownership of the vessel and therefore that she was subject to the Equipment Clause.

The last two arrests of the year were both made on the same day, 28 December. The first fell to *Brisk*, Kellett's brigantine taking the Portuguese schooner *Violante* 20 miles south of the Sherbro with a cargo of 191 slaves. For Kellett, who had taken eleven prizes in four months, this arrest must have been particularly pleasing for he had encountered this vessel before, sailing under an American flag with the name of *Mary Anne Cassard*. Now flying Portuguese colours, she was devoid of American protection and was condemned by the Anglo-Portuguese court on 10 January 1839, all 191 slaves surviving to be emancipated.

The second capture on 28 December was made later that day by *Bonetta*. Sailing in company with Kellett's brigantine on passage to Sierra Leone, she seized the Portuguese-flagged schooner *Gertrudes* off the Sherbro with a cargo of 168 slaves loaded in that river two days earlier. As was the case for *Violante*, this schooner, bound for Puerto Rico, had Portuguese papers provided by the Governor of Bissau. *Bonetta*'s prize arrived at Freetown on 2 January 1839 and was condemned eight days later, all 168 slaves surviving to be emancipated.

Chapter 12

The American Slavers:
January 1839–December 1839

In mid-January 1839 Admiral Elliot arrived at Freetown from the Cape to discover *Brisk* stricken by an outbreak of fever following her recent visit to Bolama. By the time *Melville* departed Freetown towards the end of the month seven of the sixteen men from Kellett's brigantine who had fallen ill following their brief excursion ashore had died. Having received a request from Governor Docherty to send cruisers to the northern rivers to deal with the warring tribes, the commander-in-chief suggested that a colonial schooner manned by Kroomen be employed instead. Writing to the Colonial Office to request permission to purchase such a vessel, Docherty took the opportunity to praise *Brisk*'s commanding officer.

On the afternoon of 4 January *Forester* spotted a suspicious-looking vessel whilst lying at anchor off Cape St Paul's. Campbell weighed anchor, hoisted all sail and set off in pursuit. Three hours later the schooner *Hazard* was boarded off the mouth of the River Volta. Although she was flying American colours and was registered at Baltimore, *Hazard*'s papers showed that she had immediately sailed for Havana where her ownership had been transferred to a Spaniard, Francisco Montero. Her papers, clearing her for passage to St Thomas, had been signed by the American vice-consul at Havana and the shipper of her slaving equipment was not her master but her first mate, Benito Sandez. An American who had been employed as a 'captain of the flag' had died and there were no other Americans on board the vessel at the time of her capture. *Hazard* was brought before the court on 29 January but regardless of the evidence pointing to her Spanish ownership the Mixed Commission felt unable to adjudicate on a vessel flying the Stars and Stripes and ordered her to be released.

Having departed Freetown, *Dolphin* was headed down into the Bights when she fell in with and arrested the Spanish schooner *Merced* off Cape Mesurado on 10 January. The vessel had taken the precaution of landing her slaving equipment immediately upon her arrival at the Coast, therefore the Mixed Commission were unable to condemn her under the Equipment Clause and on 11 February ordered *Merced* to be restored to her owner, Joze Urresti. They also awarded damages and costs of £85 15s against Holland. However, it would not be the last that *Dolphin*'s commander would see of this particular vessel. Reviewing the case, Palmerston now instructed the British chargé d'affaires at Madrid to propose to Spanish ministers an additional stipulation to the Equipment Clause to allow condemnation of a vessel if it could be proved she had carried such equipment during the voyage on which she was arrested.

Following her return to the Coast in late December, *Saracen*, still under the command of Lieutenant Hill, had begun cruising off the Gallinas. On 13 January her boats seized the American-flagged schooner *Florida*. As with *Hazard*, *Florida* had been registered at Baltimore but had immediately sailed for Havana where she had been sold to a well-known slaving company, Messrs. Mazanedo and Abrisqueta, who employed an American, Williamson, to act as her owner. However, her Stars and Stripes had not been flying nor had Williamson been on board the vessel at the time of her arrest. As with *Hazard*, the Mixed Commission felt unable to condemn a vessel flying American colours but in this instance Williamson took the most of the opportunity given to him and ordered the vessel to be cut up and her fixtures and fittings sold at auction.

A day after the arrest of *Florida* the brig *Eagle* was boarded by *Lily* off Lagos. Sailing under circumstances almost identical case to those of *Hazard* and *Florida*, the Mixed Commission decided not to continue with proceedings against her. Her prize master, Mr Boys, felt unable to release *Eagle* and she departed Freetown in search of *Lily*. On 21 January *Termagant*, now commanded by Lieutenant Henry Seagram, boarded the American-flagged schooner *Jago* off Cape St Paul's. Arrested on the suspicion of being a Portuguese vessel engaged in slaving, she was released by the court at Freetown, although the commissioners believed that, as was the case with *Hazard* and *Eagle*, her fraudulent use of the United States' flag could have been proven in court.

After this spate of unsatisfactory boardings of American-flagged vessels the first arrest of the year to lead to a condemnation fell to *Fair Rosamond* when she seized the Portuguese-flagged brig *Matilde* off the River Gabon on 22 January. The vessel had cleared from Havana with a boiler supposedly for clarifying palm oil, barrels to hold the oil and 3,600 boards claimed to be for the construction of a hut to store the barrels. Unsurprisingly the court declared that all this equipment was intended for use in slaving and *Matilde* was condemned on 8 March.

The next vessel seized by the Squadron, *Maria Theresa*, was similarly equipped for slaving and sailing under Portuguese colours. She was arrested by *Lily* to the east of Accra on 22 January. Owned by the slave merchants Martinez and Co. of Havana, the brigantine was condemned on 11 February. The final arrest of the month fell to *Fair Rosamond*, Oliver's cruiser arresting the Portuguese-flagged brig *Tego* off the River Gabon on 31 January. She was condemned as a Spanish vessel equipped for slaving on 19 March.

There was just one arrest by the Squadron in February. On the 9th of that month *Termagant* seized the Portuguese-flagged brig *Braganza* off Cape St Paul's. Arrested on suspicion of being a Spanish vessel equipped for slaving, 530 gold doubloons intended to pay for her cargo were discovered on board the brig. Prior to her sale at Lisbon *Braganza* had in fact been the Spanish vessel *Vigilante*, she had then been fitted out at Corunna for a slaving voyage to Lagos. *Termagant*'s prize arrived at Freetown on 20 March and was condemned under the Equipment Clause on 1 April.

In early March *Melville* arrived at Ascension from Princes. During his tour of the Bights Elliot had learned of *Dolphin*'s poor sailing qualities due to her defective copper. Elliot now wrote to the Senior Officer on the Coast, *Scout*'s Commander Craigie, to request he order Holland's vessel home for refit at the first possible opportunity. Of more pressing concern to Elliot, however, was the situation on board *Lily*, also at Ascension. Commander Reeve had taken the highly unusual step of placing both his First Lieutenant, Richard King, and his surgeon, Charles Fuller, under arrest for repeated acts of disobedience and, in King's case, writing to Elliot with allegations against *Lily*'s commanding officer. The Rear Admiral now ordered *Lily* home so that King and Fuller be tried by court martial, the second time in eight months the unfortunate sloop had been sent home from the Coast for this reason. Fuller and King's court martials were held on board *Victory* at Portsmouth in mid-May. Accused of neglect of duty, disobedience of orders and disrespectful and insulting conduct towards Reeve, both men were eventually cleared of almost all the charges made against them by *Lily*'s commander, several of which were declared by the court to be frivolous, although King was admonished to be more circumspect in future and Fuller was severely reprimanded.

On 6 March *Forester* seized the Portuguese-flagged schooner *Ligeira* off Trade Town, Campbell arresting her on suspicion of being a Spaniard equipped for slaving. On 10 March Campbell boarded another Portuguese-flagged schooner, *Serea*, off Sanguin, also on the Pepper Coast and she too was dispatched north. Upon *Ligeira*'s arrival at Freetown the Proctor for the Seizor did not feel that there was sufficient evidence to prosecute her under the Equipment Clause and she was restored to her master, departing Freetown on 24 March. Campbell had more success with *Serea*. Clearly equipped for slaving with a passport acquired at the Cape Verde Islands, she was condemned by the court on 1 April.

On 4 March *Nautilus*, still under the command of Lieutenant Beaufoy, returned to the Cape from Mauritius. On the 13th another Symondite brig-sloop, the 16-gun *Wolverine*, arrived at Sierra Leone from the Mediterranean under the command of Lieutenant William Tucker who would now assume the duties of Senior Officer on the Coast. That same day *Pelican* departed Sierra Leone for England, arrived at Spithead on 20 April having spent almost four years on the Coast. Prior to his departure Popham received a letter of appreciation from Elliot for the performance of his duties during the eighteen months he had spent as Senior Officer on the Coast, both under Elliot and his predecessor Campbell.

On 12 March *Eagle*, seized by *Lily* in January, arrived at Clarence Bay where she discovered *Buzzard* at anchor. Having heard her prize master, Boys', explanation of the proceedings at Sierra Leone, Fitzgerald decided to question *Eagle*'s master, Joshua Littig. Threatened with being sent to New York to face trial there, Littig admitted that the brigantine was a Spanish vessel and that he was not her real master. Having received this confession, Fitzgerald sent an officer and a prize crew across to the slaver to rearrest her, receiving Boys and his men as supernumeraries on board *Buzzard*. On 13 March *Buzzard* departed Fernando Po with *Eagle* in company. On the eighteenth Fitzgerald sent his boats in to the River Nun. Early the following morning they emerged from the river under the tow of another prize, the American-flagged vessel *Clara*. From the Nun *Buzzard* sailed to Princes where she fell in with *Wolverine*. The new Senior Officer on the Coast, Commander Tucker, decided that *Eagle* and *Clara* should both be sent to New York to face trial there instead of Freetown, and so he ordered *Buzzard* to escort her two prizes to America.

With the arrest on 21 March of the American-flagged schooner *Rebecca*, discovered at anchor in the Gallinas Roads, *Forester* took her third prize in two weeks of cruising off the Pepper Coast. Fitted for slaving and with an American master, George Watson, letters were soon discovered on board *Rebecca* indicating that she was in fact a Spanish vessel out of Havana. Campbell told Watson that he would be arrested and sent to his own country to face trial, upon which Watson admitted that he had been paid by *Rebecca*'s Spanish owner to take her to the Gallinas where he was to hand the vessel over to her mate, Nicholas Echevarria. *Rebecca* arrived at Freetown on 27 March. Lacking any papers to prove her ownership, American or otherwise, the court employed the 'course of trade' test and on 6 April condemned her as a Spanish vessel. Following this arrest Campbell was replaced as commander of *Forester* by Francis Godolphin Bond.

The final arrest of the month was made by *Saracen*, Hill's gun-brig seizing the Portuguese-flagged schooner *Labradora* in the Rio Pongas on 31 March. The vessel was captured in the act of loading her cargo and there were already 253 Africans on board when boats from *Saracen* arrived alongside the schooner. In the confusion of the boarding three of *Labradora*'s men made off with her boat and two slaves. Her cargo, originally intended for the schooner *Maria*, seized by *Brisk* the previous November, had been forced to endure a further four months cooped up in the barracoons on the Pongas. *Labradora* arrived at Freetown on 6 April and was condemned on the 13th, 248 slaves surviving to be emancipated.

On 8 April *Wolverine* arrested the small Portuguese schooner *Passos*, en route from the mainland to Princes with a cargo of eighty-seven slaves. Tucker, who had served as a lieutenant on board *Maidstone* and had commanded her tender *Hope* in 1826, had never seen a vessel 'so unseaworthy or so badly fitted or found'[1] on the Coast. Deeming the schooner unfit for passage north to Freetown, he took her to Princes instead. Arriving at West Bay on 10 April *Passos*'s slaves, stores and all removable gear were transferred to *Dolphin* for passage to Freetown. The following day Tucker took the schooner out to sea and sank her. *Passos* was condemned on 11 May and her surviving eighty-one slaves emancipated.

On 14 April *Brisk*, cruising between the Bissagos Islands and the mainland, boarded the Portuguese schooner *Liberal* with a cargo of forty-one slaves being taken, so it was claimed, as bona fide servants to the Cape Verde Islands. Having decided to arrest *Liberal*, Kellett now took his prize to Bolama and landed her crew. Seeing the Portuguese flag once again flying over the island and the barracoons rebuilt, Kellett went ashore with twenty-five men. The flagstaff was broken, the barracoons and the newly-erected military barracks burned and the eighteen Portuguese soldiers on the island disarmed. *Brisk*'s prize *Liberal* arrived at Sierra Leone on 22 April. The Lisbon Decree of 1836 under which it was claimed her slaves were being shipped only allowed for the transportation of domestic servants when their owner was moving from one Portuguese territory to another and the party shipping them had to be their bona fide owner. However, an examination of *Liberal*'s papers revealed that fourteen of her slaves were being shipped by the Government Secretary and Director of the Customs House at Bissau and that a further three, supposedly crew members, were owned by the Governor of Bissau. *Liberal* was condemned on 13 May and her surviving forty slaves emancipated.

On 19 April *Saracen* boarded the Russian-flagged brig *Golubtchick* off the Gallinas. Hill arrested the brig, armed with two 12-pounders and with a Spanish master and crew, under the Equipment Clause and dispatched her to Sierra Leone. However, upon *Golubtchick*'s arrival at Freetown the Mixed Commission declined to hear the case, declaring a subsequent search of the vessel by Hill, which had uncovered papers confirming her Spanish identity, as unlawful. Instead the brig was dispatched to England under the command of Lieutenant Rowlett and was handed over to the Russian chargé d'affaires at Portsmouth in mid-June. Learning of the case, Palmerston expressed his surprise that Hill's search had been deemed illegal.

Having departed Sierra Leone on 13 March *Pelican* arrived at Spithead on 20 April. Following her arrival on the Coast from Gibraltar, on 30 April the 16-gun brig *Harlequin*, Commander Lord Francis Russell, arrested the American-flagged schooner *Traveller* off New Sesters. The vessel, which had previously been boarded by *Brisk*, *Buzzard*, *Bonetta* and *Saracen*, had so far avoided detention but *Harlequin*'s inexperienced commander chose to send her to Sierra Leone. As with all previous seizures of vessels flying the Stars and Stripes the commissioners chose not to bring *Traveller* to trial and ordered her to be released. On 6 May Russell seized a second American-flagged schooner, *Merced*, arrested by *Dolphin* in January but subsequently restored to her master. Her condition being no different to how she appeared when first arrested by Holland, the Captor's Proctor subsequently advised Russell not to take *Merced* to court following her arrival at Freetown. On 17 May Russell discovered the American-flagged brigantine *Wyoming* at anchor in the Gallinas. Slaving equipment was discovered on board but, rather than take the vessel before the Mixed Commission and risk having her released back to her owner, Russell instructed Lieutenant Beddoes to take the brigantine to New York to face trial there.

On 10 May *Forester*'s boats, working their way up the River Nazareth, arrested the schooner *Rayhna Dos Anjos* as she lay at anchor awaiting her cargo. Her Spanish master was ashore and her Portuguese captain of the flag appeared to have left the vessel prior to her departure from Havana. Arrested without slaves, *Rayhna Dos Anjos* was prosecuted as a Spanish vessel, but the chief mate and cook had died en route to Sierra Leone and the third mate and a seaman who were subsequently called as witnesses claimed ignorance of the names of the master or owner of the schooner or their nationalities. A Spanish 'course of trade' having been established, *Rayhna Dos Anjos* was condemned under the Equipment Clause on 15 June.

Having made several unsuccessful arrests of American-flagged vessels, on 16 May *Harlequin* boarded the Portuguese-flagged schooner *Constanza* as she attempted to enter the Gallinas to embark her cargo. Fully equipped for slaving, *Constanza* had a Portuguese captain of the flag and her papers stated that her owner was a resident of the Cape Verde Islands, but there was evidence that her real owners were Pedro Martinez and Co. of Havana. *Constanza* arrived at Sierra Leone on 20 May and was condemned nine days later. *Harlequin*'s next prize, the schooner *Bella Florentina*, was rather unusually sailing under Tuscan colours. Seized off the River Sesters on 20 May she was dispatched to Freetown but her prize master could not confirm to the commissioners that Russell held the correct Tuscan warrant and it was therefore decided to hand the schooner back to her master. However, the vessel required repairs to be made before she could sail and she was still at Freetown in late July when *Harlequin* returned from her cruise. Her true Spanish identity having now become apparent, she was taken before the Anglo-Spanish Mixed Court and condemned on 6 August.

Forester's next prize, the Portuguese-flagged schooner *Carolina*, was arrested in Mayumba Bay on 22 May as she awaited her cargo of slaves. Her master having died prior to her arrival on the Coast, *Carolina*'s first mate had taken over command of the vessel, but he was ashore at the time of her arrest. Arrested just 3° south of the Line, *Forester*'s prize was prosecuted as a Spanish vessel but the remaining witnesses, the second mate and cook, professed ignorance on almost all the points relevant to the case and lacking further evidence, the Captor's Proctor asked for the case to be withdrawn.

Arriving off the mouth of the River Congo on 23 May *Wolverine* discovered the Portuguese-flagged brig *Vigilante* at anchor. Fitted for slaving, she had a passport from the Cape Verde Islands in which the master, Franciso Jose de Souza, appeared as the owner. Tucker arrested her as a Spanish vessel but her departure for Freetown was delayed for a day whilst *Wolverine*'s carpenter constructed a new rudder for the brig. *Vigilante* arrived at Freetown on the evening of 17 June and proceedings were begun against her the following day. Her master refuted the passport, claiming that a French merchant living in Havana, Francisco dos Santos, was the real owner of both *Vigilante* and her cargo. Her Spanish character having been ascertained, she was condemned by the court on 25 June.

Now commanded by Henry Matson, on 27 May the recently-returned *Waterwitch* arrested the Spanish felucca *Si* following a five-hour chase. Sailing from the Gallinas with a cargo of 360 slaves bound for Havana, *Si* was armed with two heavy guns and her upper works were reinforced with cork, making them impervious to musket shot. She had only heaved to after her bowsprit, mainmast and lower yard had been damaged by roundshot from *Waterwitch* which had killed one sailor and a slave. *Si* was condemned by the Anglo-Spanish Mixed Court and her surviving 359 slaves emancipated on 5 June.

On the night of 27 May *Dolphin* seized the schooner *Jack Wilding* off British Accra. The vessel, whose papers had been signed by the US vice-consul at Havana, had not been flying any colours at the time of her capture as it was night. She had an American captain of the flag and one of her passengers, the Spaniard Antonio Capo, was well known to the officers of the Squadron, having previously been master of the brigantine *General Manso*. Her crew were either Spanish or Portuguese and she was fully equipped for slaving. *Dolphin*'s prize arrived at Freetown on 27 June and her Spanish character having been confirmed, she was condemned by the Mixed Commission on 8 July.

On 12 June *Buzzard* arrived at New York with her prizes, *Eagle* and *Clara*, followed two weeks later by *Harlequin*'s prize *Wyoming*. Initially the New York District Attorney, Benjamin F. Butler, declared that all three prizes could be tried for slaving and piracy but by mid-September he had changed his mind, having come to the conclusion they were all Spanish property. Meanwhile *Eagle* had dragged her anchors in a gale and had been blown ashore on Staten Island, allowing her mate and steward to abscond. By 8 November the brigantine had been repaired and Fitzgerald departed for Bermuda in the hope of having his prizes condemned by the Vice-Admiralty court there. Shortly after *Buzzard* sailed Butler decided to re-examine his law books and *Wyoming* was subsequently brought to trial and condemned. Following Fitzgerald's arrival at Bermuda the judge declared that he had no authority to try *Buzzard*'s prizes as they were foreign vessels arrested in foreign waters and so he suggested a Mixed Court, preferably the one at Freetown. On passage to Sierra Leone the three vessels parted company during a storm, *Eagle* foundered and was lost, although her prize crew were rescued, and *Clara*'s prize master decided to make for Antigua. Once repaired she was sent to Jamaica where she was condemned as a Spanish vessel fitted for slaving.

In early June *Pylades* arrived at Plymouth from the Coast. On 8 June *Lynx* arrested the American-flagged schooner *Perry Spencer* off the River Gabon. Pointing to the irregularity of her papers, which showed that she was owned by Spanish merchants who were residents of Havana, Lieutenant Broadhead informed her master, Joseph Monroe, that his vessel must proceed to New York to face trial there, upon which Monroe hauled down his Stars and Stripes and hauled up Spanish colours in their place, declaring his vessel to be Spanish-owned and equipped for slaving. Following her arrival at Freetown the Mixed Commission once again declined to hear the case of an American-flagged vessel and, emulating *Florida*'s master earlier in the year, Monroe had the schooner cut up and sold off her masts, gear and stores at public auction.

On 14 June *Brisk* fell in with the Portuguese-flagged brigantine *Jacuhy* with a cargo of 203 slaves, roughly 280 miles west of Loango Bay. An examination of the brigantine's papers revealed that her owner was a resident of Rio de Janeiro and she was bound for Rio d'Ostras to land her cargo of slaves, thirty-seven of whom had died following their loading four days earlier. Kellett removed the members of *Jacuhy*'s crew he did not require as witnesses and, having dispatched the brigantine to Freetown, proceeded to the River Congo to land them. He then sent his boats up the river where five vessels flying Portuguese colours and one Spaniard which had already landed her slaving equipment were boarded. *Brisk* returned to sea and on 28 June gave chase to a strange brig off Mayumba Bay. The wind being light, Kellett ordered his sweeps out, keeping in contact with the brig for the next five hours until he lost sight of her during the night and hauled to the wind. Contact was re-established late the following afternoon and Kellett sent his cutter away under the command of his acting second master, William Dix. At 9.15pm Dix succeeded in boarding the brig, *Matilde*, about 60 miles north-west of the Yumba River, several of his men being wounded by musketry. The vessel was fitted with two long 18-pounders and carried a pirate flag and a Spanish ensign, although her master claimed to be Portuguese. Amongst her papers were a Havana Customs House clearance and a logbook written in Spanish. *Matilde* arrived at Freetown on 24 July and a Spanish 'course of trade' having been identified, was condemned on 12 August. *Jacuhy* was condemned by the Anglo-Brazilian court on 18 July, 196 slaves surviving to be emancipated.

On 17 June *Dolphin* made two arrests, the first of the schooner *Euphrates* as she lay at anchor off the Grand Bassa River. As it was night the vessel had no colours hoisted but her master was a naturalised American, Charles A. Molan, and her papers had been signed by the US vice-consul at Havana. Arresting *Euphrates* on suspicion of being a Spanish vessel equipped for slaving, Holland dispatched her to Freetown. However, the commissioners declined to hear the case, deeming her to be an American vessel and pointing out that, whilst Holland had been within his rights to board the schooner and examine her papers, her detention had been unlawful. The court ordered *Euphrates* to be released, however, shortly after her departure from Freetown she was re-arrested by *Harlequin* and handed over to Governor Buchanan at Monrovia who briefly employed the schooner as a colonial vessel before dispatching her to America to face trial there.

Continuing on down the Pepper Coast *Dolphin* re-encountered the Spanish schooner *Merced* as she headed for the New Sesters. Discovering her equipment to be in a similar condition as when she had escaped condemnation in February, the boarding party were just returning to their brig when they heard the cries of a man in the water. The boats were lowered and an exhausted African male was fished from the sea. He explained that he had been put in a boat with ten other slaves and several sailors from *Merced* but the boat had capsized in the darkness and the other slaves, all boys, had drowned, as none of them could swim. *Merced*'s boat crew had been able to right their vessel and bale her out but they had not let the African back on board, hitting him about his head with an oar, forcing him to swim for *Dolphin* instead. Holland hoisted all sail and set off in pursuit of *Merced*, arresting her early on the morning of 18 June. The slaver, which had only just returned to sea following her arrest and subsequent release by *Harlequin* in early May, was finally condemned by the court at the third time of asking on 8 July.

On 20 June *Harlequin* seized the Portuguese-flagged brigantine *Emprendedor* off the Gallinas. Equipped for slaving, her crew admitted that her owner was a resident of Havana. Three days later *Wolverine* arrested the similarly-named Portuguese brig *Emprehendedor* off Whydah. Along with correspondence revealing that the man claiming to be her mate was in fact her master, Tucker discovered a logbook written in Spanish. *Harlequin*'s prize was condemned on 12 July but it took longer for the Mixed Commission to reach a decision regarding *Emprehendedor* as the evidence they had been presented with, her frequent trips to Bahia, seemed to indicate that the vessel was Brazilian and so the case was passed to the Anglo-Brazilian court. The last ship to have appeared before the Anglo-Brazilian court had been *Incomprehensivel* two and a half years earlier and there were no longer any Brazilian commissioners in Freetown to hear *Emprehendedor*'s case. The lack of a Brazilian Equipment Clause proved no obstacle to the British commissioners, who cited the clause in the 1826 Convention that made it unlawful for Brazilian subjects to engage in slaving 'under any pretext or in any manner whatsoever'[2] and *Emprehendedor* was condemned on 31 August. Emboldened by this decision from the commissioners, Tucker ordered his cruiser commanders to seize any Portuguese-flagged vessel equipped for slaving they believed in reality to be Brazilian.

Mid-June had seen the return to the Coast of *Curlew* under Lieutenant George Rose, who had earlier had served as *Fair Rosamond*'s first commanding officer. Shortly after her arrival on station the brig lost two men to fever. Following her arrest of *Emprehendedor* Tucker's brig had sailed to Accra. Tucker made the mistake of allowing his men shore leave whilst *Wolverine* underwent a refit and she soon had eighteen men on her sick list, nine of whom would subsequently die from fever. At Freetown the accommodation vessel *Conflict*, moored in the Sierra Leone River since 1832, was no longer fit for purpose and the prize crews were now living ashore in a building acquired by the Squadron. In July fever appeared amongst a prize crew from *Forester*, which had been cruising off Loango, resulting in three deaths.

On 25 June *Fair Rosamond* arrested a pair of small and overcrowded Portuguese-flagged vessels ferrying slaves between Fernando Po and the mainland. The 35-ton schooner *Pomba d'Africa* had a cargo of 155 slaves from the Old Calabar, a third of whom were taken on board Oliver's cruiser to ease the crowding during her passage to Freetown. The second vessel seized by *Fair Rosamond* was a sloop-rigged boat with twenty-three slaves taken from the same river, *Sedo ou Tarde*. This tiny vessel, just 29ft in length, was unfit for the passage north so, having transferred her cargo to *Fair Rosamond*, Oliver sold the boat by auction at Princes. Following his arrival at Freetown Oliver explained this sale as being necessary to purchase provisions for the slaves. Both vessels were condemned by the Anglo-Portuguese Mixed Commission on 12 August, 126 slaves from *Pomba d'Africa* and twenty-one from *Sedo ou Tarde* surviving to be emancipated.

In the last week of June *Harlequin* took three prizes in the space of three days whilst cruising off the Pepper Coast. Russell's first arrest was the Portuguese-flagged schooner *Victoria de Libertade*, arrested as she lay at anchor off the River Sesters on 26 June. The following day a brigantine flying Danish colours, *Cristiano*, was boarded off the same river. Fitted for slaving, Russell believed her to be a Spanish vessel and dispatched her to Freetown. Relocating to the Gallinas, on 28 June *Harlequin* seized the Portuguese-flagged schooner *Sin-ygual*. Again Russell believed her to be a Spanish vessel and sent her off for adjudication. *Sin-ygual* was condemned by the court on 12 July, *Victoria de Libertade* on 18 July and *Cristiano*, her papers having proven that she was in reality the Spanish vessel *Carranzano*, was condemned on 6 August.

Around the same time that *Harlequin* made the last of her trio of captures, *Dolphin*, cruising further north, arrested the Portuguese-flagged schooner *Casualidade* with a cargo of eighty-eight slaves from the Sherbro River. Meanwhile, in the Bights, *Waterwitch* spotted a schooner standing out from Lagos and followed in her anticipated track. Falling upon her on 8 July Matson seized her following a chase of five hours. On board the Portuguese-flagged schooner *Constitucaõ* was a cargo of 344 slaves bound for Cuba. *Dolphin*'s prize *Casualidade* arrived at Freetown on 7 July and was condemned by the court on 16 July, all eighty-eight slaves surviving to be emancipated. *Constitucaõ* arrived at Freetown on 24 July having lost just two of her slaves during the passage north, the court noting the care and attention paid to the slaves by her prize master, *Waterwitch*'s mate, Clarence Taylor. *Constitucaõ*'s case was initially heard by the Anglo-Portuguese Mixed Commission but was soon transferred to the Anglo–Spanish court. Her Spanish 'course of trade' having been established, the schooner was condemned on 15 August.

Whilst cruising off Whydah on 25 July *Wolverine* fell in with the Portuguese-flagged brig *Firmeza*. Believing the vessel to be Brazilian-owned, Tucker arrested her as equipped for slaving and dispatched her to Freetown, still unsure as to whether the Mixed Commission would follow the example they had set with *Emprehendedor* in August. Two days later *Lynx* arrested the Brazilian brigantine *Simpathia* as she waited for her cargo of slaves off Popo. Having established that she was a Brazilian-owned vessel equipped for slaving, the brigantine was condemned by the Anglo-Brazilian Mixed Commission on 7 September. *Firmeza* was similarly condemned by the court a week later, the court expressing its surprise that Tucker and his officers should ever have doubted that the Commission would condemn Brazilian-flagged vessels equipped for slaving seized north of the Line.

Following a brief chase off Lagos, on 12 August *Dolphin* arrested the American-flagged schooner *Catherine*, having been forced to fire several shots to bring her to. Rather than bring her to trial before the Mixed Commission at Freetown, Holland decided to send his prize to New York under his senior mate, Mr Dundas, instead. Reviewing the case following the schooner's arrival at Freetown to water, the commissioners felt confident that *Catherine* would be condemned owing to the amount of evidence pointing to her Spanish ownership. However, following her arrival in New York, circuit court Judge Betts declared that the vessel's engagement in the slave trade had not been clearly proved and ordered her to be restored to her owner. Thankfully for Holland this decision was subsequently overruled by the Chief Justice of the Supreme Court, Roger Brooke Taney, who ordered that *Catherine* be condemned.

On 18 August *Forester* boarded the brig *Mary* off Cape Mount. Another American-flagged vessel found to be equipped for slaving, Bond arrested the brig in the belief that she was in fact Spanish and dispatched her to Sierra Leone. However, the commissioners followed their usual practice in these circumstances by declining to bring a vessel flying the Stars and Stripes to trial and instead ordered *Mary* to be released. Having discussed the matter with the Advocate-General, in the spring of 1841 Palmerston wrote to the commissioners to advise them that if evidence existed of the fraudulent use of the American flag, they ought to do their utmost to investigate the matter.

On 19 August *Dolphin* boarded the Portuguese-flagged brig *Intrepido* off Cape St Paul's. The vessel had a Portuguese captain of the flag but her papers showed that her actual owner was a resident of Bahia. *Dolphin* dispatched her prize to Freetown and continued on towards Accra where, on 23 August some of *Intrepido*'s Portuguese crew were landed and the remainder transferred from Holland's cruiser to *Fair Rosamond* for passage to Princes. *Dolphin* now returned to Cape St Paul's and on 26 August seized the American-flagged schooner *Butterfly* which was dispatched to New York via Freetown. The following day Holland arrested the Portuguese-flagged schooner *Dous Amigos* off the River Volta following a twelve-hour chase. The vessel was fully equipped for slaving and her papers had been signed by the Governor of the Cape Verde Islands. *Dous Amigos* was condemned by the Anglo-Spanish court on 24 August, the same day that *Intrepido* was condemned by the newly operational Anglo-Brazilian Mixed Commission. *Butterfly* arrived in New York in early October and was eventually condemned by a US circuit court under Judge Betts.

By the spring of 1839 Palmerston's patience with Portugal was at an end. Several years of continuous negotiations over a satisfactory anti-slavery treaty had come to nothing and with the government in Lisbon still refusing to include an Equipment Clause and allow arrests south of the Line, the Foreign Secretary decided to take matters in his own hands and began preparing a bill that would allow British naval officers to search and capture ships flying the Portuguese flag. It was clear that the various Anglo-Portuguese Mixed Commissions could not be relied on to condemn all the vessels brought before them as the Portuguese commissioners were bound to decide in favour of restoration of any seized vessels. Therefore Palmerston was advised to give the Vice-Admiralty courts powers to adjudicate upon Portuguese ships. It was also decided that the bill should include a list of 'equipment articles' in line with the several existing Equipment Clauses that would provide evidence of slaving, along with a stipulation that all condemned vessels either be bought by the Navy or broken up. Realising that, having been stripped of the protection of a Portuguese flag, slavers might dispense with flags and papers altogether, the bill also authorised Vice-Admiralty courts to adjudicate on vessels seized without nationality.

On 10 July 1839 the Slave Trade (Portugal) Bill was introduced in the House of Commons. It went through without debate but was opposed in the House of Lords by several peers including Wellington, who regarded it as a violation of international law. British courts were now being asked to adjudicate upon Portuguese ships and subjects engaged in activities subject to Portuguese law alone. Regarding the bill as hostile towards a friendly nation, Wellington declared that it would have been better if Britain had declared war against her old ally, for then the right of search and detention of foreign vessels would have been legitimate. Despite the objections of Wellington, who was lauded in the Portuguese press as a champion of slavery in Brazil, the bill became law on 24 August. Three weeks later British naval officers on the Coast were authorised to send captured Portuguese ships and those without nationality to the nearest Vice-Admiralty court (from June 1840 this would include St Helena), to hand their masters and crews over to their own authorities and to land slaves at the nearest British colony.

Kellett having been invalided home, on 26 August *Brisk*, now under the command of Lieutenant Whaley Armitage, departed the Coast for Angola and three days later *Scout* sailed for England, arriving at Spithead in early November. On 5 September *Fair Rosamond* arrested the Brazilian barque *Augusto* off Cape St Paul's. Along with her passport from Bahia, stating that the master and owner of the vessel, Xavier de Castro, was a resident of Brazil, there were various letters between the slaving firm Messrs. Almeida, Costa and Co and her agents and the masters of several slaving vessel on the Coast that were of great interest to the commissioners. *Augusto* arrived at Freetown on 3 October and was condemned as being equipped for slaving on the 19th of that month.

The Squadron's next three prizes were taken by *Bonetta* in a single day. Anchoring off Wood Point, Punta de Lena, Stoll sent his boats in to the River Congo and on 7 September they arrested three vessels flying Portuguese colours at anchor in the entrance to the river. The master of the schooner *Josephina* was ashore but her papers and those of the brigantine *Liberal* revealed that they were both owned by the well-known slaving firm Forçade and Co. of Havana. The schooner *Ligeira*'s papers stated that her owner was a resident of Bahia but there was also evidence that her owners at the time of her capture were two Spanish residents of Havana. *Josephina* and *Liberal* were dispatched to Sierra Leone and were condemned together by the Anglo–Spanish Mixed Court on 26 October. *Ligeira* was condemned by the same court on 30 October. Confirmation of all three vessels' Spanish character now meant that they could be cut up subsequent to their condemnation.

On 12 September *Wolverine* seized the Brazilian-flagged brigantine *Pampeiro* at anchor off Lagos. Equipped for slaving and owned by a resident of Bahia, her papers contained two lists of canoemen supplied to her by the Dutch at Elmina, indicating that one crew was destined for another vessel then at Lagos. Seven days later *Termagant* arrested another Brazilian brigantine, *Golphino*, as she approached the same port. The commissioners had already been made aware of both these vessels through the letters found on board the Brazilian slaver *Augusto*, arrested earlier that month, and they were condemned by the Anglo–Brazilian court at the same sitting on 20 October.

The Squadron's next arrest would have come as welcome news to Lieutenant Broadhead, although he took no part in the actual seizure. On 27 September *Waterwitch*, cruising 40 miles south-west of Lagos, boarded the Portuguese-flagged schooner *Sete de Avril*, which prior to the loading of her cargo of 424 slaves the previous day had been known as *Mary Cushing*, the American-flagged vessel arrested by *Lynx* in late March but not brought to trial. The American captain of the flag was now embarked on board the schooner as a passenger, his role having been assumed by a Portuguese, Manoel Martino, who admitted that the vessel's owners were residents of Havana. Nine slaves died prior to *Sete de Avril*'s condemnation by the Anglo–Spanish court on 2 November.

Broadhead had yet more to celebrate with his arrest, just two days after the capture of *Sete de Avril*, of the Portuguese-flagged brig *Destemida* off Winnebah. Arrested for being equipped for slaving, the brig's captain of the flag, Manoel Francisco Pinto, admitted that his vessel was owned by a resident of Bahia. On her passage out of the Bights under a prize crew commanded by Mr Frederick Slade, *Destemida* called at Princes, where she fell in with *Nautilus* and took on board a number of slaves from a prize recently taken by Beaufoy's brig. *Destemida* arrived at Sierra Leone on 9 November and was condemned by the Anglo–Brazilian court nine days later.

Nautilus's first arrest had been made whilst cruising off St Thomas on 2 October. Discovering the Portuguese schooner *Andorinha* to be carrying eight African children no older than four, the inexperienced Beaufoy allowed her master, Christovão Xavier Vellozo, to land at Princes with two of their number whom he claimed were his servants. Two days later *Nautilus* seized a small and unseaworthy launch with a cargo of sixty-one slaves off St Thomas. The vessel, *Vencedora*, was left at Princes. Half her cargo were put on board *Andorinha* and the remainder on board *Lynx*'s prize, *Destemida*. Heading north from Princes, *Vencedora* called at Cape Palmas for provisions where she fell in with *Harlequin* and her sick prize master, Mr Hunt, was replaced with Midshipman John Milbourne. Both *Andorinha* and *Vencedora* were condemned by the Anglo–Portuguese Mixed Commission on 24 December, fifty slaves from *Vencedora* surviving to be emancipated.

On 16 October *Saracen* seized the Portuguese-flagged schooner *Brilhante* off the Gallinas. Equipped for slaving, *Brilhante*'s passport had been obtained from the Cape Verde Islands and her captain of the flag, Victor da Silva, stated that the vessel was owned by a resident of Havana. Eleven days later *Waterwitch* arrested the Brazilian schooner *Calliope* 25 miles off Cape St Paul's. The schooner, also equipped for slaving, had three custom house clearances and a passport issued at Bahia. *Brilhante* was condemned by the Anglo-Spanish court on 7 November and *Calliope* by the Anglo-Brazilian court on 3 December.

Matson's next arrest came after a seven-and-a-half-hour pursuit. An hour before daybreak on 1 November *Waterwitch* spotted a suspicious-looking brig off to her north-east and gave chase. At 9.00am Matson fired a long-range shot at the brig which was then observed throwing guns, anchors, boats and spare gear overboard. At 12.30pm *Waterwitch* was close enough for her gunfire to induce the brig to hoist Portuguese colours but Matson, concerned she might attempt an escape, continued the attack for the next hour until the brig, her masts and rigging badly damaged, could no longer carry sail. Boarded around 40 miles east of Lagos, an examination of the vessel, *Fortuna*, showed that she was fully equipped for slaving, whilst her papers, including a passport issued at St Paul de Loando, revealed that she was owned by a resident of Havana. *Fortuna*'s crew were removed to Matson's vessel along with 1,150lbs of rice to make up for a shortfall in *Waterwitch*'s own provisions, a measure which later received the approval of the Mixed Commission. *Fortuna* arrived at Sierra Leone on 24 November and was condemned nine days later.

Having spent more than two years on the Coast with no arrests to her name, on 11 November *Viper*, now commanded by Lieutenant Godolphin Burslem, finally made a contribution to the suppression campaign with the seizure off Cape Palmas of the Portuguese-flagged schooner *Magdalena*. Fitted for slaving, her captain of the flag, Juan Ramon de Madariaga, admitted that he and his men were all Spanish and that the vessel was owned by a resident of Havana. *Magdalena* arrived at Freetown on 25 November, she was condemned by the Anglo-Spanish court on 3 December and ordered to be cut up.

November ended with a flurry of arrests. On the 21st *Harlequin* and *Forester* were lying at anchor together off Cape Palmas. Two of *Forester*'s boats were engaged fetching wood and water from the shore when a strange sail was spotted and *Harlequin* weighed anchor and stood out to sea, having first ordered *Forester* to remain at anchor to recover her boats. The stranger proved to be the Brazilian brigantine *Sociedade Feliz*, bound for Whydah from Bahia. She was a rich prize, so heavily laden with farina, jerk beef, beans and corn that it was impractical to make a proper search of her. She was condemned on 24 December and *Forester* subsequently put in a successful claim for a share of her bounty-money and the profits from her sale. On 27 November *Lynx* arrested the Portuguese-flagged schooner *Lavandeira* off the Gallinas. This was another vessel whose arrival on the Coast had long been expected from intercepted correspondence found on board other slavers. Her passport had been issued by the Cape Verde Islands and her Portuguese captain of the flag, Miguel Oliver, admitted that her voyage had begun and was due to end at Havana. *Lavandeira* arrived at Freetown on 2 December and was condemned on the 10th of that month. The last two arrests of the month were made by *Termagant* on consecutive days. On 28 November Seagram's vessel arrested the Brazilian brig *Conceiçao* 20 miles west of Whydah and the following day she seized the Brazilian brigantine *Julia* off the same river. Flying Portuguese colours and equipped for slaving, the brigantine's passport had been issued at Princes. Both prizes were condemned by the Anglo-Brazilian court on 6 January 1840.

Chapter 13

Attacking the Source:
January 1840–December 1841

In December 1839 Arbitrator Lewis had been granted an extension to his sick leave and it had been agreed that a sickly Judge Macaulay could go home on leave to recover his health once Lewis had returned to work. With the commissioners once again lacking clear instructions from London, by early 1840 Palmerston's new Portuguese Act had borne little fruit. Three vessels had been seized in the Indian Ocean in December, although little is known about these arrests and, as the Registrar of the Mixed Commission at Freetown, Melville, explained to a friend in the Foreign Office, just one case had been heard by the Vice-Admiralty court at Freetown. This was probably the Portuguese brig *Novo Abismo*, seized by *Bonetta* on 3 January 1840 and subsequently condemned.

In January the gun-brig *Rolla*, now commanded by Lieutenant Charles Hall, returned to the Coast following an absence of almost two and a half years. Continuing her recent run of good form, on the morning of 7 January *Viper* seized the American-flagged schooner *Laura* off Cape Mesurado. The schooner, built in Baltimore and sold to a Spaniard in Havana, was preparing to receive her cargo of slaves, laying her slave deck, adding an additional bulkhead and piercing her hatchways for iron bars, when *Viper* hove into view and Burslem sent his boats in chase. Prior to her arrest most of the schooner's Spanish papers were destroyed in the galley and her slave shackles and boiler were thrown overboard. *Laura*'s American master, Henry Hantsman, admitted he was due to hand control of the schooner over to a Spaniard, Costa, following her arrival at Cape Mesurado. Calling briefly at the American settlement of Liberia, *Viper* escorted her prize to Freetown, the two vessels arriving in harbour on the evening of 18 January. *Laura* was condemned as a Spanish vessel equipped for slaving on 28 January.

Anchoring off the River Brass on 15 January Tucker learned of an American slaver operating in the nearby River Nun and so sent Lieutenant

Dumaresq in the pinnace and *Wolverine*'s mate, Arthur Kinston in the cutter to investigate. After a lengthy pull up the river the boats fell in with the American-flagged schooner *Lark* which was boarded without resistance. The following morning, as the British were bringing their prize out of the river they sighted a second American-flagged schooner, *Asp*, and Dumaresq sent his boats away, the schooner's Spanish crew making no attempt to resist arrest. With Dumaresq leading in *Asp* and Mr Kingston following behind in *Lark*, the two schooners made their way back out of the river. As they approached the bar *Asp*'s gig and pinnace, which were being towed behind the schooner, broke adrift. The gig sank and her crew were recovered by the pinnace, which now began to drift towards the breakers. Kingston dropped anchor and, with the surf from the bar threatening to swamp *Lark*, was able to recover the pinnace as it drifted past the schooner.

Their Spanish characters having been confirmed, *Lark* and *Asp* were condemned together by the Anglo-Spanish court on 9 March. Following these two arrests in the Nun *Wolverine* had headed down into the Bights via Cape Coast Castle. Tucker arrived at Princes on 28 January, the same day *Buzzard* was reported to be at Sierra Leone following her return from Bermuda and *Nautilus* departed Freetown for England, arriving at Portsmouth in mid-March. In early February *Saracen*, then in the Gambia, received intelligence that a French-flagged slaver was about to depart from Bathurst. Relocating from the Casamance River to St Mary's, Hill seized the schooner *Senegambie* on 7 February. Equipped for slaving, it appeared that the vessel had been purchased by the French at Senegal in order to acquire slaves for military service in their colony. *Senegambie*'s owner and supercargo, M. Marbeau, was ashore at the time of her seizure. He was later arrested and remanded for trial at Bathurst. His vessel was condemned by the Vice-Admiralty court on 6 March. It is most likely that *Saracen* arrived in port in company with her prize for she was reported to be at Freetown on 1 March.

Cruising to the north of St Paul de Loando on the morning of 14 February *Columbine* spotted a strange brig roughly 14 miles ahead of her. Hoisting all sail she bore up and gave chase, passing a quantity of timber and plank that had been thrown overboard by the brig as *Columbine* slowly closed in on her. At 6.30pm the stranger finally hove to and was boarded by a boat from Elliot's cruiser. She proved to be the Portuguese brig *Primo Genito*, fully equipped for slaving. A prize crew under Lieutenant Tatham was placed on board the vessel and she departed for Ambriz, arriving there on 15 February with *Columbine* following close behind. On 17 February *Primo Genito* departed Ambriz for Simon's Bay. She arrived there on 19 March in company with *Columbine* and was condemned by the Vice-Admiralty court on 11 April.

On 21 February a boat from *Brisk*, now commanded by Lieutenant George Sprigg, seized the Portuguese-flagged brig *Raimundo Primeiro* with a cargo of nineteen slaves off Benguela. *Brisk* had been out of view below the horizon at the time of the arrest and *Raimundo Primeiro*'s prize crew spent several days in search of Sprigg's cruiser. Once reunited, the slaver's crew were put on board *Brisk* and she was dispatched to Freetown where she was condemned by the Vice-Admiralty court on 6 June. Following their vessel's departure for Freetown *Raimundo Primeiro*'s crew had been put ashore and the Foreign Office subsequently received a letter of complaint over the incident from the Portuguese minister, Baron Moncorvo.

On 27 February *Bonetta* boarded the French brig *Noemie Marie*, at anchor at Sierra Leone. Her captain was not present, being ill on shore with the vessel's papers. However, discovering a large quantity of plank and staves on board the brig, Stoll gave orders for her to be seized should she attempt to weigh. He also sent his second master, Mr Paul, to board another French vessel, the schooner *Aigle*, on board which was discovered four leaguers of water. On the evening of 29 February *Aigle* weighed and Stoll sent a boat across to examine her papers. A further search revealed twenty bags of rice and hoops to make four more leaguers. It now became apparent to Stoll that the plank on board *Noemie Marie* was intended for a slave deck and that the hoops on board *Aigle* would set up the staves on board her compatriot. Stoll and Oliver now proceeded to the Customs House where they were informed that the plank on board *Noemie Marie* had been entered on her original manifest from her clearing port in France but that the embarkation of her rice at Sierra Leone had not been noticed. *Noemie Marie*'s master, Jose Gutteill, now made a complaint over the actions of Paul and the British sailors who had searched his vessel, whilst also destroying the leaguer staves so as to appear above suspicion. Stoll released *Aigle*, fully convinced he had prevented the brig and the schooner from combining their articles to create a vessel equipped for slaving.

On 1 March Joseph Denman returned to the Coast as commander of the 16-gun brig-sloop *Wanderer*, bringing with him orders for *Harlequin* to depart for England. The following day *Wolverine* arrived at Sierra Leone, dropping anchor alongside *Bonetta*, *Saracen* and *Wanderer*. Tucker now placed Denman in charge of the Squadron's cruisers operating from Cape Verde to Cape Palmas on the Windward Coast. On 3 March the accommodation vessel *Conflict* was surveyed and found to be unfit for purpose so Tucker ordered her to be moved inshore to prevent her creating an obstacle to other vessels using the river should she founder, as now seemed highly likely. *Senegambie* was surveyed as a suitable replacement following her condemnation but was found to be unfit for Royal Navy service. On 6 March *Saracen* sailed for Portendic to support the British gum traders there.

Departing from Sierra Leone, on 3 March *Bonetta* seized the American-flagged schooner *Sarah Anne* in the River Pongas. The vessel had been hiding in a muddy creek and Stoll might have missed it had he not been led directly to the spot by a native in one of *Bonetta*'s boats. The schooner was equipped for slaving and there were just three members of her crew, two Spaniards and a Sardinian, present at the time of her capture. From documents found on board the schooner it appeared she had cleared out from Havana then headed directly to the Pongas. She was aground when seized and an attempt to warp her clear by *Bonetta*'s boats resulted in them coming under fire from the mangroves, the British responding with a volley of musketry. *Sarah Anne*'s mate, Albert Slete, who claimed to be an American, now made an appearance from the mangroves. Having arrested the schooner on suspicion of being a Spanish vessel equipped for slaving, *Bonetta* escorted her prize to Freetown, arriving in the Sierra Leone River on 6 March. The following day USS *Grampus*, Commander John S. Paine, arrived at Freetown.

Growing concern over the increased use of the American flag by slavers on the Coast, fuelled by the arrival of *Eagle*, *Clara*, *Butterfly* and *Wyoming* in New York, had led to the decision by President Van Buren to send American cruisers to Africa for the first time since the 1820s. *Grampus* and *Dolphin*, Commander Henry Bell, were instructed to deter foreigners from using the flag of the United States and to protect American vessels from molestation. The appearance off the Coast of these two vessels would result in far greater cooperation between American and British commanders than had been intended in Washington. Following *Grampus*'s arrival at Freetown Stoll handed over his prize, *Sarah Anne*, to Paine and when her master,

Raymond Foritz de Pedro, wrote requesting protection as an American citizen Paine had him arrested on suspicion on slave trading. Tucker and Paine now entered into an agreement, later repudiated in Washington, whereby the British would hand over any slaver sailing under the Stars and Stripes to the American squadron whilst Paine and Bell would hand over any Spanish, Portuguese or Brazilian slaver to the British.

On 14 March *Waterwitch* seized the Portuguese brig *Cabaca* off Ambriz. The vessel, with a cargo of two slaves, one woman and a boy, was deemed to be unseaworthy and was therefore destroyed by fire and sunk. This arrest was notable as *Cabaca*'s slaves and fittings were taken to the newly-established Vice-Admiralty court at St Helena where the brig was condemned on 11 June, just three days after the court had opened.

On 15 March the newly-launched 16-gun brig-sloop *Fantome*, Commander Edward Butterfield, arrived at Sierra Leone from England. Having provisioned, she then sailed for the Cape with dispatches for Elliot. On 21 March *Wolverine* departed Freetown for a cruise down the Pepper Coast, arriving off Cape Mesurado on 26 March where she fell in with USS *Dolphin*. The following day Tucker chased an American-flagged vessel into the New Sesters. On boarding and examining her papers she proved to be a vessel out of Havana equipped for slaving. Unable to stay and keep watch over the vessel, Tucker wrote to Paine to request he examine her. He also informed Denman to keep a close watch on New Sesters, there being an estimated 2,000–3,000 slaves in the barracoons.

On 26 March *Viper* made a rare arrest, seizing a British-flagged vessel, *Guiana*, about 250 miles east of Cape Palmas off the River Sassandra. Bound for Lagos from Bahia and loaded with trade goods, Burslem arrested the brig for acting in contravention of the 1824 Act of Parliament. She was sent for adjudication in the Vice-Admiralty court at Sierra Leone and on 12 August was sentenced to be forfeited for aiding and abetting the slave trade. In accordance with the seventh section of the act, *Guiana*'s cargo was held until a penalty double its value was paid by her owners.

April began with a flurry of arrests. Sailing under the acting command of Lieutenant Walter Pollard, on 1 April *Buzzard* seized the Portuguese-flagged schooner *Adelaide*. The following day *Wolverine*, sailing off the River Sassandra whilst on passage to the Bights, arrested the Brazilian brig *Santo Antonio Victorioso* which was bound for Lagos. On 3 April *Lynx* detained the American-flagged schooner *Octavia* off Popo under the suspicion that she was a Spanish vessel and on 4 April *Wanderer* seized a similarly-flagged brig *Eliza Davidson* 50 miles north of Sherbro Island. Discovered on board the vessel were two African children who had been embarked at the Gallinas. *Adelaide* was condemned under the Palmerston Act by the Vice-Admiralty court at Sierra Leone and *Santo Antonio Victorioso* was condemned by the Anglo-Brazilian Mixed Commission. The dates of these condemnations are not known. The Spanish character of *Lynx*'s prize *Octavia* having been confirmed, she was condemned by the Anglo-Spanish court on 5 June. *Eliza Davidson* was condemned by the same court on 18 June and her two slaves emancipated.

On 11 April *Rolla* departed Bathurst for Sierra Leone. Meanwhile, stretching far out into the Atlantic Ocean, on 12 April *Fantome* seized the Uruguayan-flagged brig *Republicano* roughly 800 miles south-west of St Helena. Her printed passport, issued by the Consulate-General of Uruguay at Rio, stated that the brig was permitted to sail from Montevideo to any other port in Uruguay; however, it had been amended by the consul to say the Canaries. *Republicano*'s captain, Joze Garcia, had also asked the consul for a certificate to cover the brig's slaving equipment, stating that the purpose of the voyage was to transport colonists from the Canaries to Montevideo. Arrested as a Brazilian vessel equipped for slaving, *Fantome*'s prize was condemned by the Mixed Commission on 5 June.

The Squadron's next arrest resulted in the largest seizure of slaves since the capture of the Spanish schooner *Sete de Avril* in September 1839, almost seven months earlier. On 18 April *Lynx* detained the Portuguese schooner *Olimpa* 250 miles south-west of Lagos, from where her cargo of 380 slaves had been loaded three days earlier. The vessel, which had cleared out from Havana, had obtained a passport at the Cape Verdes ostensibly for a voyage to St Thomas, although in reality she had made directly for Lagos. The boarding was not resisted even though the schooner was carrying eighteen muskets, a similar number of cutlasses and three pairs of pistols. *Olimpa* arrived at Freetown on the evening of 17 May. She was condemned nine days later and her surviving 370 slaves emancipated.

Cruising roughly 100 miles south-west of the Niger Delta, on the morning of 23 April *Wolverine* spotted a barque off her lee-bow and gave chase. A shot was fired ahead of the vessel but this failed to bring her to. With the wind now falling, Tucker sent Lieutenant Levigne to board the barque, which, on the appearance of *Wolverine*'s boat, hoisted British colours. Another vessel was now spotted from *Wolverine*'s mast-head bearing south-east but Tucker had now been taken several points from his original course and 12 miles to leeward, preventing him from examining the second vessel. When finally boarded, the only explanation the master of the British barque, *Bombay Packet*, gave for not shortening sail was that he did not know that *Wolverine* was a British cruiser, even though her colours were clearly visible and two shots had been fired at his vessel. Following this incident Tucker sent Elliot an angry letter bemoaning the behaviour of English masters on the Coast. In late April *Wolverine* arrived at Princes to re-fit and copper, joining *Harlequin*, *Lynx* and *Viper* which was being refitted as a brigantine. On 11 May *Wolverine* departed the island in company with *Harlequin*.

In the spring of 1840 Admiral Elliot was appointed the new commander-in-chief of the East Indies Station, departing for Singapore on board *Melville* on 30 April. After nine years of combined operations the West Africa Squadron once again became an independent command, its southern boundary being extended to Cape Frio, with the Senior Officer on the Coast, Tucker, now responsible to Admiral Edward King following his appointment as commander-in-chief of the new Cape and Brazils Station. It would, however, be several years before an officer of flag rank would arrive on the Coast to take command of the Squadron, which had increased from seven vessels in 1831, the last time a commodore had been in charge, to its current number of twelve cruisers.

Following their departure from Princes *Harlequin* and *Wolverine* parted company, Russell proceeding to Spithead whilst Tucker headed for the Gabon in order to present King Denny with a medal from Queen Victoria in recognition of the protection he had given to a boat crew from *Lynx* in 1839. On 12 May *Wanderer* arrested the Portuguese schooner *Josephina* off the River Sesters following a chase that had begun the previous evening. Dispatching her prize to Freetown, *Wanderer* now headed north, anchoring off the Gallinas on 14 May. *Josephina* was condemned by the Vice-Admiralty court in mid-May and was subsequently purchased by the Navy for use at Ascension, being renamed *Prompt* the following year.

In May *Bonetta* departed Freetown for Portsmouth, bringing to an end an arduous four-year deployment for the little brig which had seen her detain twelve vessels and emancipate just over 800 slaves. Stoll's vessel had suffered greatly from the feverish conditions prevalent on the Coast and by the time of her arrival in England in mid-June just six individuals remained on board the brig who had departed England aboard her in August 1836. Also departing the Coast for the last time was *Fair Rosamond*. Purchased by Commodore Hayes as tender to *Dryad* and then serving as a commissioned cruiser in her own right, over the course of her nine-year career she had captured eighteen slavers and emancipated 1,452 slaves. Sailing from the Cape on 21 May Oliver's brigantine called at Ascension on 2 July and Sierra Leone on 6 August, arriving at Portsmouth on 17 September. She remained in Ordinary until recommissioned for service in the Caribbean in 1841. Paid off and found to be unfit for further service, she was broken up in 1845.

On 3 June *Wanderer* seized the Portuguese-flagged schooner *Sao Paolo de Loanda* in the Gallinas on suspicion of being a Spanish vessel equipped for slaving. Owned by a Spanish resident of Cuba, *Sao Paolo de Loanda*'s passport for the Cape Verde Islands had been issued by the Portuguese consul at Havana and her Austrian captain of the flag, Mario Sgitcovich, had held the same position on board *Matilde*, seized by *Fair Rosamond* and condemned by the Anglo-Spanish court the previous March. *Wanderer*'s prize arrived at Freetown on 7 June and, her national character having been identified, was condemned on 18 June.

Relocating from the Gallinas to Cape Mount, six days after the arrest of *Sao Paolo de Loanda* Denman seized the Spanish schooner *Maria Rosaria*, sailing under a royal passport issued at Havana and en route to the Pepper Coast. Her logbook stated that she had called at the Cape Verde Islands to carry out repairs although there was no evidence of any such repairs having been made to the vessel. Fully equipped for slaving, she was dispatched to Freetown, arriving in the Sierra Leone River on 14 June. On 24 June she was condemned by the Anglo-Spanish court.

On 5 June the newly-commissioned 16-gun brig-sloop *Persian*, Commander William Quin, had arrived at Sierra Leone from Plymouth prior to taking up her cruising grounds in the Bights, her commanding officer returning to the Coast following an absence of four years. In mid-June *Brisk* arrested several slavers, all of which were taken to St Helena for adjudication by the Vice-Admiralty court there. On 10 June Sprigg's cruiser arrested the Portuguese vessel *Dictador*, two days later she seized the slaver

Coringa and on 15 June the brigantine arrested a third Portuguese vessel, *Andorinha*, with a cargo of one slave. Following her arrival at St Helena *Andorinha* was initially used as a hospital and then as an accommodation vessel for the growing population of emancipated slaves on the island. On 22 June *Persian* boarded the Sardinian-flagged schooner *Furia* at Cape Coast. Although 200 empty demijohns were discovered on board the vessel Quin was satisfied that *Furia* was engaged in legitimate commerce and, having endorsed her papers, he offered her master, Joseph Torre, any assistance he might need and invited him to dinner on board *Persian*. There was little gratitude on the part of Torre for the Foreign Office later received a complaint regarding damage to *Furia*'s cargo and theft of items from the vessel, all of which were thoroughly refuted by those involved in the boarding.

Whilst anchored off the Gallinas on 1 July *Wanderer* observed a suspicious-looking schooner off towards the north-west standing towards the river. Weighing anchor, Denman gave chase. Closing to within two miles of the schooner *Wanderer* fired several shots at the vessel to bring her to, all of which were ignored. The chase continued into the night and throughout the following day and night. At daybreak on 3 July the schooner was spotted directly ahead of *Wanderer* and after several more guns were fired she finally hove to. She proved to be *Pombinha*, a vessel fully equipped for slaving that had cleared out of Havana. *Wanderer* accompanied her prize to Sierra Leone, arriving there on 25 July. *Pombinha* was condemned by the Vice-Admiralty court on 3 August.

Sailing off Badagry on 7 July *Persian* detained the American brig *Plant*, equipped for slaving and bound for Great Popo from Havana. Amongst the correspondence found on board the vessel there was a letter from Jose Mazorra, owner of the Spanish brig *Fortuna* condemned by the court in December 1839, to the owner of *Plant*, Felis Madial, regarding the safe conveyance of slaves. Arrested on suspicion of being a Spanish vessel, *Plant* was dispatched to Sierra Leone, arriving there on 24 July. She was condemned by the Anglo-Spanish court on 1 August.

On 8 July *Dolphin*, now commanded by Lieutenant Edward Littlehales, arrived at St Helena from Portsmouth with dispatches allowing the French government to exhume Napoleon's body for burial in France. On 13 July *Waterwitch* seized the Portuguese vessel *Maria Rita* which was sent to the Vice-Admiralty court at St Helena for adjudication. Three days later *Buzzard*, now commanded by Lieutenant Reginald Levigne following Fitzgerald's return home due to ill health, seized the Spanish schooner *Carolina* at the entrance to the Rio Nunez. Equipped for slaving with a passport issued at Santiago de Cuba, her master, Pedro Salas, had commanded several slavers, *Feliz*, *Altimara*, *Atafa Primo* and *Numero Dos*, all of which had all been condemned by the Anglo-Spanish court. *Carolina* arrived at Freetown on 26 July and, following various queries by the Claimant's Proctor over the slaving equipment found on board the vessel, was condemned on 1 September.

On 16 July Francis Godolphin Bond died and was replaced as commander of *Forester*, then en route to Ascension, by Acting Lieutenant George Norcock. Cruising off the Gallinas on 21 July *Saracen* arrested the Spanish brigantine *Diana*, which was bound for Havana from Cadiz but had deviated from the course prescribed by her passport to exchange her cargo of rice for slaves on the Coast. Having discovered her slave deck already laid, her hatches pierced for iron bars, and two cooking boilers and leaguers for sixty pipes of water on board the vessel, Hill arrested *Diana* under the Equipment Clause but he could not dispatch her to Freetown immediately, having no officers spare, one being away in a boat, another ill. Consequently *Saracen*'s prize did not arrive at Sierra Leone until 28 August. Proceedings were immediately begun against the brigantine and she was condemned on 8 September. Subsequent to her condemnation the commissioners wrote to Palmerston to express their dismay that the Spanish officials at Havana and indeed Cadiz were continuing to allow slaving voyages from their ports in flagrant disregard of their treaty obligations with Britain.

On 25 July *Wanderer* departed Sierra Leone for a short trip south, taking Judge Macaulay to Banana Island, 30 miles south of Freetown, in order to recover his health prior to a return home to England. By 1 August Denman's cruiser was back at single anchor at Sierra Leone. On 9 August *Lynx* boarded the American-flagged schooner *Hero* off Whydah. Having examined the vessel's papers and searched her hold Broadhead decided to allow her on her way. The Foreign Office later received a complaint from Trist regarding the theft of some hams and damage to *Hero*'s cargo. On 14 August, as *Wanderer* was preparing to depart Freetown for Ascension, she arrested the Spanish brig *Republicano*. The vessel had been preparing to sail to Cadiz but the Collector of Customs at Sierra Leone refused to clear out the brig unless she landed one of her four leaguers of water which was deemed more than was required for her crew of eleven and five passengers. The offending cask having been landed and with her master, Felix Marengo, still ashore, Denman arrested the brig for being equipped for the slave trade. Following an examination of *Republicano* by the Surveyors to the Court the only illegal equipment found on board was a large amount of plank and spars which, it transpired, had formed part of the condemned schooner *Adelaide*, purchased at public auction by Marengo. On 24 August a joint petition from the Proctors for the Captor and the Claimant was presented to the court requesting that *Republicano* be restored to her master once the plank was landed. On 31 August the vessel departed Sierra Leone for the declared destination of Cadiz, although it was widely believed she was headed for one of the slaving ports to the northward.

Still cruising off the Gallinas, on 17 August *Saracen* seized the Spanish schooner *Sirena*. Arriving off the river with various slave-trade fittings and sixty bags of rice, the schooner, which had been issued with a Customs House Clearance from Havana, was dispatched to Sierra Leone where she was condemned by the Anglo-Spanish court along with *Saracen*'s other prize *Diana*. The final arrest of the month was made by *Fantome*, Butterfield arresting the Brazilian brigantine *Claudina* off the mouth of the River Congo on 17 August. Equipped for slaving, *Claudina*'s master, Manuel Muniz, claimed his vessel was sailing from Rio to the Azores to convey immigrants to Brazil, stopping off during her outward voyage at the slaving port of Cabinda. *Fantome*'s prize arrived at Sierra Leone on 17 September with forty-three Africans removed from three boats discovered at the mouth of the Congo that had been abandoned by their crews upon sighting the British cruiser. *Claudina* was condemned on 1 October and the Africans handed over to the Liberated African Department.

Cruising off the River Brass on 15 September *Wolverine* arrested the Spanish brigantine *Palmira*, a seizure for which very few details remain. That same day *Dolphin* arrested the American bark *Jones* at St Helena. Discovered in British waters with no papers or colours and equipped for slaving, *Dolphin*'s prize had been arrested on evidence given by two members of her crew who had apparently fallen out with her master. The vessel, which had previously been boarded by *Waterwitch*, had been at St Helena for twenty-one days, discharging and receiving cargo, therefore the commissioners at Freetown found it highly unlikely that the authorities at the island were unaware of her national identity; furthermore, no slaving equipment was found on board the vessel. Consequently the court ordered her to be restored to her owner. On 16 September *Rolla* seized the Portuguese schooner *Porto Formoso*. Equipped for slaving, her papers stated that she was bound from Havana to Montevideo, although in reality she had headed straight for the Gallinas on leaving Cuba. *Palmira* was condemned by the Anglo-Spanish court on 19 October. *Porto Formoso* was condemned by the same court on 5 November.

On 5 October *Termagant* seized the Portuguese-flagged schooner *Felicidade* off the Grand Bassa. Her passport, issued at Rio for a brigantine-rigged vessel, had an endorsement signed by the Portuguese consul at Havana, Pasqual Pluma, stating that *Felicidade* had recently been converted to a schooner. However, the vessel detained by Seagram was clearly a new vessel, indicating that Pluma had committed fraud by adapting an old Portuguese passport for use by a new American-built schooner. *Felicidade* was condemned by the Anglo-Spanish court on 24 October, the commissioners sending a copy of her doctored passport to the Foreign Office.

Sailing off Benguela on 11 October *Fantome* arrested the Brazilian brig *Onze de Novembro*, whose master, Joze Antonio Carvalho, claimed he was a lieutenant in the Brazilian Navy. Discovered fully equipped for slaving, *Onze de Novembro*'s passport stated that she was sailing from Rio to St Thomas but her actual destination was St Paul de Loando, a port she had almost reached when detained by *Fantome*. Butterfield's prize arrived at Freetown on 1 November and, following several complaints from her master regarding the circumstances of his vessel's detention and the actions of *Fantome*'s boarding crew, was condemned by the Anglo-Brazilian court on 11 November.

On 14 October *Termagant*, still cruising off the Grand Bassa, seized the Spanish schooner *Paquete Vera Cruzano*. That same day *Wolverine* arrested the Brazilian schooner *Gratido* 125 miles south of Accra. *Paquete Vera Cruzano* had a passport issued at Havana for a voyage to the Cape Verde Islands which her logbook showed she had not touched at. The passport had been endorsed with a warning for the schooner's master, Antonio Aragon, not to engage in slaving, a warning that was repeated on the vessel's muster-roll. *Paquete Vera Cruzano* arrived at Freetown on 27 October and was condemned by the Anglo-Spanish court on 5 November. *Wolverine*'s prize *Gratido* was condemned by the Anglo-Brazilian court on 16 November.

Learning of several attacks carried out against *Viper*'s boats from the Spanish slave factory at Corsico, situated on the River Gabon, in August, Commander Tucker decided to destroy the factory and remove the Spaniards from the island. Placing Lieutenant Dumaresq in charge of the cutter, gig, pinnace, whaleboat and jolly boat, on the afternoon of 7 November *Wolverine*'s boats approached the island. Coming under fire from the shore, they responded with musketry from all the boats and with several rounds from the pinnace's long gun. After ten minutes of sustained fire a Spaniard appeared waving a French flag and his hat. When Dumaresq stepped ashore with *Wolverine*'s second master, Mr Rees, to speak to the flag-bearing Spaniard, Miguel Pons, the British once again came under sustained fire, three marines falling injured. Returning fire with grape, roundshot and musketry, Dumaresq arrested Pons, who had directed the Spaniards' fire, and sent him on board the pinnace. He then landed the seamen from the boats and ordered them to burn the buildings on the island, during which process a sailor was killed and four seamen and another marine injured. With the buildings now ablaze, the British returned to their boats, remaining under fire from the Spaniards until out of range.

Two days after the assault on Corsico and still off the Gabon, *Wolverine* arrested the Brazilian brigantine *Emilia* (also known as *Flor de Rio*) and on 13 November *Waterwitch* seized a vessel without colours or papers, believed to be *Doze d'Autobro*. *Wolverine*'s prize was condemned by the Anglo-Brazilian court at Sierra Leone on 9 December. The date of *Doze d'Autobro*'s condemnation is not known but *Waterwitch*'s officers and crew were paid a tonnage bounty for her capture in December 1844.

Maintaining a close blockade along his section of the Coast, in the eight months that Denman had been in command of the Northern Division his cruisers had seized fifteen vessels, allowing just five to leave the Coast with slaves, around 1,560 Africans in total. Thirteen vessels had been condemned in the various courts of Mixed Commission and two in the Vice-Admiralty courts. South of the line, Butterfield's division had continued the system favoured by previous commanders on the Coast, that of patrol. Blockade was extremely arduous, both on men and ships, and was not entered into lightly as spending longer than two weeks at anchor was extremely detrimental to the health of a ship's crew.

In November Governor Docherty received reports that a British subject, Mrs Norman, was being held hostage with her baby by King Siacca of the Gallinas, home to various slave traders whose barracoons were filled with around 900 slaves that they were unable to move because of Denman's close blockade of the river. Denman, who was visiting Sierra Leone to water, now received a request from Docherty to assist in freeing Mrs Norman and her baby. Fresh in Denman's mind was a recent incident involving a boat from *Rolla* which had been upset in the Gallinas estuary. With her crew bailing hard, the boat eventually managed to get alongside an American merchantman who hoisted the boat on board and repaired her. The locals had then informed the American master that he should have left the boat to sink and if he gave such assistance again he would lose his trade along the river.

Collecting *Rolla* and *Saracen*, Denman headed south. On 11 November *Wanderer*, with *Rolla* in company, fell in with the Spanish brigantine *Vanguardia*. Equipped for slaving and with a passport for Trinidad de Cuba, the brigantine was dispatched to Sierra Leone where she was condemned by the Anglo-Spanish court on 9 December.

On 19 November Denman arrived off the Gallinas. Beyond its formidable bar the estuary was dotted with islands on which the now-retired trader Pedro Blanco had built his private residence, 100ft-tall lookout towers, offices, barracoons and warehouses filled with trade goods. There were nine vessels at anchor, none daring to embark slaves and risk capture by Denman's blockading cruisers. As Denman entered the river with the ships' boats, canoes laden with slaves were observed pulling from the islands further upriver, leaving the barracoons, which had housed up to 900 slaves, empty. Several canoes were captured before they disappeared into the various creeks and around ninety slaves were rescued. Denman landed on the island of Dombocorro and the slaves were fed and watered. A letter was now dispatched to King Siacca requesting a palaver and demanding the release of Mrs Norman and her child. The two hostages arrived at Dombocorro the following day, followed an hour later by the king's son, Prince Manna, and numerous chiefs, who explained that Siacca was too unwell to attend the palaver and that Manna was empowered to speak for his father. Denman now began to recount the various attacks on British shipping, the piracy and kidnappings that had occurred during the previous eight months of blockade. The Gallinas chiefs protested that none of these acts had been carried out by them or their people but by the Spaniards operating on the river. Having declared that the Spanish traders had acted against their interests, they were now informed by Denman that they must hand over the slaves that had been taken from the barracoons, which the British now intended to destroy. The chiefs went away to consider Denman's demands and the following morning agreed to hand over the slaves. However, when informed that they must also sign a treaty banning the slave trade along the Gallinas the chiefs requested more time to consider this as it would require consultation with other tribes on the river.

The Gallinas chiefs began sending Denman slaves on 22 November. Over the course of five days 841 arrived on Dombocorro, many of whom had spent twelve months in the barracoons waiting for a vessel to evade the British blockade. At the same time King Siacca's people began to raid the warehouses, removing trade goods said to be worth around £100,000. Denman now set to work burning the barracoons by firing incendiary rockets into eight of them. Anxious for their own safety, the Spanish slave traders quickly disappeared inland or, as was the case with a Señor Buron, requested passage to Sierra Leone. The last of the slaves having been handed over, King Siacca agreed to sign the treaty abolishing the Trade along the river.

Denman's successful operation caused great consternation amongst the various slave traders up and down the Coast, many of whom were now fearful for their own lives, and it was the cause of great excitement at the Foreign Office. Denman was promoted to captain and he and his men were awarded a special bounty of £4,000. Palmerston now recommended that similar operations should be carried out against all the slave trading establishments along the Coast as 'the course pursued by Captain Denman seems to be the best adapted for the attainment of the object in view'.[1] Meanwhile, having obtained safe passage back to Freetown from Denman, Señor Buron now sued him for trespass and the seizure of slaves and goods to the value of £180,000.

On 18 November *Brisk* arrived at the Cape from St Helena and on 20 November the newly commissioned 8-gun brig-sloop *Cygnet*, Lieutenant Edmund Wilson, arrived at Sierra Leone from Tenerife. On 22 November William Quin died following a short illness at St Helena and was replaced as commander of *Persian* by *Wanderer*'s mate, Thomas Symonds. A day after the death of Quin *Forester* seized the Portuguese-flagged schooner *Recurso* off the River Nun. Bearing Portuguese papers and issued with a passport from Lisbon, *Recurso*'s master, Ramon Trillo, freely admitted he was a resident of Havana, from where the schooner's present and preceding voyages had all originated. Her Spanish 'course of trade' having been established, *Recurso* was condemned by the Anglo-Spanish court on 11 January 1841.

The last arrest of November was made by *Rolla*, Hall's cruiser seizing the Brazilian brigantine *Feliz Ventura* off Cape Mount on the 29th. Carrying extra water casks, additional supplies of farina and jerked beef and ready to receive a slave deck, the brigantine had been issued with a passport for Princes and St Thomas, with instruction to call at Bahia to ship tobacco and spirits. However, upon her arrival at Bahia *Feliz Ventura*'s master had ignored her owner's instructions, loaded his own goods then made for Cape Mount. *Feliz Ventura* arrived at Freetown on 10 December and was condemned by the Anglo-Brazilian court on the same date as *Recurso*, 11 January 1841.

On 2 December *Waterwitch* seized another vessel without papers, supposed to be *Nove Irmaus*. Two days later Matson's cruiser arrested the brigantine *Julia*, a small vessel with decks only 5ft high but loaded with a cargo of 245 slaves, over half of them children. *Julia*'s crew had run their vessel ashore to avoid capture and had then abandoned it. However, prior to doing so they had warned the slaves that the British would cut their throats rather than release them. In response a large number of Africans threw themselves overboard before *Waterwitch*'s boats could reach the brigantine. Five died but many more were rescued by the efforts of British. The remaining slaves were very sickly and a further twenty-five died on the twelve day passage south to St Helena. Following her arrival at Jamestown Roads on 16 December it was reported to the Governor, Major-General Middlemore, that seventy-seven of *Julia*'s slaves were sick from dysentery and smallpox. Unprepared for an influx of so many Africans, the sick were landed, some of the healthy were transferred to *Andorinha*, whilst the others remained on board the brigantine, all of them naked apart from a few with pieces of clothing made from scavenged material such as sailcloth. As with *Nove Irmaus*, the date of *Julia*'s condemnation is not known.

On 9 December *Saracen* arrested the Spanish schooner *Boa União* off the Sherbro and on 11 December Hill's brig seized another Spanish schooner, *San Paulo de Loando*, from the same river. Both prizes were condemned by the Anglo-Spanish court on 1 February. In between *Saracen*'s two seizures *Wanderer* had arrested the Spanish schooner *Reglano* with a cargo of 350 slaves, again from the Sherbro. Issued with a passport at Havana for the Cape Verde Islands, the schooner had only briefly touched at these islands before heading for the Sherbro where she had loaded her cargo four days prior to her capture. *Wanderer*'s prize arrived at Freetown on 15 December with all 350 slaves still alive. She was condemned by the Anglo-Spanish court on 23 December, two slaves having died in the intervening eight days.

The last three seizures of 1840 were all made by *Fantome*. On 14 December Butterfield's cruiser seized the empty Brazilian schooner *Bellona* 50 miles north of St Paul de Loando. On 26 December *Fantome* arrested a launch with three slaves on board and on 31 December she seized the Portuguese slaver *Aventureiro*. The unnamed launch was sent for adjudication to the Vice-Admiralty court at St Helena and *Aventureiro* was condemned by the equivalent court at Sierra Leone. *Bellona*'s master, Francisco Pedro Ferreira, made the rather fanciful claim that his vessel was a whaler that had been blown off course towards the coast of Africa by strong winds which had also caused her to lose all her whale-tackle. His schooner lacked whaleboats but she had all the equipment associated with slaving. She was condemned by the Anglo-Brazilian court on 11 January 1841.

The first arrest of 1841 was a joint seizure made by *Waterwitch*, *Fantome* and *Brisk* of the Portuguese brig *Orozimbo* off St Paul de Loando on 8 January. The brig's papers stated that she was bound for Montevideo with a cargo of farina, beans and jerked beef, but it was clear to Butterfield that *Orozimbo* was equipped for slaving. Furthermore, Butterfield had met her first mate, Joze Antonio Soares d'Araujo, when he had sailed as supercargo on board *Onze de Novembro*, seized by *Fantome* in October 1840. A further incriminating piece of evidence was d'Araujo's passenger passport which stated that he was bound for the notorious slaving port of Cabinda. *Orozimbo* was dispatched to Freetown under the command of Lieutenant Clayton but he died of fever seven weeks prior to the brig's arrival in port on 28 March. She was condemned by the Anglo-Brazilian court on 6 April.

The next two seizures were both made by *Brisk*. On 17 January Sprigg's cruiser seized the empty slaver *Legeria* and on the same day she arrested the Portuguese schooner *Luiza* with a cargo of 420 slaves. Dispatched to St Helena, by the time *Luiza* arrived at the island on 7 February eighty-two slaves had died from smallpox and dysentery. The remaining slaves were removed to the three prize vessels then at Lemon Valley, *Andorinha*, *Cabinda* and *Julia*, whilst the former Army Ordnance stores at Rupert's Valley underwent repairs to enable the buildings to house the increasing numbers of slaves arriving on the island. The fate of *Legeria* (it is possible she was abandoned and burnt by *Brisk*) and the date of *Luiza*'s condemnation by the Vice-Admiralty court are both unknown.

On 19 January *Saracen*'s boats seized the Spanish-flagged schooner *Urraca* at anchor in the River Shebar. The vessel, bound for Cuba from Cadiz, was on her maiden voyage and her master, D. Laureano Lopez, was also her owner. Equipped for slaving with additional water casks and a slave deck already laid, she was escorted back to Freetown by *Saracen*, Hill now lacking officers or men to form a prize crew. *Saracen* and *Urraca* arrived at Freetown on 15 February and the schooner was condemned by the Anglo-Spanish court on 23 February.

On 20 January *Persian*, still under Acting Commander Thomas Symonds, arrested two Brazilian-flagged vessels south of the Line. The schooner *Bom Fin* was seized 60 miles off Cabinda and the brigantine *Nova Inveja* was arrested later that day as she attempted to enter Cabinda harbour. Both vessels were equipped for slaving and had been issued with passports for St Thomas. *Nova Inveja* arrived at Freetown on 14 February and was condemned by the Anglo–Brazilian Mixed Commission on 3 March. *Bom Fin* arrived at Freetown two weeks later and was condemned by the same court on 13 March.

On 1 February *Fantome* arrested a Portuguese-flagged launch which was discovered with one slave on board. One of the small vessels operating between Princes and the mainland, *Faesca* was condemned by the Vice-Admiralty court at St Helena. On 7 February *Saracen* seized *Augusta*, the same brig arrested by Hill in April 1839 when sailing under the name *Golubtchick*. Subsequently purchased by a British sailor, Thomas Jennings, with money forwarded to him by Zulueta & Co. of Portsmouth, the vessel, which had cleared out from Liverpool, was arrested for a second time whilst sailing under a British flag. Discovered just three miles from the location of her first arrest with a cargo of various trade goods commonly associated with the Trade, but no slaving equipment on board, *Augusta* was dispatched to Sierra Leone and condemned by the Vice-Admiralty court on 31 March. Jennings was sent to England to face trial but his case was delayed until June 1845 to enable both Hill and Denman to be called as witnesses. Disappointingly for both officers, having heard the evidence the Central Criminal Court decided to acquit Jennings of all charges.

On 8 February *Brisk* arrested the Portuguese schooner *Merzianna* with a cargo of 341 slaves off Benguela. Disease was rife on board the overcrowded vessel and by the time of her arrival at St Helena on 1 March, sixty-one slaves had died from smallpox and dysentery. The schooner was condemned on 13 March, the number of slaves who survived to see emancipation is unfortunately not known. On 9 February *Buzzard* arrested the slave vessel *Liberal* which was condemned by the Vice-Admiralty court at Sierra Leone on 14 April. Three days after this seizure Levinge arrested the Brazilian-flagged schooner *Juliania* off Whydah. Sailing from Bahia with a passport for the Azores, *Juliania*'s master, Daniel Flintes Coelho, used the well-worn excuse that his vessel had been blown off course by adverse winds and had been making for Whydah to take on provisions. Arrested for being equipped for slaving, *Buzzard*'s prize arrived at Sierra Leone on 26 March and was condemned by the Anglo-Brazilian court on 6 April.

On 13 February *Persian*, cruising off Cabinda, seized the Portuguese schooner *Dous d'Avril* which was sent to St Helena and condemned on 20 March. In an ill-advised and failed experiment, several of her crew were briefly employed as overseers on the island. On 15 February Symonds arrested the barque *Julius and Edward*. Flying Bremen colours and equipped for slaving, *Persian*'s prize was dispatched to the Hanseatic court at Bremen under the command of Lieutenant James Thurburn to face trial there. *Julius and Edward* was eventually restored to her master, R. Siedenburg, and Symonds was ordered to pay all costs and damages. The Foreign Office contested this decision on behalf of Symonds although the outcome of its appeal is unknown.

Encouraged by Denman's success at the Gallinas, in January Lieutenant Seagram had signed a treaty abolishing slavery at the New Sesters with King Freeman and in February Governor Docherty dispatched Lieutenant Hill to the Sherbro to negotiate a similar treaty with King Tucker. Sailing in company with the recently-arrived 8-gun brig-sloop *Ferret*, Lieutenant William Thomas, on 22 February *Saracen* detained the Spanish slave brig *Republicano* following a brief resistance off the mouth of the Sherbro.

The same vessel arrested by *Fantome* in April 1840 when flying Brazilian colours, *Republicano* had been purchased by the master of *Octavia* following her condemnation and had then been resold to the first-mate of *Olimpia*. Equipped for slaving, *Republicano* was condemned by the Anglo–Spanish court on 6 April.

On 24 February Hill sent a boat to procure water from the Sherbro. However, upon landing two Kroomen were taken hostage and King Tucker refused to provide water unless the British paid for it at an exorbitant rate. One of the Kroomen, Sea Breeze, managed to escape and returned to *Saracen* with signs of his brief confinement, having been placed in irons and beaten around the head. Accompanied by two boats from *Ferret*, Hill now went upstream to demand an explanation from Tucker for his unfriendly behaviour towards his boat crew and to discuss the treaty abolishing the slave trade. Upon landing, Hill and Lieutenant Thomas proceeded to the factory of the local slave trader, Henry François, which contained two barracoons capable of holding 500 slaves, to meet with King Tucker but found it deserted. A request was sent out for Tucker to meet with Hill but this was refused. Whilst Hill was waiting for a reply to a second letter several armed Africans emerged out of the bush and they explained to Hill that François had given his slaves muskets and knives in order for them to attack the British but that they would much rather give themselves up and be taken to Sierra Leone instead. Hill agreed to this request and fifty armed Africans soon appeared out of the bush. Hill had already decided to burn the barracoons but he now suggested that the Africans do it themselves to set an example to the other slaves along the river. Three Africans now proceeded to set fire to the barracoons and the accompanying buildings, razing them to the ground prior to embarking in a canoe obtained from a nearby creek. A total of fifty-one Africans were taken back to Sierra Leone and Hill subsequently learned that, as he had hoped, the day after François's factory had been destroyed another factory on the opposite side of the river was burned down by the slaves there.

As François's factory was being destroyed at the Sherbro, *Brisk*, cruising off St Paul de Loando, was busy arresting two Portuguese vessels, *Oito Decembro* and *Minerva*, the latter with a cargo of 321 slaves. Both vessels were dispatched to St Helena. *Minerva* arrived at the island on 16 March and her surviving 316 slaves were landed and taken to Lemon Valley. She was condemned by the Vice-Admiralty court on 24 March. *Brisk*'s other prize, *Oito Decembro*, was condemned by the court on 22 March.

One further arrest was made by the Squadron on 24 February, *Termagant* seizing the Spanish brig *Gabriel* off New Sesters. Having sighted the brig at daybreak, Seagram gave chase until around 10.00am when the wind fell and he sent his two remaining boats after her, Seagram in command of one vessel, the second master, Mr Sanavell, the other. Once they were within range *Gabriel* opened fire on the boats with a combination of grape and langrage from her stern guns and musketry. *Termagant*'s boats withheld their fire until within hailing distance on either quarter of the Spaniard when they poured in a well-directed hail of musketry. A boarding was attempted but the sides of the brig had been well barricaded and was easily repelled. The dingy having now been sunk, *Gabriel*'s crew directed their fire at the second boat and several crew members, Seagram included, were knocked from the rigging into the sea. As the British attempted to rescue the crew of the dingy they were assailed from *Gabriel* by blocks, arms, billets of wood and any other items her crew could lay their hands on. The sunken dingy was taken in tow and *Termagant* resumed her chase of *Gabriel* until she lost sight of the brig at dusk. The failed boarding had resulted in the deaths of three British sailors with a further seven injured, including Seagram.

After an absence of seven years from the Coast, on 28 February the paddle steamer *Pluto* departed Plymouth for Africa under the command of Lieutenant William Blount. Now ten years old, she was still as fast as the average slaver on the Coast although she could only carry enough fuel for ten days' steaming. Normally she burnt wood which, Blount noted, was less destructive to her machinery than certain types of coal. *Pluto* was soon joined on the Coast by the 28-gun frigate *Iris*, Captain Hugh Nurse, which departed Plymouth on 24 March. On 28 March *Waterwitch* departed the Cape for Mozambique and on 31 March *Lynx*, with *Wolverine* in company, made the Squadron's only arrest that month, seizing the Portuguese-flagged schooner *Liberal* following a ten-hour chase off Popo. As with the schooner *Felicidade*, seized by *Termagant* in October 1840, *Liberal*'s fraudulent passport, endorsed by the Portuguese consul at Havana, Pasqual Pluma, stated that she was six years old although she was clearly a new vessel. She was condemned by the Anglo-Spanish court on 5 May.

Following Denman's success at the Gallinas the Squadron had received instructions to burn slave barracoons wherever they were discovered, if possible with the consent of the local chiefs. (Permission was usually easy to obtain for a small subsidy.) In late April *Iris* and *Termagant* destroyed the barracoons and warehouses on the River Pongas belonging to the widow Isabella Lightbourne, the slaves they contained escaping into the bush. Lightbourne, who would continue trading slaves into the 1850s, would later write a letter of complaint to the Admiralty over the destruction of her property. On 7 May Lieutenant Blount signed a treaty with King Acqua of the Cameroons outlawing slavery in his territories. In return for this undertaking the British agreed to pay Acqua a subsidy of goods including sixty muskets, two barrels of powder, two puncheons of rum and 100 pieces of cloth every year for the next five years.

The Squadron's next arrest, following a gap of nearly two weeks, was made by *Waterwitch*, Butterfield's brig seizing the Portuguese brigantine *Euro* with a cargo of 314 slaves off Angola on 13 April. Whilst *Waterwitch* made for the Cape to be coppered, her prize sailed for St Helena, arriving there on 3 May. *Euro*'s surviving 305 slaves brought the total number of Africans on the island up to 939. In order to ease the overcrowding at Lemon Valley the nearby Rupert's Valley was now surveyed and it was reported that the existing military buildings in the bay could house around 150 Africans and an overseer.

In April *Lynx* departed Ascension for England, arriving at Spithead on 27 June with £27,000 in gold and ivory and a number of the Squadron's invalids who were taken to Haslar Hospital, Portsmouth. Meanwhile, repairs to her copper having been completed, in mid-April *Waterwitch* arrived off Ambriz from the Cape. On 27 April *Persian*, now under the command of Lieutenant Thomas Eden, arrived at St Helena and the following day *Fantome* departed Ascension to cruise off the Congo. On 30 April *Wanderer* was reported to be at Sierra Leone. The following day the first of just two arrests in May was made by *Fantome*, Butterfield's cruiser seizing a loaded Spanish schooner, *Josephina*, off Whydah. Reputed to be one of the fastest slavers on the Coast, *Josephina* had so far evaded capture by *Wolverine*, *Cygnet*, *Lynx* and *Dolphin*, her master, Manoel dos Santos, confident that the only British cruiser capable of catching her was Matson's *Waterwitch*. When Butterfield, cruising off Ambriz, spotted the schooner on the morning of 30 April several miles distant, he immediately hoisted all sail and set off in pursuit, beginning one of the most exhilarating chases the Coast had yet seen. Through expert ship-handling Butterfield slowly began to gain on his quarry, *Fantome* managing to maintain a speed of 11 knots. At 4.00pm the schooner was observed cutting away her anchors and throwing her gun and boat overboard in a last-ditch effort to avoid capture. As the sun went down the distance between the two vessels remained around six miles. At 1.00am both vessels were struck by a tremendous squall of wind and rain and the schooner was almost lost. Butterfield himself was thankful he was sailing in *Fantome* and not another less sturdily-built vessel. Under the light of the moon his sloop managed to keep sight of *Josephina*, the schooner now having lost her studding sails and booms. The gap between the two vessels began to close and by sunrise they were within gunshot of one another off the island of Annobon. Butterfield put two shots across the schooner which immediately hove to, ending a chase that had lasted twenty-four hours and covered almost 260 miles. When boarded, *Josephina* was discovered to have a cargo of 291 slaves loaded at Whydah, all of whom were in surprisingly good health. Butterfield placed his First Lieutenant in command of the schooner and she departed for Sierra Leone. This left Butterfield as the only officer on board *Fantome*, the vessel having previously lost her Second Lieutenant, Clayton, her master and surgeon to disease. *Josephina* was condemned by the Anglo-Spanish court on 20 May, 290 slaves surviving to be emancipated.

Dos Santos had assumed that he had been chased by *Waterwitch* but Matson's vessel was in fact still cruising south of the Line in company with *Fantome* and *Brisk*. On 2 May she seized a brigantine with no colours or papers that had been abandoned by her crew off Mazala, Angola. Equipped for slaving, a Portuguese flag was discovered on board the vessel along with private letters suggesting that she was *Flor de Loando*. *Waterwitch*'s prize was dispatched to St Helena and condemned by the Vice-Admiralty court. On 26 May *Brisk* arrested the last of four launches she had seized that month off the coast of Angola. The vessels were all condemned at St Helena and the thirteen slaves they had contained emancipated.

On the morning of 30 May *Dolphin*, which had not made an arrest since September 1840, was on the verge of ending her fruitless three-month cruise in the Bights to sail for Accra for provisions when a strange brig was sighted off towards the south-east. Littlehales gave chase and an hour later, with the wind now dying, he sent off his cutter and gig under the command of the mate, Mr Murray. As the boats approached the brig they raised their colours but the stranger did not show her own ensign and instead opened fire with musketry on the cutter and gig. Two British seamen were killed and Murray and another seaman received serious injuries, whilst two other sailors received minor injuries. Despite the British casualties the brig was quickly taken, two of her crew being killed and a further seven wounded during the boarding. She proved to be the Brazilian vessel *Firmé*, equipped for slaving with a slave deck laid fore and aft. Bound from Bahia to Whydah, her master, Silveiro de Brito, explained to Murray that the crew had broken open the arms chest against his orders, fearing they would lose their wages if the brig was taken. *Firmé* was dispatched to Sierra Leone and condemned by the Anglo-Brazilian court on 8 July. Meanwhile *Dolphin*, now re-provisioned, continued to cruise off British Accra and on 5 June seized the Brazilian polacca *Nova Fortuna*. Arrested under the Equipment Clause *Dolphin*'s prize arrived at Sierra Leone on 28 June and was condemned by the Anglo-Brazilian court on 20 July.

On 13 June *Fantome*, cruising 100 miles north of St Paul de Loando, seized the Portuguese brigantine *Boa Nova* with a cargo of 441 slaves bound from Ambriz to Pernambuco, Brazil. *Fantome*'s prize was taken to St Helena and condemned on 5 July, 356 slaves surviving to be emancipated. On 20 June *Waterwitch* anchored off Benguela and Matson discovered that the governor had left for Loando, leaving the slaver Joao Almeida in charge of the fort. Matson immediately began a search of the various vessels in the roads preparing to put to sea and one of these, the Brazilian brigantine *Donna Eliza*, was discovered to be fully equipped for slaving. Anxious that he had not exceeded his instructions by seizing a vessel in an open roadstead, albeit one lacking proper governance, Matson arrested the brigantine and sent her to Sierra Leone under the charge of his gunner. *Donna Eliza* was condemned by the Anglo-Brazilian court on 3 August. As anticipated by Matson, the Admiralty noted its disapproval of the circumstances surrounding her arrest.

On 23 June *Persian*'s boats, making their way along the coast off Cabinda under First Lieutenant Philip Somerville, fell in with the Portuguese brigantine *Astrea* (also known as *Astraea*). In an attempt to avoid detention the brigantine made every effort to run down *Persian*'s pinnace and gig. The marines kept up a steady fire on the brigantine which was returned with musketry and canister and grape from her long gun. One shot went through the bottom of the pinnace and it was only with great difficulty that she was kept afloat. The boats finally got alongside *Astrea* and Somerville attempted a boarding, two men being killed and another two wounded. As the lieutenant clambered up the side of the brigantine her master appeared brandishing a heavy sabre and was in the act of slashing at Somerville when he fell to the deck, shot through the forehead by one of *Persian*'s marines. Somerville clambered onto the deck, stumbling over the dead body of *Astrea*'s master, and a desperate struggle ensued for control of the vessel, eighteen British sailors against *Astrea*'s crew of fifty. By the end of the fight nineteen of the brigantine's crew lay dead, but remarkably the British had suffered no more casualties. *Astrea* was taken to St Helena and eventually condemned by the court there.

On 27 June *Fantome*'s pinnace boarded and detained a vessel with no papers, supposedly the Portuguese brigantine *Espardarte*, which was taken to St Helena and condemned by the Vice-Admiralty court. Two days later *Persian* arrested the Brazilian schooner *Flor da American* in the River Congo. The vessel was clearly equipped for slaving with extra water and a boiler. Her hold had also been filled to the top of her casks with sand to form a slave deck. Papers discovered on board proved that her master, Manoel Pereira, had been profitably connected with the slave trade for some time. *Flor da American* arrived at Freetown on 23 July and was condemned by the Anglo-Brazilian court on the 31st of the month.

On 2 July *Dolphin* seized the Portuguese schooner *Dores* off Quitta. Equipped for slaving, she was dispatched to Sierra Leone under the command of *Dolphin*'s gunner, William Penny. The following day Littlehales arrested the British-flagged schooner *Little Grace* and sent her to Freetown with a prize crew of six men commanded by *Dolphin*'s second master, Henry Burney. That same day *Wanderer* arrested the Spanish schooner *Amalia* off the Rio Grande and on 4 July *Fantome* detained the Portuguese schooner *Triumfo* with a cargo of 105 slaves, two of whom were under 7 years of age. Just 30ft in length and barely 20 tons, the vessel had a slave deck only 18in high. *Triumfo* was condemned by the Vice-Admiralty court at St Helena on 29 July. *Wanderer*'s prize, *Amalia*, was condemned by the Anglo-Spanish court at Freetown on 27 July. Unfortunately for Littlehales *Little Grace* was subsequently restored to her master and he was ordered to pay £419 in costs. *Dolphin*'s other prize, *Dores*, was not heard of again for another five weeks.

On the morning of 6 July the 12-gun brig *Acorn*, Lieutenant John Adams, was sailing roughly 400 miles south-west of Freetown en route from England to Brazil when she spotted a strange sail on her weather quarter and gave chase. The vessel she had fallen in with was the brig *Gabriel*, last seen by *Termagant* in February. The chase continued for another twelve and a half hours until 3.10pm when Adam's cruiser was close enough to *Gabriel* to open fire on the brig, which had cut away her anchors and boats to evade capture. Hoisting her Portuguese colours, *Gabriel* returned fire with her long pivot gun, Adams skilfully manoeuvring his brig to avoid most of her shots. A running battle was maintained for the next two and a half hours until *Acorn* pulled alongside *Gabriel* and a heavy fire of canister shot cleared her deck. Having lost most her sails, *Gabriel* finally struck her colours and came to. An examination of her hold revealed the vessel to be equipped for up to 800 slaves. *Gabriel*'s crew were removed to *Acorn* and she was dispatched to St Helena under the command of *Acorn*'s mate, Mr McNeill. Her crew were subsequently landed on an uninhabited part of the coast and *Acorn* resumed her passage to Brazil. Following her condemnation in September *Gabriel*, a fine-looking and fast-sailing brig, was dispatched to Rio to see if she might be of use to the Royal Navy squadron operating there.

On 10 July *Persian* arrested an abandoned brig off Cabinda, purported to be the American-built but Spanish-owned *Cipher*. Equipped for slaving, she was dispatched to St Helena and condemned by the court there on 5 August. As *Persian* was taking her prize off Cabinda *Saracen* was arriving at Plymouth from the Coast to be paid off. On 11 July *Waterwitch* called at St Helena to pick up her prize crews from *Euro* and *Flor de Loanda*, Matson then being the only officer on board the vessel. She departed the island three days later to resume her cruise off Angola. Following her capture of *Amalia*, *Wanderer* had headed north to Goree. She returned from there on 22 July, the same day that *Termagant* arrived at Bathurst from Portendic. On 29 July Seagram's brigantine departed Bathurst for a cruise to leeward, having been instructed by Denman to investigate the current state of the slave trade to the north of the Cape Verde Islands. In mid-July Captain Nurse suffered a burst blood vessel and had to be invalided home. Tucker's own vessel was due to return to England and so he moved from *Wolverine* to *Iris*, no doubt happy to move from the cramped confines of a brig-sloop to the more spacious quarters of a frigate. *Wolverine* departed the Coast under the command of Lieutenant Dumaresq, Nurse taking passage in the sloop for the voyage home. *Wolverine* arrived at Portsmouth on 21 August and Nurse was transferred to Haslar Hospital but he died the following day.

On the night of 3 August *Waterwitch*'s boats, commanded by the mate, Mr Wilcox, seized the Portuguese brigantine *Carsico* following a hard pull of six hours off Benguela. The vessel had a cargo of 392 slaves who were nearly all children and was in a shocking state, smallpox having broken out. The slaves, some barely a few months old, were all emaciated and Matson doubted that the youngest would survive the journey to St Helena. The brigantine arrived at the island under the command of *Waterwitch*'s second master, Frederick Sturdee, her sides patched up with painted canvas to prevent her sinking. She was condemned by the Vice-Admiralty court on 23 August, 380 slaves surviving to be emancipated. On this date Denman was promoted captain and returned to England on half-pay. He was replaced as commander of *Wanderer* by Lieutenant Edward Troubridge from Admiral King's flagship, *Southampton*.

On 7 August *Dolphin* was sailing off Accra when she spotted a schooner at anchor. Taking his vessel in close to investigate, Littlehales was surprised to discover that she was *Dores*, the Portuguese slaver he had seized five weeks earlier. When she was boarded it was discovered that her prize captain, Penny, and almost all of her prize crew had died from an outbreak of fever on board the schooner. *Dolphin*'s mate, Murray, who had now recovered from the wounds he had sustained during the arrest of *Firmé*, was given command of *Dores* and two sailors and three boys were transferred to her prize crew. The schooner's cabin, filthy and crawling with cockroaches, was no longer fit for habitation so Murray set up an awning on the deck for the crew to sleep under. *Dolphin* completed her provisions and on 12 August *Dores* departed on her 900-mile passage to Freetown, which Murray anticipated would last around ten days. However, sailing in light airs and with the current against them, *Dores* made little progress for the next four days and was then engulfed in a fierce storm that almost sank her. By 14 September Dores had progressed no further than the River Sesters and then she was blown backwards, anchoring at Cape Coast Castle, less than 100 miles from Accra, on 20 September. Supplied with forty days of provisions and refitted, *Dores* set off again. It would be another fourteen weeks before she finally reached Freetown.

On the morning of 25 August *Persian*, at anchor off Cabinda, observed a strange sail about six miles to the south of where she lay. Symonds sent off his boats to investigate. After a lengthy pull they boarded the Portuguese brigantine *Bella Sociedade*. The vessel, which was equipped for slaving, had been abandoned by its crew of seventeen but their boats were eventually chased down by *Persian*'s boats. When the sailors were searched they were discovered to have sixty-nine half doubloons concealed about their persons. Upon questioning, the brigantine's master, Jose de Miranda, admitted that she had been due to load 400 slaves that evening. *Bella Sociedade* was dispatched to St Helena under the command of *Persian*'s Boatswain, John Hood, and was condemned on 27 September.

In the early 1840s the Anglo-American relationship still remained fragile. To the delight of the British, in 1841 Consul Trist was recalled from Cuba for abuse of his powers, but then, following the return home of USS *Grampus*, the Paine-Tucker agreement had been declared to be illegal by Washington. In May 1841 Palmerston had clarified his earlier instructions to commanding officers on the Coast to abstain from capturing American vessels engaged in the Trade, informing the Admiralty that the mere fact a vessel hoisted an American flag should not prevent her from being stopped and boarded and having her papers examined. Palmerston now attempted to distinguish between the Right of Search and the Right of Visit, one being an intrusive examination of a ship's cargo, the other simply an examination of her papers. However, the American Ambassador, Andrew Stevenson, a slave-holding Virginian, refused to admit this distinction, leading an exasperated Palmerston to declare 'Her Majesty's Government would fain hope that the day is not far distant when the government of the United States will cease to confound two things which are in their nature entirely different, will look to things not words and … will join the Christian League'.[2]

In September there was a change of government and Lord Aberdeen replaced Palmerston at the Foreign Office. The new Foreign Secretary now adopted a more conciliatory tone, informing the American Ambassador that it had long been the right for all navies to visit merchant vessels to ascertain their real nationality, as indeed was done by American cruisers in the Gulf of Mexico. Stevenson could not argue this point and was forced to admit that there could be no objection to British cruisers visiting vessels that had fraudulently adopted the Stars and Stripes.

Another issue concerning Aberdeen was the commercial treaty with Brazil, signed in 1827, which was due to expire in November 1842. Rio was now refusing to renew the treaty unless London guaranteed lower import duties on Brazilian sugar and coffee, both slave-grown commodities. In return Rio would make the first steps towards abolishing slavery. The new administration in London headed by Prime Minister Sir Robert Peel had inherited a struggling economy and the Chancellor of the Exchequer, Sir Francis Baring, was keen to encourage trade by lowering the duty on foreign sugar. By the end of the year a draft treaty had been prepared in which the British government agreed to reduce import duties on Brazilian sugar in return for a commitment from Rio to declare all children born of slaves free (after a date still to be determined) with consideration to be given to the emancipation of all slaves in Brazil at the earliest possible date. A special mission was now dispatched to Rio to negotiate this commercial treaty along with supplementary articles to the existing anti-slave treaty which included a new Equipment Clause.

On 23 June the Niger River Expedition had departed Sierra Leone in three specially-built paddle steamers, *Albert*, *Wilberforce* and *Soudan*, carrying 300 sailors, scientists, missionaries and doctors. The purpose of the expedition, organised with the assistance of the Society for the Extinction of the Slave Trade and led by Captain Henry Trotter, was to explore the river and to introduce Christianity and legitimate commerce to the African interior, but another, less publicised, reason was to negotiate anti-slavery treaties with the local chieftains, one such being signed with the Ata (King) of Igala, soon after the expedition had reached the Niger on 10 September. Working under a blazing sun, the thermometer rarely below 90 degrees in the shade, within days of their arrival in the river the expedition was struck with fever. By 18 September seven men were dead and a further sixty were seriously ill. With the remainder of his men all showing symptoms of malaria, Trotter decided to send all the sick that could be moved back down the river on board *Soudan*. On 22 September the steamer arrived at the mouth of the River Nun and her thirty-seven fever cases were transferred to *Dolphin*. The brigantine departed for Ascension and by the time of her arrival at the island on 9 October eight more sailors had died of fever. The surviving twenty-nine invalids were now transferred to the transport *Nelson* for passage back to England.

There were just two seizures by the Squadron in September. On 2 September *Persian* arrested the Spanish schooner *Numantina* following a chase of eight hours off Cabinda. Equipped for slaving, the vessel arrived at Freetown on 5 October and was condemned by the Anglo-Spanish court on 12 October. The last arrest that month was made by *Bonetta*, which had returned to the Coast under the command of Lieutenant Francis Austen (the novelist Jane Austen's brother) in late spring. On 30 September his brigantine seized the Portuguese schooner *Acoriano Oriental*, formerly *Paquete Oporto*, following a lengthy chase off the Gallinas. *Bonetta*'s prize was condemned by the Vice-Admiralty court at Freetown on 23 October.

October saw the arrival in Freetown of Judge José Hermenegildo Frederico Nitheroy and Commissioner of Arbitration Joaquim Tomás do Amaral, ending a ten-year absence of Brazilian officials from the Anglo-Brazilian Mixed Commission. The first arrest of the month was that of a loaded slaver by *Fantome*, Butterfield's sloop seizing *Conceicao de Maria* with a cargo of 457 slaves, 350 miles south-west of St Helena on 3 October. The Portuguese-flagged brigantine was bound from Quillimane in South Africa to Pernambuco, Brazil and the slaves, 147 men, twenty-three women and 287 children had spent the last sixty-three days at sea. *Fantome* accompanied her prize to St Helena, departing there for the Cape on 6 October, a day before *Persian* arrived at the island. Shortly after the condemnation of *Conceicao de Maria* on 13 October Eden's brig-sloop departed St Helena for Ascension.

Following her return to the Coast in September *Acorn* had begun to cruise off Angola. On the morning of 15 October her pinnace, under the command of First Lieutenant Frederick Hankey, spotted a brig running close to the land off Ambriz and gave chase. The brig attempted to evade capture but was finally brought to by several volleys of musketry. On boarding she was discovered to be the Portuguese-flagged *Dous de Fevreiro*, fitted for slaving and bound from St Sebastian, Brazil, for Ambriz. She was dispatched to St Helena under the command of *Acorn*'s second master, William Brodie and condemned by the court there on 8 November. On 18 October *Acorn* was sailing in company with *Iris* when Tucker seized the Portuguese brigantine *Erculos* following a ten-hour chase off Cabinda. Equipped for slaving and possessing a clearly fraudulent passport, *Erculos* was dispatched to Sierra Leone and condemned by the Anglo-Spanish court on 10 November.

The last two arrests of October were both made by *Waterwitch*. On 20 October Matson's brig seized the Portuguese-flagged cutter *Donna Francisca* 250 miles west of St Paul de Loando. Bound from Princes for Benguela and equipped for slaving, the vessel, owned by and named after the mother-in-law of her master, Antonio d'Almeide, was condemned by the court at St Helena on 15 November. Still cruising off Loando, on 27 October *Waterwitch* seized the Brazilian barque *Ermelinda*. Equipped for slaving and armed with two 9-pounders, half of the twenty-eight people on board the vessel, formerly the Brazilian brig *Uniao*, were listed as passengers. In accordance with the treaty all persons were removed from the vessel save for her master and two seamen and she was dispatched to Sierra Leone, arriving in port on 9 December. The following day the Brazilian schooner *Galianna*, captured by *Cygnet* on 23 November under similar circumstances, arrived in port. This was the first time since 1831 that cases could be heard by a full complement of British and Brazilian commissioners and whilst the British judge, William Ferguson, favoured condemnation of both *Ermelinda* and *Galianna*, the Brazilian judge Nitheroy declared that their seizures had been illegal as no slaves had been found on board either vessel. Lots were now drawn for arbitration. On 11 January 1842 the British Arbitrator, Michael Melville, won the draw for *Galianna* and she was condemned. Nine days later Tomás do Amaral won the draw for *Ermelinda* and she was ordered to be released.

Following *Pluto*'s arrival on the Coast earlier in the year she had joined the cruisers operating in the Bights, taking advantage of the newly-constructed pier and coaling station at Princes in addition to the stations at Freetown, Fernando Po and Loando. On 27 October Blount's steamer gave chase to and seized the Portuguese-flagged schooner *Paz*. Equipped for slaving and bound from Havana for the River Brass, *Pluto*'s prize was dispatched to Sierra Leone, arriving at Freetown on 19 November. Her Spanish 'course of trade' having been established, *Paz* was condemned by the Anglo-Spanish court on 25 November.

Following her departure from Cape Coast Castle on 20 September *Dolphin*'s prize *Dores* had spent a further forty-five days at sea. Out of sight of land and with no chronometer or sextant, just an antiquated quadrant, Murray had great trouble fixing *Dores*'s position. Her sails now almost threadbare and still battling against the current in light airs, his vessel's progress remained agonisingly slow. On 4 November land was finally sighted but when the realisation dawned that his vessel was at Cape Lahou, just 260 miles west of Cape Coast, Murray despaired of ever seeing Freetown again. With just days' worth of provisions left on board Murray had little option but to return to the Castle once again. To add to Murray's misery, whilst they were in port a member of his prize crew was killed by a shark whilst bathing. Freshly re-provisioned, *Dores* departed Cape Coast, her crew augmenting their meagre diets by fishing for the skipjack, dolphins and sharks that abounded in the waters off the Coast. On 14 December *Dores* was hit by a powerful thunderstorm which threatened to swamp the vessel. Murray ordered his men below, battened down the hatches and lashed himself to the wheel. Somehow *Dores* survived the storm, battered but still afloat, and to the great surprise of many in the colony who had long presumed her lost, on 6 January she limped in to Sierra Leone, 146 days after her departure from Accra.

On 5 November *Iris* seized the schooner-rigged boat *Formigo* which was bound from Cape Lopez to St Thomas with a cargo of eighteen slaves. Arrested just to the north-east of the island with no colours or papers, the vessel, just 24ft long, was surveyed and found to be unfit for passage to Sierra Leone. Therefore she was left at Princes in the custody of *Iris*'s Head Krooman, Tom Jones, whilst her master, Antonio Silveira and her eighteen slaves were transferred to *Iris*. On 17 November *Iris* fell in with *Cygnet*'s prize *Galianna* and Silveira and the surviving seventeen slaves from *Formigo* were transferred to the schooner. Contrary to his instructions, Tucker had neglected to remove at least two of *Formigo*'s crew to give evidence to the court at Freetown. Furthermore, he did not send any of his own crew as witnesses to *Formigo*'s arrest, resulting in an avoidable delay in the case being heard. *Formigo* was eventually condemned by the Anglo-Portuguese court on 18 December, the commissioners noting their displeasure over Tucker's handling of the seizure.

Whilst at anchor off Loango on 13 November *Acorn* detained two launches containing slave cargoes of farina, beans and dried fish that were apparently intended for a Portuguese vessel which was shortly due to arrive. Once their cargo had been removed the launches were surveyed and, having found to be unfit for the journey to St Helena, destroyed. When the case came for adjudication the court at St Helena initially appeared to support Adams's decision to destroy the launches, but it later declared that his actions had been illegal as the vessels had not contained any slaves.

On 17 November *Brisk*'s boats chased a schooner off Little Mazula. Coming alongside the schooner the following day she was discovered to have been abandoned by her master and crew. Fully equipped for slaving but with no sign of any papers, the unidentified vessel was dispatched to St Helena under the command of *Brisk*'s gunner, Richard Spry, and condemned by the Vice-Admiralty court on 16 December. Five days after this arrest, *Persian*, sailing in company with *Cygnet*, detained the Spanish brig *Senhora Da Boa Viagem* following a chase of twelve hours off Lagos. Equipped for slaving, the brig was dispatched to Sierra Leone where proceedings were begun against her in the Anglo-Spanish court. However, *Senhora Da Boa Viagem*'s master, Fernando Carreiras, insisted he was Portuguese by birth and with her passport also proving suspicious the case was recommenced in the Vice-Admiralty court, the vessel eventually being condemned on 14 January. This had been *Cygnet*'s first arrest since her arrival on the Coast almost exactly one year earlier. However, having waited so long to open her account Wilson's cruiser made her next arrest the very next day, seizing the Brazilian schooner *Galianna* 110 miles south-west of Lagos.

That same morning off Ambriz *Brisk*'s boats had given chase to the well-known Brazilian slaver *Nereide*, which attempted to escape to the westwards with the aid of a fresh breeze. When they were within gunshot of the brigantine she wore round and fired her three starboard guns at the boats, then bore away and brought her port guns to bear, firing another broadside before hauling for the land, defending herself with her swivel guns and volleys of musketry from her stern. As *Brisk*'s boats continued the pursuit *Nereide* now made a dash for the beach 10 miles to the south of Ambriz but the heavy surf prevented her from being beached. She continued to run along the land until around 4.30pm when, with *Brisk*'s boats closing rapidly, she put her helm up and stood right into the beach, firing her stern guns and musketry as the British approached. The heavy surf prevented *Brisk*'s boats from getting alongside the brigantine and the British could only watch as *Nereide*'s crew, with assistance from the shore, removed her stores of water casks, sacks of farina and other goods. On 26 November *Brisk* arrived offshore and sixty rounds from her two 18-pounders ensured the brigantine's destruction.

Still cruising off Ambriz, on the morning of 2 December *Brisk* spotted a strange sail heading eastwards and gave chase. Observing that she intended to run for the shore, Sprigg fired three shots at her. The schooner immediately shortened sail and brought up. At 11.20am a boat was observed leaving the vessel with a number of men in it. When she was boarded half an hour later she was discovered to be fully equipped for slaving but with no colours or papers. Departing for St Helena, *Brisk* sailed in company with the unnamed schooner until 15 December, when, it being reported that she was unseaworthy, the decision was taken to burn her, having first removed several of her fittings to present to the court at St Helena. It appears that the cases of *Legeria*, seized by *Brisk* in January, *Nereide* and the unnamed schooner were eventually heard at the High Court of Admiralty although the outcome of these hearings is unknown.

Adding to the growing list of agreements signed with local chieftains following the precedent set by Denman at the Gallinas, on 6 December Lieutenant Blount signed a treaty with King Eyamba outlawing slavery on the Old Calabar. In return for this commitment the British promised to pay Eyamba a subsidy of 2,000 Spanish dollars per year for the next five years although this was later amended to goods worth 2,000 Spanish dollars.

In December the five great European powers, England, France, Russia, Prussia and Austria, met in London to sign a treaty declaring slavery to be piracy. The treaty, which included an equipment clause, allowed reciprocal rights of search over an area of ocean between 32° North and 45° South and from the American coast to 80° South. France subsequently refused to ratify the agreement, known as the Quintuple Treaty, no doubt due to the interference of the United States' minister in Paris, the decidedly Anglophobic General Lewis Cass, who believed that Britain was furthering her economic interests under the guise of a philanthropic act and who was also using the debate over the Right of Search to bolster his own presidential ambitions.

The Squadron's next two seizures, both by *Acorn* off St Paul de Loando, resulted in the emancipation of 646 slaves. In the early hours of 28 December *Acorn*'s boats, commanded by her master, William Barrett, arrested the Portuguese schooner *Dois Amigos*, bound from the River Coanza to Pernambuco with a cargo of 150 slaves. *Dois Amigos* was dispatched to St Helena under the command of *Acorn*'s mate, Henry Page, arriving at the island on 29 January. On the morning of 31 December *Acorn*'s lookouts reported three strange sails, two to leeward, one on the weather beam. Adams bore up for the two vessels to leeward and discovered that one was *Fantome* in chase of a suspected slaver. *Acorn* now hauled her wind for the vessel to windward, continuing the chase in light winds until around midday when Adams sent away the cutter to board the vessel, which from his position in the foretop masthead he could see was a brigantine now about 12 miles distant. At 4.00pm *Acorn*'s cutter took possession of the brigantine which proved to be the Portuguese-flagged *Minerva* with a cargo of 505 slaves. No papers could be found on board the vessel but her master, Jose de Santos Castanheira, stated that she was sailing from Ambriz to Rio. Lieutenant Frederick Hankey took command of *Minerva* for her passage to St Helena. The brigantine arrived at the island on 19 January, she was condemned on 5 February and her surviving 499 slaves emancipated.

On 29 December the 10-gun brig *Pantaloon*, Lieutenant Charles Lapidge, departed Plymouth for the Coast. Commissioned by the Duke of Portland and designed by Symonds as a yacht, *Pantaloon* had out-sailed several competing vessels in trials, resulting in her purchase by the Royal Navy in December 1831. Converted to a brig-sloop, she had initially served as tender to the Royal Yacht. Coincidentally, the final arrest of the year fell to a vessel designed by Symonds great rival, Joseph White and one that had competed against *Pantaloon* in trials. On the last day of December *Waterwitch* arrested the Portuguese vessel *Feliz Triumvirate* for being equipped for slaving. She was dispatched to St Helena and subsequently condemned by the court there.

Chapter 14

Treaties and Palavers:
January 1842–December 1843

In early 1842 there were a number of arrivals on the Coast, the first two having a family connection. On 2 January Lieutenant Henry Foote departed Plymouth for Sierra Leone in command of the 8-gun brig *Heroine* and four days later his father, Captain John Foote, arrived at Sierra Leone from Falmouth on board the 46-gun frigate *Madagascar*. Built of teak in Bombay, *Madagascar* had previous involvement in the suppression campaign, arresting several slavers off Jamaica in 1837. Following his arrival on the Coast Captain Foote took over the duties of Senior Officer from Tucker. *Heroine* and *Madagascar* would soon be joined by the gun-brig *Ferret*, now commanded by Lieutenant Josiah Oake, returning to the Coast from Plymouth following an absence of around six months.

On the morning of 4 January *Fantome*, at anchor off Ambriz, observed a brigantine to leeward. Butterfield's brig weighed, made sail and gave chase but the brigantine's crew were soon observed abandoning their vessel. *Fantome*'s cutter and jolly boat were sent away and upon boarding the vessel she was discovered to be equipped for slaving. Her identity remained a mystery, however, her papers and colours having been removed by her crew. Master's assistant William Brodie was placed in command of the brigantine for her passage to St Helena where she was later condemned.

Just two weeks into her deployment *Madagascar* made her first arrest, seizing the Spanish schooner *Presidente* following a two-hour chase off Cape Mount on 20 January. Equipped for slaving and bound for New Sesters from Havana, contrary to her passport for the Cape Verde Islands, *Presidente* was condemned by the Anglo-Spanish court on 3 February. Two days after *Madagascar*'s first arrest *Iris*, sailing off Popo, seized the well-known Portuguese slaver *Venus*, alias *Duquesa de Braganza*, which had evaded the Squadron's cruisers on numerous occasions. Having dispatched *Venus* to Sierra Leone for adjudication by the Vice-Admiralty court, *Iris* continued into the Bights, arriving at Princes in late February.

On 8 February *Waterwitch* seized four boats off the Congo containing a total of 118 slaves. The following day Matson added another boat to this total, though this vessel had no cargo. All five boats were condemned by the Vice-Admiralty court at St Helena on 16 May. On 10 February *Waterwitch* chased and ran ashore a brig 40 miles north of Cabinda. Boarding the brig, *Waterwitch*'s second master Frederick Sturdee reported that she was equipped for slaving with two Portuguese and two American ensigns. No papers were discovered aboard the vessel but she was believed to be the slaver *Himmaleh*. It proved impossible to refloat the brig so she was burnt down to her bottom timbers. On 11 July *Waterwitch*'s prize was condemned in her absence by the Vice-Admiralty court at St Helena.

Cruising off Ambriz in mid-February *Fantome* seized two loaded Portuguese slavers in the space of two days, leading to the emancipation of 818 slaves. In the early hours of 13 February Butterfield's brig arrested the Portuguese-flagged brigantine *Diligencia*, bound for Brazil with a cargo of 413 slaves. *Diligencia* parted company with *Fantome* later that day under the command of Master's Mate Horace Bullock and arrived at St Helena on 9 March. The brigantine was condemned on 31 March, 358 slaves surviving to be emancipated. Just one day after her capture of *Diligencia* Butterfield's cruiser seized the Portuguese brig *Eugenia* with a cargo of 531 slaves. Bound from Angola to Paranagua, Brazil, *Fantome*'s prize was dispatched to St Helena and condemned by the court on 18 April, 460 slaves surviving to be emancipated. This was to be *Fantome*'s final arrest on the Coast. In late May Butterfield's cruiser departed St Helena for Rio where she would spend the next fourteen months before arriving home in England in October 1843 to be paid off.

On 17 February *Pluto* departed Sierra Leone and two days later arrived at Bolama, one of the Bissagos Islands, where she detained the Portuguese cutter *Balurca*, bound for Bissau with a cargo of eight slaves, presumably a feeder vessel supplying the larger slavers departing for Brazil and Havana. *Balurca* was dispatched to Sierra Leone where she was later condemned. On 28 February *Pluto* arrived at the River Cacheu where Blount was informed that the Portuguese Governor of Bissau had given instructions not to allow foreign merchantmen entrance into the rivers Jeba and Cacheu. This was a fairly obvious attempt to prevent intelligence reaching the Squadron regarding the slavers operating in these rivers. Heading south from the Cacheu for Sierra Leone, on 8 March Blount discovered a slave factory on Hen Island (or Galinhas), one of the northernmost Bissagos Islands. Twelve round houses were destroyed, resulting in the release of around seventy slaves belonging to the governor and notorious slave trader Antonio Mattos. Mattos later claimed that his daughter had been killed in the assault but Blount denied all knowledge of this incident.

On 3 March the newly-launched 10-gun brig *Rapid*, Lieutenant Charles Earl, arrived at Cape Coast Castle from Tenerife. On that same day *Acorn* arrived at the Cape from St Helena and the 6-gun brigantine *Fawn*, Joseph Nourse, departed Simon's Bay for the Coast. Two days later *Rapid* departed the Castle for a cruise to windward. On 18 March *Fawn* detained the loaded Portuguese brigantine *Boa Harmonia* with a cargo of 274 slaves 70 miles north-west of Benguela. Dispatched to St Helena under the command of *Fawn*'s second master, Richard Elliot, *Boa Harmonia* arrived at the island on 30 March and was condemned on 18 April. The number of slaves surviving to be emancipated is not known.

On 22 March *Persian* detained the Portuguese brig *Fortuna* 50 miles south-east of Lagos following a chase lasting twenty hours. Equipped for slaving, *Fortuna* arrived at Sierra Leone on 26 April and was condemned by the Anglo–Spanish court on 4 May, the commissioners noting that *Fortuna*, owned by Feliz de Souza, had cleared from Havana in February within a few days of another brig also named *Fortuna* and owned by de Souza (this vessel had been seized by *Waterwitch* in November 1839). The standard Portuguese passports for these vessels, lacking any information regarding their build or dimensions, had been endorsed by the Portuguese consul, Pluma, but only one brig had been reported in the list of departures furnished by the commissioners at Havana.

Following his return to Sierra Leone with the seventy emaciated Africans liberated from Hen Island, Lieutenant Blount was now ordered to the River Sulima, adjacent to the Gallinas, where it had been reported to the new Governor of Sierra Leone, George Macdonald, that a Spanish slave factory was still in operation, despite the recent treaty with King Siacca. Departing Sierra Leone with a complement of twenty soldiers provided by Macdonald, *Pluto* arrived off the Gallinas on 24 March where she fell in with *Rolla*. Five boats, led by *Rolla*'s armed cutter, now entered the Sulima and early on the 25th took possession of an empty barracoon. Approaching a second barracoon the boats were fired at with roundshot and grape which fortunately caused no injuries to the British. Upon landing the now-abandoned guns were spiked and the barracoon seized. Proceeding further upriver, a newer and larger barracoon was destroyed the following day. The boats now headed back down the river and the two barracoons that had previously been seized were also destroyed. Upon examination, the adjacent storehouses were discovered to be well stocked with goods including rum, tobacco and 1,000 barrels of gunpowder. The slaves from the barracoons had been driven into the bush upon the arrival of the British but following negotiations with King Laminah 160 manacled Africans were handed over to Blount prior to *Pluto*'s departure from the river on 31 March. Hall now entered into discussions with Laminah regarding a treaty abolishing slavery on the Sulima which *Rolla*'s commanding officer later discovered was little more than a delaying tactic to allow the remaining slavers operating on the river to escape detention.

On 15 March *Pantaloon* arrived at the Gambia from Portendic. At the request of the Acting Governor, Thomas Ingram, Lapidge now sailed for the Bissagos Islands to rescue the crew of a British merchantman that had recently been shipwrecked and made prisoners by the natives. Upon her arrival in the Bissau Channel on 29 March *Pantaloon* ran aground on the Areas Shoal. As her guns were being removed onto rafts in an effort to re-float the brig-sloop she came under attack from around 150 natives in ten canoes. *Pantaloon*'s boats got in amongst them and a large number of Africans were thrown into the water and twenty-three more were taken prisoner. Seeing this, more Africans on the shore preparing to join in the assault abandoned their canoes. The prisoners having been put on board *Pantaloon*, she was successfully refloated and sailed for Bathurst. Negotiations were subsequently entered into with the King of the Pepels who agreed to exchange the shipwrecked British sailors for Lapidge's prisoners.

On 26 March *Ferret* arrived at Sierra Leone with thirty-six Africans who had been transferred from *Madagascar* which, in turn, had received them from the Dutch governor at Elmina following the loss of the slaver *Vencedora* off the fort. Having received her instructions to return home from *Prompt*, on 9 April *Pluto* departed Sierra Leone for England, arriving at Plymouth on 6 June via the Cape Verde Islands, Madeira and Lisbon. April also saw the departure from Sierra Leone of *Buzzard*, her return home bringing to an end the career of one of the most successful cruisers to operate on the Coast, the brigantine having arrested nineteen vessels over a period of seven years, emancipating almost 4,000 Africans. Following her arrival in Plymouth in May *Buzzard* was paid off. She would not return to sea and was broken up in 1843.

On 12 April *Fawn* arrested a brigantine and a coasting schooner at anchor off a beach 40 miles south-west of Benguela not described on any Admiralty map. Abandoned by their crews on the approach of *Fawn*'s boats, neither vessel had flags or papers but the brigantine was fully fitted out for slaving. Both vessels were discovered to be unfit for the passage to St Helena so Nourse ordered them to be burnt. *Fawn*'s assistant surgeon, Eustace Walsh, her purser, George Marsh and her carpenter's mate, Thomas Edwards, appeared as deponents for the survey of both vessels which were condemned by the Vice-Admiralty court at St Helena in mid-June.

On 24 April the 16-gun brig *Grecian*, Lieutenant William Smyth, recently arrived from the Cape, seized the Portuguese sumaca *Janaviva* 90 miles west of St Paul de Loando whilst en route to St Helena. Loaded with a cargo of 278 slaves and bound from Novo Redonda, 190 miles south of Loando, to Brazil, *Janaviva*'s sails and rigging were discovered to be in such a poor condition she would be unable to cope with a fresh breeze. She also lacked boats, anchors and spare stores and had only enough provisions for a further thirty-five days, therefore Smyth decided to take her under tow for the seven-week passage to St Helena. Whilst 400 miles west of Loando, on 28 April *Grecian* seized the Portuguese schooner *Minerva*. Bound for Bahia with a cargo of 126 slaves loaded at Ambriz, the schooner was discovered to be in an even poorer state than *Janaviva* and so Smyth transferred her crew and slaves to his brig, then ordered the schooner to be burnt. *Grecian* arrived at St Helena on 6 May. The following day *Janaviva* was condemned and her surviving 264 slaves emancipated, Smyth having estimated that around half that number would have died had the sumaca been allowed to complete her original passage to Brazil. *Grecian*'s other prize *Minerva* was condemned on 23 May, the number of slaves who were emancipated from this vessel is not known.

In late April *Brisk* departed the Coast for Rio. Sprigg's cruiser would remain in Brazil for just one month before sailing for England, arriving at Spithead on 9 August. On 4 May a sickly Commander Littlehales was invalided home and *Madagascar*'s Lieutenant Octavius Cumberland was appointed temporary commander of *Dolphin*, which was then at Princes along with *Termagant*, *Heroine* and *Madagascar*. On 5 May *Heroine* departed the island for Sierra Leone and the following day *Madagascar* sailed for Cabinda. Two days later *Dolphin* departed Princes for Whydah and *Termagant* sailed for England, Littlehales taking passage on board Seagram's brigantine along with the Squadron's other invalids for the journey home, arriving at Spithead on 19 July. On the same day as *Dolphin* and *Termagant*'s departure from Princes *Fawn* detained the Brazilian brigantine *St Antonio* following a short chase off Benguela. Originally an American vessel that had been issued a passport at Bahia, *St Antonio* had departed Brazil under the command of a well-known Spanish slaver, Jacintho Derizans. Equipped for slaving, two logbooks were discovered on board the brigantine, one fictitious, describing a voyage from Bahia to St Michael, the other describing the vessel's true course from Bahia to the Coast. By the time *St Antonio* arrived at Sierra Leone on 5 June both Amaral and Nitheroy had departed Freetown for health reasons. In the absence of the Brazilian commissioners *Fawn*'s prize was dealt with speedily by the court and was condemned on 14 June.

Arriving at the Bissagos Islands from the River Nunez, *Pantaloon* anchored off the south-east end of Kanyabec Island and on 19 May Lapidge sent his cutter and gig under the command of his mate, Mr Arkwright, to seize a Spanish-flagged brigantine also at anchor there. Spotting the approach of *Pantaloon*'s boats, the vessel slipped her anchor and ran herself ashore. Boarding the brigantine, *Desiao*, it was discovered that she had been abandoned by her master and the majority of her crew who had also taken some stores along with her papers and charts. Only two persons were left on board the brigantine, one passenger and one member of her crew, but the appearance of hostile natives prevented Arkwright from sending ashore for the master. Found to be equipped for slaving, *Desiao* was dispatched to Sierra Leone where on 2 June she was condemned by the Anglo-Spanish court.

Whilst Denman's attack at the Gallinas had been applauded by many including Aberdeen's predecessor Palmerston, it was doubtful that such drastic actions were covered by existing treaties and various Free Trade MPs also pointed out that the removal of goods purely on the assumption that they were to be used for buying slaves would be detrimental to legitimate trade. As a result of questions raised in the House, the new Foreign Secretary sought legal advice and in May 1842 informed the Admiralty that the Advocate-General could not 'take upon himself to advise that all the proceedings described as having taken place at Gallinas, New Cestos [Sesters] and Sea Bars, are strictly justifiable, or that the instructions to Her Majesty's naval officers are such as can with perfect legality be carried into execution'.[1] Furthermore, the Queen's Advocate was of the opinion that the blockading of rivers, the destruction of property and the removal of slaves from the territories of countries not at war with Great Britain could not be sanctioned by the law of nations or any existing treaties. Aberdeen's letter, unintentionally made public, was a shocking blow to the operations of the Squadron. As Matson later reported, the slave traders along the whole of the Coast now acted as if there had been a revolution in England: that the people were obliging the Queen to carry on the slave trade and had forced her to remove Palmerston from office. This was a falsehood only too easily believed by the local chieftains and those collecting slaves from the interior. It was reported that by December 1843 the factories on the Gallinas had all been restored and were back in full operation. For Denman the most troubling consequence of this letter was the fact that he was now to be sued for trespass and the seizure of 4,000 slaves and goods to the value of £180,000 by Señor Buron, the slaver who had begged for safe passage from the Gallinas on *Wanderer*. Other actions against Denman amounted to claims totalling £370,000. Initially the government refused to involve itself in the matter but when the action of *Buron v. Denman* finally came up for trial in February 1848 it had been agreed that Denman should be defended by the Attorney-General appearing on behalf of the Crown.

There was to be one last large-scale action against the barracoons, launched by Governor Macdonald just before the contents of Aberdeen's letter became known on the Coast. Sailing south of the Line, on 22 May *Madagascar* and *Waterwitch* arrived off Cabinda and Foote sent the boats ashore. Following a long march through the bush the British arrived at a factory with four barracoons. The barracoons and the accompanying storehouses were destroyed and 834 slaves freed, three men from *Madagascar* being killed and one injured in the operation. The goods from the storehouses were handed over to the local chieftains who agreed to a treaty abolishing slavery in their territories. Four hundred and nineteen slaves were put on board a prize recently captured by *Waterwitch*, which now departed for St Helena. The remaining 415 slaves were put on board

Matson's brig, the officers' mess having been turned over to the females whilst the officers slept on deck, the crew being put on half rations. On 31 May *Madagascar* and *Waterwitch*'s boats landed at Ambriz, here three barracoons were destroyed and a further 260 slaves released, 186 of whom were put on board *Madagascar* with Matson taking the remaining fifty-four. Once again the goods from the storehouses were handed over to the local chieftains who agreed to a treaty abolishing slavery. *Waterwitch* now departed for St Helena with her 469 slaves whilst *Madagascar* headed for the Congo, at some point transferring her 186 slaves to an unnamed prize for transportation to Sierra Leone.

On the morning of 21 May *Dolphin* was cruising 560 miles south-west of St Thomas in company with *Iris* when she spotted and gave chase to a loaded American-flagged schooner that eventually ran herself ashore at Whydah to avoid detention, her cargo being landed with assistance from the shore. The heavy surf prevented *Dolphin* from getting close to the slaver so Tucker instructed Cumberland to send some of his Kroomen across to the vessel to recover her papers and ensigns. *Dolphin*'s entire compliment of fifteen Kroomen now volunteered to swim across to the schooner. When they reached the vessel the African sailors came under fire from natives on the shore armed with muskets. *Dolphin*, which had now re-anchored to windward of the wreck, replied with roundshot and grape and Cumberland sent his boats, under the command of the mate, Mr Cockraft, to recover the Kroomen. From the papers retrieved from the vessel it was determined that she was the American-flagged schooner *Illinois*, boarded just days earlier by *Iris* at Whydah. When Tucker questioned the masters of two merchant vessels then at Whydah, *William Ludvig* and *Emperio*, he discovered that the vessel had departed the port on 21 May flying Spanish colours. Having put a shot through *Illinois*'s hull to prevent her being re-floated, *Dolphin* returned to sea. On 29 May Cumberland seized the Portuguese-flagged brig *Minerva* following a chase of twelve hours off Great Popo. Fully equipped for slaving she was dispatched to Sierra Leone where she was eventually condemned by the Vice-Admiralty court.

On 28 May *Fantome* arrived at St Helena prior to her departure for Rio. The following day *Rolla* stopped off at Ascension en route to England, having spent three rather ineffective years on the Coast. That same day *Grecian*, sailing in company with *Acorn*, detained an unnamed brig which was dispatched to Sierra Leone and subsequently condemned by the Vice-

Admiralty court. On 10 June *Grecian* arrived at St Helena and the following day *Pantaloon* departed Bathurst for the Rio Nunez. On 27 June *Acorn* made two arrests off Benguela. The first was of the Brazilian brigantine *Sao Joao Baptista* which was seized following a short chase and sent to Sierra Leone where she was condemned on 14 September. Adams's second arrest that day was of the Portuguese brigantine *Marianna*, bound from Mauá, Brazil, to Ambriz. The vessel was dispatched to St Helena under the command of *Acorn*'s master, William Ellis, arriving at the island on 18 July. She was condemned by the Vice-Admiralty court on 5 September.

On 3 July *Madagascar* seized the Portuguese schooner *San Jose* off Cape Palmarinhas, 30 miles south-west of St Paul de Loando. Equipped for slaving, she had departed Pernambuco for Mozambique in early May but according to her master, Luis Goncalves Ferreira, had been forced to bear up for St Paul de Loando due to her leaky condition. However, following a survey the schooner's hull was found to be in a sound condition, save for a freshly-made hole with an auger lying next to it. *San Jose* was condemned on 10 October.

By mid-1842 the Palmerston Act had been responsible for the detention of ninety-one slave ships and smaller feeder vessels in the Vice-Admiralty courts at Freetown and St Helena. Whilst Palmerston had been highly critical of Portugal's continuing involvement in the slave trade, his replacement, Aberdeen, considered the country an important ally and wished to see the Act, which he considered hostile in the extreme, replaced by a treaty. Lisbon was also eager to see the Act replaced by a treaty, albeit one of limited duration. A breakthrough in negotiations was finally reached when Aberdeen offered an additional article whereby the two governments agreed to consult one another if the proposed treaty began inconveniencing legitimate trade. The new Anglo-Portuguese treaty, signed in Lisbon on 3 July, finally included the long sought-for Equipment Clause. Vessels could now be searched and detained on the high seas south of latitude 37° N. However, British cruisers had no right to search vessels at anchor in the roadsteads of Portuguese possessions or within cannon shot of their shore batteries. The treaty also included an agreement to open new Anglo-Portuguese Mixed Commissions at Boa Vista (Cape Verde Islands) and St Paul de Loando. On 25 July Lisbon issued a decree describing slavery as piracy and setting out severe penalties for those found to be involved in the

Trade. Two weeks later the Palmerston Act was suspended in respect of those vessels flying the Portuguese flag.

On 7 July *Acorn*, sailing in company with *Grecian* and *Brisk*, seized the brigantine *Oito de Decembro*, 125 miles north of Benguela. Equipped for slaving but with no flag or papers, the vessel was dispatched to St Helena in company with *Grecian*, both vessels arriving at the island on 16 July. Smyth's statement regarding the seizure was added to that of Adams and *Oito de Decembro* was condemned on 4 August. In March 1844 notice was given that *Brisk* would receive her share of the tonnage bounty for the arrest of the brigantine.

On 12 July *Madagascar*'s boats detained the Brazilian barque *Ermelinda Segunda* in the River Coanza, 60 miles south of St Paul de Loando. Emerging from the river with their prize, one of *Madagascar*'s boats was upset when crossing the bar and her crew of twelve men were all drowned. Lieutenant Kenyon was placed in command of the barque and both vessels headed north, arriving at the River Congo in late July. Learning of a factory at Cabinda operating in violation of the recent treaty, Foote now dispatched Kenyon to the port to burn the barracoons and release the slaves, sending him *Madagascar*'s marines and Kroomen to assist in the task. Kenyon arrived at Cabinda on 9 August. Four barracoons were destroyed and 118 slaves embarked on *Ermelinda Segunda* for passage to St Helena, one seaman being killed in the operation and two marines mortally wounded. Foote had ordered Kenyon to remove the goods that had been given to the local chieftains in return for their agreeing to the recent treaty, but Kenyon decided against this in an effort to maintain cordial relations, only removing seventy-two barrels of gunpowder. Battling against contrary winds with the barque in a leaky state, Kenyon had to put in at Princes where temporary repairs were made to *Madagascar*'s prize. However, arriving at Fernando Po on 3 October the barque was surveyed and found to be unfit to put to sea again. The slaves were therefore landed and placed under the care of *Soudan*'s surgeon whilst Kenyon proceeded to Sierra Leone aboard the steamer with two witnesses from *Ermelinda Segunda*, her master, Joaquim Maria Cordeiro and her cook. *Soudan* arrived at Freetown on 12 December. On 21 December *Ermelinda Segunda* was condemned in her absence by the Anglo-Brazilian court. Departing the Congo *Madagascar* sailed for St Paul de Loando where Foote remonstrated with the Portuguese governor for being secretly involved in the slave trade, a claim the governor strenuously denied.

On 22 July Lieutenant Phillip Bisson was appointed commander of *Dolphin* and Cumberland returned to *Madagascar*. That same day *Waterwitch* seized the Portuguese slaver *Triumfo* 375 miles south-west of St Thomas. Bound from Rio to Loango, the vessel was discovered to be in a very leaky state and was burnt at sea 180 miles south of St Thomas on 27 July. Cruising off Ambriz on 7 August *Waterwitch* seized the Portuguese brigantine *Bella Indianna*, en route from Rio to Angola. The vessel was dispatched to St Helena under the command of Master's Mate Richard Burstall, arriving there on 22 August. *Waterwitch*'s next prize was another Portuguese vessel, the lateen-rigged schooner *Nossa Senhora da Juda*, detained off Dandie with a cargo of sixty-three slaves by one of Matson's boats. The vessel was discovered to be unfit for passage to St Helena so her slaves and crew were transferred to *Waterwitch* and then to *Acorn* which was en route to the island. *Waterwitch*'s three prizes were all condemned by the Vice-Admiralty court on 22 September.

With the replacement of Palmerston with the more conciliatory Aberdeen at the Foreign Office there had been a long-overdue thaw in Anglo-American relations. In August the British envoy, Lord Ashburton, and the American Secretary of State, Daniel Webster, signed a treaty in which the American government agreed to send a squadron to patrol the West Coast of Africa for the next five years. The treaty did not specify the number of ships, only that the squadron should be of at least eighty guns. Following their return from the Coast Webster had interviewed the commanders of USS *Dolphin* and USS *Grampus* who recommended fifteen cruisers working in company with the British. Paine also recommended that his agreement with Tucker allowing a mutual Right of Visit be adopted. The American government felt this was a step too far and instead the treaty included an agreement for joint cruising. If a vessel flying the Stars and Stripes was encountered she would be boarded by an American cruiser but if the vessel hoisted any other colours she would be boarded by the British cruiser. However, with no Equipment Clause in force American cruisers could only stop fully-laden slavers. To avoid the fevers prevalent on the Coast the decision was taken to base the American squadron at the Cape Verde Islands, almost 1,000 miles to the north of Freetown and even further away from the slaving hotspots in the Bights than the British base at Sierra Leone.

On 11 August *Madagascar* gave chase to a suspicious-looking brigantine which was run on shore by her crew off Pointe-Noir, 60 miles north of Cabinda. Heavy surf prevented Foote's boats from reaching the vessel but a number of Africans were observed leaping from the brigantine into the water. The boats returned on 15 August to discover the vessel totally wrecked. The British went ashore but could discover no more information regarding the vessel from the natives. A year later an American sailor serving on board *Madagascar*, Francis Evans, told Foote that he had been working at a factory at Pointe-Noir belonging to the slaver Pedro Melegado and that on 10 August 1842 a Spanish brigantine, *Roberto*, had arrived off Little Loango and shipped between 500 and 600 slaves. The following day Evans had observed *Madagascar* in pursuit of the vessel, which had then run herself on shore. Evans had then assisted in removing the slaves to safety. Foote presented this new information to the Anglo–Spanish court and *Roberto* was finally condemned on 24 January 1844, seventeen months after she had been wrecked.

Having spent almost three and a half years on station, the majority of which as Senior Officer, in August a sickly Tucker was replaced as commander of *Iris* by *Persian*'s Thomas Eden and invalided home on board the ageing merchantman *Reliance*, which had stopped off at St Helena en route from India to England. Departing St Helena in early September, *Reliance* battled against light and contrary winds, finally entering the English Channel in November, by which time Tucker's health had greatly improved. Thrown towards the French coast by a fresh gale, on the night of 13 November *Reliance* ran aground on a deserted area of coast 20 miles to the west of Boulogne, the force of the impact breaking the ship's back. Tucker now went to the assistance of a midshipman, Mr Ford, whose leg had been broken by the falling foremast. With the water rapidly rising, Tucker and the ship's carpenter, Robert Dickson, dragged Ford to the safety of the poop deck whilst the crew set off signal flares. Shortly after, *Reliance*, rolling from side to side in the heavy swells, broke in half. Dickson decided to swim for safety whilst Tucker remained by Ford. The ship rapidly filled with water and within minutes was a complete wreck. Tucker was drowned along with Ford and 107 other members of crew, just six seamen, Dickson included, surviving to be picked up.

On 20 August *Pantaloon* seized the slaver *Eugenia* which was sent to St Helena but ordered to be restored on 26 October. The reasons for the Vice-Admiralty court reaching this decision are not known. On 22 August the newly-launched 3-gun brigantine *Spy*, Lieutenant George Raymond, departed Plymouth for the Coast. Six days later *Waterwitch* detained the schooner *Gentil Africano* off Novo Redondo. She was condemned by the court at St Helena on 12 December.

Following a twelve-hour chase off Whydah, on 4 September *Cygnet* seized the Brazilian brigantine *Resolucao*. Dispatched to Freetown, *Cygnet*'s prize arrived in harbour on 29 September and was condemned on 8 October. The final arrest of September was made by *Waterwitch*, her boats detaining the brigantine *Duquesa de Mindillo* in Elephant Bay, south of Benguela, as she was preparing to load a cargo of 400 slaves on 21 October. Dispatched to St Helena, she was condemned on 17 November.

On 7 October *Cygnet* arrested the slave vessel *Pureza de Conceicao* in the Bights. Three days later Wilson's brig detained *Se Deos Quizor*. Both vessels were condemned by the Vice-Admiralty court at Sierra Leone in mid-March 1843. On 14 October *Grecian* seized the slaver *Amizade Feliz* which was condemned at St Helena on 16 January 1843. *Grecian* followed up this seizure with the arrest of *Princesa Dona Francisca* alias *Maria Carolina* on 18 October, this vessel being condemned by the St Helena Vice-Admiralty court on 27 February 1843.

On 14 October *Dolphin* departed Ascension for England. Five days later a sickly Lieutenant Bisson died at sea. *Dolphin* arrived at Spithead on 19 November and was paid off. She would not return to the Coast for another six years but her next deployment was off the coast of Brazil where she detained several slavers which were sent for adjudication by the Vice-Admiralty court at British Guiana.

On 24 October *Rapid* seized the Portuguese-flagged schooner *Quelhe Importa* with a cargo of 447 slaves 250 miles south of Cape Palmas. Bound for Brazil, the schooner appeared to be a new vessel although her passport was six years old. Sailing with a Portuguese captain of the flag, Juan Antonio Gonçalves, the evidence pointed to the schooner and her cargo being the property of merchants in Brazil but there was sufficient proof of her

Portuguese nationality for her to be condemned by the Anglo-Portuguese court at Freetown on 9 November, 440 slaves surviving to be emancipated.

Cruising in the Bights on 17 December *Persian* made the Squadron's final arrest of the year, her boats seizing the Portuguese brig *Maria Segunda* which was dispatched to Sierra Leone for adjudication. The circumstances surrounding her arrest are unclear and on 15 February 1843 the Vice-Admiralty court ordered the vessel to be restored to her master, Eden incurring costs of £22 4s 10d.

Upon coming into office Aberdeen had found the Instructions issued to officers on the Coast to be inadequate and often contradictory. There were now no less than thirty treaties with various foreign governments in operation and copies of new treaties were often sent to the Coast with no Instructions at all. Aberdeen ordered a review and in December the Government set up a commission consisting of Captain Denman, the lawyer and abolitionist MP Stephen Lushington, James Bandinel of the Slave Trade Department and William Rothery, legal adviser to the Treasury, to draw up new Instructions for the guidance of officers on the Coast. In response to the debate within the Navy over the effectiveness of close blockade versus offshore cruising, the committee also investigated the tactics currently employed in the suppression campaign. Perhaps unsurprisingly the report, published in the spring of 1844, suggested a comprehensive adoption of the tactics of close blockade employed by Denman at the Gallinas. The new Instructions prepared by Denman would now help officers on the Coast navigate their way through the minefield of legalities required to ensure a vessel was successfully condemned and, just as importantly, that they were not held personally responsible for wrongful arrests. As a result of the committee's investigations the government agreed to increase the size of the Squadron and within a year of the report's publication the number of cruisers on the Coast had almost doubled to twenty-one vessels

1843 began with an incident that might have been avoided had Denman's *Instructions for the Guidance of Naval Officers Employed in the Suppression of the Slave Trade* already been available. Having spent a quiet couple of months following her arrival on the Coast, on 4 January *Spy* was cruising off Whydah when around midday she passed within a cable's-length of an American-flagged barque which, by the appearance of her rig and the number of black sailors amongst her crew, Lieutenant Raymond took to be a Spanish vessel engaged in the slave trade. *Spy* immediately tacked and stood for the barque. Closing on the vessel, *Rhoderick Dhu*, Raymond hailed her but was then forced to fire a shot to bring her to. A boat was sent across to the barque with twelve men and an officer, Mr Louttid, who, according to the barque's master, Mr Sims, was the last man to board. Louttid now demanded to see *Rhoderick Dhu*'s papers. Once they had been examined and Louttid was satisfied she was an American vessel he returned to *Spy*. Sims, who had experienced boardings from other British cruisers without incident, later complained that Raymond, Louttid and his crew had been insulting in their behaviour toward him and his men and that the boarding had been unjustified. Upon questioning, Raymond agreed that his language had been peremptory but only as a result of Sims's refusal to heave to (*Rhoderick Dhu*'s master had told Raymond he did not wish to bring his vessel to in the strong current) and his insulting language. For his part Louttid claimed that his foot had slipped as he had attempted to board the barque, resulting in him being the fourth man on deck, not the last. Sims stated that the British had been on board *Rhoderick Dhu* for forty-five minutes but Louttid insisted the boarding party had spent less than fifteen minutes aboard the vessel. Examining all the evidence, Aberdeen considered that there had been insufficient grounds for the boarding and wrote to the American Ambassador, Edward Everett, to convey his serious displeasure at Louttid for allowing the boat crew to leave their vessel and his governments sincere regret that the visit ever took place. It was later explained by Foote that he had neglected to give Raymond the correct instructions from the Admiralty regarding the boarding of American vessels upon the British officer's arrival on the Coast.

By the time of *Spy*'s next encounter with two suspected slavers three weeks later she was under the command of a lieutenant from *Madagascar*, Samuel Brickwell. The circumstances surrounding this change of command are unclear but Raymond would not return to the brigantine. Cruising 60 miles south-west of Whydah on 24 January, *Spy* seized the Brazilian brig *Clio*. Fully equipped for slaving with over forty water casks, she was dispatched to Freetown for adjudication. That same day Brickwell seized the Brazilian-flagged brigantine *Bom Fim*. Similarly equipped for slaving, the brigantine had cleared out of Bahia with a passport for a port further along the coast of Brazil but had instead made for the West Coast of Africa and was detained by *Spy* following a nine-hour chase off Great Popo. *Bom Fim* arrived at Sierra Leone on 25 February and was condemned by the Anglo-Brazilian Mixed Commission on 6 March. *Clio* arrived in port on 12 March and was condemned by the same court on the 21st of that month.

On 18 March *Cygnet* detained another Brazilian slaver, the schooner *Brilhante*, just a few miles off Whydah. Equipped with a slave deck laid fore-and-aft over thirty-nine water casks, the vessel had no trade cargo; instead her papers revealed that she had 354 doubloons to purchase slaves, 240 of which were discovered concealed amongst the baggage and the persons of *Brilhante*'s officers and crew in the most extraordinary manner. Along with those hidden in trunks or mattresses, some had been buried in wax and made to resemble poultices, others concealed in squares of soap or sewn between the soles of shoes. Having been dispatched to Sierra Leone, *Cygnet*'s prize was condemned on 6 May.

Whilst Raymond's boarding of *Rhoderick Dhu* had caused offence to the American government, elsewhere similar operations were running more smoothly. Between 16 January and 1 April *Ferret* boarded four American vessels, the schooners *Providence* and *Kathleen*, the barque *Reaper* and the brig *Mary Pauline*, all without incident. Following these boardings the Squadron's next arrest was made by *Waterwitch* which had spent most of February at Simon's Bay. Returning to the Coast, on 27 April Matson's cruiser seized the slaver *Almeida* which was sent to St Helena and condemned by the court there on 1 June. (The precise location of this arrest is not known.) Shortly after this capture *Waterwitch*, badly in need of repair, departed the Coast for England, arriving at Portsmouth on 29 June.

Sailing from Sierra Leone in mid-February *Madagascar* headed north to the Cape Verde Islands prior to a run down the Coast. On 4 May a dinner was held on board the frigate at Cape Coast Castle for the departing Lieutenant-Governor of Gold Coast, George Maclean, who was to be replaced by *Saracen*'s Lieutenant Hill. The following day *Madagascar* departed Cape Coast for the Bights before heading south to Ascension where in early June she fell in with *Ferret* and the steamer *Soudan*, now laid up as her horsepower had been discovered to be insufficient for use as a cruiser. *Albert* was then at Sierra Leone having the rusting iron rivets in her hull replaced and with the departure for England of both her sister-ship *Wilberforce* and *Pluto* the previous year the Squadron currently had no steamers in operation on the Coast.

On 29 May *Spy*, sailing under her third commander in four months, Lieutenant Edward Earle, arrested the Brazilian schooner *Esperanca* off Little Popo. The vessel, out of Bahia, had a passport for Paranagua, further along the Brazilian coast, but had instead made for Whydah. Fully equipped for slaving and capable of carrying a cargo of 250 slaves, *Esperanca*'s hold was at no point higher than 2ft 10in and amidships barely 1ft 11in. The schooner was dispatched to Sierra Leone and arrived in port on 22 June. Once again the Brazilian and British commissioners failed to come to agreement as to whether a vessel before them should be condemned. However, the British judge was happy to accept arbitration as Amaral was still absent from court and *Esperanca* was condemned on 18 July. Following this decision Nitheroy took another two months' leave.

Whilst en route to Ascension *Persian* seized the Portuguese-flagged schooner *Andorinha* 750 miles north of the island on 13 June. Bound from Espirito Santo, Brazil, to St Thomas and fully equipped for slaving but with no papers, *Andorinha* was taken to Ascension to fit her out for passage to Sierra Leone. Whilst at the island her master, Antonio Laite, slit his throat, having first revealed the nationality of his vessel to be Portuguese. *Andorinha* arrived at Sierra Leone on 2 July and was condemned by the Anglo–Portuguese court on 13 July.

Approaching Whydah on the evening of 27 June *Cygnet* spotted a schooner under American colours in the roads. Immediately suspicious, Wilson stood towards the schooner which now weighed anchor and made sail along the coast. Passing within hail of the schooner, Wilson told her to prepare for a boarding then sent an officer across to examine her papers. She proved to be the American-built schooner *Leda*, en route from Bahia to Lagos. Her master, William Pearse, did not wish his log to be signed and the boarding officer immediately returned to *Cygnet*. In August it was reported by the British consul in Bahia, Edward Porter, that *Leda* had disembarked a cargo of slaves in the vicinity of that port. Pearse had subsequently abandoned his vessel on the coast and arrived at Bahia on board a Swedish brig.

On 29 June *Waterwitch* arrived at Portsmouth from the Coast. Four years' service in the harsh African climate had taken its toll on both the vessel and her crew, thirteen of her complement of sixty men having died during her deployment. Following a survey of the brig the Master Shipwright,

Richard Blake, declared her to be 'in a worse state than I ever saw any vessel
… there is scarcely an edge of plank perfect; she is completely sap rotten
… In fact, I have no doubt when the plank is taken off within and without
board, that there will not remain an original timber sufficiently sound to
continue in the ship.'[2] It was eventually agreed that *Waterwitch*'s original
builder Joseph White would undertake the vessel's repairs at his own yard
at Cowes on the Isle of Wight at considerably less expense than if they had
been carried out at the Royal Dockyard.

On 5 July the ageing 10-gun brig-sloop *Espoir*, Lieutenant Arthur
Morrell, departed Plymouth for the Coast. Heading in the opposite
direction, exactly one month later *Acorn* departed Simon's Bay for England,
arriving at Plymouth in late September. On 8 August *Spy* seized the brig
Furia off Lagos following a chase of twelve hours. Fully laden with a cargo
of 532 slaves but sailing without a flag or ship's papers, *Furia*'s master,
Joze Soares Monteiro, stated that his vessel had cleared out of Bahia and
was bound from Lagos to Brazil. Following her arrival at Sierra Leone on
10 September *Furia* was condemned by the Anglo-Brazilian court and her
surviving 529 slaves emancipated.

In late August *Cygnet* arrived at Ascension prior to her departure for
England. Wilson still had the 240 doubloons seized from *Brilhante* for which
the commissioners were holding him personally responsible and was eager
for instructions on how to dispose of the money. On 5 September *Spy* was
cruising off Whydah when she fell in with a suspicious-looking schooner
that eventually ran herself ashore 35 miles to the east of Whydah following
a chase of four hours. Boarding the vessel, *Spy*'s purser, Francis Cole, her
gunner, John Devonshire and her carpenter's mate, Henry Ward, found
her to be fully equipped for slaving, having water casks laid fore and aft
beneath a slave deck and vast quantities of farina, rice and other provisions.
They also discovered a flag and papers proving her to be the Brazilian
schooner *L'Egeria*, ostensibly bound from Bahia to Rio Grande, Brazil,
but in reality headed for Whydah. The vessel was no longer seaworthy and
so the surveyors set fire to her then returned to *Spy*. However, their boat
was upset when crossing the bar and *L'Egeria*'s logbook and ship's papers
were lost. On the evidence of Devonshire and Ward the schooner was
condemned by the Anglo-Brazilian court at Sierra Leone on 24 January
1844. The condemnation of an unloaded Brazilian slaver was now possible
following the issue of new Instructions by Aberdeen four months earlier.

The intransigence of the Brazilian commissioner Nitheroy had led to various delays in the proceedings of the Mixed Commission when dealing with Brazilian vessels found to be equipped for slaving. Disagreements between the two judges resulted in decisions being made by either the British or Brazilian arbitrators, with the ultimate fate of the vessel, condemnation or restoration, depending on chance. Governor MacDonald, who was performing the duties of British judge following the return home of Michael Melville in late March, now wrote to Aberdeen to request that cases should only be submitted to arbitration when there were disagreements over the nationality of a vessel. Having taken the advice of the Advocate-General, Sir John Dodson, in mid-September Aberdeen instructed the British commissioners to resist the call for arbitration in cases where a Brazilian vessel was found to be equipped for slaving, as they were engaged in an illegal trade and therefore liable to capture and condemnation. Learning of Aberdeen's instructions on his return to Sierra Leone following two months' leave, Nitheroy immediately resigned his post. On the day after his resignation, 10 November, the Brazilian brigantine *Independencia*, seized by *Madagascar* on 8 August was condemned without the usual difficulties by the Anglo-Brazilian court.

In early September the American squadron formed as a result of the Webster-Ashburton Treaty arrived at Porto Grande on the island of St Vincent in the Cape Verdes. The squadron comprised four vessels, the frigate *Macedonia*, the brig *Porpoise* and the sloops *Saratoga* and *Decatur*. Commodore Matthew Perry flew his flag on board *Macedonia*, a vessel captured from the British during the war of 1812 and still bearing her original figurehead. The intentions of the American government had been made clear by the Secretary of the Navy, Abel Upsher, who instructed Perry to make the protection of legitimate trade, not the suppression of the slave trade, his primary concern and at their first meeting Perry would explain to Foote that joint cruising would be impossible due to the great disparity in numbers between the British and American squadrons. Although provided with the names and locations of several slavers from Foote, Perry had seemingly already made his mind up on the subject and would later report 'I cannot hear of any American vessel being engaged in the transportation of slaves, nor do I believe there has been one so engaged for several years'.[3] However, there was some co-operation between the two squadrons. In October Lieutenant Grey reported to Foote that *Porpoise*, Lieutenant Stellwagen, had offered to remain off New Sesters to look after *Bonetta*'s boats during their operations upriver and to give them any assistance they required.

On 14 September *Heroine* seized the Brazilian-flagged brigantine *Conceicao Flora* off Cape Palmarinhas. The brigantine had been at anchor prior to her detention and the appearance of *Heroine* had caused some confusion on deck. Having hauled for the wind and let go all her braces, it initially appeared to Foote that she intended to run herself ashore. When boarded it was discovered that the vessel, bound from Rio to Benguela via Loando, was equipped with more water casks than necessary for use by her crew but not sufficient for a cargo of slaves. *Heroine*'s prize was dispatched to Sierra Leone, arriving in harbour on 9 October. The Claimant's Proctor stated that *Conceicao Flora* was bound for Benguela to procure cattle and that her over-sized main hatchway was as a result of her previous employment as a sugar droguer. In reply the Seizor's Proctor stated that the excessive amount of water, the lack of a logbook, manifest, any money to purchase cattle and her suspicious movements ought to be ample reasons to condemn the brigantine. On 18 October the British commissioners, George Macdonald and James Hook, announced their decision to restore *Conceicao Flora* to her owner, the slaver Antonio Guimaraes, but to deny him any demurrage, losses or damages that had occurred as a result of her detention.

On 19 September *Espoir* made her first contribution to the suppression campaign, seizing the Brazilian-flagged cutter *Aguia* as she lay at anchor in Cabinda Roads. Equipped for slaving, the vessel was dispatched to Sierra Leone for adjudication. It being established that *Aguia*'s owner, Joao Antonio Cogoes, was a Brazilian-born resident of Havana, his vessel was condemned by the Anglo-Spanish court on 10 November and ordered to be cut up and sold in separate lots as stipulated in the treaty.

On 22 October *Ferret* departed the Gallinas. The following day she arrived off the Sherbro where she fell in with *Eleanor*, an American-flagged barque out of Havana. Boarding the vessel, purportedly bound for Cape Mesurado, Oake learned from a British member of her crew that two evenings prior, another vessel, *Volador*, had discharged her cargo of tobacco and rum into *Eleanor* and that the three Spaniards discovered on board the barque actually belonged to *Volador* and were accompanying their cargo to the Gallinas. Having allowed *Eleanor* to continue on her voyage, on 18 November *Ferret* arrived off Cape Mount where she fell in with *Bonetta*, for whom she had instructions to return to England. Oake now learned that *Volador* had taken on board a cargo of slaves from West Bay on Sherbro Island and that *Eleanor* had landed a slave cargo at the Gallinas.

Returning to her cruising grounds off Angola from Ascension, on 28 October *Madagascar*, sailing in company with *Espoir*, seized the Brazilian-flagged polacca *Prudentia*. Four days later, whilst off Juma Bay, 150 miles south of Cabinda, *Madagascar*'s launch, commanded by Lieutenant Charles Brickdale, arrested another Brazilian vessel, the brigantine *Loteria*, following a chase of five hours. Both vessels were dispatched to Sierra Leone, *Loteria* via Ambriz. *Prudentia* arrived in port on 13 December. Originally registered as a Genoese vessel, she was bound from Rio to Gibraltar via the east coast of Africa. Her master, Joao Luiz da Silva, admitted he had chartered the vessel for 3,500 dollars, 500 dollars more than he had actually paid for her. Further investigations revealed that her crew of ten, all Spanish or Portuguese sailors, were being paid 20 milreis per month, an amount never paid in legitimate Brazilian trade. However, these peculiarities were not thought sufficient evidence by the British commissioners to condemn the vessel and on 6 February she was ordered to be restored without damages. *Madagascar*'s other prize, *Loteria*, arrived at Freetown on 29 November. The vessel had cleared out of Rio with a passport for Campos on the Brazilian coast but her master, Felicianno Gomez, claimed his brigantine had been blown towards the coast of Africa by strong winds. Clearly equipped for slaving and also carrying an American ensign and pennant, *Loteria* was condemned by the Anglo-Brazilian court on 15 December.

On 3 November *Rapid* seized a schooner flying no colours 120 miles south-east of St Thomas. The vessel, *Temerario*, had cleared out of Santos, Brazil in August and had made directly for Cape Lopez where, on 31 October, she had loaded a cargo of 298 slaves. Her master, Joaõ Suares, claimed that he had left the schooner's flag and papers ashore but Earl suspected these had been thrown overboard upon Suares first sighting his brig. *Temerario* was dispatched to Freetown, arriving in port on 24 November having lost fifteen of her slaves during her passage north. Due to the overcrowded situation on board the vessel the slaves were landed immediately but a further four died in hospital prior to the vessel's condemnation by the Anglo–Brazilian court on 2 December.

Following a chase of four hours *Heroine* seized the Brazilian-flagged brigantine *Imperatrix* 90 miles north-west of St Paul de Loando on 12 November. Attempting to evade capture her master, Jozé Maria Pereira, had ordered the mast wedges to be knocked out in order to give the poles more play. Fully equipped for slaving but with none of her equipment included in her manifest, *Imperatrix* had cleared out from Rio with a passport for Campos but had instead made for Loando. *Heroine*'s prize arrived at Sierra Leone on 2 January and was condemned by the Anglo–Brazilian Mixed Commission on the tenth of that month.

Cruising off Porto Novo, on 20 November *Spy* seized the Brazilian schooner *Linda* which had departed Bahia with a passport for Santa Catarina, further south on the Brazilian coast, but which had instead made directly for Whydah. Equipped for slaving, *Linda* was dispatched to Sierra Leone where she was condemned by the Anglo–Brazilian court on 29 December.

The final arrest of the year fell to *Espoir*, Morrell's sloop chasing a vessel without colours 100 miles north-west of St Paul de Loando on 29 November. Discovered with a cargo of 525 slaves, the brigantine, *Helena*, had no papers or anyone acting in the capacity of master. Only able to spare a few hands to form a prize crew, Morrell found it necessary to remove all of *Helena*'s crew except her boatswain who, having only recently joined the vessel, could provide little information other than the fact that his brigantine had sailed from Pernambuco, her cargo had been loaded at Ambriz and that her chief mate had thrown her Brazilian ensign and papers overboard prior to capture. *Helena* arrived at Freetown on 29 December. Due to her small size and overcrowded state mortality was high, eighty-three slaves dying on the passage north. A further sixteen died subsequent to the vessel's arrival in port, 426 slaves surviving to be emancipated when *Helena* was condemned on 4 January 1844.

Chapter 15

The End of the Trade: 1844–1867

In 1839 the British and Foreign Anti-Slavery Society had been founded by the Quaker Joseph Sturge. That same year Wilberforce's official successor, Sir Thomas Fowell Buxton, founded the Society for the Extinction of the Slave Trade, which had the Prince Consort as its patron. As a Quaker, Sturge opposed the use of force in suppressing the Trade, whilst Buxton held that the only way to eradicate slavery was through the civilisation of Africa. To this end he suggested establishing agricultural settlements at Fernando Po, Lokoja and elsewhere. With the backing of the Melbourne government, Buxton organised an expedition up the Niger with the intention of persuading the local chieftains to turn from slavery to legitimate commerce such as the production of palm oil. The disastrous expedition, which ended with the deaths of forty-eight Europeans from malaria, spelled the end for Buxton's society. Soon after came news of Aberdeen's letter putting a stop to the Navy's attacks on the barracoons. Whilst slaving had all but been eradicated north of the Line, it still flourished at Cabinda, Angola and the Congo and, according to Buxton, it had now doubled in size. Buxton estimated that the suppression campaign being carried out on the African, Brazilian and West Indies Stations and elsewhere involved one-fifth of Britain's naval strength with an annual cost to the taxpayer of £750,000. Regardless of these costs, he still thought that even more ships, especially steam vessels, should be sent to the Coast. However, after nearly forty years of anti-slavery operations with no apparent end in sight, others now began to question the costs of the Squadron, to the nation both in monetary terms and in terms of lives lost, in pursuit of a seemingly impossible goal.

On 24 June 1845 the MP for Gateshead, William Hutt, launched a motion in Parliament calling for a withdrawal of the cruisers from the Coast. Hutt argued that after nearly forty years of operation the West Africa Squadron had most evidently failed to stop the slave trade which was, in fact, on the increase. The country could ill afford the expense of maintaining the

Squadron and the Navy could not continue to lose 'her best and bravest in order to carry on this idle and mischievous project'.[1] Finally, with more slaves being packed on board vessels and less care being taken of them, Hutt argued that Britain's attempts to suppress the Trade actually made conditions on board the slave ships worse than they had been before. The Prime Minister, Peel and the First Sea Lord, Sir George Cockburn, rose in defence of the Squadron and the motion was voted down, but for Hutt this was not the end of the matter. Later that year he moved and carried a motion requiring a return of the cost of the suppression campaign on the Coast for the period 1839–44. The figures showed that the cost in wages, provisions and wear and tear of ships totalled over £655,000. The expenses of the various mixed courts totalled £103,000 and during this six-year period, 385 officers and men had died from accident or disease or had been killed in action and a further 495 had been invalided out of the service. This equated to around one-third of the Squadron's manpower.

As a member of the Free Trade group, which demanded cheap food and raw materials such as sugar and cotton to maintain Britain's economy, Hutt contended that Britain could reject these slave-grown commodities on moral grounds if she wished but the Trade would still continue and the cotton and sugar would go to her rival France instead. Others with vested interests now joined in the debate. A group of pacifists led by Sturge opposed the use of force for whatever purpose, whilst another group led by the Scottish philosopher Thomas Carlyle contended that slavery was not the evil it had been made out to be. There were also former members of the Squadron such as Sir Henry Huntley who agreed with Hutt that operations on the Coast were increasing the sufferings of the slaves. These 'Anti-Coercionists', as they became known, continued their attacks on the Squadron and on 22 February 1848 Hutt moved that another Select Committee be appointed to consider the best means for suppressing the slave trade. His motion was agreed to and he was appointed chairman. The committee heard from hundreds of witnesses including Palmerston, Hotham, who advocated cruising at sea to keep the Squadron healthy, and Denman and Matson who both called for a return to close blockade. Hutt's committee published its report in August 1848, declaring that, in the face of contradictory evidence, no alteration to current policy was to be made and that the Select Committee be reappointed to look at the matter again after the summer recess. In the meantime the House of Lords set up its own committee, proposed by Bishop Wilberforce, which also heard evidence from Denman, Matson and Hotham. Having reconvened, Hutt's committee remained undecided through several sittings until Hutt used his casting vote to call for the disbanding of the Squadron. Countering this, Bishop Wilberforce's committee now issued its report which advocated the continuance of government policy, stating that the withdrawal of cruisers from the Coast would result in a great and immediate increase in the slave trade and that, furthermore, abandoning the suppression campaign would be a blow to the nation's honour.

Undaunted by the Lords' report, on 19 March Hutt addressed the Commons, proposing that Britain be released from her treaties with foreign states requiring her to maintain cruisers on the Coast. Defending himself from attacks in the press, Hutt dismissed the evidence of naval officers such as Denman and Matson, stating that, in spite of Britain's best efforts, the export of slaves was increasing and that they were now cheaper in Brazil than when their import had been unrestricted. The Navy, Hutt declared, employed thirty to forty ships in its suppression campaign at a cost of around £700,000 a year. No other state would support Britain's efforts, indeed she was in constant quarrels with France and the United States. Hutt's motion was seconded by Henry Baillie and most notably supported by Gladstone, who stated that to completely suppress the Trade Britain would have to double the Squadron, obtain treaties with France and the United States and compel Brazil and Spain to fulfil their own treaty responsibilities, all of which he considered highly unlikely. Hutt was opposed by Henry Labouchere, President of the Board of Trade, and Sir Robert Inglis, who disagreed with his estimate of £700,000 a year, thinking the true figure less than half that, arguing that Britain ought to maintain a squadron on the Coast to protect her trade and should not renounce her treaty obligations simply in order to save money. It was past midnight when the Prime Minister, Lord John Russell, rose in defence of the Squadron, declaring that the country could not abandon a thirty-year task, could not abandon Africa, nor surrender the protection of commerce that was regarded as essential in all other parts of the world. Citing the recent work done by the Navy to end the centuries-old scourge of Algerian piracy, Russell declared 'if we are to give up this high and holy work, and proclaim ourselves no longer fitted to lead in the championship against the curse and the crime of slavery, that we have no longer a right to expect a continuance of those blessings, which, by God's favour, we have so long enjoyed'.[2] At 2.15am the House divided: 154 members voted for Hutt's motion and 232 against it.

With over a third of the House having voted in favour of Hutt's motion (the debate was not conducted on party lines) it was now clear to the Government that if it did not redouble its efforts against the Trade it might not survive another debate. In May a questionnaire was sent out to the officers of the Squadron to obtain their views on how to improve anti-slavery measures. Nearly all decided in favour of close blockade and thought the destruction of barracoons effective. They considered the best type of vessel for service on the Coast to be the 200-ton Symondite brig or 300-ton screw steamer with pivot guns amidships. They also suggested more coaling and victualling stations at Accra, St Helena and Cabinda. Over the following months the Squadron's strength was increased, more treaties were negotiated with local chieftains and fresh diplomatic efforts were made with foreign powers. The following year the Government authorised an attack on the slaving hotspot of Lagos.

In March 1844 the paddle steamers *Penelope*, Captain William Jones, and *Prometheus*, Commander John Hay, had departed Plymouth for the Coast where they would meet up with the paddle steamer *Hydra*, Commander Horatio Young, recently arrived from Cork. By the end of the year these vessels would be joined by the paddle steamers *Growler*, *Ardent* and *Gorgon* from the coast of Brazil. The number of steamers on the Coast remained fairly constant until the year following Hutt's select committee, when the number rose from eight to fifteen. For most of this period the majority of these vessels were of the wooden-hulled paddle-box type. They were generally dirty and unreliable and their paddle-boxes interfered with the traditional broadside mounting of guns, further reducing their effectiveness as cruisers. Many were converted sailing vessels like *Penelope*, a Fifth Rate frigate which had been cut in half and extended by 63ft to enable two steam engines and coal bunkers to be installed. Others were designed independently of their steam engines, paddle boxes and associated machinery. *Gorgon*, for example, was designed for 220hp engines but actually received 350hp power plants, making her sit much lower in the water than originally intended. It was not until 1850 and the appearance on the Coast of the screw steamers *Archer*, *Niger* and *Wasp* with their heavier armament and lower fuel consumption that steam vessels finally came into their own and at last began making an impact on the suppression campaign.

Following his arrival on the Coast Captain Jones assumed command of the Squadron from Foote who returned home on board *Madagascar*. Hoisting his broad pennant on board *Penelope*, the newly-appointed commodore appeared to have misinterpreted his instructions from the Admiralty for he now decided to leave patrolling south of the Line entirely in the hands of the Portuguese, who had a squadron of just five vessels based on the Coast. Noting his surprise at this move, in his annual report to Aberdeen the British consul at St Paul de Loando, Edmund Gabriel, stated that during the course of 1845 Royal Navy vessels had captured forty-three slavers south of the Line to the Portuguese Navy's nine. (Five of the British seizures were loaded slavers, resulting in the emancipation of 2,095 slaves.) Gabriel thought there were two reasons for this imbalance in captures, firstly the inadequate number of Portuguese cruisers tasked with anti-slavery duties and secondly the apathetic attitude of the Portuguese commanders who considered slavery as little more than contraband traffic and who lacked any financial incentive to arrest suspected slavers as their government did not award bounties for condemned vessels.

Having spent two years in command of the Squadron, in March 1846 a sickly Commodore Jones departed Sierra Leone on board *Penelope*. He died from fever at Haslar Hospital, Portsmouth, on 24 May. Jones was replaced as Commander-in-Chief of the Squadron by Commodore Sir Charles Hotham, flying his broad pennant on board the returning *Penelope* in December. As he later informed Hutt's Select Committee, Hotham arrived on station having given no previous thought to the task at hand. He did not think to visit any of the slave centres on the Coast but cruised off them from time to time, whenever he had 'nothing else particular to do'.[7] Hotham's instructions to his officers were confidential, reducing the ability of co-operation between cruisers. Furthermore, officers were not allowed to make alterations to their vessels, such as adjusting their rigging or removing unwanted stores to improve their handling. During his time in command of the Squadron Hotham consulted no one who happened to be serving under him as he was of the opinion that commodores did not seek the opinions of junior, albeit experienced, officers. As previously noted, Hotham disagreed with Denman and Matson's ideas of close blockade, feeling it was ruinous both to the health and morale of his men. He also believed that he had too few ships to patrol over 2,000 miles of coast and institute blockades at the same time. In his considered opinion, regardless of whether he kept his vessels in close blockade or allowed them to cruise offshore, the slavers would still evade capture. Hotham's critics pointed out that most of the Coast had by now been cleared of the slavers, the places that required blockading were all well-known and new ones could easily be discovered by the intelligence network that supplied information to the Squadron. Defending his record on his return home, Hotham pointed out that during his period in command the Squadron had seized 143 slavers compared to the 100 vessels of his predecessor, Jones, who had held his command for a similar length of time.

On 13 March 1845 the Anglo-Brazilian Treaty of 1817 was due to expire and the Brazilian Foreign Minister, Ernesto Ferreira França, served notice to the British Minister in Rio, Hamilton Hamilton, that his government had no desire for it to be renewed. The mutual Right of Search would end and the Mixed Commissions in Rio and Freetown, which had been allowed to operate for fifteen years after the abolition of the Brazilian slave trade in 1830, would continue to function for just another six months, in order to adjudicate on ships captured prior to 13 March. França emphasised that his government was prepared to reach agreement on a new treaty, this time on Brazil's terms.

Aberdeen learned of the Brazilian government's decision in May. Beginning with his 'misguided' letter to the Admiralty regarding Denman's operations in the Gallinas, the new Foreign Secretary had received severe criticism over his handling of the suppression campaign from his predecessor, Palmerston. Now, examining the treaty of 1826 which still remained in effect, Aberdeen soon found his way out of a 'most complicated and embarrassing'[4] situation. The first article of this treaty stated that slaving by Brazilian subjects would be deemed and treated as piracy. The law of nations allowed the warships of any nation to search and seize any pirate vessel discovered on the high seas, regardless of their flag, therefore Aberdeen now informed Hamilton he intended to enforce Britain's right, enshrined in the 1826 treaty but largely forgotten, to treat the Brazilian slave trade as piracy. Aberdeen asked the Queen's Advocate, Sir John Dodson, the Attorney-General, Sir William Follett and the Solicitor

General, Sir Frederick Thesiger, to investigate the matter and on 30 May the Law Officers reported that under the 1826 treaty Britain had acquired the right to seize all Brazilian subjects found on the high seas engaged in the slave trade and to treat them as pirates. Legislation would be required to establish which courts should adjudicate on captured vessels and how to deal with their crews, cargoes and slaves (this task would eventually fall to the Vice-Admiralty courts) and therefore the Law Officers began to prepare a bill, known as the Slave Trade (Brazil) Bill, for its passage through Parliament.

With the free traders voicing their opposition to the Navy's anti-slavery operations in the Commons, Aberdeen's bill was introduced in the Lords where it went through without debate. In the Commons the bill received the support of the majority of the opposition. Palmerston gave his support and the Duke of Wellington, a fierce opponent of Palmerston's Act, gave his consent, having been persuaded that Aberdeen's bill differed from the earlier bill in that it simply allowed Britain to exercise powers that Brazil had conceded under the 1826 Act rather than giving powers to Britain that Brazil had refused to give by treaty. As was expected, the bill was opposed by the free traders and it survived a late scare when the former Solicitor General and Attorney General, Sir Thomas Wilde, pointed out that the slave trade had never been declared to be piracy by the Brazilian government and doubted whether the 1826 treaty alone gave British courts the right to deal with Brazilian subjects and their property. Wilde was absent for the bill's third reading on 1 August and a week later the Aberdeen Act received royal assent.

Enforcement of the new Act fell to Hotham who now had twenty-five cruisers at his disposal. In the last three months of 1845 the Squadron seized twenty-seven Brazilian vessels. The following year forty-nine vessels were arrested, in 1847 this figure rose to seventy-eight and in 1848, the final year of Hotham's command, ninety vessels were seized under the Aberdeen Act. More than half the captured vessels were adjudicated in the Vice-Admiralty court at St Helena, the remainder at Sierra Leone or the Cape. There were no Brazilian representatives at any of these courts and the Brazilian consuls at Sierra Leone, St Helena and the Cape were given no instructions other than to protest formally against the illegality of the capture whenever a Brazilian vessel arrived for adjudication.

In the 1840s members of the free trade movement had begun agitating for a reduction of the heavy duties on products entering Britain from outside her colonies and in 1844 Peel had reduced the duty on foreign, free-grown sugar. In June 1846 Peel's Conservative government had collapsed following the introduction of a bill repealing the Corn Laws. The new Whig Prime Minister, Lord John Russell, now introduced a bill proposing the gradual reduction of duties on foreign sugar, including Brazilian and Cuban slave-grown sugar, so that by 1851 duties on both foreign and colonial products would be equalised.

Palmerston, recently returned as Foreign Secretary under Russell's government, argued that the reduction in duties on slave-grown sugar would not increase the Brazilian slave trade as its volume was determined more by Britain's suppression campaign than by her commercial policy and, whilst she had discarded 'fiscal coercion', the blockade of the Coast remained in place. Most members of the Anti-Slavery Society were by now supporters of free trade and in the Lords only Brougham, Chief Justice Denman (Captain Denman's father) and the Bishop of Oxford, Samuel Wilberforce, argued against the bill which was eventually passed by twenty-eight votes to eleven.

In Cuba the introduction of the Act had little immediate impact on the importation of slaves. In 1845 the island had imported less than 2,000 slaves. In both 1847 and 1848 this figure was around 1,500. The chief factors behind the low number of imports were fears of further slave revolts similar to those which had occurred on the island in 1843 and 1844, leading to brutal reprisals by the island's Governor, Captain-General Leopoldo O'Donnell, and the return of Martinez de la Rosa – who had been Spain's signatory to the Anglo-Spanish Treaty of 1835 – as her Foreign Minister in 1844. A friend of Canning, de la Rosa introduced a bill in the Cortes defining penalties for those involved in the slave trade. The bill caused widespread panic in Cuba and for several years the Trade was brought to a virtual standstill, with several sugar planters selling up and moving to Texas.

Whilst the effects of the Sugar Act on the Cuban trade had been negligible, the same could not be said for the Brazilian slave trade. In 1845 22,700 slaves had been imported into the country, but with sugar exports rising from 22 per cent to 28 per cent this figure rose sharply to 62,600 the following year. Imports would remain at similarly high levels until

1850 when Palmerston sent a squadron into Brazilian territorial waters to detain slave ships at their point of departure. British intervention also coincided with the emergence of the Pure Brazilian Party with their open hostility towards the Trade which was in the hands of twenty to thirty rich Portuguese merchants, outsiders who controlled the supply and price of the slaves which every Brazilian planter needed, who lent money where they saw fit and who clearly had the government in their pockets.

In February 1848 the long-delayed case of *Buron v Denman* finally came up for trial. At first the Government had tried to wash its hands of the whole affair by claiming that it was purely a private matter but after lengthy discussion Denman and his associates including his father, the Chief Justice, successfully argued that, as his action in the Gallinas had been carried out in the course of his duty and with the subsequent approval of the Admiralty, it should be defended with the Attorney-General appearing on behalf of the crown. At the trial the defence argued that Buron did not own the slaves as that was against Spanish law and therefore he could not claim compensation for their loss. In addition Spain had signed a treaty with Britain allowing British naval officers to arrest any Spaniard in possession of slaves. In relation to the trade goods, Denman had been specifically authorised to destroy Buron's warehouses by Siacca, on whose ground they stood, and the goods had subsequently been appropriated by the King of the Gallinas, therefore Buron should make his claim against Siacca not Denman. Having heard the evidence the judges now directed the jury to find Denman not guilty.

The successful outcome of this case encouraged other officers on the Coast to return to the work begun by Denman in 1840, but now with the precaution of ensuring that treaties with local chieftains agreeing to their actions were in place first. Although the two men had disagreed over the question of close blockade, Commodore Hotham was happy to follow Denman's lead and assembled a squadron of seven cruisers (*Penelope, Favourite, Sealark, Waterwitch, Bonetta, Dart* and *Pluto*) to attack the Gallinas barracoons, largely rebuilt following the original raid. On the morning of 3 February 1849 the ships' boats crossed the Gallinas bar and 300 men landed on Dombocorro Island, where they quickly took possession of the barracoons and factories there. Captain Jones now took *Penelope*'s boats up the south-eastern creek to a trading post known as Solyman and destroyed a further three factories, whilst Captain Murray destroyed the factories at Tineh before returning to Dombocorro. On the morning of 4 February the barracoons on Dombocorro were destroyed. Having obtained written statements from two of the principal chiefs declaring that they had violated the treaty with Denman and therefore agreed to his actions, Hotham now declared a blockade on the coast from Solyman Point in the south to Cazee in the north that was supported by the commanders of both the French and American squadrons. The Gallinas chiefs quickly turned against the Spanish slave-traders and ordered them out of the river. Fearful of attacks from the inland chiefs who did all the procuring of slaves but saw little of the profits, the merchants were soon writing to the officer in command of the blockading cruisers, Lieutenant Hugh Dunlop, pleading for safe passage to Brazil. By the end of the year it was reported that there were no foreign slave traders in either the Sherbro or the Gallinas.

On 22 April 1850 the Foreign Office advised the Admiralty that under both the Palmerston and the Aberdeen Act the Royal Navy was free to search, detain and arrest any vessel found engaged in the slave trade under the Brazilian flag, or without any nationality, anywhere within Brazilian territorial waters as well as on the high seas. The Admiralty had already promised to reinforce the South American Station, commanded by Admiral Barrington Reynolds, which for several years had been tied up monitoring the situation between the warring navies of Argentina, Paraguay and Uruguay in the River Plate area. When the steamer *Sharpshooter*, Commander John Bailey, arrived off Rio in June 1850 she was bearing correspondence which included the letter of 22 April from the Foreign Office.

With a force of just four vessels, Bailey's *Sharpshooter*, the steam sloops *Rifleman*, Commander Stephen Crofton, *Cormorant*, Commander Schomberg, and his own flagship, the frigate *Southampton*, at his disposal, on 22 June Reynolds ordered his squadron to enter Brazilian ports to seize any vessels they discovered fitted for the slave trade. The following day *Sharpshooter* cut out a slaver from the port at Macaé, her boats emerging with their prize having been fired on from a nearby fort and with musketry. On 30 June *Cormorant* cut out three vessels at Paranaguá. As they were being towed out to sea Schomberg's steamer came under fire from the fort at the mouth of the river and one British seaman was killed and two wounded. Having received minor damage, *Cormorant* engaged the fort as she made her way through the narrows. Discovering that two of his prizes were unseaworthy, Schomberg burned both in view of the fort and dispatched the third to St Helena where all three prizes were eventually condemned.

Although the Foreign Office instructions of 22 April had advised caution and the avoidance of incidents, Reynolds would subsequently receive approval for his operations from Palmerston and the First Lord of the Admiralty, Sir Francis Baring. However, aware that the Brazilian Foreign Minister, Paulino Jose Soares de Sousa, was about to address the Chamber of Deputies on the matter of the slave trade, on 14 July Reynolds ordered a halt to the search and arrest of Brazilian vessels in their home ports. In his speech Paulino stated that the recent incidents in Brazilian waters were a result of the failure of all Brazilian governments to fulfil their obligations to the treaty of 1826. Presenting a detailed account of Britain's anti-slavery campaign over the preceding fifty years, Paulino asked the Chamber: 'When a powerful nation like Great Britain is evidently in earnest, can Cuba and Brazil stand out?'[5] Paulino explained that there would come a day, not too far distant, when the Trade would no longer exist and that his country should begin looking for suitable alternatives to African labour. With the prior knowledge that Reynolds had already suspended naval operations close to Brazilian ports, Paulino announced that the commanders of coastal forts would be ordered to prevent by force any further seizures of Brazilian ships in Brazilian waters and that once the British squadron's attacks had ceased he would show the Brazilian government's 'firm, frank sincere and loyal intention'[6] to fulfil her obligations under the Treaty of 1826. An anti-slavery bill, first introduced by the Minister of Justice, Eusébio de Queiroz, in September 1848 quickly passed through the Chamber. It was accepted on 13 August and sent to the Emperor. On 4 September the bill became law. The importation of slaves into Brazil was now to be treated as piracy. Vessels which were fitted out for slaving or which had landed slaves were liable for seizure. Owners, masters and members of crew who had assisted in the landing of slaves or who had obstructed the authorities were liable to between three and nine years' imprisonment and corporal punishment under the anti-slavery law of 1831.

By November it was being reported that the Trade in the south-east of the country was virtually at a standstill, but it still flourished in the north-east, particularly out of Bahia and Pernambuco. As a consequence, on 11 January 1851 the British minister in Rio, James Hudson, informed Paulino that the suspension of the orders of 22 June had been revoked. The following day every available Brazilian steamship was dispatched on anti-slavery duties. During the first four months of the year only two landings of slaves were reported along the entire coast of from Pará to Rio Grande do Sul and on 14 July Palmerston was able to announce to the Commons that the Brazilian Trade was virtually at an end.

By the late 1840s the Trade out of Whydah had all but dried up following several years of close blockade but Lagos, an island situated six miles from the mainland and protected by a dangerous bar, was proving much harder for the Squadron to police. In an effort to promote legitimate trade in the region, in mid-June 1849 the British government had appointed the Governor of Fernando Po, John Beecroft, as Consul of the Bight of Benin and Biafra, with jurisdiction over Whydah, which belonged to King Gezo of the Dahomey, and Lagos, under the control of his rival, King Kosoko, who had recently come to power having overthrown his brother, Akintoye. Following his appointment Beecroft visited Gezo to persuade him to give up the slave trade and concentrate on legitimate commerce such as palm oil instead. However, Gezo declined the offer, explaining that slaving was still a much more lucrative venture than palm oil and that he was not about to give up the Trade whilst it still flourished out of Lagos.

Having failed in his attempts to regain his crown with the assistance of the local slave-traders, in 1851 Akintoye wrote to Beecroft for assistance. Beecroft now suggested to Palmerston that if the British helped Akintoye to return to power he might be persuaded to sign a treaty abolishing slavery. Palmerston went one step further, deciding to capture Lagos should Beecroft's plan fail and the Admiralty gave instructions for the Commander-in-Chief of the West Africa Squadron, Commodore Bruce, to carry out any such attack at his own discretion. Without Bruce's prior knowledge, Beecroft and Akintoye now embarked on the steamer *Bloodhound* for a palaver with Kosoko, sailing for Lagos along with *Philomel*, *Harlequin*, *Waterwitch* and the steamers *Niger* and *Volcano*. Beecroft and Kosoko met on 20 November, the British consul offered Kosoko the standard treaty of trade and friendship that including the abolition of the slave trade offered to all chieftains on the Coast over the past twenty years but Kosoko flatly refused and was deaf to all further discussion. The British now retired to assess the situation and decide on their next course of action. Beecroft had been instructed by Palmerston to request a second interview with Kosoko, backed up by force, if his first failed. At this second interview he was to intimate that the British would back Kosoko's rival Akintoye if he failed to sign the treaty being offered. Bruce's second-in-command, Commander Forbes of *Philomel*, agreed that a naval escort would now be necessary to obtain this second interview and on 25 November a gig, flying a white flag and carrying John Beecroft, led *Bloodhound*, also flying a white flag with Akintoye on board, and the steamers *Niger* and *Volcano* towing twenty-one boats containing 306 armed seamen and marines into the approach channel to Lagos. Little resistance was expected but as soon as the flotilla crossed the bar it came under accurate musketry from the shore. The British continued to fly the white flag and held their fire. Coming abreast of Lagos Island the musketry intensified, then, as she reached a point almost opposite Lagos town *Bloodhound* ran aground and was fired at by a heavy battery of guns on the island. Having withstood this barrage for twenty minutes, Bruce finally ordered the white flag to be lowered and returned fire. A landing party was sent ashore to capture the battery but was forced to retreat, having set fire to several buildings. During the night *Bloodhound* was refloated and the following morning the British withdrew, having lost two officers killed and two officers and fourteen men injured.

When news of the failed attack reached London Beecroft was reprimanded for acting without consultation with Bruce. However, by then the Squadron's commander-in-chief had already launched a second attack on Lagos. In late November Kosoko's men had gone ashore and burned a village to the east of the river entrance in preparation for a combined attack from land and sea over Christmas. Having decided that the failure of the first attack had been down to a lack of firepower, Bruce assembled a force comprising *Bloodhound*, the 12-gun paddle steamer *Penelope*, Captain Henry Lyster, the 4-gun paddle steamer *Sampson*, Captain Lewis Jones, the screw steamer *Teazer*, mounting two guns and Beecroft's iron galley *Victoria*, fitted out as a rocket boat for the occasion. Arriving off Lagos on 24 December the attack was carried out following a day of rest on 26 December. Lyster was given overall command of the landings with Jones being placed in charge of the boats which were to be protected by *Bloodhound* and *Teazer*. Kosoko had been expecting a second attack and as the boats, containing 400 sailors and marines, approached the beach the

British could see that the enemy defences had been fortified with stakes, trenches and stockades. The boats came under intense fire from the shore and as the flotilla approached Lagos Island *Teazer* ran aground near the south end of the island where she came under sustained fire from two enemy 12-pounders. Unable to bring any of his own guns to bear, Lyster now ordered the boats to attempt a landing to spike Kosoko's guns. Two hundred men went ashore and drove the enemy from their first line of defence but could not force them from the second. However, they managed to spike an abandoned battery before returning to their boats with heavy casualties. *Bloodhound* had also run aground to the north of the island, firing on the enemy positions with her one available gun, and Lyster launched a second landing to spike the enemy guns. As the British hacked their way through the bamboo stakes lining the foreshore they came under intense musketry and were forced to withdraw. Later that day *Bloodhound* and *Teazer* were both re-floated, the dead were buried and the wounded sent to the ships waiting outside the bar.

The following morning the boats made a landing on the north-western end of the island, covered by *Bloodhound*, *Teazer* and *Victoria*, one of the galley's rockets landing in the enemy's main powder magazine. The palace was soon observed to be on fire and the town in flames. Throughout the course of the day hundreds of canoes were observed putting off for the mainland loaded with household goods. By sunset it was clear that Kosoko had fled and that the town had been abandoned. The following morning a landing party went ashore and spiked and dismantled Kosoko's guns which were then dumped in deep water. Akintoye and his men were brought over from the west bank of Lagos harbour and Akintoye entered discussions with the local chiefs for them to return and accept him as their king. On 1 January the newly re-instated King Akintoye signed an anti-slavery treaty on board *Penelope*. The export of slaves was forbidden and no slave trader was to live in Lagos. Any slaves awaiting export were to be handed over to the British and taken to Sierra Leone. At a cost of fifteen men killed and seventy-five men injured, slaving out of Lagos was now at an end. Further south it was confined to an area some 200 miles either side of the Congo. In 1861, amid more political unrest, Lagos was annexed as a British colony.

Under the governorships of Federico de Roncali and José Gutiérrez de la Concha, the Trade to Cuba began to increase in the early 1850s. When the Crimean War broke out in October 1853 the British withdrew their best cruisers from the Coast in order to serve in that campaign. This saw a reduction in vessels from nineteen in 1853 to fourteen in 1856. The Cuban traders took the most of this opportunity and the import of slaves into that country increased from 13,911 slaves in 1853 to 16,992 in 1858, reaching 30,473 the following year. The majority of this trade was carried out in American-built vessels which either sailed direct to the Coast or via Cuba. During a period of eighteen months from 1859 to 1860 eighty-five slavers, capable of transporting up to 60,000 Africans, had been fitted out at New York. Anxious not to give the United States any reason to annex Cuba, the Royal Navy refrained from any overtly aggressive behaviour towards American vessels in her territorial waters. As a result of several misguided boardings in the Caribbean, in July 1858 the Foreign Secretary, Lord Malmsbury, finally gave up Britain's long-contested Right of Search over American-flagged vessels. Later that year Commodore Charles Wise, Commander-in-Chief of the West Africa Squadron, complained that eleven of the twenty-three vessels that had lately escaped his blockade were known to be American slavers that he could not touch. Having fought a long and hard battle against the British Right of Search, in 1860 the United States sent its own cruisers to Cuba where it was reported that they conducted searches of Spanish and French vessels, even though the US Government did not have any mutual right of search treaties with these countries.

When Abraham Lincoln was nominated as presidential candidate by his abolitionist Republican Party in May 1860 the Trade with Cuba was still flourishing. In March 1861 Lincoln was elected President and a month later Confederate forces fired on Union troops at Fort Sumpter, beginning the American Civil War. Whilst the constitution of the breakaway Confederate States of America had actually banned the slave trade, the Southern States claimed the right to extend slavery into the new territories of the West. Eager to prevent Britain siding with the Confederacy, in March 1862 Lincoln's Secretary of State, William Seward, responded favourably to an approach from the British Ambassador, Richard Lyons, regarding an anti-slavery treaty, his one stipulation being that the draft treaty should appear to have come from his own government. In early April Lincoln signed the Washington Treaty. The treaty, which agreed a reciprocal right of search and trials in mixed courts, was unanimously ratified by the US Senate later that month. The British and American squadrons, which by now had resumed joint cruising, received their new warrants in November. By the end of the year the Cuban Trade out of the Congo was at a standstill with not a single vessel claiming the protection of the Stars and Stripes. In December 1862 General Domingo Dulce was appointed Captain-General of Cuba. Like his predecessor, Francisco Serrano, he was firmly against the Trade and made it clear that he would not hesitate to use his powers to destroy those involved in it. In 1859 around 9,000 slaves had entered the country, in 1863 that figure fell to around 1,000. In 1864 and 1865 only two cargoes were said to have been landed on the island, totalling around 1,400 slaves. The following year the British consul at Havana reported that the Cuban Trade was virtually at an end.

Since the first arrests of slave ships by British cruisers off Cuba in 1824 all emancipated slaves taken from captured vessels had been hired out by the Cuban government in gangs to any estate owner that applied for them. English consuls on Cuba had long complained that these *emancipados* were being treated exactly as slaves by the planters and that they were also being re-sold to slaveowners. In 1865 the Spanish government finally removed the power to assign *emancipados* from the Captain-General. All emancipated slaves were now to be taken back to Fernando Po or the African mainland. Finally yielding to both internal and international pressure, the following year a bill was introduced in the Spanish Cortes for the suppression of the slave trade. The bill passed the Senate in April but due to several delays was not made law until May 1867 and was not promulgated in Cuba until September 1867. In 1869 all *emancipados* were declared free and the system of labour gangs abolished.

From 1864 the yearly reports from the British commissioners and consuls at Sierra Leone, St Helena and St Paul de Loando began stating that no new cases had been adjudicated in their courts and by 1867 it was clear that the Atlantic slave trade had effectively come to an end. That year Sir Hervey Bruce put forward a motion in the Commons to withdraw the West Africa Squadron from the Coast as it was 'no longer expedient',[7] now that the Trade had been abolished in Cuba and the United States. Seconding his motion, Admiral Walcot stated that naval officers had never liked the task imposed on them but they had always been ready to sacrifice their lives in the performance of their duties. Opposing the motion, Sir John Hay stated it was still necessary to maintain a small force on the Coast to prevent a revival of the Trade and to protect legitimate commerce. The motion was defeated but three years after this debate the Squadron was finally amalgamated with the Cape Squadron.

In November 1865 the anti-slavery campaign's chief architect Lord Palmerston died aged 81. That same year Viscount Cardwell, speaking during a debate on the campaign in Parliament, declared 'I own I do not know a nobler or brighter page in the history of our country'.[8] Writing in 1869 the historian William Lecky stated: 'The weary, unostentatious, and inglorious crusade of England against slavery may probably be regarded as among the three or four virtuous pages comprised the history of nations.'[9] For almost exactly sixty years Britain had fought to bring the Atlantic slave trade, a trade that had existed for over three and a half centuries, to an end. Fought almost entirely single-handedly, the campaign had cost around £40 million (equivalent to £2 billion today) and the lives of more than 2,500 British seamen. Against these costs the West Africa Squadron intercepted around 1,600 vessels, freeing an estimated 160,000 Africans from slavery.

For the first thirty years of the campaign the Navy had employed the tried-and-tested tactics of offshore cruising, skills it had honed during the recent wars with France, to intercept slave ships before their cargoes were subjected to the horrors of the Middle Passage. The first anti-slavery treaties were signed with Spain and Portugal in 1817, these allowed for the creation of the Mixed Commissions, they banned the Trade north of the Line but only allowed for loaded slavers to be seized. It was not until the introduction of the Equipment Clause that unloaded slavers could be arrested. Holland was the first country to accept the clause in 1822. Spain followed in 1835 but it was not until 1839 that Portugal accepted the clause, and then only under duress. It was her failure to negotiate a new, more comprehensive treaty with Portugal that led Britain to reinterpret the 1817 treaty and introduce the Palmerston Act in 1839. Unladen slavers under Portuguese colours or no colours at all were now arrested for acting piratically and condemned by the Vice-Admiralty courts. The following year saw a shift in tactics on the Coast. The close blockade employed by Denman, combined with his attack on the Gallinas barracoons, saw the first real blows against the Trade, further enforced by the growing number of treaties signed with local chieftains to abolish slavery in their dominions in return for minor subsidies, usually of trade goods. Further such actions against the barracoons were suspended when the new Foreign Secretary, Aberdeen, questioned the legality of Denman's attack. A case was brought against Denman by the slave trader Buron but it was not until 1848 that it was finally brought to court and dismissed, allowing the attacks on the barracoons to recommence.

Although Britain and America had both abolished the slave trade in 1807, relations between the two countries were at a low ebb following the war of 1812 and Washington had no intention of allowing American-flagged vessels to be boarded by British cruisers. America would occasionally dispatch her own cruisers to the Coast to police the Trade and there were brief periods of co-operation with their British counterparts but the American suppression campaign remained largely ineffective. Slavers seeking the protection of false flags now abandoned the Portuguese ensign and turned to the Stars and Stripes. In 1842 Britain and America signed a treaty by which each nation undertook to maintain a minimum force on the Coast. That same year Portugal bowed to the inevitable and finally agreed to the addition of an Equipment Clause in its treaty with Britain.

In 1825 Brazil had declared her independence from Portugal. Free of Portugal's treaty obligations with Britain, she nevertheless signed a convention the following year agreeing to the terms of the 1815 treaty which would also prohibit the importation of slaves after 1829 and allow for the existence of the Mixed Commissions. Without prior warning but not altogether unexpectedly, when this treaty expired in 1845 the Brazilian government refused to renew it. In response the British Government once again relied on a creative interpretation of the earlier treaty to treat the Brazilian slave trade as piracy, thereby allowing the condemnation of Brazilian-flagged vessels in Vice-Admiralty courts. Even with this new act in place the import of slaves into Brazil increased dramatically in the late 1840s, fuelled largely by the Sugar Act. In 1850 British ships entered Brazilian territorial waters to seize suspected slave ships under the Aberdeen Act. Unwilling and unable to go to war over these incursions and with its own increasingly vocal abolition movement, later that year Brazil brought in new anti-slave trade legislation. However, slavery itself was not abolished until 1888.

The proximity of Cuba to America had prevented the Royal Navy acting as aggressively as it had off the coast of Brazil and successive captain-generals had turned a blind eye to the import of slaves into their country.

It was not until the appointment of General Geronima Valdez to that post in 1842 that the administration finally took a stand against the Trade. By 1851 imports were at a record low but the introduction of the Sugar Bill and the appointment of captain-generals less inclined to control the Trade meant that by the end of the decade imports, mostly from south of the Line and under the American flag, were higher than they had ever been. In 1862 the Lincoln Administration finally signed an anti-slavery treaty with Britain which allowed for the Right of Search and the trial of suspected slave ships in courts of Mixed Commission. Whilst these Anglo-American Mixed Commissions never actually heard any cases, the abolitionist Henry Brougham justifiably considered the new treaty 'in many respects the most important event that had occurred during the period of his sixty years warfare against the African Slave Trade'.[10] By the end of the decade the Atlantic slave trade was at an end and in 1871 the courts at Freetown were abolished, having heard their last case in 1864.

Whilst the Foreign Office was engaged in making treaties with the various slaving powers it was, of course, the responsibility of the Royal Navy to enforce these treaties. When the suppression campaign had begun Britain was still at war. Half of all British seamen were impressed, a quarter were volunteers and a quarter were provided by the quota system, whereby each county had to provide a set number of men for the Navy, normally men who had been facing trial for minor crimes. Men joined a vessel when it was commissioned and only left it when it was paid off. Returning home aboard the brig *Lynx* in June 1842 Captain Broadhead complained that eleven men out of his complement of seventy-five had not been out of his ship for three and a half years. It was hard to maintain discipline over men such as these and they often broke into the spirit rooms of captured slavers. Returning exhausted to Freetown on board these vessels the prize crews went ashore and got blind drunk on local spirits. Having escaped the contagious slave diseases of dysentery or opthalmia, after a night asleep in the gutter these men inevitably fell ill from yellow fever or malaria, the causes of which were still not known at that time. It had, however, been well understood that those on boat service up the rivers and creeks of the Coast were at greater risk from these diseases than the men on vessels cruising further out at sea. Commanded by an officer and crewed by a dozen men, a ship's boats, her cutter, gig or jolly boat would be sent, often for weeks at a time, to explore the furthest reaches of a river while the parent ship remained at anchor or cruising out to sea. Armed with muskets and knives and provisioned with water and ship's biscuits, it was the job of the boats to search the river for any slavers that might be awaiting their cargoes.

Once a vessel had been seized it needed to be dispatched to the nearest court for adjudication. This was no easy task, presenting its own problems and dangers to those placed in command of the arrested vessel. Only if the capturing vessel was a frigate could a commissioned officer be appointed as prize master: usually the task fell to a midshipman, master's mate or warrant officer. Given command, invariably for the first time and with just a small prize crew, these men, often barely out of their teens, had to contend with the navigation of an unfamiliar ship over thousands of miles using whatever rudimentary navigational instruments were to hand in the prize, along with the watch of prisoners, possible attacks by pirates and, if the vessel were carrying a cargo, the care of several hundred emaciated and sickly Africans.

Whilst undoubtedly harsh, service on the Coast gave junior officers the chance for independent command along with the possibility of prize money and there was fierce competition over the command of the Squadron's fastest cruisers. With little in the way of recreation on the Coast the impromptu races between vessels created an enjoyable diversion from the monotony of blockade or endless cruising and also helped hone the skills of their crews for when they next gave chase to a supposedly faster slave vessel. The superior seamanship of the British sailor, not to mention his courage under fire, usually resulted in successful arrests, often against the odds and to the surprise of the slaver captains. Inured to most things by the horrors of war, officers who had previously given little thought to the rights and wrongs of slavery were appalled by the suffering they witnessed first-hand on board these vessels and many developed a desire to do all in their power to bring an end to this cruellest of trades.

Having abolished the slave trade, Britain rather arrogantly believed that the rest of the world would simply fall in line and follow its lead. Instead the subsequent suppression campaign was opposed by the nations of France, Spain and Portugal who saw it as little more than an attempt by Britain to prevent her rivals from taking economic advantage through their continued involved in the Trade. As we have seen, for the first thirty years at least, this apparent grab for economic supremacy had involved the use of no more than a half a dozen cruisers off the coast of Africa, the majority of which were worn out or otherwise unsuited to the task at hand, and the suppression campaign had little impact on the trade of these countries which continued largely unabated until the 1840s. Contrary to the accusations by these foreign powers, there is little evidence that the campaign was anything other than a moral crusade. Run with seemingly little enthusiasm by the Admiralty, by its termination it had cost Britain around £2 billion in today's money and the lives of around 2,000 seamen, one of the country's most valuable assets. As a British merchant, writing to *The Times* in March 1845 noted, the country had spent £40 million abolishing and suppressing the Trade 'yet does no one nation under Heaven give us credit for disinterested sincerity in this large expenditure of money and philanthropy. Whether the calm verdict of posterity will redress this injustice, time alone can show.'[11]

Long before the Nuremberg trials or the drafting of the UN Charter and the Universal Declaration of Human Rights, the Mixed Commission Courts at Sierra Leone and elsewhere had sat in judgement over crimes against a section of a civilian population, Africans sold into servitude. Facing opposition at almost every turn, Britain had done more than any other nation to atone for its involvement in the Trade. The hard fought-for treaties she signed with other slaving nations during the seventy-year suppression campaign and the ensuing legislative bodies that were set up helped pave the way for international human rights law as we know it today. The role the Mixed Commissions played in the formation of these laws has largely been forgotten, as indeed has the role played by the Royal Navy in the ending of the Trade. The campaign involved no memorable fleet actions worthy of public acclaim, just one long, hard battle against the slavers, and when it was over the officers and men of the West Africa Squadron returned to Britain with little acknowledgement or thanks for their role in helping to bring the Atlantic slave trade, which had existed for over 350 years, to an end.

Appendix I

Chronology of the Suppression Campaign

1807	Abolition Act: slave trade made illegal in Britain.
1808	First Royal Navy cruisers sent to West Coast of Africa on 'Particular Service'.
1810	First Anglo-Portuguese Treaty: Portugal to load slaves at her own ports only.
1811	Slave trading made a felony in Britain.
1814	Slave trade made illegal in Holland.
1815	Second Anglo-Portuguese Treaty.
1817	Spain prohibits slave trading north of the Equator.
1818	Anglo-Dutch, Anglo-Spanish and Anglo-Portuguese Mixed Commissions open in Sierra Leone.
1819	Formation of the West Africa Squadron.
1820	Slave trade made illegal in Spain.
	Slave trade deemed to be piracy in the United States.
1822	Holland, Spain and Portugal agree that empty vessels can be condemned on proof they have carried slaves.
1822	Equipment Clause accepted by Holland.
1824	Slave trading deemed to be piracy in Britain.
1826	Anglo-Brazilian Treaty: slave trade to be illegal after 1829.
1831	West Africa and Cape Squadrons combined.
1833	Slavery abolished throughout the British Empire.
1835	Equipment Clause accepted by Spain.
1839	Equipment Clause accepted by Portugal.
1840	West Africa and Cape Squadrons separated.
	Denman's action against the Gallinas barracoons.
	American cruisers arrive off West Coast of Africa.
1842	Anglo-Portuguese Treaty: additional Mixed Commissions added in Luanda, Boa Vista and Cape Town.
	Webster-Ashburton Treaty: regular American squadron established, good Anglo-American co-operation.
	Lord Aberdeen's letter regarding the possible illegality of the Gallinas action.
1845	Murder of British prize crew on board *Felicidade*.
	Felicidade trial: crew acquitted of murder on appeal.
	Hutt's Select Committee appointed to investigate effectiveness of suppression campaign.

1848   *Buron v Denman* trial: court finds in favour of Denman.
1849   Hotham's action against the Gallinas barracoons.
1850   Hutt's motion calling for an end to anti-slavery patrols defeated in Parliament.
       Admiral Reynolds' squadron arrests slave ships in Brazilian waters.
       Brazil enforces new anti-slave trade legislation.
1851   British capture of Lagos.
1853   Brazilian slave trade effectively at an end.
1861   British annexation of Lagos.
1862   Anglo-American Treaty: mutual Right of Search and creation of Mixed Commission courts.
1865   Slavery abolished throughout the United States.
1867   Amalgamation of West Africa Squadron with Cape Squadron.
1869   Abolition of slavery in Cuba.
1871   Closure of the courts at Sierra Leone.

Appendix II

Commanders-in-Chief Appointed to the West Coast of Africa

(Vessels on Particular service)
1809–11   Commodore Edward Columbine
1811–13   Commodore Frederick Irby
1814–15   Commodore Thomas Browne
1816–18   Commodore Sir James Yeo

(Formation of West Africa Squadron)
1818–21   Commodore Sir George Collier
1822–3   Commodore Sir Robert Mends
1824–7   Commodore Sir Charles Bullen
1827–30   Commodore Francis Collier
1830–2   Commodore John Hayes

(West Africa and Cape Squadrons combined in 1832)
1832–4   Rear Admiral Frederick Warren
1834–7   Rear Admiral Patrick Campbell
1837–40   Rear Admiral George Elliot

(West Africa and Cape Squadrons separated in 1840)
1840–1   Captain William Tucker
1842–3   Captain John Foote
1844–6   Commodore William Jones
1847–9   Commodore Sir Charles Hotham
1850–1   Commodore Sir Arthur Fanshawe
1852–3   Commodore Sir Henry Bruce
1854–56   Commodore John Adams
1857–9   Commodore Henry Wise
1860–2   Commodore William Edmonstone
1863–5   Commodore Arthur Eardley-Wilmot
1866–9   Commodore Geoffrey Hornby

Further Reading

Bethell, Lesley, *The Abolition of the Brazilian Slave Trade* (Cambridge, 1970).

Edwards, Bernard, *Royal Navy versus the Slave Traders: Enforcing Abolition at Sea, 1808–1898* (Barnsley, 2007).

Grindall, Peter, *Opposing the Slavers: The Royal Navy's Campaign against the Atlantic Slave Trade* (London, 2016).

Lloyd, Christopher, *The Navy and the Slave Trade: The Suppression of the African Slave Trade in the Nineteenth Century* (London, 1949).

Martinez, Jenny S., *The Slave Trade and the Origins of International Human Rights Law* (Oxford, 2012).

Rees, Siân, *Sweet Water and Bitter: The Ships that Stopped the Slave Trade* (London, 2009).

Ward, W.E.F., *The Royal Navy and the Slavers: The Suppression of the Atlantic Slave Trade* (New York, 1970).

Notes

Prologue
 1. Edwards 2007, p. 140.

Chapter 1: Slavers and Abolitionists
 1. Edwards 2007, p. 159.
 2. Ibid., p. 25.
 3. Ibid., p. 20.
 4. Crow 1830, p. 42.
 5. Thomas 1887, p. 308.
 6. Edwards 2007, p. 31.
 7. Thomas 1997, p. 494.
 8. Wilberforce 1838, p. 218.
 9. Thomas 1997, p. 551.
10. Ibid., p. 552.
11. Edwards 2007, p. 45.

Chapter 2: Early Operations: November 1807–November 1814
 1. Grindal 2016, p. 132.
 2. Ibid., p. 133.
 3. Lloyd 1968, p. 63.
 4. Ibid.

Chapter 3: Hagan versus the Slavers: December 1814–December 1819
 1. Grindal 2016, p. 160.
 2. Thomas 1997, p. 585.
 3. Ibid.
 4. Ibid.
 5. Grindal 2016, p. 177
 6. Ibid., p. 197.
 7. Ibid., p. 200.
 8. Ibid., p. 202.
 9. Martinez 2012, p. 47.
10. Ibid.
11. Grindal 2016, p. 214.
12. Ibid., p. 218.
13. Ibid., p. 219.

Chapter 4: The American Squadron: January 1820–February 1822
1. Brooks 2010, p. 90.
2. Edwards 2007, p. 75.

Chapter 6: Captain Owen's Island: January 1825–June 1827
1. Edwards 2007, p. 96.
2. Grindal 2016, p. 291.

Chapter 7: The *Black Joke*: June 1827–December 1829
1. Rees 2009, p. 123.
2. Grindal 2016, p. 323.
3. Ibid., p. 339.
4. Rees 2009, p. 138.
5. Ibid.
6. Grindal 2016, p. 333.
7. Ibid., p. 337.
8. Ibid., p. 162.
9. Rees 2009, p. 150.
10. Walsh 1830, p. 482.
11. Ibid., p. 490.
12. Rees 2009, p. 142.

Chapter 8: The Brazilian Trade: January 1830–November 1831
1. Edwards 2007, p. 10.
2. Rees 2009, p. 157.
3. Leonard 1833, p. 105.

Chapter 9: Commands Combined: December 1831–September 1834
1. Grindal 2016, p. 430.
2. Lloyd 1968, p. 73.
3. Leonard 1833, p. 260.
4. Ibid.
5. Rankin 1835, p. 119

Chapter 10: The Spanish Equipment Clause: September 1834–December 1836
1. Pollock 1838, p. 518.
2. Ibid., p. 519.
3. Ibid.

Chapter 11: The Fever Coast: January 1837–December 1839
1. Rees 2009, p. 169.
2. Grindal 2016, p. 619.

Chapter 12: The American Slavers: January–December 1839
1. Grindal 2016, p. 650.
2. Ibid., p. 659

Chapter 13: Attacking the Source: January 1840–December 1841
1. Lloyd 1968, p. 97.
2. Ibid., p. 54.

Chapter 14: Treaties and Palavers: January 1842–December 1843
1. Lloyd 1968, p. 97.
2. Sharp 1858, p. 440.
3. Lloyd 1968, p. 179.

Chapter 15: The End of the Trade: 1844–1867
1. Lloyd 1968, p. 107.
2. Ibid., p. 113.
3. Ibid., p. 121.
4. Bethell, 1970, p. 255.
5. Lloyd 1968, p. 145.
6. Ibid., p. 146.
7. Lloyd 1968, p. 182.
8. Ibid., p. 183.
9. Edwards 2007, p. 185.
10. Martinez 2012, p. 146.
11. Rees 2009, p. 308.

Bibliography

Primary Sources

National Archives, Public Record Office, Kew
ADM 51 Captains' Logbooks:
ADM 51/2912 *Thistle*.
ADM 51/3339 *Pluto*.

ADM 52 Masters' Logbooks:
ADM 52/4020 *Arethusa*.
ADM 52/4177 *Myrmidon*.

ADM 53 Ships' Logbooks:
ADM 53/459 *Dolphin*.
ADM 53/1523 *Wanderer*.

ADM 101 Surgeons' Journals:
ADM 101/100/1/5.

FO 84 Foreign Office: Slave Trade Department and Successors:
FO 84/437.
FO 84/440.
FO 84/441.
FO 84/443.

British Newspaper Archive (Online)
Belfast News Letter (23 August 1833).
Caledonian Mercury (4 October 1832).
Devizes and Wiltshire Gazette (3 May 1838).
Evening Mail (4 August 1824/21 November 1831).
Hampshire Advertiser (25 August 1838).
Hampshire Chronicle (21 October 1822).
Illustrated London News (26 November 1842/7 January 1843).
Morning Advertiser (14 October 1835/13 November 1837/19 March 1838).
Morning Post (14 July 1824/16 December 1826/4 August 1829/4 October 1832/7
    May 1838).
Naval and Military Gazette (14 December 1833/21 March 1835/18 February
    1837/16 September 1837/5 August 1843).

Public Ledger and Daily Advertiser (20 May 1833).
Saunder's News-Letter (5 January 1826/14 May 1829).
Sydney Gazette (7 December 1841).
The Taunton Courier (30 September 1840).
West Kent Guardian (19 March 1836).
Wexford Conservative (25 July 1835).

Edited Collections of Reports, Letters and Memoirs

Anonymous
British and Foreign State Papers: 1820–1843 (London, 1830–58).
The Christian Observer, Vol. XIII (London, 1814).
The Christian Observer, Vol. XX (London, 1821).
Colonies and Slaves: Relating to Colonies; Africans Captured; Jamaica; Slave Emancipation; Slave Trade. Vol. XIX (Oxford, 1831).
Correspondence with the British Commissioners at Sierra Leone, the Havana, Rio de Janeiro and Surinam Relating to the Slave Trade 1826–1844 (London, 1826–44).
Journals of the House of Lords, Volume LII (London, 1818).
Nineteenth Report of the Directors of the African Institution (London, 1825).
An Order of the King in Council for Consolidating the Several Laws Recently Made for Improving the Condition of the Slaves in his Majesties Colonies (London, 1830).
Papers Presented to Parliament in 1821, Vol. III (London, 1821).
The United States Congressional Serial Set: First Session of the Twenty-Eighth Congress: Vol. IV (Washington, 1844).
The United States Congressional Serial Set: Second Session of the Twenty-Eighth Congress: Vol. IX (Washington, 1845).
The Sixth Annual Report of the American Society for Colonizing the Free People of Colour of the United States (Washington, 1823).
House of Lords: The Sessional Papers 1801–1833. Vol. 158 (London, 1823).

Named Authors
Boteler, T., *Narrative of a Voyage of Discovery to Africa and Arabia, Performed in His Majesty's Ships Leven and Barracouta, from 1821 to 1826* (London, 1833).
Crow, H., *Memoirs of the Late Captain Hugh Crow of Liverpool* (London, 1830).
Haggard, J., *Reports of Cases Argued and Determined in the High Court of Admiralty Volume 1: 1822–1825* (Boston, 1853).
Holman, J., *Travels in Madeira, Sierra Leone, Tenerife, St Jago, Cape Coast, Fernando Po, Princes Island* (London, 1840).
Huntley, H., *Seven Years' Service on the Slave Coast of Western Africa* (London, 1850).
Keppel, H., *A Sailor's Life Under Four Sovereigns* (London, 1899).
Leonard, P., *Records of a Voyage to the Western Coast of Africa in His Majesty's Ship Dryad* (Edinburgh 1833).

Rankin, F.H., *The White Man's Grave: A Visit to Sierra Leone in 1835. Vol. II* (London, 1836).
Sharp, J. (ed.), *Memoirs of the Life and Services of Rear-Admiral Sir William Symonds, Surveyor of the Navy from 1832 to 1847* (London, 1853).
Walsh, Rev. R., *Notices of Brazil in 1828 and 1829. Vol. II* (London, 1830).
Zulueta, P., *Trial of Pedro de Zulueta, Jun., On a Charge of Slave Trading, Under the 5 Geo. IV, Cap. 113* (London 1844).

Secondary Sources

Anonymous
The British and Foreign Anti-Slavery Reporter Vol. I. 1840 (London, 1969).
The Foreign Slave Trade: A Brief Account of its State, of the Treaties that Have Been Entered into and of the Laws Enacted for its Protection (London, 1837).
The Nautical Magazine and Naval Chronicle for 1838 (London, 1838).
The United Service Magazine and Naval and Military Magazine 1838 Part II (London, 1838).
The United Service Magazine and Naval and Military Magazine 1839 Part II (London, 1839).
A View of the Present State of the African Slave Trade (Philadelphia, 1824).

Named Authors
Allen, J., *Battles of the British Navy, Vol. II* (London, 1852).
Beattie, P.M. (ed.), *Recapricorning the Atlantic: Special Issue of the Luso-Brazilian Review: Volume 45, Number 1* (Wisconsin, 2008).
Bethell, L., *The Abolition of the Brazilian Slave Trade* (Cambridge, 1970).
Birrell, T., *Mariners, Merchants-Then Pioneers* (Bli Bli, 1993).
Brooks, G.E., *Western Africa and Cabo Verde, 1790s-1830s: Symbiosis of Slave and Legitimate Trades* (Bloomington, 2010).
Bryant, J.M., *Dark Places of the Earth: The Voyage of the Slave Ship Antelope* (New York, 2015).
Canney, D.L., *Africa Squadron: The US Navy and the Slave Trade, 1842–1861* (Washington, 2006).
Du Bois, W.E.B., *The Suppression of the African Slave-Trade to the United States of America, 1638–1870* (Harvard, 1896).
Edwards, B., *Royal Navy Versus the Slave Traders: Enforcing Abolition at Sea, 1808–1898* (Barnsley, 2007).
George, C., *The Rise of British West Africa, Comprising the Early History of the Colony of Sierra Leone, the Gambia, Lagos, Gold Coast etc.* (London, 1968).
Giffard, E., *Deeds of Naval Daring; or Anecdotes of the British Navy* (London, 1867).
Gray, J.M., *A History of the Gambia* (Cambridge, 1940).
Grindall, P., *Opposing the Slavers: The Royal Navy's Campaign against the Atlantic Slave Trade* (London, 2016).

Howard, W.S., *American Slavers and the Federal Law: 1837–1862* (California, 1963).

Johnson, J. (M.D.), *The Medico-Chirurgical Review: Volume Two* (London, 1825).

Kingston, W.H.G., *Blue Jackets; Or, Chips of the Old Block* (London, 1854).

Kohn, G.C. (ed.), *Encyclopedia of Plague and Pestilence: From Ancient Times to the Present* (New York, 2008).

Lloyd, C., *The Navy and the Slave Trade: The Suppression of the African Slave Trade in the Nineteenth Century* (London, 1968).

Luskey, B.P., & Woloson, W.A. (eds), *Capitalism by Gaslight: Illuminating the Economy of Nineteenth Century America* (Philadelphia, 2015).

Marshall, J., *Royal Naval Biography; Or, Memoirs and Services of All the Flag-Officers, Superannuated Rear-Admirals, Retired Captains, Post-Captains and Commanders* (London, 1823).

Martinez, J., *The Slave Trade and the Origins of International Human Rights Law* (Oxford, 2012).

McAleer, J., & Petley, C. (eds), *The Royal Navy and the British Atlantic World, c. 1750–1820* (London, 2016).

Nascimento, A., *Histórias da Ilha do Príncipe* (Oeiras, 2010).

O'Byrne, W.R., *A Naval Biographical Dictionary, Vols. 1 & 3* (London, 1849).

Pearson, A.F., *Distant Freedom: St Helena and the Abolition of the Slave Trade, 1840–1872* (Liverpool, 2016).

Pollock, A.W.A., *The Nautical Magazine and Naval Chronicle for 1837* (London, 1837).

Rees, S., *Sweet Water and Bitter: The Ships that Stopped the Slave Trade* (London, 2009).

Slight, H. & J., *The Chronicles of Portsmouth* (London, 1828).

Taylor, B.K., *Sierra Leone: The Land, its People and History* (Dar es Salaam, 2011).

Thomas, H., *The Slave Trade: The Story of the Atlantic Slave Trade, 1440–1870* (New York, 1997).

Upham, N.G., *Opinion in Case of the Barque Jones* (London, 1854).

Waites, B., and Goodrich, A., *Slavery and Freedom* (Milton Keynes, 2007).

Ward, W.E.F., *The Royal Navy and the Slavers: The Suppression of the Atlantic Slave Trade* (New York, 1970).

Wilberforce, R.I. and S., *The Life of William Wilberforce vol. 1* (London, 1838).

Winfield, R., *British Warships in the Age of Sail, 1714–1792* (Barnsley, 2007).

——, *British Warships in the Age of Sail, 1793–1817* (Barnsley, 2007).

——, *British Warships in the Age of Sail, 1817–1863* (Barnsley, 2007).

Other Sources

http://www.pbenyon.plus.com/18-1900/Index.html (Accessed January 2017–January 2019)

https://threedecks.org (Accessed January 2017–January 2019)

Index

Vessels are British unless indicated otherwise. Slave vessels are not listed unless substantial mention has been made of them in the text.

76,

ı,

9,